Supercook's
SUPERSAVERS COOKBOOK

Marshall Cavendish

Editor: Pepita Aris
Designer: Pedro Prá-Lopez

Contributors: Pepita Aris
            Joan Hood
            Louis Jordaan
            Norma MacMillan
            Jeni Wright

Published by
Marshall Cavendish Books Limited
58 Old Compton Street
London W1V 5PA

© Marshall Cavendish Limited 1980, 1981, 1982, 1983, 1984

First printing 1980
Second printing 1981
Third printing 1983
This printing 1984

Printed and bound in Hong Kong by Dai Nippon Printing Company

ISBN 0 85685 839 0

Contents

Photography

Bryce Attwel – 88

Rex Bamber – 178, 253

Patrick Cocklin – 205

John Cooke – 76, 136

Delu/PAF International – 80, 90,
100, 131, 226

Alan Duns – 20, 24/25, 30, 32, 36, 45, 50/51, 52,
53, 54, 60, 62, 65, 70, 71, 84, 93, 96, 97, 98, 110,
112, 118, 119, 121, 124, 125, 127, 145, 171,
176, 193, 197, 202, 213, 231, 236, 246 (below)

Melvin Grey – 10, 71, 94, 116, 217, 243

Gina Harris – 115, 214, 235

Anthony Kay – 9, 13/14, 55

Paul Kemp – 19, 37, 39, 70, 75, 78/79, 91, 104,
117 (below), 128/129, 132/133, 142, 150/151,
185, 186/187, 189, 195, 216, 229, 239, 256

Don Last – 48, 89

Mike Leale – 83

John Lee – 87, 190

David Levin – 12, 27, 29, 43, 47, 61, 66, 103,
112, 117, 123, 130, 158, 161, 165, 177, 183,
184, 188, 206, 219, 225, 233, 240, 242, 244,
245, 246 (above), 247, 249, 250, 251, 252, 254

Max Logan – 26, 56

Frederick Mancini – 22/23, 57

David Meldrum – 109, 196, 210, 228

Key Nilson – 113

Roger Phillips – 28, 29 (above), 34, 35, 44,
46/47, 64, 67, 68, 71 (above), 72, 74, 81, 82,
85, 99, 101, 102, 105, 106, 112, 120, 135, 138,
139, 140, 141, 144, 147, 148, 154, 156, 157,
162, 163, 168, 172, 173, 175, 180, 194, 198/199,
209, 211, 215, 221, 224, 227, 234, 237, 238

Iain Reid – 58, 59, 108, 111, 149, 153, 201

David Smith – 86, 92, 166/167

Paul Williams – 7, 107, 122, 220, 222, 223

George Wright – 41, 134, 200

Saving Money

'The necessity of practising economy should be evident to everyone, whether in the possession of an income no more than sufficient for a family's requirements, or of a large fortune which puts financial adversity out of the question. We must always remember that to manage a little well is a great merit in house-keeping.' (Isabella Beeton: *The Book of Household Management*.) Though the average family is more prosperous now than it was when Mrs. Beeton was writing more than a hundred years ago, her words are still true. Being economical in the kitchen does not necessarily imply poverty, nor does it mean skimpiness and frugality. It means good planning so as to get the best value for money and time spent. This should have the happy effect of enriching your cooking as things that might otherwise get neglected or thrown away can make a contribution.

A sensible, attractive, well-balanced diet for all members of the family uses food in season, at its cheapest, freshest and best quality. Buying wisely is the first step in economical budgeting. The second is to plan your time and cooking intelligently, so that a lot of labour is not spent in saving a few pence. With a little thought, leftovers and byproducts can make their contribution for a more varied and stimulating diet.

Economical cuts of meat and the less expensive kinds of fish and vegetables are just as rich in protein, vitamins, fats and minerals as more expensive ones. They do require more thought and care in preparation and cooking, however. Meat, in parti-cular, must be cooked by the methods most suited to the inexpen-sive cuts, or it will be unpalatable.

Meat is a major expenditure for the average family, as the majority of main course dishes are based on meat in one form or another. In the Western world meat is one of the major sources of first-class protein and most people have grown to expect meat at least once during the day.

Economical Cuts of Meat

BEEF

Economical roasts and large cuts of meat are *topside, flank, brisket, buttock, silverside, top ribs* and *middle ribs,* (in the US *chuck eye, shoulder, flank, brisket, rump, round, tip, cross ribs* and *short ribs*). Though not top quality, the meat is generally lean and there is not a great deal of waste. Cuts with a higher proportion of fat or gristle may well be sold at a lower price to make them more attractive. Apart from the ribs these cuts are usually sold boned and rolled and the price quoted is therefore for the trimmed weight. Though lean the meat is muscular and sometimes coarse in texture and all these cuts need to be braised or pot roasted with some liquid.

Sear these large cuts of beef quickly in fat or oil to seal in the juices and give the meat a good colour, then add liquid, vegetables and herbs and seasonings. Use home-made beef stock, wine, beer or cider, diluted with water if desired. Root vegetables will add flavour and body to the finished gravy. Fresh herbs—grow your own on a windowsill if you have no garden—will improve flavour and a bouquet garni (*page 254*) can be tucked in beside a pot roast.

Use a heavy-bottomed, deep casserole dish or dutch oven with a tight-fitting lid for pot roasting. Cover the meat with greased greaseproof or waxed paper, then with the lid, as this helps to create moisture. Cook on top of the stove or in a low oven at 160°C (325°F) gas mark 3. Use the pot liquid to make gravy. Pot roasts improve if left overnight before serving; the fat can be skimmed off and the flavours of the gravy have time to penetrate the meat.

Marinating both adds flavour and helps tenderize meat. Full-bodied red wine and stout (beer) are excellent, but fruit juice and other acids also help while onions, garlic, herbs and spices add flavour. Marinades are on *page 255*: choose the one to suit the time you have on hand and the occasion.

Salting or pickling in brine have become less fashionable in recent years, but some butchers still sell meat treated this way, which can then be boiled. It is also possible to do it yourself at home, if you like the flavour.

Stewing cuts of beef are *chuck steak, shin, neck, blade, clod* and *sticking* (in the US *chuck, shank, arm, blade, flank, short plate* and *round*). Cut in cubes, chunks or strips, these are usually sold under the general term of 'stewing' or 'braising' steak. They require long, slow cooking to make them tender and the ratio of liquid to meat should be at least 275ml/½ pt (1¼ cups) to every 450g (1 lb). These are very versatile cuts and can be used for a great variety of dishes.

Minced (ground) beef is a byproduct of the other cuts and often comes in two grades. Useful for a variety of dishes, it can be stretched by adding rice, pasta, vegetables etc, or can be used as a stuffing for vegetables, crêpes etc.

Entertaining: do not automatically shun economy cuts of beef when entertaining. Some of the classic stews, with a rich flavour, are made with these cuts, while the addition of a few colourful vegetables can with thought turn an inexpensive cut into something special.

On the other hand you need not automatically rule out the more expensive cuts because your budget is limited. The overall cost of the dish need not be high if good quality meat is used economically. Top rump (sirloin) or even the cheaper topside (boneless rib) can be thinly sliced and stuffed with sausage meat, kidneys, breadcrumbs, herbs and spices to make an economical dinner party main course. Rump steak (filet mignon) may sound extravagant, but if small steaks are wrapped in puff pastry, the cost per head will not be prohibitive.

LAMB

The price of lamb fluctuates according to the season far more than other meat. Where local, home-produced lamb commands a high price, you will find it cheaper to buy imported lamb. The more economical cuts of lamb have large amounts of fat and bone, so care must be taken in preparation and cooking.

Economical roasts of lamb are *shoulder* and *breast*. Though shoulder is far less expensive than the prime cuts, such as leg, loin and best end of neck, many people prefer it for its sweeter flavour and more succulent texture. Shoulder does contain a fair proportion of fat and bone, so buy 350g (¾ lb) meat on the bone for each person. Shoulder is one of the few economy cuts that can be roasted on the bone. Nevertheless, it will go further if boned, stuffed and rolled.

Breast of lamb is fatty, so look for the leanest available and if possible have the butcher bone it for you. Stuffings, with fruit such as dried apricots, prunes, grated orange and lemon rind, will help to break down the fat content, while the addition of breadcrumbs, onions and garlic will help flavour and stretch the meat. Roll the stuffed meat, rub it with seasoned flour and brown on all sides. Then slow roast or braise in the oven.

For casseroles, stew and pies, economical cuts are *middle neck chops, scrag end* (sometimes called 'apple rings'), *chump chops* and *boned shoulder* (in the US *neck slices, riblets, shank* and *boned shoulder*). Shoulder boned and cut into cubes is most useful for stews and curries while the meat is of good enough quality to grill (broil) as kebabs. Shoulder makes a much cheaper alternative to leg or loin. Middle neck and scrag (neck slices and riblets) are both fatty and have a high proportion of bone, so allow for this when calculating the meat per portion.

Dishes using these cuts are best cooked a day ahead. Chill in the refrigerator then skim off any surface fat. Cooling and reheating also improves the flavour.

PORK

Pork is a best buy all the year round, though prices can dip to their lowest in summer. It is a rich meat with plenty of flavour, so smaller quantities per person are served, compared with other meat.

Economical cuts are *blade, hand and spring, spare ribs* and *belly* (in the US *blade, picnic shoulder, spare ribs* and *butt*). All these cuts have a high proportion of fat, so choose the leanest available. Cooked correctly, however, the meat is sweet and full of flavour and compares well with the more expensive loin and leg.

The roasting cuts are blade and hand and spring (picnic shoulder). These are awkward in shape and therefore difficult to carve, so try to get your butcher to bone them. Ask him to leave on the skin if you like crackling. Score, brush with oil and rub with coarse salt then roast at a high temperature for crisp crackling. For an economical family roast, stuff, roll and tie these joints at home.

Spare ribs and belly (butt) can be roasted whole, but they are usually better portioned so that the meat can crisp. These cuts are excellent in a sweet and sour or barbecue sauce.

Unlike beef and lamb, pork is not frequently casseroled or braised, probably because the amount of fat makes the stew excessively rich. Spare rib chops (country style rib chops) can be boned and cut into cubes for casseroles and are used frequently in Chinese dishes. The boned meat can be minced (ground) for meat loaves, rissoles, pâtés etc or used for stuffing, for example in cannelloni. It can also be mixed with minced (ground) beef or veal.

Salted belly (butt) can be bought at some butchers or delicatessens, but is less common than it used to be. It is nearly all fat, but is useful as a flavoursome ingredient in vegetable dishes and soups. Like back fat, it can be used for lining pâté moulds. Bacon can be substituted for salt pork when it is unavailable.

BACON AND HAM

Bacon and gammon tend to be more economical than ham, which has a longer salting and curing process. If used wisely, however, all three meats are economical, as there is little waste.

Economical bacon cuts are *middle* and *corner gammon, slipper* and *collar*. Heavily smoked and cured hams, knuckles and hocks should be soaked in cold water before cooking to remove excessive salt. Cook in water or cider with vegetables and flavourings, allowing about 25 minutes per 450g (1 lb) plus 25 extra minutes. Drain, skin, and slice to serve.

Streaky rashers (fatty slices) are the most economical of all bacon slices, unless they are mostly fat. The best buy is probably *middle rashers* in that they combine a good versatile proportion of fat and lean bacon at a relatively low price. Bacon slices can be grilled (broiled) or fried, or added to stews and casseroles and used in pies and stuffings. A little bacon will help to turn a pulse (dried legume) or vegetable dish into a main course, adding flavour and interest. *Bacon chops* are also relatively economical in that they are usually lean with very little waste.

Escalopes (scallops) of meat can be rolled up with a tasty stuffing of nuts, bread, onion and herbs. As well as making the meat go further, the stuffing makes an elegant 'olive' of meat.

VEAL

Veal is usually scarce and rarely economical. If the price is not too high the most economical cuts to buy would be *shoulder, knuckle, best end of neck* (US *shank*) and the *breast*. All these cuts are awkward to deal with on the bone, so try to buy them boned and rolled.

Braising and slow pot roasting will ensure maximum tenderness. As with beef, brown the meat and then cook with liquid and vegetables etc. As with lamb, the dish is best cooled and reheated.

Veal trimmings are sold as *stewing* or *pie veal*. Both economical and versatile, this can be used like stewing beef. Use with strongly flavoured ingredients, as veal can be bland on its own. Stewing veal can be minced (ground) and used as an alternative to, or mixed with, minced (ground) pork or beef. It does not have as much flavour as either of these two.

Tripe is rich in calcium and gelatine. Partly cooked when bought, it makes a stew with the consistency of certain shellfish.

Escalopes (scallops) of veal are thin steaks cut diagonally across the grain of the meat. Though the price per weight is high, there is no waste. The amount per person is also very small. They can be rolled and stuffed, when they are called 'olives' or 'veal birds' because their appearance when rolled is like a small bird. About 450g (1 lb) is ample for four people so, with a substantial filling, they make a fairly economical main course for a dinner party.

POULTRY AND GAME

Chicken is one of the most economical meats available. Widely available all the year round, both fresh and frozen, it constitutes one of the best meat buys. There is relatively little fat on chicken, and very little waste in terms of gristle and bones (the latter can always be used in soups and stocks). It is a versatile meat which can be prepared in many ways: *whole chickens* can be served for the weekend roast, *chicken portions* make economical mid-week meals either grilled (broiled), fried, casseroled or roasted, and both make excellent main course dishes for dinner parties. Individual *chicken breasts, thighs* and *drumsticks* make portion control easier to manage and this cuts down on cost.

Older *boiling fowls* are cheapest by weight, but do not attempt to cook them in any way other than by long, slow stewing with vegetables and herbs for flavour.

Turkey is now widely available throughout the year, and is ceasing to be only for festivals. Many butchers and supermarkets sell *boned and rolled turkey roasts* and individual *turkey portions*. There is little or no waste on these cuts, which makes them economical both for family meals and entertaining. You can also buy exactly the quantity you require without having to invest in a whole bird.

Rabbit portions can be bought as an alternative to chicken portions. They are widely available at butchers and supermarkets, usually frozen, at roughly the same price as chicken. Prepare and cook as for chicken portions.

Ducks and geese are still fairly scarce, and so relatively expensive when compared with chicken and turkey. They are best reserved for 'special occasion' cooking, since not only is their price high, but they also tend to be bony, with a high proportion of fat. A duck, however, can be stretched to serve more people than the 4–5 it feeds normally (see duck pie).

Game prices fluctuate according to the season, and unless you are lucky enough to live in the country where you have access to local game in season, it is unlikely that you will consider it an economical form of meat. Under other circumstances, game is better kept for special occasions.

OFFAL (VARIETY MEATS)

The internal organs and extremities of beef, lamb, pork and veal are often neglected in the cook's repertoire. This is unfortunate, because most of them are nutritious, easy to cook and extremely economical.

Brains are probably the least well-liked of all animal by-products, largely due to their appearance raw. They are cheap to buy, however, and are considered to be a culinary delicacy by the discriminating French because of their delicate texture. Soak them in cold water for about 4 hours before use, then drain and remove all membranes and gristle. The brains are prepared by first poaching in water with added lemon juice for about 10 minutes, then blanching in ice-cold water. Popular ways of cooking them are frying in breadcrumbs or batter. Allow about 450g (1 lb) brains for 4 people.

Heart: calf's and sheep's hearts are fairly small and each one will serve 1–2 people on average. Ox (beef) heart is large and will serve 4–6 people. To prepare heart, wash well, then cut off all arteries and tendons. Small hearts are best opened up inside and then stuffed, and braised or casseroled. Ox (beef) heart tends to be tough and muscular, and is therefore better sliced and added to casseroles and stews which need long, slow cooking.

Kidney: although sometimes strong-tasting and therefore not very popular, kidneys should be used more often in cooking because they are very rich in iron and protein, and contain vitamin A, nicotinic acid and some minerals. Lamb's kidneys are the smallest and, like calf's kidneys, they have a delicate flavour. Pig's kidney is larger, with a stronger flavour, while ox (beef) kidney is the largest and strongest tasting of them all. First remove the fat which surrounds the kidneys, then skin them and cut out the fatty cores. Lamb's and calf's kidneys are usually fried or grilled (broiled), whereas pig's kidneys are usually added to pies and casseroles. Ox (beef) kidney needs long, slow cooking, and is therefore usually sliced or chopped before adding to stews; it is a cheap extender of beef.

Liver is a versatile meat, as well as being rich in iron, protein and vitamins A and B. Calf's liver is considered a delicacy; since there is no waste and portions are small it is not particularly expensive.

Lamb's liver is widely used for frying and grilling (broiling) because of its mild flavour and tender texture; it is usually cheaper than calf's liver. Pig's liver has a stronger flavour and is more often used in pâtés and terrines. It is cheaper than lamb's liver, however, and can be eaten fried, grilled (broiled) or casseroled if it is soaked in milk or salted water for a few hours before cooking—this helps to temper its strong flavour. Ox (beef) liver benefits from this soaking before use, as it is the strongest and toughest of all the livers; it is really only suitable for long, slow braising. Chicken livers, now widely available frozen in supermarkets, are good fried and make a very economical pâté.

Oxtail: strictly speaking, oxtail should not be classed as offal (a variety meat), but most butchers sell it as such. It is normally sold skinned and chopped into 5cm (2 in) pieces ready for use in casseroles, soups and stews. It has very bony meat with a large proportion of fat, and one whole oxtail will serve only about 4 people, despite the fact that it looks so large. It is best to leave cooked oxtail overnight, preferably in the refrigerator after cooling, then the fat can be skimmed off with a slotted spoon before reheating.

Sweetbreads: there are two kinds of sweetbread, those from the stomach (pancreas) and those from the throat, the latter being more widely available. Calf's sweetbreads are the most economical, while lamb's sweetbreads are considered to be a delicacy. To prepare sweetbreads, soak in cold water for 1–2 hours, then drain. Bring to the boil in water with added lemon juice. Cook for 2 minutes, and then plunge into ice-cold water. Remove all the membranes and cook according to the individual recipe.

Tripe is the stomach lining of the bullock which has been partially cooked and blanched before it reaches the butcher's shop. It is both economical and rich in calcium and gelatin, with small amounts of iron and vitamins A and B. It does not have much flavour of its own and the consistency is rather like some shell fish, for example abalone. The honeycomb variety seems to be fairly popular. Before cooking tripe, check with your butcher how long it needs still to cook as preparation methods vary. Then cook it slowly in the oven with highly-flavoured ingredients.

Trotters (feet) are often grouped with offal. They are cheap to buy and are a good way of making jellied stock and adding body to warming winter stews, though there is almost no meat on them.

Seasonal Fish

Note: entries in brackets refer to fish which, in season, are good buys in the United States.

Like animal byproducts, fish is a much under-rated food. This is unfortunate, because it can be a relatively inexpensive source of first-class protein (containing nearly as much as meat), and is also a good source of iron, vitamins and minerals. Fish is also a versatile food: there are many different varieties, each with its own distinctive flavour and texture, and there are numerous ways in which they can be prepared. The price of fresh fish varies considerably, both according to the time of year and the location, so it is wise to check prices closely before buying.

White fish such as cod and haddock used to be among the most economical of fish to buy in countries bordering the Atlantic, but due to changes in fishing laws over the past few years, and also the increasing scarcity of these fish because of high demand, this is no longer the case. Fishing authorities are keen to introduce the more unusual varieties to help fill the gap in the market, but the consumer is very slow to accept this change. Many of these lesser-known fish are extremely ugly in appearance and have awkward shapes when whole. Once boned and cut up, however, they have good, flavoursome flesh and are more reasonable in price than the better-known varieties. Among the most economical fish generally available are:

(*Bluefish* is common along the Atlantic Coast of the United States and in the Gulf in winter, spring and summer. The average size of bluefish to be found in the markets runs about 1.5–2.5kg/3–6 lb. Its flesh is very meaty with a distinctive flavour which requires little seasoning. Bluefish are best served baked, broiled or fried.)

Blue Ling is available in summer and is well worth searching out. It is reasonable in price, yet can be used as a substitute for cod in most recipes.

(*Butterfish* are available on the American East Coast during spring, summer and fall, but are usually too small to be cut into fillets. Since they only weigh between 100–450g ($\frac{1}{4}$–1 lb), they are best bought and cooked whole. They are caught in large quantities and therefore are a good buy when in season. They are a fat-fleshed fish which may be quickly broiled or sautéed.)

(*Carp* is a freshwater fish available throughout the year in the United States. They may be purchased whole, weighing between 900g–3.5kg (2–8 lb), or cut into fillets. Soak them in cold water for 3 hours before boiling, baking or frying.)

(*Catfish* is a freshwater fish usually sold in the inland American states and is available throughout the year. Catfish vary in size from $\frac{1}{2}$–19kg (1–40 lb) and sometimes larger. The fish should be skinned before cooking and tastes better either baked or fried.)

(*Cod* are caught in the colder northern waters of the Atlantic. The weight varies from 3–35kg (3–75 lb). Though not a cheap fish, it is one of the most popular, and is very versatile in the number of ways it can be prepared. Salt cod is widely available in the US and makes a delicious casserole ingredient. Soak it overnight in several changes of cold water before use.)

Coley (also known as saithe) is classed as a white fish and makes an excellent alternative to cod or haddock because it is similar in shape, size and texture. The fish flesh looks rather grey on the fishmonger's slab, but it does whiten in cooking and this can be helped by sprinkling the fish with lemon juice. Coley is a useful fish for making economical dishes such as fish pies, croquettes and fish cakes, in which its colour is not so noticeable.

Conger Eel is not as cheap as it used to be, but still is economical. It has a rich flavour and needs long, slow cooking. Eels are sold live by some fishmerchants, particularly in the traditional English working class areas, where jellied eels are considered a delicacy. Cut into cutlets, eel should be cooked slowly in the oven in a sauce or stock; it is also the traditional fish for fish soups such as *bouillabaisse*. (In the United States eels are often sold live or smoked throughout the year.)

Dab is a small fish in the same family as plaice, but much cheaper. At their cheapest and best from April to November in the north Atlantic, dabs are usually fried whole; they are rather too small to be filleted like plaice. Use them in recipes for plaice as an economical alternative.

Flounder is another fish similar to plaice, yet cheaper in price. Use either whole or as fillets in any recipe calling for plaice.

(*Haddock* belongs to the cod family and can be used for cod recipes. Comparatively expensive, it can be bought fresh, filleted and in steaks. Smoked haddock is excellent in recipes requiring small quantities of fish and is therefore an economical purchase.)

Hake: while Atlantic hake is expensive in European markets, it is possible to buy imported South African or Pacific hake at a more reasonable price. Use in any recipe for cod. It has a firm, white flesh like cod, but a more distinctive flavour.

Herring is available all the year round, but best buys are to be had from spring to late autumn (fall). The flesh is close-textured, with a rich distinctive flavour, therefore individual portions need not be large. Herring can be bought whole or filleted and can be baked, grilled (broiled) or fried. For an economical family meal, they may be boned and stuffed, then baked in the oven. They are also excellent salted, smoked or pickled. Soft herring roes make an economical starter, snack or brunch when fried and piled on hot buttered toast.

Huss is also known as rock salmon, cat fish, rock fish and dog fish. These fish are not all exactly the same, but are usually grouped together under one name to save confusion. They are in good supply all year round and are medium-priced. Unidentified fish inside batter will probably be one of this group. The flesh has a slight pinkish tinge and is usually sold in steaks or fillets. It is best deep-fried, poached or grilled (broiled).

Mackerel is an oily fish which is excellent value for money. It is available all year round, but is at its best in winter and spring. One large fish will feed 2. The flesh is firm with a pronounced flavour, and individual servings need not be large. Prepare and cook as for herring. Smoked mackerel is inexpensive.

Megrim is one of the more unusual fish, but reasonable in price. It is a flat fish similar to dab, and can be used in any recipe calling for plaice, though it can be difficult to obtain.

Mock Halibut is more correctly called Greenlands halibut. Do not confuse it with ordinary halibut, which is rather expensive. Mock halibut is an excellent white fish with a firm texture, and can be used in any recipe for white fish.

Monkfish is also known as angler fish. Although available all year round, this fish is at its best from October to January in the northern hemisphere. One of the more unusual fish, it has a very ugly head, which is therefore usually removed before it is displayed for purchase. Monkfish are good value, with firm succulent flesh, the flavour of which is often compared to lobster. The tail of the monkfish is used as mock scampi. It is well worth asking for this fish, which can be cut into steaks and grilled (broiled), fried or baked.

Mullet: both red and grey mullet are available. Red mullet is considered the superior of the two and is at its best in the summer months. Grey mullet is best from July to February in the northern hemisphere. Both fish are usually cooked whole, either baked, grilled (broiled) or fried.

(*Ocean Perch* is a mild flavoured fish often sold frozen in the US. It is economical and can be adapted to many recipes.)

(*Porgy* is common along the Atlantic coast of the US and in the Gulf. Weighing 225–900g ($\frac{1}{2}$–2 lb) they are usually sold whole.)

(*Redfish* is one of the cheaper fish and a good all-rounder because its firm flesh can be poached, stewed or baked with a stuffing. Available as whole fish or fillets from June to December in the northern hemisphere, it is well worth trying for its favourable price.)

(*Scrod* are young cod or haddock, weighing from 700–900g (1$\frac{1}{2}$–2 lb). They can be used in any recipe calling for white fillets.)

(*Shad* is a delicious fat-fleshed fish, available during the fall, winter and spring in the US. They weigh between 700g–2.5kg (1$\frac{1}{2}$–6 lb) and may be baked, grilled (broiled), boiled or fried. They are usually sold whole, but sometimes fillets are available. These are preferable since the bone structure of shad is very complicated and plentiful. Shad roes are a delight, usually sold by the pair. They are less expensive at the end of the season when they are most abundant. Shad roes are delicious simply sautéed in butter for 6–7 minutes on each side.)

(*Smelt* are fat-fleshed, rich-flavoured small fish, usually only weighing in at about 100g ($\frac{1}{4}$ lb). They are available throughout the US in the fall, winter and spring. They may be baked or

broiled, but most people like them fried crisp in butter or oil. Split them and remove the bones before cooking.)

Sprats belong to the same family as the herring, and are very cheap when available. Fry or grill (broil) small whole ones, then serve them for a starter as an inexpensive alternative to whitebait. (*Trout* is a delectable freshwater fish, varying in size from $\frac{1}{2}$–9kg 1–20 lb. The smaller fish are usually served whole with the head and tail intact. Fresh trout are available during the spring, summer and autumn (fall). Because they are now farmed and sold frozen the price has dropped. Smoked trout may be purchased throughout the year, but is one of the more expensive smoked fish.)

(*Weakfish*, also known as sea trout, is available on both the Atlantic and Pacific coasts of the US. They are a lean fish, reasonable in price, and can be used in any recipe calling for white fish.)

Whiting is also known as marling. Available all year round, it is at its best in the winter months. One of the cheapest white fish, it is similar to cod, but smaller. Use it whole or as fillets in any recipe calling for white fish.

Fish heads and backbones are often thoughtlessly discarded. The next time you buy a whole fish and have it filleted, remember to take the head home too. After all, you have paid for it, so do not let it be thrown out. Place it in a pan with cold water to cover, add a few vegetables like an onion, carrot and stalk of celery and boil it for about half an hour. The heads and shells of prawns (shrimp) can be used the same way. This broth will make a good base for sauce, soup, chowder, or for poaching the fish (see court bouillon *page 253*).

Smoked fish can make an economical meal. While *smoked haddock* and *cod* are by no means cheap, a little goes a long way, particularly when combined with other ingredients, for example, in kedgeree.

Better value than these are *smoked mackerel*, which are widely available. Smoked mackerel is a rich, meaty fish with a distinctive flavour. It can be served filleted as an economical appetizer with lettuce, lemon wedges and brown bread and butter, or it can be combined with other ingredients such as cream cheese and mayonnaise to make a deliciously rich pâté. *Bloaters* and *kippers* (smoked herring) also make economical pâtés which are just as tasty as their more expensive counterpart, smoked trout pâté, if not more so.

Smoked cod's roe is also economical: it need only be used in very small quantities because of its strong flavour. It can be served on its own as an appetizer with lettuce, lemon wedges and brown bread, but is perhaps at its best and most economical made into taramasalata with oil and lemon juice.

Pickled fish in the form of marinated herrings or 'rollmops' are reasonably priced, and they make an inexpensive starter when sliced with raw onions and served topped with sour cream or plain unsweetened yogurt and snipped chives. They can also be used as part of mixed hors d'oeuvre.

Canned fish such as anchovies, mackerel, pilchards, salmon, tuna and sardines should not be overlooked for their use in cooking. They are so often regarded only as an ingredient to serve straight from the can with a salad, that many cooks forget how useful they are in recipes for fish pies and stuffings.

Seasonal Vegetables

ROOTS

Beetroots or beets are available all the year round, but the new season's beets come in the 3 summer months. Wash them carefully under cold running water, but do not pierce the skin. Boil until the skins will rub off. Serve cold in salads with vinaigrette or hot with white sauce or sour cream.

Use seasonal root vegetables for warming winter casseroles.

Carrots are available all year round and make a cheap winter vegetable. The new season's carrots are available from March, in the northern hemisphere, throughout the summer. Top and tail them, then scrape or peel according to age. Leave young carrots whole; slice or quarter large ones. Serve grated raw carrot cold in salads. Serve hot carrots with butter or white sauce, to accompany roasts, soups and stews etc.

Celeriac or celery root is available from early autumn (fall) to the end of winter. Peel, then slice, dice or grate the root. Sprinkle with lemon juice to prevent discolouration. Boil or parboil, then sauté in butter. The slices can be served hot with white sauce, they can be braised or cooked in soups and stews or puréed. Serve the raw, grated root in salads, especially with mayonnaise.

Jerusalem artichokes, sometimes called sunchokes, are available from early winter to early spring. Scrub and boil in the skins or peel, keeping them in water with a little added lemon juice to prevent discolouration. Then boil or steam them, or purée for soup. Deep fry the artichokes or serve with white or cheese sauce.

Onions: this bulb is available all the year round, but inexpensive, home-produced onions are on the market from the end of summer. Peel and leave whole or chop, slice or grate according to the recipe. Boil, fry, braise or roast this versatile, flavoursome vegetable or serve sliced rings raw in salads.

Parsnips are available from the end of summer until the end of the following spring. Top and tail the root, then peel. Slice or cut into

chunks. Boil and mash, or fry as 'chips' (French fries). Bake or roast small whole ones. Serve hot in white sauce, or in casseroles, soups and stews, or make mashed parsnip fritters.

Potatoes are available all the year round, usually as the cheapest of all vegetables, but the new season's crop comes in at the beginning of summer. Scrub new potatoes, peel old ones or scrub if baking. Boil, sauté, deep-fry, bake or roast them. Serve boiled potatoes mashed or creamed, or diced cold in salads. Serve new potatoes with butter and mint. They are also used in casseroles, soups and stews and mashed potato makes a good pie topping.

Radishes: this spicy, colourful root is available from spring right through the summer. Top and tail, then leave whole or slice. They are usually served raw in salads or used for garnishing, but can be boiled whole and served with a white or parsley sauce.

Swedes (or Rutabagas as they are called in the United States, where they are often sold coated with wax to preserve freshness) are 'neeps' in Scotland, where they are a national dish. They are available from early autumn (fall) right through the next eight months. Peel then slice thickly or cube. Boil or roast around meat. Serve hot with butter and seasonings. The root can also be served mashed or puréed and in casseroles, soups and stews.

Sweet potatoes are available all the year round, but prices will depend on where you live. Scrub or peel them, then boil and serve hot like potatoes, or with sugar and spices for a dessert.

Turnips are available all the year round, but the new season's root comes in mid-spring. Peel and leave young ones whole; slice large roots. Boil or roast around meat or serve like swedes.

LEGUMES

Broad (lima) beans are available from June in the northern hemisphere for the summer. Remove the beans from the pods and boil, then serve cold in salads, or hot with cream or white or parsley sauce.

French or green beans have the same season as broad (lima) beans. Top and tail them and slice if large. Boil, then serve cold in vinaigrette or hot with butter and chopped herbs.

Runner (snap) beans succeed the other types of beans about a month later. Top and tail them, then slice diagonally. Serve like green beans.

Peas: new peas come at the beginning of summer. Pod and boil or steam. Serve hot with butter and mint, or petit pois (tiny new ones) cooked but cold in salads. Purée well-plumped peas and use for soup. Soup can also be made from the discarded pods.

Mange-tout or snow peas are the very young pods of peas. The French name means 'eat-all', which exactly describes them.

Remove any stalks then boil briefly or stem. Never really inexpensive, they can be stretched by mixing with new potatoes.

LEAVES AND BUDS

Broccoli: the unopened flower buds make a vegetable of delicate flavour. Various types are available, according to where you live. Sprouting broccoli are small flower heads that grow all the way up the side of the stalk; they are available in spring and again in autumn (fall) in Europe. A large single white head looks like a cauliflower, but is available in mid-winter. The large purple headed variety originated in South Africa. Calabrese is a green broccoli originating in Italy. Remove the hard stalks from any type, then divide into florets if desired. Boil or steam and serve hot with butter or white or cheese sauce.

Brussels sprouts are available from early autumn (fall) right through until well into the spring. Trim away damaged leaves then cut across through the base stalk. Boil briefly and serve hot with butter, chestnuts, nutmeg and black pepper, or purée.

Cabbage is available all the year round in different shapes, either green, red or white. Cut it into quarters, separate the leaves or shred them. Boil or stir-fry. Serve hot with butter, nutmeg, black pepper or caraway seeds. Casserole red cabbage with apple, onions and sugar or pickling spices. Use white cabbage in salads, such as coleslaw. Use cabbage leaves for lining casseroles etc or serve stuffed. 'Spring greens' are available from December in the northern hemisphere until spring has run its course. Separate into leaves then use as for cabbage.

Cauliflower is available all the year round, but prices fluctuate according to weather conditions. Remove hard stalks, then divide into florets if desired or cook whole. Boil, or steam if in florets. Serve with white or cheese sauce, or make into soup or a soufflé. Serve cooked florets cold with vinaigrette or young florets raw as a crudité with a dip.

Celery is available all the year round, but prices fluctuate: winter celery is whiter. Scrub individual stalks, then leave whole or halve or chop. Boil or braise. Serve hot with a white or cheese sauce. Celery can also be used in soups and is invaluable in stews.

Chard is variously known as Swiss chard, seakale beet, silver beet and seakale spinach. Use the cooked leaves like spinach. The centre stalks can be served alone (like asparagus) in butter sauce.

Kale is a hardy northern type of cabbage, available from before Christmas for about five months in the northern hemisphere. Discard the hard stalks, then shred the curly leaves. Boil, braise or steam and serve with butter or white sauce.

Leeks, the national badge of Wales, have a delicate flavour. They can be difficult to obtain in the United States. In Europe the season lasts from the end of summer right through to the beginning of the next. Trim and split lengthwise, then wash thoroughly under cold running water. Leave whole or slice. Boil or braise and serve with white or cheese sauce or in a soufflé. They are also used in casseroles, soups and stews. Serve boiled leeks cold with vinaigrette dressing.

Lettuce is available all year round, but can be expensive or of poor quality in winter. Separate the leaves and wash thoroughly. It is usually served raw in salads, but can also be boiled or braised. Outside leaves can be added to cooking peas or made into soup.

Spinach is available all the year round but fluctuates in price.

15

Pull off hard stalks and then wash the leaves, either twice over or under cold running water. Cook without water in a covered pan or steam. Serve chopped or puréed with butter, cream and nutmeg. It is also used in crêpes, soufflés, soups and quiches.

VEGETABLE FRUITS

Aubergines or Eggplants are available all the year round but are only economical in summer and early autumn (fall). Wipe, then top and tail them. To remove the bitter juices, slice thinly, sprinkle with salt and leave for 30 minutes. Drain and rinse under cold, running water, then pat dry. Shallow or deep fry. Bake in casseroles or stuff halves. Serve in moussaka, ratatouille and eggplant Parmesan.

(**Avocados** are available most of the year in warmer climates, and even in colder climates you can take advantage of an imported glut. Peel and slice to serve raw in salads, or halve and remove the stone or pit and fill the cavity with chicken, meat or seafood salad. Always sprinkle with lemon juice to prevent discolouration. The flesh, mashed with lemon juice, can be used as a dip or as a dessert.)

Courgettes or Zucchini are known by their French name in Britain and by their Italian name in the United States. Available all the year round, they are only inexpensive in summer and early autumn (fall). Top and tail them, leaving smaller ones whole and slicing larger ones into rings. Cut in half lengthwise if stuffing. Boil, steam or shallow fry, coated in dried breadcrumbs if desired. Deep-fry in batter. Serve in casseroles and dishes such as ratatouille. They can be stuffed and baked. Serve boiled courgettes cold in salads.

Cucumber is available all the year round, but is only economical in summer. It is usually served raw in salads, but can be cut into matchstick strips or balls with a melon baller and fried in butter. It can also be halved lengthwise, the seeds removed and stuffed, or cut across into chunks and hollowed out to make cups for stuffing.

Marrow, Marrow Squash or Baking Zucchini is available from midsummer until well into the autumn (fall). Cut it in half and remove the seeds. Keep the halves for stuffing or braising, or peel then slice thickly or dice. Boil or sauté in butter. Serve hot with butter and herbs or with white or cheese sauce.

Peppers (Bell Peppers), both green and red are available all the year round, but are only economical in summer and early autumn (fall). Remove the stem, core and seeds. Leave whole then stuff and bake. Slice or chop then fry or use in casseroles, soups and stews or use raw in salads.

Pumpkins are ripe in September and October in the northern hemisphere. Cut into quarters, remove the skin and seeds. Then cut into thick slices. Parboil, then fry in butter or boil or roast. Serve boiled pumpkin mashed or puréed. It is also used in soups and sweet pumpkin pie.

Sweetcorn is cheapest at the end of summer. Boil or steam whole corn-on-the-cob, then serve with butter. Or remove the kernels from the cob, then boil or use in casseroles, soups and stuffings.

Tomatoes are in season from March right through to October in the northern hemisphere. Serve raw in salads. For concassé tomatoes, dip in boiling water then in ice-cold water. Peel off skins then remove seeds and juice. Chop the remaining flesh roughly. Fry or grill (broil) halves, bake or stuff whole ones, or steam whole. Use also in casseroles, soups, stews etc.

Seasonal Fruit

TEMPERATE TREE FRUIT

Apples, both dessert and cooking types are available all the year round, with the new season's fruit coming in after midsummer. This is a most versatile fruit, both raw and cooked. Peel, core and slice cooking apples then stew or purée, or bake whole. Use in pies, puddings and desserts and also some savoury dishes, particularly with pork.

Apricots are available at a reasonable price during the summer months even in areas too cold to grow them. Serve whole ripe apricots raw as dessert fruit, or peel and halve, then remove the stones (pits). Use raw in desserts or poach halves and use in pies, flans and tarts etc.

Cherries are ripe in the second half of the summer. Remove the stalks and stones (pits) too if desired. Cook in compôtes, pies and puddings. Use cooking types for jam making.

Crabapples are ripe in early autumn (fall) and are only used for jelly making.

Damsons are cheapest at the end of summer. Remove stalks (and stones, if desired) and then stew or use in pies, puddings, jams and jellies.

Greengages are another end-of-summer fruit. Halve and remove the stones, then use in pies or preserves.

Peaches are available during the summer months at a reasonable price. Serve whole ripe peaches raw as a dessert fruit, or peel and halve, then remove the stones. Slice and use raw in desserts or poach the halves or slices. They are excellent in flans, tarts and with ice-creams.

Pears are available most of the year and locally-grown ones from the end of the summer to after Christmas in the northern hemisphere. Dessert pears are eaten raw, either whole or peeled and sliced and used in fruit salads etc. Cooking varieties are often left whole and are poached in syrup, or peeled and sliced and used in pies and tarts.

Plums are a late summer and early autumn (fall) fruit. Remove the stalks, then eat raw as a dessert fruit, either whole or halved with the stones removed. Use cooked in flans, pies and puddings. They make excellent jams, pickles and chutney.

BERRIES AND LOW-GROWING TEMPERATE FRUIT

Bilberries and/or Blueberries are available in the summer months. Stew and use in pies, puddings and ice-cream. They are also used in jam and jelly making.

Blackberries are ripe from late summer into autumn. Hull then stew or use in pies and other puddings. They are also used in jam and jellymaking.

Currants of all three colours, black, red and white, are ripe in late summer. Remove the stalks, then use in compôtes and other puddings and desserts. Use blackcurrants in ice-creams and sorbets (sherbets), jams, jellies and fruit syrups.

Gooseberries are in season from midsummer. Top and tail, then stew or use in pies, puddings, jams and jellies.

Loganberries are in season the last two summer months. Hull then use in pies and tarts. They are also used in jam and wine making.

Melons are cheaper during the summer months, but prices vary according to variety. They are always served raw, either for a starter or dessert course. Large melons are sliced into quarters, smaller varieties are halved or left whole. The flesh can be scooped into balls for fruit salad or used in water ice.

Raspberries are in season the last two summer months. Hull, then eat raw with sugar to taste or use in fresh fruit salads and other desserts. Also use in ice-creams, sorbets and water ices and in jam and jelly making. Puréed raspberries are used as a sauce.

Rhubarb is available from the beginning of the year in the northern hemisphere for six months. Trim and cut into chunks, then stew or use in pies, puddings and tarts. It is also used in jam making.

Strawberries have a four month season, starting before midsummer. Hull, then eat raw with sugar to taste or use in fresh fruit salads, or other desserts. They are also used in ice-creams, sorbets (sherbets) and water ices and in jam making.

TROPICAL AND WARM CLIMATE FRUIT

Bananas are available all the year round, but prices fluctuate according to season. Bake in the skins or peel then poach in syrup or grill (broil) with brown sugar. Slice and use raw in puddings and desserts, or used mashed banana in puddings and teabreads. Green bananas (plantains) are used in savoury West Indian dishes.

Grapes are available all the year round but are generally cheaper in the summer months. Seedless grapes have a very short summer season. Grapes are mostly eaten raw as a dessert fruit or used in puddings and desserts, particularly as a decoration. Halve and remove seeds if desired.

Grapefruit are available all the year round, but prices fluctuate according to the season. They are mostly eaten halved and raw on their own for breakfast or as a starter. They can also be used in desserts, such as fruit salads and squeezed for juice.

Lemons are available all the year but prices fluctuate. Lemon rind and juice are used extensively in cooking for both sweet and savoury dishes. Lemon slices, rings and quarters are used for decoration and garnishes and also for drinks.

Limes have a summer season and are used like lemons.

Mandarin oranges, Satsumas and Tangerines are available in the four winter months. Peel and eat them raw as a dessert fruit, or in fresh fruit salads and similar desserts.

(**Mangos** are at their cheapest in summer. Peel and slice or serve raw in fruit salads and desserts.)

Oranges are available all year round, but prices fluctuate. This versatile fruit is mainly eaten raw as a dessert fruit. It is used raw or cooked in desserts. Orange rind and juice are used extensively in cooking, both sweet and savoury.

(**Pawpaws or Papayas** have usually travelled and therefore may not be cheap. Serve raw as for melon. They are also used in oriental cookery.)

Pineapples are usually at their cheapest and best during the summer months. They are usually eaten raw as a dessert fruit, either cut into rings or segments. Use diced pineapple in fruit salads and other desserts, ice-creams, sorbets and water ices. They are occasionally used in savoury dishes, particularly with ham, bacon and pork.

(**Pomegranates** are available in the autumn (fall) months. Eat them raw on their own or use in fresh fruit salads.)

Eat fruit in season, and preferably raw, for maximum vitamins.

Freezing

A freezer not only helps you to save time and money, but enables you to preserve food in a way that best retains colour, flavour and nutritional value. You can save time by turning daily shopping trips into weekly or even monthly ones. You can save money by buying in bulk and taking advantage of seasonal and special offers. You can save time and money by batch cooking.

BULK BUYING

There is a temptation when buying in bulk to snap up anything that is cheap. But if the family do not like it, or if you buy so much that you cannot get through it within its recommended storage life, then it is not a good bargain whatever the price. Nor is it a good buy if it is cheap because it is of poor quality. Food for the freezer must be of the highest quality. The freezer will store food safely but it cannot magically improve it. Put tired old produce in and that is precisely what you will get out. Bearing all this in mind, what is worth buying in bulk for the freezer?

Meat and poultry: probably your largest outlay of money will be on meat so think carefully before you indulge in whole or half carcasses. Remember that as well as fat and bones you are going to get a number of cuts you probably never use. You might do better to see what your local butcher can offer in the way of discount on the cuts you normally use and buy those in bulk. If by buying a larger quantity you can make an even bigger saving, consider sharing your bulk buy with one or two families.

Ask your butcher to bone and roll any roasts as they take up less freezer space that way. Get him to pack, label and if possible, freeze the meat, as this will make another saving in time and money for you.

Watch if there are seasonal fluctuations in the price of meat; pork is sometimes cheaper in the summer and stewing meat may also be reduced in price.

Chickens can often be bought on special offer or in quantity at farms at a worthwhile saving. If you are freezing them yourself, divide some of them into portions. These are useful for quick meals and are cheaper than buying chicken portions. Pack the giblets and livers separately or, better still, turn them into stock and pâté ready to freeze.

Mince (ground meat) can be used in such a variety of dishes that it is worth buying in bulk and will usually cost a little less that way. Ask your butcher to package and freeze it in amounts suitable for your family's needs. Alternatively, bulk buy fresh mince. Use some of it to make hamburgers. Invest in a hamburger press and plan always to make your own; they will work out cheaper than commercially packed ones. Cook the rest of your bulk buy with onion, tomatoes and seasonings and freeze in portions to use in shepherd's pies, lasagne and moussaka.

Fish: this must be frozen within 24 hours of being caught so do not be tempted to bulk buy, unless you live on the coast where you can buy direct from the boat.

Fruit and vegetables: the best sources of supply for these (with the obvious exception of your own garden) are the many pick-your-own farms, or farm shops. Shop produce will not be freshly harvested so may not be worth freezing, with the possible exception in Britain of seasonally cheap, imported foods such as aubergines (eggplants), peppers, possibly peaches, pineapples and melons.

If you are buying ready-frozen vegetables, buy the large packs rather than the smaller ones. Either repackage in family-size portions when you get home, or remember to measure out by the cup or weigh the amount you need when you cook them to avoid waste. It is difficult to judge the quantity when tipping from a large bag.

BATCH COOKING

As well as buying in bulk you can bake in bulk to save time and money. It takes very little extra time and effort to make a batch of cakes rather than one and you will be making fuller use of your oven heat. The same goes for pies, casseroles and other cooked dishes. You save money, too, as you will not be so easily tempted to buy expensive convenience foods when you are in a hurry if you have a supply of your own in the freezer.

You can batch bake by setting aside one day every month or so to cook a selection of meat and fish dishes and a range of pies and cakes. Alternatively, you can simply make double or triple quantities of your day-to-day cooking and freeze the surplus, so that by the end of a week you have another one or two weeks' supply of cooked dishes in the freezer.

PACKAGING

Food for the freezer must be carefully packed in moisture/vapour-proof wrappings to exclude as much air as possible so that the food does not dry out and lose flavour and texture. There is no need to invest in a lot of expensive packaging. Plastic bags will do for most things; choose ones in heavy gauge and preferably gusseted. Foil is useful, too, particularly for moulding around awkward shapes. But as often as possible aim for square or rectangular shapes, as these can be stacked without leaving gaps and so use every bit of freezer space.

These 'brick' shapes can be made in two ways. You can put a plastic bag into a square or rectangular carton like a fine sugar box, fill the bag with whatever you are going to freeze—soup, purée, fruits in syrup—stand it on a baking tray in the freezer and when hard remove the carton, seal the plastic bag and return it to the freezer. The other way is to pour a quantity of stew or mince (ground beef) or sauce into a roasting pan, stand it in the freezer and when firm mark it into squares. When fully frozen divide it up and pack each 'brick' in a plastic bag or wrap it in foil. This cuts down on the need for rigid containers.

Casseroles and pie dishes can be lined with foil and the contents removed in the foil when frozen solid. The parcel will fit back into the correct container when needed. This way you can avoid buying foil containers.

Make use of 'free' cartons, too. Yogurt, cream and margarine pots, ice-cream containers all can be reused provided they are thoroughly cleaned and, as an added precaution, sterilized with boiling water or any solution used to sterlize babies' feeding bottles. If the lids are damaged or missing, top with a double layer of foil and seal with freezer tape.

FREEZING PREPARED DISHES

Prepared dishes make a marvellous standby for occasions when

you have neither the time nor the inclination to cook, and they can be batch baked, saving you time.

Soups and sauces: both these can be made in bulk then frozen in 275ml ($\frac{1}{2}$ pt) and 575ml (1 pt) quantities. It is best to add cream or milk to soup when reheating. Sauces take time to make, so are worth doing in bulk to freeze. They can be in the form of complete sauces—meat or tomato for use with pasta—or basic sauce—white and brown to which other ingredients are added later. As sauce made with ordinary flour tends to curdle when reheated after freezing, it is best to use cornflour (cornstarch) for thickening. Freeze in 'bricks' as described under packaging.
Storage time: Soups: 3 months; sauces: 6 months.
To use: reheat gently from frozen.

Pâtés: chicken livers (from a bulk buy of chicken) or pig's liver make good cheap pâtés. Make a large one in a loaf pan then slice it before freezing, separating each slice with waxed paper. You can just take out the number of slices you need and there is no waste.
Storage time: 1 month, if it contains bacon or garlic, 3 months for others.
To use: thaw a slice at room temperature for about an hour.

Fish: small amounts of leftover cooked fish can be made into fish cakes or kedgeree—a useful standby for quick snack meals.
Storage time: 1 month.
To use: fish cakes and kedgeree can be reheated from frozen.

Casseroles: undercook these slightly as the reheating will complete the cooking. Make sure there is sufficient sauce or gravy to cover the meat so it does not dry out in the freezer. Thicken after thawing to eliminate the risk of curdling and do not forget to adjust the seasoning before serving. Before freezing cool the casserole and remove any surface fat. You can freeze it in its dish, then, when hard, tip it out onto a piece of foil, wrap and return it to the freezer. When using it unwrap while still frozen and return it to its dish for reheating. Alternatively you can 'brick' freeze it and thaw before reheating.
Storage time: 3 months.
To use: reheat slowly from frozen or thaw overnight in refrigerator and reheat.

Sweet desserts and pies: suet (lard) and sponge mixtures can be made and frozen raw or cooked. Add dried fruits, nuts, coffee or chocolate flavourings. Jams and syrups are best served with the pudding; they tend to make it soggy if put in the bottom of the container for freezing.

Two-crust pies should have the lower crust brushed with egg white or sprinkled with cake crumbs, to prevent the pastry becoming soggy, before filling. Fruit crumbles can be frozen raw or the crumb mixture frozen separately. Mousses and trifles can be frozen in individual containers: useful for packed lunches and picnics.
Storage time: 3 months for all puddings.
To use: puddings, pies, crumbles: cook from frozen; mousses and trifles: thaw in refrigerator.

Bread, cakes and scones (biscuits): bread freezes beautifully and a supply in the freezer saves shopping trips. Most cakes freeze well but try to avoid synthetic flavourings and go lightly with spices as these tend to change during freezing and taste unpleasant. Cakes can be cut in wedges and wrapped individually or the slices separated with waxed paper and the cake wrapped as a whole. This is useful for packed lunches or for rationing the consumption. Scones (biscuits) go stale quickly after baking, so batch bake then freeze in plastic bags.
Storage time: bread and scones (biscuits): 6 months; cakes: 4 months.
To use: bread, cake and scones: thaw at room temperature.

Sandwiches: if any of the family buy snack lunches, homemade sandwiches will prove cheaper. Plan a sandwich-making session, perhaps once a month, pack them into daily batches and freeze. Avoid hard boiled eggs—they go rubbery; mayonnaise—it curdles; salad vegetables—they go limp. Sandwiches taken from the freezer in the morning will be thawed by lunchtime and taste freshly made.
Storage time: 2 months.
To use: thaw at room temperature.

Baby foods: save money by making up your own supply of meat, vegetable and fruit purées. Freeze in ice-cube trays or small cartons in one-meal portions. Be particularly careful about hygiene when preparing baby foods and sterilize all equipment.
Storage time: 3 months.
To use: reheat from frozen or thaw in refrigerator.

19

Economy Hints

SHOPPING WISELY

If you are housekeeping on a budget, and few people are not, careful shopping is essential. If you shop wisely in the first place, then no matter what you do afterwards, you are more than half-way there. Before leaving home, plan menus and write shopping lists. This should save you from impulse purchases (one of the pitfalls of supermarkets) and will avoid wasting unwanted food, particularly fresh produce. If you want to take advantage of a special offer, strike out the item on your list for which it can be substituted.

To shop economically, it is essential to achieve a happy balance between the large supermarket/hypermarket/freezer centre type of shop and the local tradesman, market or farmer. Try at least to cut down on the number of shopping trips you make, both to economize on time and travelling expenses and to avoid temptation.

Buying in bulk at the supermarket will definitely save money if carried out sensibly. Large packets, bottles and cans will not work out cheaper, however, if the family tires of whatever is in them, or if you use more of an expensive product because it is there, or if the food goes stale before you reach the end. Bulk buy tried and tested items. Household cleaning items and basic foodstuffs such as coffee, tea and sugar are the most obvious candidates.

Supermarkets can also save you money on 'own brands', which are usually cheaper than name brands—though a special offer may change this. Shop around for best buys in different supermarkets and keep a sharp eye open for bargains. Read the labels on cans, bottles and packets very carefully, comparing weight for weight and price for price. What looks like a bargain may not actually be so.

Plan your shopping to buy fresh produce such as fruit, vegetables, fish, meat and even dairy foods at the appropriate shops. This will be cheaper than buying supermarket prepacks, which may not be exactly what you want. Local tradesmen specialize in the bulk purchase of their own particular type of merchandise and can offer a lower price to their customers.

STOCKING UP

If you do not have a freezer there are still numerous other ways in which fresh produce can be stored. Nor do you pay a storage charge, as you must with a freezer.

There are a few important points to remember when preserving fresh produce, by whatever method mentioned below. Always use produce that is in first-class condition, neither under-ripe nor over-ripe, nor with any trace of blemish or mould. Preserves made with inferior quality produce will not keep well and, in most cases, will simply become mouldy and inedible. This will also be the case if they are not stored correctly. Follow the recipe instructions to the letter for covering and sealing jars and bottles, and choose a cool, dry, airy storage place that is free from damp and away from any heat source such as a central heating boiler or radiator. If these few basic rules and principles are followed, you will find that preserving is not only good economy, it is also a most rewarding and satisfying occupation.

Preserving is the most obvious way to store fresh fruit and

vegetables, either in the form of jams, jellies, curds, mincemeat and marmalade, or as bottled fruit, sauces and syrups, chutneys, pickles and vinegars. Homemade preserves are definitely cheaper than their commercial counterparts, and they taste better too. It is certainly worth spending time and energy on preserving during the peak growing season.

Bottling (Canning) fruit and vegetables is another way of storing and is cheaper than freezing even if you have a choice. You will need to invest in the necessary equipment first time around, but this will more than pay for itself if used correctly and often.

Salting is an old-fashioned method of preserving vegetables such as cabbage and green beans, but nevertheless it is still efficient and worthwhile if you have a glut of homegrown produce and have preserved sufficient in other ways.

Drying is a useful method of preserving for fruit, vegetables and herbs. Apples can be dried successfully in rings and such fruits as peaches, plums and apricots are usually dried in halves. Beans, mushrooms and onions are good vegetables to dry, and all herbs are successfully preserved by this method.

Cool Storage: some fruit and vegetables can be stored simply by being kept in a cool, dry place, such as an attic above the house insulation or in a garage or cellar. Apples, pears, root vegetables and nuts can all be stored this way. They should be picked or harvested when in peak condition, then spread out in a single layer on trays or racks and, if possible, kept in the dark. Make a point of inspecting such produce at regular intervals and remove any that has gone mouldy or rotten, or it will quickly spread to the surrounding produce.

Home-cooking is another worthwhile occupation, both in terms of saving money and eating food that actually tastes better. Homemade cakes, bread, biscuits (cookies), buns and pies, for example, can be made for a fraction of the cost of bought ones, and the quality simply cannot compare. Homemade soups are also more economical than using cans and packages, they freeze well and have far better flavour and consistency, not to mention nutritional value. Home cooking in general is to be preferred to opening cans and packets and living on convenience foods and frozen meals, but the wise cook needs to watch her expenditure on time and fuel, as well as of money.

Cooking Economically

Animal protein food tends to be the most expensive item in the housekeeping budget, therefore the first way to save money is to substitute something else for part of it. Remember if you are cooking for the same group of people regularly, the most important thing is to vary the menu. Try not to repeat the same idea too often.

Pasta is about 12% protein, with more protein than potatoes, bread or rice. Egg noodles, macaroni, shells and twists can be added to soups, meat casseroles, stew and minced (ground) beef to stretch the meat and make it go further. Up to half the amount of meat can be replaced with pasta, in most dishes, without spoiling them. Lasagne, cannelloni and ravioli can be used in layers or stuffed with meat, poultry or cheese to make the latter go further.

Rice: long-grain rice contains 8–9% protein, and the more expensive brown rice contains more than this. Long-grain rice makes an excellent and filling base for stuffing red and green peppers, cabbage and vine leaves, beef and veal 'olives' or 'birds', chicken and turkey etc. It can also be used in dishes such as risotto, cold rice salads, kedgeree and the Indian dish polo. Rice is the main ingredient and the quantity of meat, fish or poultry need only be small.

Dried pulses (legumes) include chick peas, haricots (navy beans), red kidney beans, lentils, butter (lima) beans, black-eye peas, dried or split peas and soya beans. Soya or TVP (Textured Vegetable Protein) contains protein equal to that found in meat or fish, and all beans and peas are only deficient in those amino acids which are found in whole grains. All you have to do is to combine them with brown bread or a grain like rice and you will get quality protein for a fraction of the cost of meat or fish. Many familiar or famous dishes are based on this idea: for example baked beans on toast and risi e bisi and kitchri (see recipes).

Dried beans and peas of all sorts provide useful bulk in meals without being all carbohydrate. They also make excellent inexpensive soups, as they can be puréed in a blender with the cooking liquid and vegetables. Many famous dishes like Boston baked beans and French cassoulet (see recipes) use beans to replace or extend meat. Both beans and peas make good salads.

Lentils make an interesting purée cooked as dhal (see recipe) and can be made into croquettes, patties or rissoles, either on their own or with meat or soya protein (hamburger helper). Hummus, the Middle Eastern dip made from puréed chick peas, makes an inexpensive starter well under the cost of meat or fish pâté.

Nuts can be used in moderation in stuffings and casseroles and to make croquettes, rissoles and cutlets. They are expensive for their weight, but they are a valuable source of protein and fat.

Starchy foods containing some protein: other popular foods for stretching stews are *forcemeat* or *stuffing* balls. These usually contain some meat or bacon with breadcrumbs and onions added. *Dumplings*, made of flour and shredded suet (lard) add bulk to a soup or stew and, if flavoured with herbs, are delicious in themselves. *Scone (biscuit) topping*, or 'cobbler' as it is known, is cut in circular shapes and placed on top of the casserole which is then baked until they rise and brown. Grated cheese can be added to the dough.

Pastry is probably the most popular meat extender ever invented. Both under and over meat, fish and dairy mixtures, in its many delicious types, it provides a crisp contrast to meat, as well as extending it.

Potato is a great meat-stretcher, both for topping pies like shepherd's pie and for making croquettes and potato cakes. It still makes a major contribution to children's diets, supplying about 25% of all protein in the United States and about 30% in parts of Europe. Casseroles can be topped with a combination of mashed potato and carrot or other vegetable such as swedes (rutabagas) or Jerusalem artichokes. *Rings of French bread*, spread with garlic or herb butter, can also be placed on a beef casserole: cook in the oven until crisp and golden.

Soya protein (TVP), which is treated to give it a consistency not unlike meat, is widely available in cans and packets and can be used as an addition to minced (ground) beef. With the addition of onions, garlic, herbs and spices, it makes a tasty family meal.

Vegetarian meals should never be considered inferior to meat or fish ones. This type of cookery is both varied and interesting and even meat-eating families can well eat one meatless meal a week. You will find that a little vegetarian cookery stimulates your imagination to produce more interesting vegetable side dishes too.

Milk contains protein, fat, minerals, vitamins A and B and nicotinic acid. In 575ml/1 pt ($2\frac{1}{2}$ cups) milk there is roughly the same amount of protein as 75g (3 oz) meat or 2 eggs. Milk plays an important part in budget cooking; in terms of value for money there are very few foods which can equal it.

Milk makes an inexpensive, nutritious drink alone or with the addition of chocolate, coffee or fruit juice. Made into white, béchamel or cheese sauce, or with added eggs to make custard, milk adds extra nutritional content to both savoury and sweet sauces. Added to soups, it gives them extra food value. With very small quantities of cereal it makes milk puddings such as rice, sago and tapioca puddings. It will also make junket, blancmange and milk jelly.

Mock cream can be made with milk, unsalted butter and gelatin for a fraction of the cost of fresh dairy cream (see recipe). In countries where milk is pasteurized rather than homogenized, 'top of the milk' can often replace thin cream or stretch thick cream.

Eggs are an excellent source of protein, fat and minerals, and the cook interested in economy should know that a medium-sized egg has roughly the same amount of protein and fat as 50g (2 oz) fairly fat meat.

Eggs can be made into nourishing meals in the form of omelets, quiches, soufflés etc, apart from the more obvious ways of frying, boiling, coddling, poaching and scrambling. They can also be used to enrich sauces and soups, beaten into mashed potato with milk and butter, stuffed or coated with mayonnaise for an inexpensive starter to a dinner party, or curried for a quick, inexpensive main course dish. They can be baked in potatoes or a nest of spinach, or surrounded with sausagemeat and made into Scotch eggs. Finely chopped hard-boiled (hard-cooked) eggs, quarters or slices make a nutritious garnish for soups and vegetable dishes.

An inexpensive yet nutritious breakfast or children's snack can be made by coating slices of bread in a mixture of eggs and milk, then frying them in butter. Eggs are also useful in making desserts, where they are not so noticeable for those who dislike them. **Cheese** is a valuable source of protein, fat, calcium, phosphorus and vitamins A and B, and 25g (1 oz) cheese contains as much protein as 75g (3 oz) lean meat, and it is very versatile.

Grated hard cheese mixed with breadcrumbs, pasta, mashed potato or beaten eggs makes a nutritious topping for most savoury dishes, either baked in the oven or cooked under the grill (broiler). Cheese also makes a substantial main course dish in a quiche, pie or charlotte instead of, or in addition to, meat or poultry. In the form of a thick coating sauce, it can also make a main course mixed with vegetables, pancakes or fish. Cheese fondue can make an inexpensive dinner party meal if half Emmenthal or Gruyère and half Cheddar are used instead of all Swiss cheese as usual. For an unusual dinner party appetizer that is not unreasonably expensive, deep-fry individual portions of Camembert and serve hot with a sharp preserve such as gooseberry or cranberry jelly.

Cheese is also useful in adding that something 'extra' to your baking—add it to scones (biscuits) and fruit loaves, individual buns, pastry and breads etc.

Yogurt: many party dishes are topped with soured cream, or include fresh cream in the sauce. Both these items are expensive to buy, yet plain, unsweetened yogurt makes a perfectly acceptable alternative. Yogurt retails at about half the cost of fresh and sour cream and homemade yogurt (*page 249*) works out at roughly a third of the commercial price.

Luxury foods need not be entirely dismissed from the cook's repertoire simply because he or she is sticking to a budget. Top rump (top round), topside (sirloin) or even rump steak (filet mignon) can be sliced very thinly when making beef olives (birds) and, provided that an economical and fairly substantial stuffing is used, the overall cost of the meal will not be unreasonable. Instead of veal, use pork or turkey escalopes (scallops). Beef Stroganoff is

one of the most popular of all classic dishes for dinner parties, but if you are sticking to a budget, why not use very thin slivers of lamb's liver instead and make liver Stroganoff?

Delicatessens are worth patronizing for 'ends' of cooked meats such as garlic sausage, salami and smoked ham, which are often sold more cheaply, because they will not go into the slicing machine. Use them chopped in quiches, salads and stuffings etc. End pieces of smoked salmon are often cheaper than sliced salmon: these make a delicious quiche with cream cheese (see recipe).

LEFTOVERS

If you are cooking for a family on a budget, forward planning of menus is very important. Buy enough for the first meal to have what you need left over for the second. Think of it as a sensible form of chain cooking, rather than as being mean with the housekeeping money!

As a general rule a small roasting cut is poor value for money because it dries out. Buy a larger one and use the leftovers from Sunday's roast to make a Monday meat and vegetable pie. Slice the meat thinly, then arrange in layers in an ovenproof dish with seasonal vegetables. Pour over cheese sauce or (leftover) gravy, then bake in the oven until the vegetables are tender. Alternatively, mince (grind) or chop the leftover meat finely and use it in such dishes as moussaka and cottage or shepherd's pies. If the amount of minced meat looks too small, then it can be used to stuff vegetables such as aubergines (eggplants) and tomatoes, combined with other ingredients as necessary.

When using leftovers, more than just a little imagination and ingenuity are required, to disguise the fact that they are leftovers.

Cooked poultry or meat can be chopped finely and combined with a thick béchamel sauce to make rissoles. It can be shredded or diced and used in pies if there is a lot. A slice or two of bacon can be used to help. If there is not much meat, use it for an omelet or crêpe filling.

Stock or gravy and vegetables can be strained or blended to make soup. Use milk for the liquid if there is no gravy. Bones and carcasses can be used to make stocks and soups. Parsley stalks and the pared rind of citrus fruits can be used for flavouring sauces. Stale bread can be made into white or dried breadcrumbs, then used in stuffings or as a coating for fried foods. In slices it can make croûtons, charlottes or bread and butter puddings with the addition of fruit. Stale cheese should be grated and kept in a plastic container in the refrigerator for toppings, sauces, omelets and cheese on toast. If small quantities of an ingredient like anchovies, that mean opening a can, are required plan your menus to include the leftover portion in the next day or two.

Clever cooks with a thought to helping themselves, deliberately cook twice the amount they need and chill or freeze the portions that are not eaten on the day. This saves time and fuel but also saves energy, as you are 'half way there' to another meal. Obvious examples are useful all rounders like tomato sauce and shortcrust pastry. You will barely notice the time it takes to make the second pastry case, and you will be grateful later to have one ready to fill. Most families do not object to eating a popular stew on two successive nights. Less obvious examples are ready-cooked rice, mashed potatoes and cooked pulses (legumes). This principle is very familiar to freezer owners who can use the freezer as a storecupboard for leftovers.

MAKING THE MOST OF MEAT

To taste delicious, the cheaper cuts of meat must be cooked by methods which enhance their good points. Do not try to pass them off as something they are not by roasting, frying or grilling (broiling). The result can only be disappointing. The best methods of cooking these cuts are usually braising, stewing, pot roasting and boiling. Long, slow cooking is the essence of success; this will tenderize the tougher sinews and allow the juices and flavours to make a rich gravy, which is one of the pleasures of this type of dish. An inexpensive larger cut such as brisket or shoulder can be slow roasted, however, if it is first wrapped in kitchen foil, because the enclosed moisture will help to tenderize the meat.

Tough sinews can be broken down by beating the meat with a mallet or rolling pin before cooking. Marinating and/or cooking in wine, wine vinegar, lemon juice or some other form of acid also helps to break down the sinewy tissues in meat.

Modern cooking methods can also help. A pressure cooker is a worthwhile investment for its saving on fuel and in the cook's time. Its basic principle is that steam is forced into the food under pressure; this speeds cooking and tenderizes at the same time.

The electric slow cooker or crock pot is another popular appliance. It will stew safely without risk of drying out for up to 12 hours—a boon for the cook who is out all day and could not otherwise prepare casseroles and stews. It also uses only the same amount of fuel as a light bulb, so the fuel saving could be considerable if it was used frequently instead of the oven. Like the pressure cooker it cannot brown meat, so for a richer flavour meat must be browned in a frying-pan first.

Spring

Soups and Starters

Greek Egg and Lemon Soup

SERVES 6

75g/3 oz (½ cup) long-grain rice, washed
1.7L/3 pt (7½ cups) chicken stock
4 medium-sized eggs
juice of 2 lemons
salt
freshly ground black pepper
30ml (2 tablespoons) chopped parsley

Put the stock in a large saucepan and bring it to the boil. Add the rice and simmer over low heat for 15 minutes until the rice is tender. Remove the pan from the heat.

Break the eggs into a bowl and beat lightly. Gradually add the lemon juice, beating continuously. Add a few spoonfuls of stock and mix well. Stir this mixture into the stock.

Return to a low heat and warm through but do not let it boil or it will curdle. Season, and add parsley. Serve immediately.

Cooking time: 20 minutes

●Fish stock or court bouillon can also be used to make this soup and it makes a delicious way of using up a leftover item. Omit the lemons if they were included in the court bouillon.

Seafood Cocktail

Serving a fish cocktail in a wine glass gives you an effect without spending money. If you have wine glasses which are rarely used—wedding presents, perhaps—here is the opportunity to get them out. The chiffonade of lettuce helps to spread the fish, while the Italian tuna mayonnaise gives extra flavour.

SERVES 4

225g/1 pt (½ lb) boiled, unpeeled prawns (small shrimp)
175g/6 oz (¾ cup) peeled, finely diced potatoes
1 strip of lemon rind
4 lettuce leaves
100g (3½ oz) canned tuna
2 egg yolks
25ml (5 teaspoons) lemon juice
200ml/7 fl oz (1 scant cup) olive oil
5ml (1 teaspoon) capers
30ml (2 tablespoons) tomato ketchup
salt
freshly ground black pepper
paprika

A light, clear beetroot soup, bortsch may be served either hot or cold, with sour cream swirled on top.

Peel the prawns (shrimp), reserving the bodies. Put the shells into a small pan with the lemon rind. Cover with water and simmer for 20 minutes. Strain, discarding the shells, and then cook the potatoes in the fish stock until they are cooked but not oversoft—about 5 minutes. Drain and leave to cool.

Make the mayonnaise (*page 250*). Chop the capers finely and stir in the tuna and its oil, flaking it. Add the tomato ketchup.

Shred the lettuce and make a bed in the bottom of each glass. Add a prawn to each one and then divide the potato between the glasses. Spoon over most of the mayonnaise. Pile in the remaining prawns, spooning a little mayonnaise on top. Dust heavily with paprika. Refrigerate until needed.

Cooking time: 55 minutes plus chilling time

●White fish can be used instead of tuna. Cook it with beetroot to colour it.

Bortsch

This famous Russian soup can be served hot or cold.

SERVES 6

450g (1 lb) uncooked beetroot (beets)
¼ × small cabbage, finely shredded
25g/1 oz (2 tablespoons) butter
1 onion, chopped
850ml/1½ pt (3¾ cups) chicken stock
5ml (1 teaspoon) caraway seeds
5ml (1 teaspoon) sugar
salt
freshly ground black pepper
juice of 1 lemon
60ml/4 tablespoons (¼ cup) dry white wine (optional)
30ml (2 tablespoons) sour cream

Cook the beetroot (beets) for 1½ hours in boiling salted water until tender. Reserve 275ml/½ pt (1¼ cups) of the cooking liquid. Cool the beets then slip off the skins. Grate the beets and reserve any juice.

Simmer the cabbage for 8–10 minutes in the reserved liquid. Meanwhile melt the butter in a large pan and fry the onion for 5 minutes. Add the chicken stock to the onion and bring to the boil. Add the cabbage and its cooking liquid, the beets and the juice, the caraway seeds, sugar and seasonings. Simmer for 10 minutes, removing any scum that rises to the surface. Add the lemon juice and the wine and bring to the boil.

To serve, pour the soup into a soup tureen and garnish with swirls of sour cream.

Cooking time: 2¼ hours

● To serve the soup cold, stir in 150ml/ ¼ pt (⅔ cup) sour cream instead of the smaller quantity used for the hot soup. Chill for 3 hours.

Heavenly Soup

Soups with eggs are nourishing and adding eggs is a quick way of improving a canned consommé. The cheese looks like little fluffy clouds on top, reminiscent of baroque church painting which earns it its name.

SERVES 6
1.1L/2 pt (4½ cups) good chicken stock
30ml (2 tablespoons) white breadcrumbs
2 eggs, separated
30ml (2 tablespoons) grated Parmesan cheese
salt
freshly ground black pepper

Heat the stock. Meanwhile whisk the egg whites until stiff then whisk in the yolks until well blended. Stir in the bread-crumbs, cheese and seasonings.

Add the egg mixture a spoonful at a time to the hot stock. Cook 5–8 minutes then serve.

Cooking time: 10 minutes

● Stracciatella is another useful egg soup. The Italian name means 'little rags' because the egg appears as little shreds in the stock. Half a beaten egg, left over from glazing pastry, can be used up in this way. Add another egg, 7.5ml (1½ teaspoons) fine semolina and 15ml (1 tablespoon) grated Parmesan cheese. Combine these in a cup than add to 700ml/1¼ pt (3 cups) hot chicken stock. Whisk with a fork then allow to cook for 4–5 minutes.
● Two eggs can be used and the semolina can be omitted.
● If you have relied heavily on a stock cube for the broth, add dry sherry to the stock in the proportion of 50ml/2 fl oz (¼ cup) to 450ml/16 fl oz (2 cups) stock.

Kipper Pâté

Make the pâté in advance and chill it; eat within 48 hours. Serve it with toast as first course or with salad for a light lunch.

SERVES 6
400g (14 oz) kipper or herring fillets, poached
175g/6 oz (¾ cup) curd or cream cheese
1.5ml (¼ teaspoon) paprika
salt
freshly ground black pepper
lemon juice
30ml (2 tablespoons) thin cream

Mash the kipper fillets with a fork and remove any bones as you do this. Work the cheese to a paste and add paprika and seasoning. Mix the kipper flesh and the cheese until well blended. Mix in a few drops of lemon juice to taste. Stir in cream and seasoning to taste.

Pile the mixture on to a plate or turn it into a small dish and level the top.

Preparation time: 10 minutes plus chilling time

● Make a party version for 4 with buckling, if you can get it. Cut the tops off 4 lemons, scoop out the inside and use these to hold the pâté. Make the pâté with 1 large buckling—about 200g (7 oz)—100g/¼ lb (½ cup) butter, 15ml (1 tablespoon) lemon juice and plenty of black pepper and stuff the lemon shells. Chill ½ hour before serving.

Carrot and cream cheese pâté is a good way to use up old or blemished carrots. It is excellent spread on toast.

Carrot and Cream Cheese Pâté

SERVES 4
700g (1½ lb) carrots, chopped
350g (¾ lb) full fat cream cheese, at room temperature
15ml (1 tablespoon) fresh parsley, chopped
salt
freshly ground black pepper
a few chives, chopped to garnish
sprigs of watercress
½ × cucumber, sliced

Cook the carrots in boiling salted water 7–10 minutes, then drain in a colander for a few minutes.

Mash or purée the carrots and leave until cold. Beat in the cheese a little at a time so that it blends in evenly. Add the parsley, seasoning and chives. Line a 12.5cm (5 in) long pâté dish or 450g (1 lb) loaf tin (pan) with greaseproof or wax paper. Pack in the mixture and chill for 3 hours.

Invert the pâté on to a serving dish. Remove the paper and smooth the pâté with a knife if necessary. To garnish, arrange slices of cucumber along the top and watercress sprigs along the sides.

Cooking time: 30 minutes plus 3 hours chilling time

Spring Vegetable and Chicken Soup with Dumplings

This meal-in-a-bowl can be half prepared the day before.

SERVES 6
1.4kg (3 lb) chicken
2 onions, quartered
6 large carrots, 3 chopped and 3 cut into matchsticks
2 celery stalks, chopped
2 bay leaves
6 peppercorns
2.3L/4 pt (5 pt) water
salt
freshly ground black pepper
FOR THE DUMPLINGS
125g/¼ lb (1 cup) plain flour
5ml (1 teaspoon) baking powder
½ egg, lightly beaten
50ml/2 fl oz (¼ cup) milk
salt
freshly ground black pepper

Put the chicken into a saucepan. Add the onions, chopped carrots, celery, bay leaves, peppercorns and water and bring to the boil. Reduce the heat and simmer for about 1½ hours until the chicken is tender.

Remove the pan from the heat and transfer the chicken to a chopping board. Strain the soup and discard the vegetables and seasoning. Allow the soup liquid to stand in a bowl until the fat rises to the surface. The easiest way is to refrigerate overnight, until the fat solidifies.

Allow the chicken to cool enough to handle—leave overnight if making the soup over two days. Remove and discard the chicken skin. Strip the meat from the bones and chop it into bite-sized pieces. Cover and set aside. Remove the fat from the soup. Return the broth to the pan and bring to the boil. Add the matchstick carrots to the pan and reduce heat. Simmer for 5–6 minutes.

Meanwhile, make the dumplings. Sift the flour, baking powder and some salt. Gradually beat in the egg and milk to make a firm dough. Using floured hands, form the dough into 6 balls.

Increase the heat so that the soup boils. Add the dumplings to the soup, cover and cook over moderate heat for 5 minutes or until they are fluffy and have risen to the top of the soup. Add the reserved chicken meat and allow to heat through. Check the seasoning and serve hot.

Cooking time: 1½ hours plus ½ hour cooling then 10 minutes to finish

This cream of mushroom soup uses a delicately-flavoured béchamel as a base to economize on thick cream.

Cream of Mushroom Soup

SERVES 4
50g/2 oz (4 tablespoons) butter
225g (½ lb) mushrooms, trimmed and sliced
salt
freshly ground black pepper
575ml/1 pt (2¼ cups) béchamel sauce (page 252)
75ml/3 fl oz (⅓ cup) thick cream

Melt the butter in a heavy-bottomed saucepan. When the foam subsides, add the mushrooms and sauté for 3 minutes. Reserve a few slices of mushroom for the garnish. Add the béchamel sauce to the pan and simmer for 20 minutes.

Purée the mixture in a blender or through a food mill. Reheat the soup. To serve, stir in the cream and garnish each bowl with the reserved slices of mushroom.

Cooking time: 30 minutes

Vichyssoise

This classic chilled potato and leek soup is made from the humblest ingredients. Serve it cold for maximum effect, but it is also good hot.

SERVES 6
50g/2 oz (¼ cup) butter
225g/½ lb (1 cup) potatoes chopped
2 leeks, cleaned and chopped
1 large onion, chopped
1 celery stalk, chopped
salt
freshly ground black pepper
850ml/1½ pt (3¾ cups) chicken stock
250ml/½ pt (1 cup) thin cream
1 small bunch of chives, chopped

Melt the butter in a heavy-bottomed saucepan. Add the vegetables and sauté for 10 minutes. Add the stock and simmer for 20 minutes until the vegetables are tender. Purée the vegetables in a blender or through a food mill and season well.

Chill for 3 hours. Before serving swirl in the cream and garnish with chives.

Cooking time: 45 minutes plus 3½ hours chilling

Spicy Hot Grapefruit

SERVES 4

50g/2 oz ($\frac{1}{4}$ cup) soft brown sugar
1.5ml ($\frac{1}{4}$ teaspoon) allspice
2.5ml ($\frac{1}{2}$ teaspoon) cinnamon
15ml (1 tablespoon) butter, softened
15ml (1 tablespoon) dark rum or sherry
2 large grapefruit, halved and flesh loosened

Heat the grill (broiler) to hot. Combine the sugar and spices. Add the rum and butter and beat the mixture with a wooden spoon to form a paste.

Spread a quarter of the paste over each half grapefruit. Grill (broil) for 6–8 minutes or until the paste has melted and is bubbling. Serve hot.

Cooking time: 15 minutes

Above: make this Chinese chicken and mushroom soup when you are boiling a chicken. Although dried mushrooms are expensive, a little goes a long way.

Left: although it is made from such simple ingredients, leeks and potatoes, Vichyssoise is one of the world's most famous cold soups. It was created in America, but by a French chef, who named it after his home town, Vichy.

Chinese Chicken and Mushroom Soup

Dried mushrooms are available from Chinese supermarkets but if they are unobtainable, use 100g ($\frac{1}{4}$ lb) button mushrooms instead. The success of this soup really depends on the quality of the stock—preferably home-made.

SERVES 6

50g (2 oz) dried mushrooms
1.15L/2 pt (5 cups) chicken stock
100g($\frac{1}{4}$ lb ($\frac{1}{2}$ cup) cooked chicken meat, skinned and shredded
salt
freshly ground black pepper
sprigs of watercress

Soak the dried mushrooms in hot water for 20 minutes. Bring the stock to the boil. Drain the mushrooms and add to the stock. Add the chicken meat and simmer for 5 minutes. Check the seasoning. To serve, spoon into soup bowls and garnish with sprigs of watercress.

Cooking time: 30 minutes

Cheese and sour cream soufflé, called alivenci in Italy, is light and unusual. Soufflés can be prepared quickly from a wide variety of staple items, and do not necessarily include cheese.

Eggs and Cheese

Spinach Roulade

This unusual type of soufflé makes a good first course for 6 or an economical supper or lunch for 4. It is good on its own but can also be served with a cheese or tomato sauce.

SERVES 4
4 large eggs, separated
225g/½ lb (1 cup) spinach purée
50g/2 oz (½ cup) Cheddar cheese, grated
salt
freshly ground black pepper
15ml (1 tablespoon) grated Parmesan cheese
FOR THE FILLING
25g/1 oz (2 tablespoons) butter
25g/1 oz (¼ cup) plain flour
175ml/6 fl oz (¾ cup) milk, warm
1 medium-sized onion, chopped
150g/5 oz (⅔ cup) cottage or curd cheese, drained

Heat the oven to 190°C (375°F) gas mark 5. Line a 33 × 23cm (13 × 9 in) Swiss roll tin (jelly roll pan) with foil and brush it with oil or melted butter, and then sprinkle the inside with flour and turn out the excess.

Dry the spinach purée in a pan over low heat, turning with a wooden spoon until all the water has evaporated. Lightly beat the yolks and stir in. Fold in the Cheddar cheese and season.

Whisk the egg whites until they stand in stiff peaks. Fold into the spinach mixture and pour into the prepared tray. Bake for 15–20 minutes until firm but springy to the fingertips.

Meanwhile make the filling. Melt the butter and stir in the flour off the heat. Cook briefly then stir in the warm milk. Cook, stirring, for 2 minutes. Add the onion and cook for 10 minutes. Add the cottage cheese and heat through without boiling.

Remove the spinach cake from the oven and invert it on to a clean towel. Lift off the tray and gently peel away the foil. Spread the filling to within 2cm (¾ in) of the edge and roll up like a Swiss (jelly) roll. Roll on to a warm serving dish with the seam underneath. Sprinkle over the Parmesan. Serve immediately.
Cooking time: 25 minutes

● Leeks can replace the spinach. Chop 225g (½ lb) cooked leeks and reheat with 15ml (1 tablespoon) béchamel or mornay sauce. Add the eggs to make the roulade, bake then fill with thick tomato sauce. Or if you prefer a creamy filling, make a thick béchamel with cooked, chopped mushrooms, cooked chicken or fish added.

Cheese and Sour Cream Soufflé

Soufflé is a classic dish, always impressive, but made from very simple ingredients. In this Italian recipe cream cheese adds extra protein. This is an ideal dish to serve before or after a well-prepared hot vegetable dish to make a complete meal.

SERVES 4
15g/½ oz (1 tablespoon) butter, softened
15ml (1 tablespoon) plain flour
225g (½ lb) cream cheese, at room temperature
90ml (6 tablespoons) sour cream
3 large eggs, separated
90ml (6 tablespoons) milk
2.5ml (½ teaspoon) salt

Heat the oven to 180°C (350°F) gas mark 4. Grease an 18cm (7 in) soufflé dish with the softened butter. Add 5ml (1 teaspoon) of the flour to the dish and shake so that the flour coats the inside.

Beat the cream cheese with a wooden spoon until soft and creamy. Beat in the sour cream, using a wire whisk. Beat in the egg yolks one at a time. Gradually incorporate the remaining flour, the milk and salt. Beat well.

Whisk the egg whites until they form stiff peaks. Fold the whites into the cheese mixture and turn into the prepared soufflé dish. Bake for about 35 minutes, until the top is risen and light brown then serve.

Cooking time: 40 minutes.

A soufflé is an excellent emergency standby: more impressive as a way of using leftovers than folding them into a crêpe and quicker than covering them in pastry.
● For surprise cheese soufflé, omit the cream and cream cheese and make a white sauce with 225ml/8 fl oz (1 cup) milk and 15ml (1 tablespoon) each butter and flour. Add 50g/2 oz (½ cup) grated cheese and stir in 50g (2 oz) cubed Gruyère (Swiss) cheese with the egg whites.
● For ham soufflé finely mince or chop 225g (½ lb) ham and stir into 225ml/ 8 fl oz (1 cup) white sauce with a pinch of cayenne. Use an extra egg white.
● For herring roe soufflé, mash 225g (½ lb) soft herring (shad) roes and fold into 150ml/¼ pt (⅔ cup) béchamel sauce with 25g/1 oz grated Gruyère (Swiss) cheese and a pinch of cayenne.
● For tuna soufflé use 150g/5 oz (⅔ cup) drained, mashed canned tuna with 275ml/ ½ pt (1¼ cups) white sauce and a dash of anchovy essense (paste), or substitute 175g/6 oz (¾ cup) cooked white fish.
● For sweetcorn soufflé, drain a 225g (8 oz) can well. Make 275ml/½ pt (1¼ cups) thick white sauce, using 40g/1½ oz each butter and flour (3 tablespoons butter with 6 of flour) plus 275ml/½ pt (1¼ cups) milk. Flavour with 5ml (1 teaspoon) each onion juice and parsley. Use an extra egg white.

Omelette aux Fines Herbes

SERVES 2–3
6 eggs
salt
freshly ground black pepper
30ml (2 tablespoons) cold water
22ml (1½ tablespoons) fresh mixed herbs, chopped
15ml (1 tablespoon) butter

In a mixing bowl beat the eggs, salt and pepper, water and herbs together. In a large omelet pan melt the butter. When the foam subsides, pour in the egg mixture. Stir the eggs then leave them for a few seconds until the bottom sets. Reduce heat to low.

Using a spatula, lift the edge of the omelet and tilt the pan at the same time so that the liquid mixture escapes under the edge. Put the pan flat until the egg sets. Lift the edge of the omelet and flip it over to fold in half. Transfer to a heated serving dish and cut into 2–3 portions to serve.
Cooking time: 8 minutes

Eggs Benedict

Ham is included in this variation of a classic recipe. You can make your own crumpet (English muffins) for breakfast (page 239) instead of pancakes. The dish will also make a substantial television supper.

SERVES 4
8 thick slices cooked ham
8 crumpets (English muffins)
30ml (2 tablespoons) butter
8 hot poached eggs
hollandaise sauce *(page 251)*

Heat the grill (broiler) to high. Place the ham slices under the grill and grill (broil) for 2–3 minutes on each side. Keep warm. Toast the crumpets and spread with butter. Add a slice of ham to each crumpet and place a poached egg on top.

Transfer to 4 warmed serving plates. Spoon a little of the sauce over each egg and serve at once.

Cooking time: 10 minutes

Sardine Rarebit

Sardines are added to a traditional rarebit for extra protein for a quick light meal.

SERVES 6
6 slices thin bread, toasted
175g (6 oz) cream cheese
225ml/8 fl oz (1 cup) milk
30ml (2 tablespoons) tomato paste
5ml (1 teaspoon) Dijon mustard
salt
pinch of cayenne pepper
1 large egg
15ml (1 tablespoon) butter
6 canned whole sardines, drained and halved

Place the cream cheese and milk in a small saucepan. Set the pan over moderate heat, and stirring all the time, heat the mixture until all the cheese has melted. Remove pan from heat and set aside. Preheat the grill (broiler) and make the toast.

Beat together the tomato paste, mustard, salt, cayenne pepper, egg and butter. Add this mixture to the milk and return to heat. Cook, stirring, for 2–3 minutes. Remove from the heat. Divide the mixture and spread it over the toast. Lay 2 sardine halves on each slice of toast. Grill (broil) for 2–3 minutes until the cheese is bubbling. Transfer to a serving plate and serve immediately.

Cooking time: 10–15 minutes

Mozzarella Pizza

This quantity will make one 30cm (12 in) pizza. As a lunch or supper dish, it is a generous quantity for two, served with a salad. For a lighter first course divide the pizza into 4 or make 4 small pizzas.

SERVES 2
5ml (1 teaspoon) oil
$\frac{1}{3} \times$ traditional white bread dough *(page 234)*
800g (1 lb 14 oz) canned tomatoes, drained
salt
freshly ground black pepper
5ml (1 teaspoon) dried oregano or marjoram
100g ($\frac{1}{4}$ lb) Mozzarella cheese
50g (2 oz) canned anchovy fillets
12 black olives

Brush a baking sheet with oil. Knock back the dough and knead into a ball shape. Put the dough on the baking sheet and flatten it to measure about 30cm (12 in) in diameter. Raise the edge slightly to make a ridge to prevent the topping from spilling.

Put the tomatoes in a saucepan, add half the herbs and bring to the boil. Simmer for 3 minutes, stirring to break up the tomatoes. Leave to cool slightly.

Cut the Mozzarella into thin slices. Drain the anchovy fillets and reserve the oil. Pour the tomato mixture over the dough. Place the slices of Mozzarella on top and arrange anchovy fillets in a lattice pattern on top. Decorate the squares with olives. If time permits, rest in the refrigerator for 30 minutes.

Meanwhile heat the oven to 230°C (450°F) gas mark 8. Drizzle the reserved oil over the pizza. Sprinkle remaining herbs on top. Bake for 20–25 minutes until the pizza is well risen and bubbling.

Cooking time: 35–75 minutes

Eggs Benedict are a classic American breakfast dish, prepared from crumpets (English muffins), eggs and ham.

Meat and Poultry

Beef and Cheese Roll

This is minced (ground) beef with a difference; serve with buttered noodles and a salad and accompany by a hot tomato sauce (page 254). Use Gouda cheese if you cannot get Mozzarella.

SERVES 6
50g/2 oz (1 slice) white bread, crusts removed
75ml/3 fl oz ($\frac{1}{3}$ cup) milk
700g (1$\frac{1}{2}$ lb) minced beef
2 medium-sized eggs, lightly beaten
10ml (2 teaspoons) mustard powder
salt
freshly ground black pepper
2.5ml ($\frac{1}{2}$ teaspoon) dried thyme
1 onion, finely chopped
30ml (2 tablespoons) fresh parsley, chopped
15ml (1 tablespoon) plain flour
225g ($\frac{1}{2}$ lb) Mozzarella cheese, thinly sliced
30ml (2 tablespoons) melted butter
parsley sprigs to garnish

Soak the bread in the milk and squeeze out the excess. Combine the bread, meat, eggs, mustard, salt, pepper, thyme, onion and parsley in a bowl and knead together.

Spread out a piece of foil on a baking sheet and dust with flour. Spread the meat on it about 2cm ($\frac{3}{4}$ in) deep. Press with the back of a spoon to make a compact rectangle. Cover and chill for 1 hour.

Heat the oven to 180°C (350°F) gas mark 4. Uncover the meat and place the cheese over it. Use the foil to help you roll up the meat just like a Swiss (jelly) roll. Transfer the roll to a shallow baking tin (pan), with the seam underneath. Brush it with the melted butter and bake for 45–50 minutes for medium-rare, 1 hour for well-done.

To serve, transfer the roll to a heated serving dish and garnish with the parsley. Serve hot accompanied by a tomato sauce.
Cooking time: 5 minutes plus 1 hour chilling time, then 45–50 minutes
● For a spicy beef and cheese roll, add 30ml (2 tablespoons) tomato paste, 5ml (1 teaspoon) Worcestershire sauce and a few drops of Tabasco sauce.

Bacon Cooked with Apples and Onions

This quickie for emergencies turns bacon rashers (slices) from a breakfast dish into a substantial meal.

SERVES 4
30ml (2 tablespoons) oil
450g (1 lb) onions, sliced
450g (1 lb) cooking apples, cored and sliced
freshly ground black pepper
350g ($\frac{3}{4}$ lb) bacon slices, cut into 12mm ($\frac{1}{2}$ in) pieces
15ml (1 tablespoon) fresh parsley, chopped

Heat the oil in a large saucepan. Add the onions and fry them until transparent. Stir in the apples, cover and cook for about 10 minutes or until the apples are soft.

Meanwhile fry the bacon until crisp, stirring so that it does not stick. Drain the bacon on absorbent paper. Season the apple and onion mixture with pepper, mix in the bacon and turn into a warmed serving dish. Sprinkle the parsley over and serve hot.
Cooking time: 30 minutes

Chinese Spareribs

SERVES 4
60ml/4 tablespoons ($\frac{1}{4}$ cup) oil
1 garlic clove, chopped
1 small onion, peeled and finely chopped
15ml (1 tablespoon) fresh ginger root, chopped
900g (2 lb) pork spareribs, separated into single bones
salt
15ml (1 tablespoon) sugar
50ml/2 fl oz ($\frac{1}{4}$ cup) soy sauce
50ml/2 fl oz ($\frac{1}{4}$ cup) dry sherry
freshly ground black pepper
150ml/$\frac{1}{4}$ pt ($\frac{2}{3}$ cup) chicken stock

Heat the oil in a heavy-bottomed pan. Fry the garlic, onion and ginger for 2–3 minutes, stirring all the time. Add the ribs, season with salt, and fry until browned, about 5 minutes. Remove ribs.

Add the sugar, soy sauce, sherry and a sprinkling of pepper. Stir-fry for 3 minutes. Add the stock and bring to the boil. Add the ribs and stir them until coated with the sauce. Cover and simmer for 20 minutes. Remove the lid and simmer for a further 10 minutes. This can all be done ahead if desired.

Meanwhile heat the oven to 190°C (375°F) gas mark 5. Arrange the ribs in a roasting tin (pan) and spoon over any remaining sauce. Leave in the oven for 5–10 minutes until the surface of the meat is dry. Transfer to a heated serving plate, spoon over any pan juices and serve hot.
Cooking time: 1 hour

Goulasch

Potatoes are included in this goulasch to make it a one-pot meal.

SERVES 6
45ml (3 tablespoons) cooking oil
900g (2 lb) chuck steak, trimmed and cubed
450g (1 lb) onions, sliced
5ml (1 teaspoon) caraway seeds
1 garlic clove, chopped
30ml (2 tablespoons) paprika
salt
freshly ground black pepper
175ml/6 fl oz ($\frac{3}{4}$ cup) hot stock
1 bay leaf
450g (1 lb) potatoes, peeled and sliced
150ml/$\frac{1}{4}$ pt ($\frac{2}{3}$ cup) sour cream

Heat the oil in a large heavy-bottomed saucepan. Brown the meat, in batches, stirring frequently. Keep warm. Add the onions to the pan and fry for about 8 minutes or until transparent. Stir in the garlic, paprika, caraway seeds, salt and pepper. Return the beef to the pan and mix well. Add the stock and bay leaf to the pan, bring to the boil, cover and simmer for 1 hour.

Add the potatoes and simmer for another hour. To serve, discard the bay leaf, check seasoning and remove from the heat. Pour over the sour cream.
Cooking time: 2$\frac{1}{2}$ hours

Curried Tripe

Tripe is usually sold parboiled and need only be soaked for 60 minutes in cold water with a spoonful of vinegar to prepare it for cooking.

The cooking time for tripe varies tremendously, depending on how it has been prepared before cooking. To make sure the tripe is tender, cook the dish in advance and reheat it when required. Serve the tripe as it is with rice or thicken the sauce with a little flour and serve it with boiled potatoes.

SERVES 6
15ml (1 tablespoon) cooking oil or lard (shortening)
450g (1 lb) onions, chopped
2 garlic cloves, chopped
1 chilli, seeded and chopped
15ml (1 tablespoon) curry powder
5ml (1 teaspoon) ground turmeric
2.5ml ($\frac{1}{2}$ teaspoon) coriander, crushed
900g (2 lb) prepared tripe, cut into strips 5cm (2 in) long
575ml/1 pt (2$\frac{1}{2}$ cups) stock
salt
freshly ground black pepper

Heat the oil in a large saucepan. Fry the onions until transparent. Add the garlic, chilli, curry, coriander and turmeric. Fry for an additional 3 minutes. Add the tripe and enough stock to cover. Bring to the boil, reduce heat and simmer for 1–2 hours until the tripe is tender. Check seasoning.

Cooking time: 1 hour soaking, then 2 hours

● You can use $\frac{1}{2}$ × curry paste on *page 254* to replace the curry powder, coriander and turmeric.

Rabbit with Prunes

SERVES 4
1 rabbit, skinned and portioned
225g ($\frac{1}{2}$ lb) prunes
575ml/1 pt (2$\frac{1}{2}$ cups) cold tea, strained
50g/2 oz ($\frac{1}{4}$ cup) dripping
15g/$\frac{1}{2}$ oz (2 tablespoons) plain flour
275ml/$\frac{1}{2}$ pt (1$\frac{1}{4}$ cups) game or chicken stock
salt
freshly ground black pepper
FOR THE MARINADE
1 onion, skinned and chopped
150ml/$\frac{1}{4}$ pt ($\frac{1}{3}$ cup) medium sherry
5ml (1 teaspoon) powdered thyme
1 bay leaf
30ml (2 tablespoons) olive oil
2.5ml ($\frac{1}{2}$ teaspoon) allspice

Prunes lend flavour to the rather bland white meat of a rabbit. In this recipe the rabbit is marinated in sherry and cooked in the prune juice. Drink a cheap red wine with it for a guest meal and use this in the dish.

Combine all the marinade ingredients and add the rabbit pieces. Pour the tea over the prunes. Leave the prunes and the rabbit to marinate for 8 hours or overnight.

Heat the oven to 180°C (350°F) gas mark 4. Remove the rabbit from the marinade and pat dry. Strain and reserve the marinade. In a large flameproof casserole or dutch oven heat the dripping. Add the rabbit pieces and brown on all sides. Remove the rabbit from the pan. Sprinkle the flour into the pan and allow to brown. Add the strained marinade and stock. Return the rabbit to the pan. Add the prunes and any soaking liquid left. Add seasoning. Bring to the boil. Cover and cook in the oven for 1$\frac{1}{2}$–2 hours, until the rabbit is tender.

If there is too much liquid at the end of cooking time, remove the rabbit and prunes and reduce the liquid by rapid boiling. Return the rabbit and prunes to the pan and serve.

Cooking time: 8 hours marinating then 2$\frac{1}{2}$ hours

Lattice Tart Milanese

This is an excellent Sunday night supper dish when you need to stretch a little beef.

SERVES 6
hard-cheese shortcrust *(page 241)*
25g/1 oz (2 tablespoons) margarine
100g (¼ lb) bacon trimmings, chopped
450g (1 lb) minced (ground) beef
1 garlic clove, chopped
225g (½ lb) onions, chopped
225g (½ lb) canned tomatoes, drained
5ml (1 teaspoon) mixed dried herbs
15ml (1 tablespoon) tomato paste
salt
freshly ground black pepper
75g/3 oz (1 cup) grated cheese
FOR THE OPTIONAL DECORATION
4 tomatoes, halved
OR 4 anchovy fillets, split lengthwise
OR 10 black olives
OR 10 cap mushrooms plus 30ml (2 tablespoons) margarine

Heat the oven to 200°C (400°F) gas mark 6. Put a baking sheet on a centre shelf.

To make the filling, melt the margarine in a frying-pan and add the bacon trimmings. Sweat for 2 minutes. Add the garlic and onion and fry for 8–10 minutes until softened. Add the minced (ground) beef and fry a further 8–10 minutes, stirring with a wooden spoon. Turn off the heat, add the drained tomatoes, paste and herbs and stir to incorporate and break up the tomatoes. Season well and leave to cool slightly.

Roll out the pastry, reserving the trimmings, and line a greased 28cm (11 in) oval gratin dish, or 20cm (8 in) flan tin (pie plate). Pile in the filling, distributing it well around the dish. Smooth with the back of the spoon. Roll out the pastry trimmings and cut into strips 2cm (¾ in) wide. Arrange these in a lattice across the dish, dampening the ends and sticking on to the pastry rim. Scatter the grated cheese over the top.

Arrange a garnish in the centre of each diamond if desired. Arrange half a tomato cut side down or half an anchovy fillet, split lengthwise, in a loop. Alternatively, place one black olive or a mushroom cap, gill side up; dot the mushrooms with small pieces of margarine and season lightly.

Place the tart on a baking sheet. Bake for 40 minutes for a ceramic dish; 30 minutes for a metal container. Serve hot.
Cooking time: including making the pastry, 1½ hours

Chick Peas with Spanish Sausage

Chick peas contain protein but lack colour and flavour and this is added by pimento and spicy sausage. Chorizos are dried sausages which need cooking. If you cannot buy them, look for any other spicy sausage.

SERVES 6
350g/¾ lb (2 cups) chick peas, soaked overnight in water to cover
850ml/1½ pt (3¾ cups) stock
bouquet garni
450g (1 lb) chorizo sausage
100g (¼ lb) canned pimento
1 large onion, chopped
2 garlic cloves, chopped
30ml (2 tablespoons) oil
2.5ml (½ teaspoon) oregano
salt
freshly ground black pepper

Drain the chick peas. Transfer them to a large saucepan. Pour over the stock and add the bouquet garni. Bring to the boil. Cover and simmer for 1½–2 hours, until tender.

Meanwhile chop the sausages roughly. Drain the pimento, reserving the liquid, and cut into strips.

Heat the oil in a large frying-pan. Add the onion, garlic and sausages. Cook for 8–10 minutes until the onions are soft.

Drain the chick peas and discard the bouquet garni. Add the chick peas, pimento and its juice, oregano and seasoning to the onions. Mix well and cook for 10 minutes. Serve hot.
Cooking time: 2¼ hours

● A cheaper but less meaty version can be made with dry sausage—salami, cabanos etc. You will need 175g (6 oz) diced salami. The method is slightly different. Fry the onions, then add the other ingredients, using 400g (14 oz) canned tomatoes instead of pimento, half the given quantity of stock and adding 15ml (1 tablespoon) each of red wine vinegar and paprika. Add salt at the end of cooking. Stew as in the recipe. Serve this as a main course for 4–5 or a cold appetizer for 8.

Chick-peas combine well with a highly-spiced Spanish sausage and pimentos.

Coq au vin is a classic dish; red wine adds flavour to cheap chicken.

Reduce the heat and leave sauce to simmer.

Meanwhile melt the remaining butter in the frying-pan. When the foam subsides add the mushrooms and cook for 4–5 minutes. Stir them into the sauce and return the chicken to the casserole. Garnish with the parsley.

Cooking time: 2 hours

Beef Carbonnade

Beer and onions make a good combination added to beef. This is a good dish to make when left with several half-empty, flat cans of beer after a party. There are many variations of this recipe; potatoes are sometimes included or the meat is marinated before cooking.

SERVES 6
15ml (1 tablespoon) oil
900g (2 lb) chuck steak, trimmed and cubed
450g (1 lb) onions, peeled and sliced
3 garlic cloves, peeled and chopped
150ml/¼ pt (⅔ cup) stock
400ml/14 fl oz (1¾ cups) beer
salt
freshly ground black pepper
15ml (1 tablespoon) soft brown sugar
bouquet garni
bay leaf
15ml (1 tablespoon) cornflour (cornstarch)
25ml/1 fl oz (2 tablespoons) wine vinegar

Heat the oil in a frying-pan. Add the fat trimmings from the meat and sweat them so that they give up their fat. Remove and discard them. Brown the meat in batches in the pan then transfer to a flameproof casserole or large saucepan. Fry the onions and garlic until they begin to turn golden and add to the pot. Heat the stock and beer in the frying-pan, stirring around the pan to scrape up the sediment. Add to pot.

Put the pot over a low heat. Add salt and pepper, sugar, bouquet garni and bay leaf. Cover and simmer gently for 2–2½ hours until the meat is tender.

Skim off any surface fat. Blend the cornflour (cornstarch) with the vinegar. Add a few spoonfuls of the stew liquid. Mix and stir into the stew. Simmer and allow the sauce to thicken. Discard the bouquet garni and bay leaf. Check the seasoning and serve.

Cooking time: 2½–3 hours

Coq au Vin

As chicken has become weekly family fare, it tends to be neglected for entertaining. Cooked in red wine it makes a classic dish, worthy of any party.

SERVES 6
100g (¼ lb) bacon, chopped
75g/3 oz (5 tablespoons) butter
6 chicken pieces
salt
freshly ground black pepper
575ml/1 pt (2½ cups) red wine
575ml/1 pt (2½ cups) warmed chicken stock
15ml (1 tablespoon) tomato paste
2 garlic cloves
bouquet garni
15ml (1 tablespoon) oil
18 small onions, peeled and left whole
25g/1 oz (2 tablespoons) butter
25g/1 oz (¼ cup) flour
225g (½ lb) mushrooms, sliced
30ml (2 tablespoons) fresh parsley, chopped

Heat the oven to 180°C (350°F) gas mark 4. Put one-third of the butter in a large frying-pan over medium heat. Add the bacon and fry it until lightly browned. Transfer the bacon to a casserole. Pat the chicken pieces dry, then fry them for 5–7 minutes until lightly browned. Transfer to the casserole and sprinkle on salt and pepper.

Heat the wine and stock together, then add to the casserole with the tomato paste, garlic and bouquet garni. Cover and cook in the oven for 30 minutes.

Melt half the remaining butter in a frying-pan. When the foam subsides add the oil. Fry the onions for about 10 minutes over a medium heat, turning them in the pan to brown on all sides.

When the chicken has been cooking for 30 minutes, remove the casserole from the oven and add the onions. Return the casserole to the oven and cook for 30–45 minutes until the chicken is tender.

Remove the chicken and bacon to a warm dish while you finish the sauce. (If the casserole is not flameproof tip the sauce into a saucepan.)

Boil the sauce rapidly to reduce to about 575ml/1 pt (2½ cups). Add the flour and butter, combined to make a beurre manié, a little at a time, stirring. Cook the sauce for a few minutes. Check the seasoning.

Spooned Beef

This is an ideal recipe to make when you are out all day. It only takes 5 minutes to prepare and is unlikely to spoil if you are late home. It can also cook 8–9 hours all night while you sleep. Sealing the lid to the pan is an old country custom to prevent steam evaporating from the dish during long cooking. It is particularly suitable for those whose pans and lids have received a few knocks and no longer fit tightly. The pig's foot is optional, but the gravy will not set without it.

As a substitute for wine, vinegar is used. You will not, of course, get the same result as a bottle of burgundy would give, but the acid does help to tenderize the meat. The proportions for a wine substitute are given after the recipe.

SERVES 5
1 pig's trotter (foot)
1kg (2 lb 3 oz) braising beef in 2–4 pieces
bouquet garni
2 fat garlic cloves, chopped
1 medium-sized onion, roughly chopped
10 peppercorns
50ml/2 oz ($\frac{1}{2}$ cup) black olives, stoned (pitted) (optional)
350ml/12 fl oz ($1\frac{1}{2}$ cups) warm beef stock
30ml (2 tablespoons) tomato paste
15ml (1 tablespoon) lemon juice
45ml (3 tablespoons) red wine vinegar
4ml ($\frac{3}{4}$ teaspoon) sugar
15ml (1 tablespoon) salt
60ml (4 tablespoons) flour made into a paste with 30ml (2 tablespoons) water

Heat the oven to 120°C (250°F) gas mark $\frac{1}{2}$. Fit the pig's foot into a casserole dish and press the meat around it in a single layer. Push the bouquet garni in beside the meat. Cover with a thick layer of garlic, onion, and peppercorns.

Add the tomato paste, lemon juice, vinegar, sugar and salt to the warm stock. Pour this over the meat. Sprinkle over the olives if using.

Cover the dish with the lid and plaster flour paste round the gap between the lid and the pan to make it airtight. Cook for 6–8 hours. The dish can be eaten hot.

The meat can be left to cool completely in the sealed pan. For a better appearance, remove the trotter while the dish is still warm, picking any meat on it off the bone and returning the meat to the dish. Adjust the meat in the bottom of the dish and leave overnight in the refrigerator. The liquid should set around the meat, which will be soft enough to serve with a spoon and will portion without a knife.
Cooking time: 6 hours or more

● Vinegar can be used to make a passable wine substitute—for cooking purposes only, alas! Add 5ml (1 teaspoon) wine vinegar to each 25ml/1 fl oz ($\frac{1}{8}$ cup) liquid used in the recipe, plus 5ml (1 teaspoon) sugar for every 450ml/16 fl oz (2 cups) liquid.

Beef in Fruit Sauce

Fresh ginger and citrus fruit give this Chinese stew its distinctive flavour. Use reconstituted orange juice. To be authentic, serve it with beansprouts and boiled rice.

SERVES 6
30ml (2 tablespoons) oil
1 onion, peeled and chopped
2 garlic cloves, peeled and chopped
15ml (1 tablespoon) fresh ginger root, finely chopped
1.4kg (3 lb) beef skirt (flank steak), trimmed and cubed
juice of 1 lemon
60ml (4 tablespoons) soy sauce
350ml/12 fl oz ($1\frac{1}{2}$ cups) orange juice
45ml (3 tablespoons) red wine vinegar
500ml/18 fl oz ($2\frac{1}{4}$ cups) light stock or water
salt
freshly ground black pepper

Heat the oven to 150°C (300°F) gas mark 2. Heat the oil in a flameproof casserole. Fry the onion, garlic and ginger for 3 minutes. Add the beef and cook for 5 minutes, stirring all the time.

Add the remaining ingredients and bring to the boil. Cover and cook in the oven for $3\frac{1}{4}$–4 hours until the meat is tender. Check seasoning and serve hot.
Cooking time: 4 hours

Pork Tenderloin Milanese

Danish Samsöe cheese is often cheaper than real Swiss Gruyère, which is the classic cheese for this type of dish.

SERVES 3
275–350g (10–12 oz) tenderloin of pork
freshly ground black pepper
3 slices of ham
100g ($\frac{1}{4}$ lb) Samsöe (Swiss) cheese
6 sage leaves, finely chopped
30ml (2 tablespoons) Marsala, Cinzano bianco or sweet white wine

Hold the tenderloin steady with your free hand. With a sharp knife, starting 10cm (4 in) from the end, shave off a thin escallop of pork at an angle. Cut another

For a Chinese-style meal, cook beef in a fruit juice such as orange juice.

escallop from behind the first. As the slices get longer, turn up the knife before the end of the tenderloin, so that all the middle slices are cut diagonally across the meat. Like this you will get 12 small medallions of meat. If you are short, halve one of the bigger ones.

Spread out the escallops, grind over black pepper and beat them with a steak bat, mallet or a rolling pin to flatten. Halve the ham slices and cover 6 escallops. Slice the cheese into 6 and cover the ham. Put the remaining escallops on top.

Melt the butter in a frying-pan over medium heat and when the foaming stops put in the meat sandwiches. Fry for 4 minutes then turn over with a spatula. Press the spatula down on top of each sandwich in turn to make sure it is bonding. Fry for 3 minutes. Pour in the wine and add the sage leaves. Sprinkle over the salt. Bring to the boil, then cover with a lid and simmer about 1 minute.

Transfer the escallops to a serving dish. Stir the pan to free any sediment and pour the juice over the escallops and serve.
Cooking time: 15 minutes

Roast Birds with Apples and Cider

If you live in the country where pigeons are a farm pest, they can be very inexpensive. With cider and apples, these make a dish of party proportions.

SERVES 4
4 pigeons (Cornish game hens), oven-ready
75g/3 oz (5 tablespoons) butter
2 onions, chopped
4 carrots, scraped and finely diced
2 cooking apples, peeled, cored and sliced
2 slices bacon, chopped
30ml (2 tablespoons) plain flour
575ml/1 pt (2½ cups) stock
salt and freshly ground black pepper
450ml/16 fl oz (2 cups) dry cider
FOR THE GARNISH
15ml (1 tablespoon) butter
2 cooking apples, peeled, cored and sliced into rings
4 fatty bacon slices

Heat the oven to 180°C (350°F) gas mark 4. If using pigeons, cut through the breastbones and backbones of the pigeons with a sharp knife. Using kitchen scissors cut away the backbones and discard. This is not essential, but will make eating easier.

In a large flameproof casserole or dutch oven melt half of the butter. When the foam subsides add the onions, carrots, apples and bacon and cook, stirring, for 8 minutes or until the onions are soft. Using a slotted spoon, remove the onion mixture and keep warm.

Heat the remaining butter and when the foam subsides add the birds and fry for 3–4 minutes until lightly browned. Remove the birds with a slotted spoon and keep warm. Off the heat, add the flour to the pan and stir to form a paste. Add the stock gradually, stirring all the time. Season and add the cider. Return to the heat and bring to the boil. Return the birds and the onion mixture to the pan. Cover and cook in the oven for about 1 hour until the birds are tender.

During the last 10 minutes of cooking time heat the grill (broiler). To prepare the garnish, melt the butter in a frying-pan. When the foam subsides add the apple rings and fry for 3–4 minutes before turning them over. Remove from the pan with a slotted spoon and drain on absorbent paper. Cut each bacon slice in half. Roll up and secure with a cocktail stick (pick). Grill (broil) for 3–4 minutes, turning them, until crisp. Keep warm.

Remove the casserole from the oven. Arrange the birds on a heated serving dish. Pour a little sauce over them and serve the rest separately. Garnish with apple rings and bacon rolls.
Cooking time: 1½ hours

Liver with Mushrooms

Lamb's liver can be used for this recipe or the cheaper pig's liver. The sage and bacon match its strong flavour.

SERVES 4
450g (1 lb) pig's liver, thinly sliced
a little milk
2 slices of bacon, cut into matchsticks
225g (½ lb) mushrooms, sliced
6 fresh sage leaves, chopped
1 garlic clove, chopped
40g/1½ oz (3 tablespoons) butter
15ml (1 tablespoon) lemon juice
salt and freshly ground black pepper

Soak the pig's liver for 2 hours in milk, then discard the milk and pat the liver dry with absorbent paper.

Heat the butter in a heavy-bottomed pan and sweat the bacon until the fat runs out. Remove to a plate. When the foam

subsides, add the liver and cook for 4–5 minutes on each side, depending on how you like the liver. Remove the liver from the pan and keep warm.

Add the remaining ingredients and cook for 3–4 minutes, stirring all the time. Return the bacon and heat through. Serve hot, arranging the liver on a serving plate and spooning the mushrooms on top.
Cooking time: 2 hours soaking, plus 20 minutes

Irish Stew with Parsley Dumplings

All stews containing a lot of fat and bone are best cooked, cooled and reheated. This gives you an opportunity to remove fat from the top and to discard any bones which are entirely bare of meat. Reheat the stew and make sure that the liquid is boiling before you put in the dumplings.

SERVES 4
900g (2 lb) scrag or middle neck of lamb
30ml (2 tablespoons) plain flour
salt and freshly ground black pepper
2 large onions, sliced
225g (½ lb) potatoes
15ml (1 tablespoon) pearl barley
2.5ml (½ teaspoon) mixed dried herbs
400ml/14 fl oz (1¾ cups) water
FOR THE DUMPLINGS
50g/2 oz (¼ cup) shredded suet
100g/¼ lb (1 cup) self-raising flour
15ml (1 tablespoon) fresh parsley, chopped
salt and freshly ground black pepper

Toss the lamb in seasoned flour. Put the meat, onions, potatoes, barley and dried herbs in a large saucepan and slowly bring to the boil. Remove any scum that forms with a slotted spoon. Reduce the heat, cover and cook for 2½ hours.

Thirty minutes before the end of cooking time, make the dumplings. Mix the suet, flour, parsley and seasoning together. Mix in enough water to make an elastic dough. Divide the dough into 8 balls.

Bring the stew to the boil and drop the dumplings into the liquid. Replace the lid and leave to boil for 20–25 minutes. They will rise to the surface when cooked. Serve immediately.
Cooking time: 2¾ hours, plus optional overnight cooling, plus 40 minutes

Irish stew with parsley dumplings.

Fricassée of Veal

Stewing or pie veal is a comparatively inexpensive buy and will make a glamorous dish.

SERVES 6
1 kg (2 lb 3 oz) stewing or pie veal, cubed
175g (6 oz) bacon
100g/¼ lb (½ cup) butter
100g/4 fl oz (½ cup) oil
1 large onion, sliced
1 garlic clove, chopped
salt
freshly ground black pepper
350ml/12 fl oz (1½ cups) chicken stock
bouquet garni
12 small onions, peeled
175g (6 oz) mushrooms, sliced
15ml (1 tablespoon) flour
30ml (2 tablespoons) lemon juice
125ml/4 fl oz (½ cup) thick cream or thickened yogurt (*page 249*)
6 thick slices of white bread without crusts and cubed
5ml (1 teaspoon) paprika

Melt 25g/1 oz (2 tablespoons) butter with 30ml (2 tablespoons) oil in a large heavy-bottomed pan over moderate heat. Fry the bacon for 2 minutes until it begins to sweat. Fry the chopped onion and garlic, stirring for 5 minutes. Add the veal and cook for 10 minutes over moderately high heat until set but not browned. Season lightly with salt and pepper. Stir in the flour, until absorbed by the onions and cook briefly. Add the stock and bouquet garni, cover and simmer for 1 hour. Add the peeled onions and simmer a further 30 minutes.

Meanwhile melt 25g/1 oz (2 tablespoons) butter and 60ml (4 tablespoons) oil in a frying-pan and fry the croûtons until crisp and golden. Sprinkle over the paprika. Remove and keep warm, then add 50g/2 oz (4 tablespoons) butter and fry the mushrooms.

Fold the mushrooms and croûtons into the veal, followed by the lemon juice and cream or yogurt. Check the seasonings.
Cooking time: about 2 hours

● Veal Marengo is a colourful variation. Add 225g (½ lb) canned tomatoes, chopped, 30ml (2 tablespoons) tomato paste and omit the cream. About 150ml/¼ pt (⅝ cup) white wine or 75ml/3 fl oz (⅜ cup) dry white vermouth will improve the dish further.

● Sweetbreads can be substituted for the veal. Allow 700g (1½ lb) sweetbreads for 6 people. Soak in cold water for 1 hour, or until thawed if frozen. Bring to the boil in water with added lemon juice or vinegar, then remove from the pan, trim off membranes and use for either the fricassée recipe or the tomato variation. Reduce the stewing time to 15 minutes. Add 15ml (1 tablespoon) lemon juice and garnish with chopped parsley.

● For an attractive garnish, cut the croûtons into larger triangles or diamonds. Fry, then arrange around the dish, rather than incorporating them with the meat. One corner can be dipped into melted butter and then into finely chopped parsley. Arrange around the serving dish with the parsley ends pointing outward.

Lamb Stew with Spring Vegetables

Vegetables are included in this stew; vary them to suit what is available. A meaty and a cheap cut of lamb are combined together for taste and economy. Skim the fat from the dish as it accumulates or skim it off when the dish is cooked.

SERVES 6
450g (1 lb) boned shoulder of lamb, cubed
450g (1 lb) breast of lamb, boned and cubed
30ml (2 tablespoons) oil
10ml (2 teaspoons) sugar
22ml (1½ tablespoons) plain flour
salt
freshly ground black pepper
575ml/1 pt (2½ cups) stock
15ml (1 tablespoon) tomato paste
3 large tomatoes, peeled, seeded and chopped
1 garlic clove, chopped
1 bouquet garni
12 button (pearl) onions, peeled
450g (1 lb) small new potatoes, peeled
6 small carrots, scraped
6 small turnips, peeled

Heat the oven to 150°C (300°F) gas mark 2. Heat the oil in a large flameproof casserole or dutch oven. Brown the meat, stirring it from time to time. Spoon off excess fat. Sprinkle the sugar over the meat and continue frying until lightly caramelized. Off the heat, sprinkle on the flour, salt and pepper. Return to the heat, cook for 3 minutes, stirring until the flour is pale brown.

Heat the stock and dissolve the tomato paste in it. Add to the meat, garlic tomatoes and bouquet garni. Cover and cook for 1 hour in the oven.

Skim off the fat and discard the bouquet garni. Add the vegetables to the pan, cover and cook for 30–40 minutes until the vegetables are tender. To serve, skim off fat if necessary, check seasoning.
Cooking time: 2 hours

Chilli Con Carne

This is a big, inexpensive, hot meal in one pot and all you need is bread to mop up the juices plus a refreshing cool salad.

SERVES 8
450g (1 lb) red kidney beans, soaked overnight in water to cover
450g (1 lb) onions
2 cloves
4 garlic cloves, peeled and chopped
bouquet garni
6 large dried chillis
30ml (2 tablespoons) oil
900g (2 lb) minced (ground) beef
1 red (bell) pepper, seeded and chopped
30ml (2 tablespoons) tomato paste
salt
bay leaf
275ml/½ pt (1¼ cups) beef stock

Put the kidney beans and soaking liquid into a heavy-bottomed pan. Add more water, if necessary, to cover the beans. Peel one onion and stick the cloves into it. Add this to the beans with half the garlic. Bring the pot to the boil and add the bouquet garni. Cover and simmer for 1 hour.

Meanwhile soak the chillis in a cup of hot water for 1 hour. Reserve the chilli water. Pull the stalks from the chillis and discard. Split the chillis open, under cold running water, and flush away all the seeds. Finely chop the skins and add to the chilli water.

Peel and chop the remaining onions. Heat the oil in a large saucepan and fry the onions and garlic until soft. Remove the onions and keep warm. Add the meat and red (bell) pepper. Stir with a fork to break up the meat and fry for 5 minutes. Return the onions to the pan, cover and simmer for 10 minutes.

Drain the beans and reserve the liquid. Discard the bouquet garni and the whole onion. Add the beans to the meat. Dissolve the tomato paste in the chilli water and add to pan. Add salt and bay leaf and bring to the boil. Add the beef stock to the pan and simmer for 15–30 minutes or until the beans are tender. Add some of the reserved bean liquid to the pan if the beans start drying up. Serve hot.

Cooking time: overnight soaking, then 1½–2 hours

●A quicker, though more expensive, version of this recipe for 4–5 people can be made using cubed pork shoulder instead of beef plus items you may have in store. Use 2 onions only and a green (bell) pepper. After frying, add about 300g (10 oz) canned, condensed tomato soup, 1 large celery stalk, chopped, 450g (1 lb) canned red kidney beans and 1.5ml (¼ teaspoon) hot chilli powder. Simmer for 15 minutes.

Tandoori chicken is marinated in spices and yogurt before cooking, which give it the red colouring. This is the ideal way to put flavour into insipid frozen chicken.

Tandoori Chicken

This is the ideal recipe to put flavour into a frozen chicken.

SERVES 4
4 chicken portions, skinned
salt
freshly ground black pepper
30ml (2 tablespoons) butter
15ml (1 tablespoon) lemon juice
FOR THE MARINADE
40g (1½ oz) fresh ginger root, peeled and chopped
2 garlic cloves, peeled and chopped
150ml/¼ oz (⅔ cup) plain yogurt
5ml (1 teaspoon) sesame seeds, crushed
5ml (1 teaspoon) coriander seeds, crushed
5ml (1 teaspoon) cumin seeds, crushed
2.5ml (½ teaspoon) red food colouring
FOR THE GARNISH
lemon wedges
fresh coriander leaves or watercress

Mix all the ingredients for the marinade together. Prick the chicken pieces all over with a fork, then spread the mixture over them. Cover and leave in a cool place for 8 hours.

Heat the grill (broiler) to medium. Transfer the chicken pieces to the grill (broiling) pan, fleshy side down, and dot with butter. Grill (broil) for 12–15 minutes. Turn the chicken pieces over and grill for 8–10 minutes, basting the chicken with the pan juices during this time. Check by piercing with a skewer that the chicken is tender: if the juices that run out are completely colourless, the chicken is cooked. Transfer to a warm serving dish. Garnish with lemon wedges and fresh coriander leaves. Serve immediately.

For a main course, serve with boiled rice, cucumber and yogurt salad and home-made chutney. It is however, sometimes served as a first course before a curry.

Cooking time: 8 hours marinating, then 30 minutes

Fish and Shellfish

Herring and Apple Salad

Salt herrings are used in this salad, so you need to start a day in advance to soak them. The apples are not peeled as the red skins add a touch of colour.

SERVES 6
2 salt herrings
275ml/½ pt (1¼ cups) sour cream or yogurt
30ml (2 tablespoons) fine sugar
30ml (2 tablespoons) tarragon vinegar
2 large potatoes, cooked and chopped
2 red-skinned apples, cored and diced
1 small onion, chopped
1 small pickled cucumber, cut in rounds
2 celery stalks, chopped
TO SERVE
lemon wedges
brown bread, sliced and buttered

Place the herrings in cold water and leave in a cool place for 12 hours. Drain the herrings and pat dry with absorbent paper. Trim heads and tails, if present, and extend the belly cavity to the tail. Open the fish out and peel off the skin. Remove the fillets and discard the backbone. Cut the fillets into small pieces, removing any fine bones.

Turn the sour cream into a bowl and add the sugar and vinegar. Mix well. Add all the ingredients to the sour cream mixture. Check seasoning. Chill for at least 3 hours before serving with lemon wedges and brown bread and butter.

Preparation time: 12 hours soaking, then 20 minutes plus chilling time

Baked Stuffed Mackerel

SERVES 6
6 mackerel, cleaned and boned
75g/3 oz (1 cup) oatmeal or rolled oats
175g/6 oz (¾ cup) butter
1 onion, finely chopped
freshly ground black pepper
2.5ml (½ teaspoon) ground bay leaves
salt
15ml (1 tablespoon) wheatgerm

Heat the oven to 190°C (375°F) gas mark 5.

Wash and pat the fish dry. Mix the oatmeal and half the butter with a fork. Add the onion. Season with pepper, bay leaves and salt. Mix well.

Pack this stuffing into the fish, lay them on a large piece of buttered foil. Dot with the remaining butter. Fold the foil over the fish and crimp above them. Bake for 15–20 minutes.

Heat the grill (broiler). Open the foil, sprinkle the fish with wheatgerm and crisp under the grill (broiler).

Cooking time: 35 minutes

Mock Scampi

This mock scampi is a very good substitute for the real thing. Serve it with 275ml/½ pt (1¼ cups) tartare sauce or mayonnaise verte (page 250) and brown bread as a first course.

SERVES 4
450g (1 lb) tail piece of monk fish (tile fish fillets), cut into strips
15ml (1 tablespoon) plain flour
salt
freshly ground black pepper
2 small eggs, lightly beaten
100g/¼ lb (⅓ cup) dried white breadcrumbs
oil for deep frying
TO GARNISH
fresh parsley sprigs
wedges of lemon

Add 10ml (2 teaspoons) water to the eggs and beat together. Arrange the eggs, the seasoned flour and the breadcrumbs in separate dishes next to the fish strips.

Using tongs, dip each piece of fish in the flour, shaking off the excess, then into the egg mixture and finally into the breadcrumbs. Cover and refrigerate for 1 hour.

Heat the oven to 180°C (350°F) gas mark 4. Put some absorbent paper on a baking tray. Prepare a deep fat fryer and heat the oil to 190°C (350°F) or until a cube of bread will brown in 60 seconds. Deep-fry a quarter of the fish for 1–2 minutes until the coating turns golden brown. Transfer the cooked fish to the baking tray and keep warm in the oven.

Continue until all the fish is fried.

Transfer to a heated serving dish, garnish with parsley and lemon wedges and serve immediately.

Cooking time: 1 hour firming, then 25 minutes

Tuna Fish Gratin

SERVES 4
45ml (3 tablespoons) margarine
1 onion, finely chopped
60ml (4 tablespoons) plain flour
425ml/¾ pt (1⅔ cups) milk
1.5ml (¼ teaspoon) dried dill
200g (7 oz) canned tuna, flaked
salt
freshly ground black pepper
25g/1 oz (½ cup) fresh breadcrumbs
40g/1½ oz (⅓ cup) Cheddar cheese, grated

Melt the margarine in a pan and fry the onion until soft, about 8 minutes. Blend in the flour and cook, stirring for 1 minute. Off the heat, add the milk gradually, stirring all the time. Return to the heat and bring to the boil, stirring. Add the dill, the tuna and the oil from the can. Season to taste. Heat the grill (broiler).

Turn the mixture into an oven-proof dish. Mix the breadcrumbs and the cheese and sprinkle over the fish. Put under the heat for 5 minutes or until the top is golden brown.

Cooking time: 20 minutes

Haddock with Almonds and Lemon

SERVES 4
4 haddock fillets, skinned
45ml (3 tablespoons) lemon juice
salt
freshly ground black pepper
40g/1½ oz (6 tablespoons) plain flour
50g/2 oz (¼ cup) butter
1 garlic clove, crushed
25g/1 oz (¼ cup) slivered almonds
15ml (1 tablespoon) finely grated lemon rind
1.5ml (¼ teaspoon) cumin

Fish gougère is made from cheese-flavoured choux pastry. Quicker and easier to do than you might imagine, it makes an interesting light dish.

On a large plate, sprinkle the haddock with the lemon juice and season lightly. Set aside for 10–15 minutes. Remove and pat dry, reserving the lemon juice.

Dip each haddock fillet in flour. Melt the butter in a frying-pan. Cook the garlic clove, stirring, for 1 minute. Add the haddock fillets to the pan and cook for 4–5 minutes, until lightly browned, before turning them over. Remove the fillets from the pan and keep warm.

Stir in the almonds, lemon rind, cumin and reserved lemon juice. Cook, stirring for 2 minutes. Return the fillets to the pan and cook until the flesh flakes when tested with a fork, about 8 minutes.

To serve, transfer the fish to a heated serving plate. Discard the garlic and pour the sauce and almonds over the fish.
Cooking time: 20 minutes

Fish Gougère

Gougere is cheese-flavoured choux pastry, unusual, with a luxury touch, but very cheap to make. Combined with the fish it makes a delicious light lunch dish.

SERVES 6
choux pastry *(page 244)*
25g/1 oz ($\frac{1}{4}$ cup) Parmesan cheese, grated
25g (1 oz) Gruyère cheese, diced
freshly ground black pepper
FOR THE FILLING
225g ($\frac{1}{2}$ lb) haddock fillet, skinned
40g/1$\frac{1}{2}$ oz (6 tablespoons) plain flour
salt
freshly ground black pepper
30ml (2 tablespoons) oil
1 large onion, finely chopped
1 garlic clove, chopped
275ml/$\frac{1}{2}$ pt (1$\frac{1}{4}$ cups) chicken stock
15ml (1 tablespoon) tomato paste
1 small green (bell) pepper, seeded and cut into strips
2.5ml ($\frac{1}{2}$ teaspoon) dried basil

Make the filling first; cut the fish into bite-sized pieces. Put the flour in a plastic bag and add seasoning. Toss the fish in seasoned flour and reserve any left-over flour. Heat the oil in a pan and fry the onions until soft. Stir in any remaining flour. Cook for 2 minutes.

Stir in the stock and the tomato paste. Bring to the boil and cook for 2–3 minutes. Remove from heat. Add green peppers, fish, basil and seasoning to the sauce and set aside.

Heat the oven to 200°C (400°F) gas mark 6. Make the choux pastry, adding the grated and diced cheeses after the eggs, and season with pepper.

Place spoonfuls of the pastry around the edge of a buttered baking dish. Pour the filling into the centre and bake for 30–35 minutes until golden brown and puffy. Serve hot.
Cooking time: 1 hour

● Several other fillings can be used, combined with 275ml/$\frac{1}{2}$ pt (1$\frac{1}{4}$ cups) béchamel sauce. Try 225g ($\frac{1}{2}$ lb) chicken with 100g

(¼ lb) sautéed mushrooms, or make up the weight of meat with half and half ham and chicken.

● Use 225g (½ lb) diced ham combined with 100g (¼ lb) sweetcorn.

Herrings in Butter

SERVES 6
6 herrings, filleted
50g/2 oz (½ cup) plain flour
salt
freshly ground black pepper
75g/3 oz (5 tablespoons) butter
15ml (1 tablespoon) lemon juice
15ml (1 tablespoon) fresh parsley, chopped

Wash the fillets under cold running water and pat dry. Season the flour with salt and pepper. Dip each fillet in the flour until it is well coated. Set aside.

Heat the butter in a frying-pan. When the foam subsides, add the fillets and cook for 3 minutes on each side or until lightly browned and the flesh flakes easily.

Transfer the herrings from the pan to a heated serving dish. Spoon over the lemon juice and then the pan juices. Sprinkle with parsley and serve.

Cooking time: 10 minutes

Frying in butter shows off the fresh taste of this economical fish and gives a crisp finish to the skin.

Cold Mackerel with Mustard

SERVES 2–4
2 large mackerel, gutted
15ml (1 tablespoon) lemon juice
75g/3 oz (5 tablespoons) butter
22ml (1½ tablespoons) Dijon mustard
2 egg yolks
15ml (1 tablespoon) cider or wine vinegar
salt and freshly ground black pepper
30ml (2 tablespoons) mixed fresh herbs

Heat the oven to 180°C (350°F) gas mark 4. Grease a large piece of foil with oil. Lay the mackerel on it and sprinkle the lemon juice over the fish. Wrap the fish in the foil and bake for 20 minutes.

Meanwhile prepare the sauce. Cream the butter with a wooden spoon. Combine the mustard, egg yolks, vinegar and salt and pepper. Mix well then gradually beat this mixture into the creamed butter. Stir in the herbs. Season then chill.

Remove the mackerel from the oven and open carefully. Pour the cooking juices into a bowl and reserve.

Remove the skin from the mackerel by gently scraping with a knife, but do not break the flesh. Cut each fish into four fillets and remove the bones. Arrange the fish on a large shallow serving dish.

Strain the reserved juices over the fish and allow to cool to room temperature. Chill for at least 2 hours before serving with the mustard sauce.

Cooking time: 25 minutes plus 2 hours cooling

Japanese Sardines

Sardines, cooked and flavoured with ginger and garlic, make a delicious first course served with brown bread and butter. As a meal for 2, serve with a stir-fried vegetable, such as shredded cabbage with lemon juice.

SERVES 2–4
125ml/4 fl oz (½ cup) soy sauce
50ml/2 fl oz (¼ cup) vinegar
30ml (2 tablespoons) lemon juice
25g (1 oz) fresh ginger root, peeled and chopped
2 garlic cloves, crushed
450g (1 lb) fresh sardines, washed and dried
30ml (2 tablespoons) olive oil

Combine the soy sauce, vinegar, lemon juice, ginger and garlic in a small mixing bowl. Arrange the sardines in a shallow baking dish and pour the soy sauce mixture over the sardines. Leave in a cool place to marinate for 2 hours.

Heat the grill (broiler) to a high heat. Remove the sardines from the marinade and discard it. Pat the sardines dry. Line the grill (broiling) pan with foil and brush it with half the oil. Place the sardines in the pan and brush them with the remaining oil.

Cook the sardines for 3–5 minutes depending on their size, turning them once to brown the other sides.

Cooking time: 2 hours marinating then 5–8 minutes

Rice and Pasta

Jambalaya

SERVES 6
15ml (1 tablespoon) vegetable oil
3 bacon slices, chopped
1 onion, finely chopped
2 celery stalks, chopped
350g/¾ lb (2 cups) long-grain rice, washed
575ml/1 pt (2½ cups) chicken stock
salt and freshly ground black pepper
pinch of cayenne pepper
1 bay leaf
1 large green (bell) pepper, pith removed, seeded and chopped
400g (14 oz) canned tomatoes
100g (¼ lb) ham, chopped
225g (½ lb) peeled prawns or shrimps
225g/½ lb (1 cup) cooked chicken, chopped
15ml (1 tablespoon) parsley, chopped

In a large saucepan, fry the bacon in the oil over moderate heat for 5 minutes, stirring occasionally. Remove the bacon from the pan with a slotted spoon and set aside.

Add the onion to the pan and cook, stirring, for 8 minutes until soft. Add the celery and rice. Cook, stirring, for 3 minutes. Pour the chicken stock into the pan. Add seasoning, cayenne and bay leaf. Bring to the boil, reduce the heat and simmer for 10 minutes.

Add the green (bell) pepper and tomatoes with their juice. Cover and simmer for 5 minutes. Stir in the ham, prawns, chicken and reserved bacon. Cover and cook for 5 minutes until the rice is tender.

Turn out the jambalaya to a warm serving dish and sprinkle the parsley over.
Cooking time: 50 minutes

Lamb and Apricot Polo

SERVES 6
175g/6 oz (1 cup) long-grain rice
100g/¼ lb (½ cup) butter
1 onion, chopped
350g (¾ lb) boned shoulder of lamb, cubed
2.5ml (½ teaspoon) cinnamon
25g/1 oz (3 tablespoons) seedless raisins
100g (¼ lb) dried apricots
salt
freshly ground black pepper

Risotto is a great standby for an emergency. Combined, as here, with chicken livers and mushrooms, it makes an authentic Italian dish, which can be produced in about half an hour. Extra items, like ham and peppers, can be added.

Parboil the rice for 8 minutes in salted water. Drain, rinse with cold water and set aside.

Melt half the butter in a frying-pan. Add the onion and fry until soft, about 8 minutes. Add the meat and stir to coat with butter. Sprinkle the cinnamon over, add raisins and apricots. Cover with water. Bring to the boil, cover and simmer for 1½ hours until the meat is tender.

Grease a flameproof casserole or dutch oven with the remaining butter. Put a quarter of the rice in the bottom of the pan. Spoon a third of the lamb mixture over this. Add more rice and then lamb and repeat the layers so that you finish with a layer of rice on the top.

Fold a clean towel into four. Put this over the pan and put the lid on top. Place over a low heat and steam for 20 minutes until the rice is tender.
Cooking time: 2 hours 15 minutes

Chicken Liver Risotto

SERVES 4
50g/2 oz (¼ cup) butter
1 onion, finely chopped
100g (¼ lb) mushrooms, sliced
275g/10 oz (1¼ cups) long-grain rice
575ml/1 pt (2½ cups) chicken stock
8 chicken livers, chopped
30ml (2 tablespoons) parsley, chopped
50g/2 oz (½ cup) grated Parmesan cheese

In a large, heavy-bottomed saucepan melt three-quarters of the butter over moderate heat. Cook the onion, stirring, occasionally for 8 minutes. Add the mushrooms and cook for 3 minutes. Heat the stock.

Add the rice to the onion mixture. Stir constantly for 2–3 minutes until the rice is well coated. Add the stock. Bring to the boil, reduce the heat and leave uncovered to cook for 15–20 minutes. All the liquid must be absorbed and the rice tender.

Meanwhile, melt the remaining butter in a small frying-pan and cook the chicken livers for 10 minutes. When the rice is cooked stir in the chicken livers and the parsley. Sprinkle Parmesan cheese over.
Cooking time: 30 minutes

Ham and Rice Salad

SERVES 4

175g/6 oz (1 cup) long-grain rice
450ml/16 fl oz (2 cups) water
5ml (1 teaspoon) salt
350g/$\frac{3}{4}$ lb ($\frac{3}{4}$ cup) cooked gammon (ham), diced
$\frac{1}{2}$ cucumber, diced
60ml/4 tablespoons ($\frac{1}{4}$ cup) mayonnaise (page 250)
salt
freshly ground black pepper
1 small lettuce
6 tomatoes, quartered

Put the rice, water and salt in a saucepan and bring to the boil. Stir once, then cover the pan and simmer very gently for 15 minutes, or until the rice is tender and has absorbed the water. Spread out the rice on a large platter to get cold.

Add the gammon, cucumber, mayonnaise and seasoning to the cold rice and mix well. Arrange the lettuce leaves on a serving platter and pile the ham and rice mixture in the centre. Garnish with the tomato wedges.

Cooking time: 25 minutes plus cooling

Kitchri

A mixture of rice with beans in this dish gives a perfectly balanced protein meal. Serve with poppadums, which you can buy ready-made, salad and a home-made chutney.

SERVES 6

45ml (3 tablespoons) vegetable oil
1 large onion, chopped
4 garlic cloves, chopped
5ml (1 teaspoon) turmeric powder
2.5ml ($\frac{1}{2}$ teaspoon) dried ginger
5ml (1 teaspoon) curry powder
5ml (1 teaspoon) cumin seeds
1.5ml ($\frac{1}{4}$ teaspoon) chilli powder
1 large potato, diced
4 tomatoes, blanched, skinned and chopped
350g ($\frac{3}{4}$ lb) mung beans, soaked overnight and drained
350g/$\frac{3}{4}$ lb (2 cups) brown rice, washed
575ml/1 pt (2$\frac{1}{2}$ cups) milk
575ml/1 pt (2$\frac{1}{2}$ cups) water
salt
freshly ground black pepper
45ml (3 tablespoons) lemon juice
1 tomato for the garnish

Heat the oil in a large heavy-bottomed saucepan over moderate heat. Fry the onion and garlic for 5 minutes. Stir in the spices. Fry for 3–4 minutes.

Add the potato and tomatoes. Stir in the mung beans and rice. Fry for 5 minutes, stirring. Add the milk and water, salt and pepper. Bring to the boil, cover the pan, reduce the heat and cook for 40 minutes until the rice and beans are tender. Check seasoning and add the lemon juice. Transfer to a heated serving dish and garnish with the sliced tomato.

Cooking time: overnight soaking then 1 hour

Spaghetti with Bacon and Egg

SERVES 6

450g (1 lb) spaghetti
15ml (1 tablespoon) vegetable oil
salt
45ml (3 tablespoons) butter
100g ($\frac{1}{4}$ lb) lean bacon, chopped
45ml (3 tablespoons) thick cream
3 eggs
100g/$\frac{1}{4}$ lb (1 cup) grated Parmesan cheese
freshly ground pepper

Fill a 4.5L (1 gal) saucepan two-thirds full

of water. Add the oil and 15ml (1 tablespoon) salt and bring to the boil. Push the spaghetti down into the water as it softens. Reduce the heat when froth appears and cook for about 8 minutes. Check the spaghetti by biting a piece and take care not to overcook it.

Meanwhile, heat 15ml (1 tablespoon) butter in a frying-pan. When the foam subsides, add the bacon and cook for about 5 minutes until crisp. Remove the pan from heat and stir in the cream. Set aside.

In a medium-sized mixing bowl lightly beat the eggs and half the Parmesan together. Drain the spaghetti in a colander

and put it into a large well-heated serving dish. Add the remaining butter and, using two spoons, toss the spaghetti in it. Add the egg mixture and toss again. Stir in the bacon, toss and season with salt and pepper. Serve immediately accompanied by the remaining cheese.
Cooking time: 20 minutes

Spanish Chicken with Rice

SERVES 4
30ml (2 tablespoons) vegetable oil
3 bacon slices, chopped
4 chicken pieces
30ml (2 tablespoons) flour
salt
freshly ground black pepper
2 onions, chopped
1 garlic clove, crushed
400g (14 oz) canned tomatoes, drained
75g (3 oz) canned pimentoes, drained
10ml (2 teaspoons) paprika
575ml/1 pt (2½ cups) water
100g/¼ lb (⅔ cup) long-grain rice
150g/5 oz (⅔ cup) frozen peas
30ml (2 tablespoons) fresh parsley, chopped

Heat the oil in a flameproof casserole or dutch oven. Fry the bacon for about 5 minutes until crisp. Remove with a slotted spoon and set aside.

Season the flour with salt and pepper. Dip each piece of chicken in the flour to coat it. Place in the pan over moderate heat and fry turning until golden on all sides. Remove the chicken pieces and set aside.

Heat the oven to 180°C (350°F) gas mark 4. Drain off most of the oil in the pan. Return it to a moderate heat. Add the onions and garlic and fry, stirring, for 2–3 minutes.

Place the chicken on the onions, add the bacon, tomatoes, pimentoes, paprika and seasoning. Pour the water over and stir in the rice. Bring to the boil. Cover and cook in the oven for 30 minutes.

Add the peas to the pan and cook for a further 10 minutes or until the chicken is tender. Serve with the parsley sprinkled over it.
Cooking time: 1¼ hours

Kitchri, a mixture of rice and beans, flavoured with curry and ginger, is the Indian dish from which the better-known kedgeree is derived.

Cannelloni hot from the oven.

Cannelloni

SERVES 4
16 cannelloni tubes
15ml (1 tablespoon) olive oil
225g (½ lb) Mozzarella cheese, diced
225g/½ lb (1 cup) Ricotta or cottage cheese, sieved
75g/3 oz (⅓ cup) cooked ham, chopped
2 large eggs, lightly beaten
salt
freshly ground black pepper
tomato sauce *(page 254)*
25g/1 oz (¼ cup) Parmesan cheese

Fill a large saucepan two-thirds full of water. Add salt and oil and bring to the boil. Add the cannelloni tubes and boil for 13–15 minutes until they are just beginning to soften.

Meanwhile, heat the oven to 200°C (400°F) gas mark 6. Combine Mozzarella, Ricotta, ham and eggs. Mix well and add seasoning to taste. Wring out a clean towel in cold water. Grease an oven-proof dish.

Drain the tubes and lay out on the towel. Using a teaspoon, fill each tube with the cheese mixture. Transfer the tubes to the greased dish. Pour the tomato sauce over and sprinkle with the Parmesan. Bake for 15–20 minutes. Serve hot.
Cooking time: 40 minutes

● Gouda can be substituted for Mozzarella. Chopped, drained spinach can also be used half and half with the cheese, omitting the ham. Flavour this well with nutmeg.

● If you have no cannelloni tubes, boil lasagne and cut it into strips, then roll it up.

Vegetables

Vegetable Curry

Use any combination of vegetables for this: aubergines (eggplants), carrots, cauliflower, turnips, beans, green (bell) peppers, potatoes, spring onions (scallions) and okra can all be mixed together.

SERVES 4
60ml (4 tablespoons) cooking oil
5ml (1 teaspoon) mustard seeds
1 onion, finely chopped
1 green chilli, seeded and chopped
15ml (1 tablespoon) fresh ginger root, finely chopped
2 garlic cloves, chopped
7.5ml (1½ teaspoons) ground turmeric
15ml (1 tablespoon) ground coriander
700g (1½ lb) mixed vegetables, sliced
salt
225g/½ lb (2 cups) fresh coconut, grated
175ml/6 fl oz (¾ cup) water
30ml (2 tablespoons) fresh coriander leaves, chopped (optional)

Heat the oil in a large saucepan over high heat. Add the mustard seeds, ginger and garlic and fry for 30 seconds. Add the chilli and the onion, reduce the heat and fry slowly, stirring occasionally, until the onion is cooked, about 8–10 minutes.

Add the turmeric and ground coriander and cook for 1 minute. Add the vegetables and mix well with the spices. Add the water to the coconut in a blender and purée the mixture. Add this to the vegetables.

Season the vegetables with salt. Cover and simmer for 30 minutes or until vegetables are tender. If the mixture shows signs of drying out, add a spoonful of water at a time. To serve, sprinkle the coriander leaves on top.

Cooking time: 45 minutes

Vegetable curries can be varied to use whatever is in season. The subtle Indian spices lend interest to what might otherwise be a dull selection of winter roots.

Caraway Beets

SERVES 4
450g (1 lb) small round beetroot (beets), washed
75g/3 oz (5 tablespoons) butter
10ml (2 teaspoons) caraway seeds
salt

Place the beets in boiling salted water and cook for 30 minutes. Meanwhile heat the oven to 180°C (350°F) gas mark 4. Place the butter in an ovenproof dish and put it in the oven to heat.

Drain the beets and pat dry with absorbent paper. Slip off the skins and cut off roots and tops. Cut beets in half. Place the beets, cut side down, in the sizzling butter. Scatter the caraway seeds over and baste the beets with the butter. Roast for 1 hour, basting from time to time but do not turn the beets over. Serve hot and spoon the caraway butter over.

Cooking time: 1½ hours

Carottes à la nivernais

SERVES 6
1.15kg (2½ lb) old carrots, scraped
1 onion, finely chopped
salt
22ml (1½ tablespoons) sugar
75g/3 oz (5 tablespoons) butter
60ml (4 tablespoons) beef stock
freshly ground black pepper

Cut each carrot lengthwise into four pieces. Pare away hard yellow core. Cut into 2.5cm (1 in) lengths.

Melt the butter in a heavy-bottomed pan. Add the onions, cover and fry over a low heat for 15 minutes. Shake the pan occasionally to prevent the onions sticking to the bottom.

Meanwhile bring to the boil 850ml/ 1½ pt (3¾ cups) water. Add the salt and sugar. Add the carrots, cover and lower heat. Cook for 5–6 minutes. Drain the carrots. Add the carrots to the onions and mix together. Add the stock. Cook uncovered until the stock has nearly all disappeared. To serve, transfer to a warm serving dish and grind over a generous quantity of black pepper.

Cooking time: 45 minutes

Vegetable Rissoles

SERVES 4
100g/¼ lb (⅔ cup) red lentils
1 large onion, finely chopped
1 celery stalk, finely chopped
2 small carrots, trimmed and grated
50g (2 oz) French (green) beans, cooked and finely chopped
50g/2 oz (1 cup) fresh white breadcrumbs
3 eggs
7.5ml (1½ teaspoons) salt
5ml (1 teaspoon) pepper
5ml (1 teaspoon) mixed dried herbs
75g/3 oz (¾ cup) dry white breadcrumbs
50ml/2 fl oz (¼ cup) vegetable oil

Cook the lentils 20–30 minutes or until soft. Stir frequently during the last stage and cook uncovered to drive off the water and make a dry purée. Place the lentils, onion, celery, carrots, beans, fresh white breadcrumbs, 2 eggs, salt and pepper and mixed herbs in a mixing bowl. Mix well until all the ingredients are thoroughly combined. Set aside for 30 minutes.

Divide the mixture into 8 and shape each portion into a ball and then flatten it slightly. Lightly beat the remaining egg. Dip each rissole in the egg and then in the breadcrumbs until thoroughly coated. In a medium-sized frying-pan heat the vegetable oil. Add the rissoles and fry them for 10 minutes on each side or until golden brown. Drain the cooked rissoles on absorbent paper, transfer to a heated serving dish and serve hot.

Cooking time: about 1½ hours

Green Beans with Apples and Almonds

SERVES 4
850ml/1½ pt (3¾ cups) water
salt
450 (1 lb) French (green) beans, trimmed and halved
75g/3 oz (6 tablespoons) butter
1 onion, thinly sliced and pushed into rings
2 cooking apples, peeled, cored and chopped
25g/1 oz (¼ cup) almonds, flaked

In a large saucepan bring the water to the boil and add salt and beans; simmer until they are just tender—depending on the beans, this should take about 10 minutes. Drain the beans and set aside.

In a frying-pan melt the butter. Add the onion and the apples and cook, stirring occasionally, for 10–12 minutes until apples are tender.

Stir in the beans and almonds and reduce heat to low. Cook for 5 minutes, stirring occasionally. Transfer to a warmed serving dish. Serve hot.

Cooking time: 30 minutes

Sweet and Sour Carrots and Parsnips

SERVES 6
450g (1 lb) parsnips, chopped
450g (1 lb) carrots, chopped
15ml (1 tablespoon) margarine
45 ml (3 tablespoons) malt vinegar
25g/1 oz (2 tablespoons) soft brown sugar
salt

Melt the margarine in a heavy-bottomed saucepan. Add the vegetables and turn them to coat with fat. Fry the vegetables, stirring, until they start to brown.

Add the vinegar, brown sugar and salt. Stir, cover and cook for 45 minutes over a low heat. Remove the lid and cook vegetables, turning them occasionally, until they begin to caramelize. Check the seasoning and serve.

Cooking time: 60 minutes

Cabbage with Sour Cream

SERVES 4
30ml (2 tablespoons) butter or margarine
1 onion, sliced
1 garlic clove, crushed
5ml (1 teaspoon) caraway seeds (optional)
1 Savoy cabbage, shredded
5ml (1 teaspoon) paprika
275ml/10 fl oz (1¼ cups) sour cream

Heat the oven to 180°C (350°F) gas mark 4. Melt the butter or margarine in a heavy-bottomed saucepan. Add the onion and garlic and sauté until the onion is soft. Add the cabbage and stir. Cook for about 5 minutes.

Transfer the cabbage to an ovenproof dish. Stir the paprika into the sour cream and pour over the cabbage. Add the caraway seeds if using. Bake for 20 minutes and serve hot.

Cooking time: 30 minutes

Champ

This traditional Irish dish is an attractive variation of mashed potatoes.

SERVES 6
150ml/¼ pt (⅔ cup) milk
10 spring onions (scallions), finely chopped
700g (1½ lb) potatoes, boiled and mashed
salt and freshly ground black pepper
15ml (1 tablespoon) parsley, chopped
50g/2 oz (4 tablespoons) butter, melted

Scald the milk (bring almost to boiling point), add the onions, cover and simmer for 10 minutes until the onions are tender. Drain the onions, reserving the cooking liquid. Add the onions to the mashed potatoes. Over a low heat, add the salt, pepper and parsley. Mix well and season, adding the reserved milk if necessary to make a stiff purée.

To serve, transfer to a heated serving plate and make a well in the centre. Pour the butter in the well and serve.

Cooking time: 15 minutes

Desserts

Fruit Fritters

Deep-fried fruit makes an economical and filling pudding and is quick to do, once the batter is made.

SERVES 4
yeast batter *(page 245)*
2 apples, peeled and cored
2 bananas, peeled
grated rind and juice of 1 lemon
15ml (1 tablespoon) brown sugar
15ml (1 tablespoon) sweet sherry or Madeira
flour
oil for deep frying
FOR THE ORANGE SAUCE
grated rind and juice of 2 oranges
100g/¼ lb (½ cup) fine sugar
60ml/4 tablespoons (¼ cup) water

While the batter is resting, prepare the fruit. Cut the apples into rings and the bananas into diagonal slices. Sprinkle over the lemon rind, lemon juice, sugar and sherry. Leave for 20–30 minutes.

Meanwhile, make the sauce. Combine all the ingredients and simmer for 10 minutes. Reheat when ready to serve.

Heat the oil in a deep fat fryer to 180–190°C (350–375°F) or until a cube of bread browns in 60 seconds. Dredge the fruit in flour then shake off the excess. Dip the fruit in the batter and deep-fry in batches until all the fruit is cooked. Drain on absorbent paper and keep warm until ready to serve. Serve hot with orange sauce.
Cooking time: 45 minutes

●Dried fruit, such as soaked prunes with an almond in the centre, can also be used. Serve these with vanilla sugar and curls of chocolate, shaved from a bar with a potato peeler.

Lemon Meringue Pie

SERVES 6
¾ × sweet rich shortcrust pastry *(page 241)*
peel and juice of 1 large lemon
30ml (2 tablespoons) granulated sugar
275ml/½ pt (1¼ cups) water
30ml (2 tablespoons) cornflour (cornstarch)
2 large eggs, separated
15g/½ oz (1 tablespoon) unsalted butter
pinch of salt
100g/¼ lb (½ cup) fine sugar

Heat the oven to 200°C (400°F) gas mark 6. Roll out the pastry and line an 18cm (7 in) flan tin (tart pan). Bake blind *(page 61)* for 15 minutes.

Put the lemon peel, granulated sugar and water in a pan over medium heat. Stir to dissolve the sugar and bring to the boil. Boil for 1 minute then remove from the heat. Dissolve the cornflour (cornstarch) in the lemon juice. Remove the lemon peel from the sugar syrup and mix in the starch and juice. Add the egg yolks and butter and stir over low heat until the mixture thickens.

Remove the cooked pastry case from the oven and reduce the heat to 150°C (300°F) gas mark 2. Add a pinch of salt to the egg whites and whisk until stiff peaks are formed. Whisk in half the fine sugar, then fold in the remainder with a wooden spoon. Spoon the lemon filling into the pastry case. Pile the meringue on top, being careful to seal the edges of the crust. Make peaks with the spoon. Bake 20–30 minutes until the meringue is golden brown on the outside. Cool completely before refrigerating; serve chilled.
Cooking time: 45 minutes plus chilling

●Equally delicious is banana meringue pie. Slice 2 bananas into the baked pastry case. Beat the egg yolks with 50g (2 tablespoons) fine sugar, a small pinch of salt and 15ml (1 tablespoon) each cornflour (cornstarch) and butter. Scald 350ml/¾ pt (1½ cups) milk and pour a little on to the yolk mixture. Blend then return to the hot milk. Cook, stirring until the custard thickens and add the vanilla. Pour the custard over the bananas and leave to cool. Top with meringue and 30ml (2 tablespoons) shredded almonds.

Queen of Puddings

SERVES 4
425ml/¾ pt (1⅔ cups) milk
30ml (2 tablespoons) butter
grated rind of 1 lemon
3 large eggs, separated
75g/3 oz (1½ cups) fresh white breadcrumbs
30ml (2 tablespoons) raspberry jam
100g/¼ lb (½ cup) fine sugar

Fruit fritters, coated in yeast batter and deep-fried, makes a popular family pudding and any type of fruit can be used, which makes it a good emergency dessert. It can be produced in under an hour, even when the batter is rested for ½ hour—the correct time—in the middle.

Heat the oven to 180°C (350°F) gas mark 4. Heat the milk, butter and lemon rind in a saucepan until the butter melts. Mix the egg yolks with 30ml (2 tablespoons) sugar. Stir in some of the milk and when smooth add the rest of the milk.

Put the breadcrumbs in the bottom of a 1.1L/2 pt (1 qt) ovenproof dish. Pour the custard over the crumbs. Bake for 25–30 minutes to set.

Reduce the heat to 140°C (275°F) gas mark 1. Spoon the jam over the custard. Whisk the egg whites until stiff. Gradually whisk in the remaining sugar. Spoon the meringue over the custard, spreading it completely to the edge of the dish. Bake for 30 minutes until the meringue is pale brown. Serve hot or chilled.

Cooking time: 1¼ hours

Date Puffs in Syrup

SERVES 6
150g/5 oz (1¼ cups) plain flour
10ml (2 teaspoons) bicarbonate of soda (baking soda)
salt
2.5ml (½ teaspoon) cinnamon
15ml (1 tablespoon) butter
100g/¼ lb (¾ cup) dates, stoned and chopped
15ml (1 tablespoon) golden syrup or honey
125ml/4 fl oz (½ cup) milk
FOR THE POACHING SYRUP
575ml/1 pt (2½ cups) water
225g/½ lb (1 cup) sugar
2.5cm (1 in) piece of ginger root, peeled

To make the poaching syrup, bring the water to the boil in a saucepan with a lid. Add the sugar and stir to dissolve. Add the ginger.

Sift the flour, soda, salt and cinnamon for the batter. Add the butter and rub it into the dry ingredients. Stir in the chopped dates, golden syrup or honey and milk to make a smooth batter.

Adjust the heat so that the poaching syrup is slowly boiling. Working quickly, drop spoonfuls of the batter into the syrup. Cover the pan and cook for 25 minutes. Do not disturb the pan during this time and do not lift the lid.

To serve, discard the piece of ginger and spoon into individual serving dishes with some of the syrup. Serve hot.

Cooking time: 35 minutes

Quick Lemon Cheesecake

SERVES 8–10

18cm (7 in) whisked sponge cake
(*page 246*)

2 squares lemon jelly plus 60 ml
(4 tablespoons) water OR 2.5ml
($\frac{1}{2}$ teaspoon) gelatin dissolved in the
same amount of water

3 large eggs, separated

150ml/$\frac{1}{4}$ pt ($\frac{2}{3}$ cup) milk

grated rind and juice of 2 lemons

25g/1 oz (2 tablespoons) fine sugar

450g (1 lb) cream cheese

150ml/$\frac{1}{4}$ pt ($\frac{2}{3}$ cup) thick cream

icing (confectioners') sugar to decorate

If using jelly squares, cut them into pieces and place in a saucepan with the water. Dissolve over gentle heat, stirring. Alternatively, sprinkle the gelatin over the water, leave to soak 5 minutes then dissolve in the same way.

Beat the egg yolks with the milk and stir the jelly liquid into the milk. Add the lemon rind, lemon juice and sugar. Chill until about to set—about 1 hour.

Meanwhile split the sponge cake. Place half in the bottom of an 18cm (7 in) spring-form cake tin (pan). Beat the cream cheese until smooth. Add the milk jelly a little at a time.

Lightly whip the cream and fold it into the mixture. Whisk the whites until they form soft peaks. Fold into the jelly mixture. Spoon the mixture over the sponge bottom and top with the other sponge half. Chill for 3 hours.

Release the spring and transfer the cake to a serving plate. Dust with sifted icing (confectioners') sugar and serve.
Cooking time: 5 minutes plus 4 hours chilling in 2 periods

Jam and Sour Cream Crêpes

SERVES 4

sweet crêpes (*page 245*)

60ml (4 tablespoons) butter for frying

175g/6 oz ($\frac{3}{4}$ cup) apricot jam

45ml (3 tablespoons) brandy or sherry

50g/2 oz ($\frac{1}{2}$ cup) icing (confectioners')
sugar, sifted

50g/2 oz ($\frac{1}{2}$ cup) hazelnuts, chopped

225ml/8 fl oz (1 cup) sour cream

In a small saucepan warm the apricot jam and brandy. Stir until the jam has melted and the mixture is thin. Remove from heat

and keep warm. Mix the hazelnuts and the icing (confectioners') sugar together.

Make the crêpes and keep warm until you are ready to serve. Divide the jam between the crêpes, spreading it with a knife. Fold or roll the crêpes and arrange them on a serving plate. Top each with a dollop of sour cream and sprinkle over the sugar and nuts.
Cooking time: about 1 hour, including making batter and crêpes

Danish Peasant Girl with a Veil

SERVES 6

700g (1$\frac{1}{2}$ lb) cooking apples, peeled, cored
and sliced

5ml (1 teaspoon) lemon juice

45ml (3 tablespoons) brown sugar

45ml (3 tablespoons) water

4 thick slices brown bread

15ml (1 tablespoon) ground cinnamon

75g/3 oz (5 tablespoons) butter

150ml/$\frac{1}{4}$ pt ($\frac{2}{3}$ cup) thick cream

50g (2 oz) plain dessert (semi-sweet)
chocolate squares, grated

Put the apples in a heavy-bottomed pan with the lemon juice, sugar and water. Cover and cook over a low heat for 25 minutes or until tender.

Meanwhile, cut the crusts from the bread and reduce the bread to crumbs. Melt the butter in a pan over low heat. When foam subsides add the crumbs and fry until brown and crisp. Sprinkle the brown sugar and cinnamon over the crumbs. Remove from heat and mix well.

In a glass serving dish layer the cooked fruit and crumbs ending with a layer of crumbs. Set aside to cool. Cover the dish

Danish apple 'peasant girl with a veil'.

and chill for at least 1 hour. Pour the cream over the dessert and sprinkle the chocolate on top just before serving.
Cooking time: 30 minutes plus chilling

Apple Yogurt Fool

SERVES 6

450g (1 lb) cooking apples, peeled, cored
and chopped

50g/2 oz ($\frac{1}{3}$ cup) raisins

2.5ml ($\frac{1}{2}$ teaspoon) mixed spice

425ml/$\frac{3}{4}$ pt (2 cups) plain yogurt

green food colouring

TO SERVE

30ml (2 tablespoons) Demerara or
granulated brown sugar

30ml (2 tablespoons) chopped nuts

Put the apples in a saucepan with the raisins, 30ml (2 tablespoons) water and the mixed spice. Bring to the boil then simmer gently until the apples are tender. Transfer to a fruit bowl and chill until cold.

Stir in the yogurt and a few drops of food colouring. Spoon into individual glass dishes and sprinkle over the sugar and nuts. Chill until required.
Cooking time: 15–30 minutes plus chilling

● Oranges also make a delicious fool. Use your own home-made yogurt (*page 249*). Remove peel and pith from 8 oranges and chop. Combine in a blender with 575ml/1 pt (2$\frac{1}{2}$ cups) yogurt and 30ml (2 tablespoons) honey. Top the dessert with 60ml (4 tablespoons) chopped almonds.

French Apple Tart

$\frac{3}{4}$ × **sweet shortcrust pastry** *(page 241)*
275ml/10 fl oz (1¼ cups) very thick, sweet apple purée or apple sauce
450g (1 lb) dessert apples, peeled and cored
60ml (4 tablespoons) golden syrup or honey
rind and juice of 1 lemon
60ml/4 tablespoons (¼ cup) redcurrant or crabapple jelly
30ml (2 tablespoons) water

Heat the oven to 200°C (400°F) gas mark 6. Line a 23cm (9 in) flan tin (tart pan) with the pastry. Chill briefly then bake blind (*page 61*) for 15 minutes. Leave to cool.

In the bottom of the cold pastry case spread the cold apple purée or sauce—this must be thick; if it seems at all runny, dry it by stirring in a pan over low heat and then leave until cold before using.

Put the golden syrup or honey in a small heavy-bottomed pan. Heat gently and stir in the lemon rind and juice.

Cut the apples into thin slices. Cover the purée or sauce with rings of overlapping apple slices, starting with the outside and working towards the centre. Pour the lemon syrup over the apples. Bake for 20 minutes to cook the apples. Leave to cool.

Heat the redcurrant or crabapple jelly with the water. Brush the cold apples with jelly and leave to set.

Cooking time: 45 minutes plus chilling

●Oranges make a delicious variation. Add the finely grated rind of 2 oranges to the apple purée, then peel and slice 3 large oranges into rings, removing pith and pips (seeds). Use these to top the tart. Glaze with 45ml (3 tablespoons) melted apricot jam but do not bake.

Crème Brulée

This rich glazed custard serves a small quantity of cream to a lot of people. It can be served in one dish or in separate ramekins.

SERVES 6
575ml/1 pt (2½ cups) thin cream
a vanilla pod
4 medium-sized egg yolks
15g/½ oz (1 tablespoon) granulated sugar
50g/2 oz (¼ cup) fine sugar

Pour the cream into a heavy-bottomed saucepan and add the vanilla pod. Heat until the edge of the cream is covered with bubbles. Remove from heat and leave to infuse.

Prepare a double boiler. Cream the egg yolks and granulated sugar in the top, off the heat. Remove the vanilla pod from the cream. Pour the cream on to the egg yolks, stirring all the time.

Put the pan over boiling water and cook, stirring, for about 10–15 minutes until the custard thickens. Strain into a flameproof serving dish. Chill for at least 4 hours.

Heat the grill (broiler) to a high heat. Sprinkle the fine sugar over the custard; add extra sugar if the surface area is large. Put under the grill (broiler) until the sugar melts and starts turning brown: be careful not to burn it. Cool then chill before serving.

Cooking time: 30 minutes plus 6 hours chilling in two periods

●A layer of fruit can be included at the bottom of the dish to stretch the dessert to feed 8.

A classic French apple tart.

Crumbles or crumb-topped puddings are perfect for chilly spring days, when the first forced rhubarb appears. The pudding can be flavoured with chopped ginger or stir in the grated rind and the peeled segments of a medium-sized orange.

Budget Chocolate Mousse

The flavour of cocoa is every bit as rich as chocolate itself. This rich, dark mousse is based on an egg custard and costs so little that you could afford to lavish cream on top if desired.

SERVES 6–7
50g/2 oz ($\frac{1}{2}$ cup) cocoa powder
350ml/12 fl oz (1$\frac{1}{2}$ cups) milk
3 medium-sized eggs, separated
15ml (1 tablespoon) gelatin
60ml (4 tablespoons) water
5ml (1 teaspoon) instant coffee
100g/$\frac{1}{4}$ lb ($\frac{1}{2}$ cup) fine sugar
90ml (6 tablespoons) thick cream

Sift the cocoa into a small pan and use some of the milk to make a smooth paste. Add the rest of the milk and stir till mixed. Bring to the boil and simmer 1 minute, stirring.

Prepare a double boiler. Beat the yolks and the sugar together in the top pan with a hand whisk. Pour in the hot milk. Heat over hot water, stirring, until the custard thickens.

Strain the custard into a cold bowl. Cover tightly with plastic wrap to prevent a skin forming on the surface. Fill a large bowl or sink half full of cold water and stand the custard in it to cool—about 15 minutes.

Put the spoonfuls of water in the pan vacated by the chocolate milk. Sprinkle in the gelatin and leave to soften for 5 minutes. Place over low heat. Scrape down any remaining chocolate into the liquid. Add the instant coffee and stir until this dissolves. Cool to room temperature then stir the gelatin liquid into the custard. Beat well to mix. Cover again with plastic wrap, leave to cool then refrigerate to chill to the point of setting.

Whisk the whites until they stand in soft peaks and fold in the cold chocolate custard. Spoon the mixture into custard cups or spare wineglasses. Chill in the refrigerator to set completely. When set, whip the cream until thick and pipe a rosette on top of each mousse.

Cooking time: 2 hours plus chilling time

Rhubarb Crumble

SERVES 6
1kg (2$\frac{1}{4}$ lb) rhubarb, chopped
grated rind and juice of 1 lemon
15ml (1 tablespoon) stem or crystallized ginger, finely chopped
75g/3 oz ($\frac{1}{2}$ cup) brown sugar
FOR THE CRUMBLE
150g/5 oz (1$\frac{1}{2}$ cups) plain flour
pinch of salt
65g/2$\frac{1}{2}$ oz ($\frac{1}{3}$ cup) butter, diced
50g/2 oz ($\frac{1}{4}$ cup) Demerara or granulated brown sugar

Heat the oven to 190°C (375°F) gas mark 5. Grease a 1.15L/2 pt (1 qt) pie dish with butter.

To make the crumble, sift the flour and salt into a large mixing bowl. Rub in the butter until the mixture resembles breadcrumbs. Stir in the sugar.

Put the rhubarb in a bowl and add the lemon rind, juice, ginger and sugar. Mix well and spoon into the prepared dish. Cover the rhubarb with the crumble topping and bake for 25–30 minutes. Serve hot or cold.

Cooking time: 35 minutes

● The grated rind and chopped flesh of an orange can be used instead of the ginger and lemon.

Apricot Mousse

Apples and egg whites—both inexpensive—are used in this recipe to stretch a more expensive dried fruit. The syrup left over from stewing the fruit can be used as a fruit sauce to serve with hot puddings or ice-cream.

SERVES 6
225g ($\frac{1}{2}$ lb) dried apricots, soaked overnight
rind and juice of half a lemon
2 medium-sized cooking apples, peeled, cored and sliced
about 15ml (1 tablespoon) fine sugar
2 large egg whites
15ml (1 tablespoon) toasted almonds, hazelnuts or grated chocolate

Put the apricots and the soaking liquid in a saucepan. Add the rind and juice of the lemon, and the cooking apple. Stew gently until fruit is tender—about 20 minutes.

Drain the fruit and discard the lemon rind. Purée the mixture in a blender or through a food mill. Sweeten to taste with the sugar, then cool completely.

Whip the egg whites until stiff, then fold into the purée. Spoon into individual serving dishes and garnish with the almonds, hazelnuts or chocolate.

Cooking time: overnight soaking, then about 60 minutes

Cakes, Biscuits and Cookies

Brownies

MAKES 16 SQUARES

100g/$\frac{1}{4}$ lb ($\frac{1}{2}$ cup) butter
175g (6 oz) semi-sweet chocolate (squares)
30ml (2 tablespoons) water
100g/$\frac{1}{4}$ lb ($\frac{1}{2}$ cup) sugar
5ml (1 teaspoon) vanilla extract
100g/$\frac{1}{4}$ lb (1 cup) self-raising flour
pinch of salt
2 eggs
50g/2 oz ($\frac{1}{2}$ cup) walnuts, chopped

Heat the oven to 160°C (325°F) gas mark 3. Grease a 20cm (8 in) square baking tin (pan). Put the chocolate, water and butter in a medium-sized saucepan over low heat. Melt the chocolate, stirring all the time. Remove from the heat and stir in the sugar and the vanilla. Set aside and allow the chocolate to cool to room temperature.

Sift the flour and salt into a mixing bowl. Gradually stir in the cooled chocolate mixture. Add the eggs and beat well. Fold in the walnuts. Pour into the baking tin. Bake for 30–35 minutes or until a skewer comes out clean. Leave to cool and cut into squares.

Cooking time: 45 minutes

Dried Apricot Bars

MAKES 16 SQUARES

100g/$\frac{1}{4}$ lb ($\frac{1}{2}$ cup) margarine
100g ($\frac{1}{4}$ lb) dried apricots, soaked overnight
50g/2 oz ($\frac{1}{4}$ cup) fine sugar
175g/6 oz (1$\frac{3}{4}$ cups) plain flour
2.5ml ($\frac{1}{2}$ teaspoon) baking powder
1.5ml ($\frac{1}{4}$ teaspoon) salt
2 medium-sized eggs, lightly beaten
225g/$\frac{1}{2}$ lb (1$\frac{1}{4}$ cups) brown sugar
2.5ml ($\frac{1}{2}$ teaspoon) vanilla extract
75g/3 oz ($\frac{3}{4}$ cup) walnuts, chopped
50g/2 oz ($\frac{1}{2}$ cup) icing (confectioners') sugar

Heat the oven to 180°C (350°F) gas mark 4. Grease a shallow 20cm (8 in) square baking tin (pan).

Cream the margarine and fine sugar together until light and fluffy. Rub half the flour into the mixture. Press into the baking tin (pan). Bake for 25 minutes or until the pastry is lightly browned.

Drain the apricots and chop them into small dice. Meanwhile, sift the remaining flour with the baking powder and salt. Mix the eggs and the brown sugar together. Gradually add the egg and sugar mixture to the flour. Stir in the vanilla, chopped apricots and walnuts and mix well. Spread this over the cooked pastry and bake for 30 minutes.

Remove the tin (pan) and allow to cool. Cut into 16 squares and roll them in the icing (confectioners') sugar.

Cooking time: total 1 hour 10 minutes, plus cooling time

Brownies are the American child's cake.

Sachertorte

SERVES 10

100g/¼ lb (½ cup) butter

175g/6 oz (¾ cup) fine sugar

6 egg yolks

175g (6 oz) semi-sweet chocolate (squares)

5ml (1 teaspoon) vanilla extract

75g/3 oz (¾ cup) plain flour

pinch of salt

8 egg whites

FOR THE GLAZE

175g/6 oz (¾ cup) apricot jam

10ml (2 teaspoons) lemon juice

FOR THE ICING

100g/¼ lb (½ cup) icing (confectioners') sugar

45ml (3 tablespoons) cocoa

30ml (2 tablespoons) water

2.5ml (½ teaspoon) vanilla extract

75g/3 oz (5 tablespoons) butter

50g (2 oz) milk chocolate

Heat the oven to 180°C (350°F) gas mark 4. Grease and line a 23cm (9 in) deep, round cake tin (pan).

Beat the butter until creamy. Add the sugar and mix until fluffy. Beat in the egg yolks one at a time. Break the chocolate into pieces and melt in the top of a double boiler. Remove from heat and stir in the vanilla. Mix the melted chocolate into the butter mixture.

Sift the flour and salt and fold into the chocolate mixture. Whisk the egg whites with a pinch of salt until stiff. Fold them into the chocolate mixture using a metal spoon. Transfer to the prepared cake tin (pan) and cook in the centre of the oven for 1 hour.

When cooked, the cake should spring back when lightly pressed. Allow the cake to cool in the tin for 5 minutes. Turn out onto a wire rack and leave until completely cold. Cut the cold cake horizontally into two layers.

Heat the apricot jam and lemon juice. Strain and leave to cool slightly. Spread half the jam over the bottom layer. Place the other layer on top and lightly brush the top and sides with the remaining jam.

To make the icing, put the fine sugar, cocoa and water in a saucepan and bring to the boil. Boil for 1 minute stirring all the time. Remove from heat, stir in the vanilla. Beat in the butter a little at a time. Leave to cool slightly. Coat the top and sides of the cake with icing and leave to set.

Melt the milk chocolate. Put into a piping bag with a fine writing nozzle and pipe 'Sacher' across the top. Leave to set before cutting the cake.

Cooking time: total 1 hour 20 minutes, plus 2 hours cooling and final setting

Sachertorte, from Vienna, is one of the world's great chocolate cakes; it has an apricot jam layer inside.

Carrot Cake

SERVES 8

900g (2 lb) carrots, grated
100g/$\frac{1}{4}$ lb ($\frac{1}{2}$ cup) margarine
5ml (1 teaspoon) cinnamon
5ml (1 teaspoon) nutmeg
2.5ml ($\frac{1}{2}$ teaspoon) salt
150g/$\frac{1}{4}$ lb ($\frac{1}{2}$ cup) granulated sugar
150ml/$\frac{1}{4}$ pt ($\frac{1}{2}$ cup) golden syrup or honey
4 medium-sized eggs, beaten
15ml (1 tablespoon) baking powder
225g/$\frac{1}{2}$ lb (2 cups) plain flour
50g/2 oz ($\frac{1}{2}$ cup) mixed chopped nuts

Heat the oven to 180°C (350°F) gas mark 4. Grease a 23cm (9 in) deep, loose-bottomed round cake tin (pan) and line it with foil, allowing a deep turn-up to prevent the batter leaking out before it starts to set.

Cream the margarine with the spices and salt it. Add the sugar and beat well. Warm the syrup then measure and pour on to the butter mixture, stirring all the time. Stir in the grated carrot and eggs, a little at a time. Sift the baking powder with the flour and beat into the carrot mixture. Add the chopped nuts.

Turn into the cake tin (pan) and bake about 1$\frac{1}{4}$ hours. Test by inserting a skewer

It is an old 18th century idea to use a cheap readily-available vegetable, instead of expensive dried fruit. Carrot cake has a dense, moist consistency similar to good bread pudding or cheesecake; it keeps well.

that the centre is cooked; it should come out clean if the cake is cooked through. Cover the top with foil if the cake is overbrowning.

Leave the cake to cool in the pan for 15 minutes before turning out. Cool completely on a wire rack and remove the foil.
Cooking time: 1$\frac{1}{2}$ hours plus cooling time

Chocolate Roll

Whisked sponges are among the cheapest of cakes—and are a light delight—because they contain no butter. You can therefore afford a filling of thick, sweetened cream, if desired.

MAKES 8 SLICES

65g/2¼ oz (⅔ cup) plain flour

small pinch of salt

15g/½ oz (2 tablespoons) cocoa

3 large eggs

75g/3 oz (5 tablespoons) plus 60ml (4 tablespoons) fine sugar

30ml (2 tablespoons) icing (confectioners') sugar, sifted

FOR THE FILLING

75g/3 oz (5 tablespoons) butter

175g/6 oz (1¾ cups) icing (confectioners') sugar, sifted

10ml (2 teaspoons) instant coffee

30ml (2 tablespoons) hot water

Heat the oven to 200°C (400°F) gas mark 6. Line a 33 × 23cm (13 × 9 in) Swiss roll tin (jelly roll pan) with greaseproof (wax) paper. Mitre the corners and fit the paper into the pan neatly, then brush with oil.

Sift the flour and salt together. Beat the eggs and 75g/3 oz (5 tablespoons) fine sugar over a pan of hot water until thick, then whisk off the heat for about 5 minutes until cool. Fold in the sifted flour and cocoa. Pour into the prepared tin (pan) spreading it evenly. Bake 8–10 minutes.

Meanwhile, spread a kitchen towel and cover it with a piece of greaseproof or waxed paper a little larger than the cake tin (pan). Sprinkle the paper with 30ml (2 tablespoons) fine sugar. Remove the baked sponge from the oven and turn it out immediately onto the sugared paper.

Gently peel away the baking paper. With a sharp knife, trim the crisp edges from the cake: this makes rolling easier. Make a cut halfway through the cake, about 25cm (1 in) from the edge, across the narrow end of the cake. Sprinkle 30ml (2 tablespoons) fine sugar over the cake.

Now roll up the cake (see steps, *page 246*). Press the cut end over and hold it down with one hand. Fold the bottom paper over the end of the cake and roll up firmly with the paper inside, using the cloth to help you. Hold the cake in position, seam-side down, on a wire rack for a few minutes then leave to get completely cold.

Meanwhile make the filling; beat the butter with a fork and blend in the sifted sugar. Dissolve the instant coffee in the water and beat in. Chill the butter cream.

Unroll the cold sponge and spread the butter cream to within 6mm (¼ in) of the edges. Roll up the cake, using the paper to help. Press to secure and dredge with the sifted (confectioners') sugar.
Cooking time: 35 minutes, plus chilling

● Use the whisked sponge on *page 246* and roll up with jam or jelly.

Apple Muffins

MAKES 12

15ml (1 tablespoon) oil

225g/½ lb (2 cups) plain flour

2.5ml (½ teaspoon) salt

10ml (2 teaspoons) baking powder

50g/2 oz (¼ cup) sugar

2.5ml (½ teaspoon) ground cinnamon

1.5ml (¼ teaspoon) nutmeg

1.5ml (¼ teaspoon) mixed spice

2 large eggs

50g/2 oz (¼ cup) butter, melted

150ml/¼ pt (⅔ cup) buttermilk

15ml (1 tablespoon) lemon juice

2 medium-sized dessert apples, peeled, cored and grated or finely chopped

Heat the oven to 230°C (450°F) gas mark 8. Grease a deep 12-bun tin (muffin pan).

Sift the flour, salt, baking powder, sugar, cinnamon, nutmeg and mixed spice into a large mixing bowl. Beat the eggs until pale yellow in colour. Beat in the butter, buttermilk and lemon juice. Stir this mixture into the flour and mix quickly until just combined. Fold in the apple.

Spoon the batter into the muffin pan and bake for 15–20 minutes or until a skewer inserted into a muffin comes out clean. Cool the muffins in the pan for about 5 minutes then transfer to a plate.
Cooking time: 35 minutes

Black Pepper Cookies

MAKES 36

175g/6 oz (¾ cup) butter

4ml (¾ teaspoon) freshly ground black pepper

4ml (¾ teaspoon) ground cinnamon

1.5ml (¼ teaspoon) ground cloves

7.5ml (1½ teaspoons) vanilla extract

225g/½ lb (1 cup) fine sugar

1 egg, lightly beaten

175g/6 oz (1½ cups) self-raising flour

1.5ml (¼ teaspoon) salt

75g/3 oz (¾ cup) cocoa powder

Heat the oven to 190°C (375°F) gas mark 5. Grease a baking sheet.

Put the butter, black pepper, cinnamon, cloves and vanilla into a medium-sized bowl and thoroughly mix together, using a wooden spoon. Gradually beat in the sugar and the egg, beating until creamy.

Sift the flour, salt and cocoa into the butter mixture. Mix to form a stiff dough. Lightly flour your hands and roll the dough in walnut-sized balls. Place the balls on the baking sheet leaving at least 3cm (1¼ in) between them. With the heel of your hand press each ball flat so they are about 6mm (¼ in) thick. Bake for 12–15 minutes. Cool on a wire rack.
Cooking time: 25 minutes

Pineapple Upside-down Cake

SERVES 6–9

150g/5 oz (⅔ cup) butter

30ml (2 tablespoons) soft brown sugar

1 medium-sized fresh pineapple, peeled, cored and cut into 9 rings, or 9 small, canned pineapple rings, drained

9 glacé cherries

100g/¼ lb (½ cup) sugar

2 eggs

175g/6 oz (1½ cups) self-raising flour

45ml (3 tablespoons) milk

angelica, cut into leaf shapes

Heat the oven to 180°C (350°F) gas mark 4. Grease a 20cm (8 in) square cake tin (pan). Cut 25g/1 oz (2 tablespoons) butter into pieces and dot the bottom of the tin (pan). Sprinkle the brown sugar over. Arrange the pineapple rings in the tin (pan). Place a cherry in the centre of each ring.

In a medium-sized mixing bowl, beat the remaining butter until soft and creamy. Add the sugar and cream it until light and fluffy. Add the eggs, one at a time, beating well after each addition. Sift the flour and fold into the batter. Stir in enough milk to make a batter of dropping consistency. Spoon the batter on to the pineapple rings, smooth the top and bake for 50–60 minutes until the cake is lightly brown and a skewer comes out clean.

Allow the cake to cool in the tin for 5 minutes. Run a knife around the edge. Invert over a serving dish. Decorate each cherry with angelica leaves. Serve immediately or leave to cool.
Cooking time: 1 hour 10 minutes

Right : pineapple upside-down cake

Quiches and Savoury Pies

Crisp pastry provides an attractive contrast to a moist filling. It is easy to make, economical and extends the protein in the final dish. There is no need to serve rice or potatoes if pastry forms part of the main dish. The pastry can act as a container for the food, as in quiches or savoury tarts and their smaller versions, boat-shaped barquettes and tartlets. Pastry may also be a topping, as in a one-crust pie, or it can wrap right around the food, as in double-crust pies, turnovers, parcels, rolls and pasties.

Quiches and savoury pies are a wonderful standby for the cook. They can usually be cooked in advance and can be eaten cold or reheated. They are excellent party food and are just the thing for a picnic, as they need the minimum of eating utensils. Remember that, for successful picnic food, they must not be runny in the middle, but must be firm enough to retain a wedge-shape when cut.

Pastry types: shortcrust is the most versatile of all pastries, suitable both for lining pastry cases and making pie toppings. The basic proportions are half the weight of fat to flour and just enough water to bind the pastry, though a pastry richer in fat gives a better result (recipes are given on *page 241*). This pastry can be enriched by adding egg yolks to bind it or by adding cheese, herbs or spices to flavour it, to complement the filling. This is particularly successful for a savoury flan (tart). For a two-crust pie, which has pastry both beneath and above the filling, use a fat- or egg-enriched shortcrust, but do not use cheese shortcrust as it could crack.

Flaky pastry makes a wonderful, light pie topping, while the decorations made from the trimmings will rise most attractively (though shortcrust can also be used for topping pies.) Flaky pastry can be made successfully at home, but it is very time consuming to do, so either make a big batch and keep it in the freezer or buy it ready-made and frozen (or as a packaged mix). To ensure that the pie crust rises successfully, roll the pastry when cold and return the pie to the refrigerator for at least $\frac{1}{2}$ hour after shaping, to allow the pastry to rest and chill.

Pastry cases: to make a pastry case, first line the tin (pan) or a ring standing on a baking sheet with the pastry, as shown in the step-by-step pictures. The filling may be added and the whole thing then cooked, but it is more usual to bake the crust first in order to crisp it, so that the filling cannot make it soggy. It may be completely or partially baked. The case is always baked for 10 minutes with the lining inside (as shown in the pictures). The lining is then removed and the pastry is returned to the oven for a number of minutes to cook partially or fully. The recipe will give you the total number of minutes.

The difference between a savoury flan (tart) and a quiche is that in a quiche the filling of cheese, vegetables etc is covered with a savoury custard which is then baked. A savoury flan (tart) can have a meat, fish or vegetable filling, often with béchamel sauce, but does not contain beaten eggs. Both types can be served hot or cold. A fully-cooked pastry case can also be used as a container for mayonnaise mixtures or savoury ingredients in cold sauce—béchamel or aspic—which is not cooked further.

Covered pies: a single-crust pie has only a topping of pastry, as shown in the pictures on *page 66*. Lift a large topping by wrapping around the rolling pin and then unrolling it over the dish. For a two-crust pie, the pie dish or tin (pan) is first lined inside with pastry. The filling must be cooked—and cold—if it requires a longer cooking time than the pastry, but can be raw if it requires the same time. Fill the pie, cover it and seal the edges. Decorate the pie, pierce the top to allow steam to escape and glaze the crust with a mixture of salt and beaten egg for a golden finish.

Make a fresh chicken and ham quiche: the recipe is on page 62.

Lining and Baking a Pastry Case

1. Roll out the pastry on a lightly-floured surface to about 4cm (1½ in) wider all around than the diameter of the ring or tin (pan).

2. To lift the pastry without breaking, roll around the rolling pin and centre it over the ring. Unroll carefully over the ring, then ease into place.

3. Working from the centre outward, press the pastry into shape, using a bent forefinger, to fit snugly around the bottom edge and up the sides.

4. To remove excess pastry and leave a clean edge, bend the surplus over the rim, then roll the rolling pin across the top of the rind to cut it off.

5. To finish the edge and ensure a good fit, press around the rim and into the fluted sides (if these are present) with your index finger.

6. Lightly prick the base in several places with a fork to release any trapped air. This will prevent the base rising during cooking.

7. Cut out a circle of waxed paper or foil 8cm (3 in) larger than the ring. Place inside the pastry and fill with beans, piling some around the rim.

8. Place the ring on a baking tray and bake at 200°C (400°F) gas mark 6 on the shelf above centre for 10 minutes. Then lift out the lining and beans.

9. To partially bake, return to the oven for 3–5 minutes until the pastry is set. To fully crisp, bake for a further 5–10 minutes until coloured.

Quiche Lorraine, with bacon and cream, has many imitations, but few peers: it is the classic of its type.

Mushroom Lattice Quiche

This simple, decorative tart will feed 4–5 as a lunch or supper dish or 6 as a starter.

SERVES 4–5
rich shortcrust pastry *(page 241)*
225g ($\frac{1}{2}$ lb) mushrooms, sliced
50g/2 oz (4 tablespoons) butter
25g/1 oz (3 tablespoons) grated Parmesan cheese
2 medium-sized eggs
1 egg yolk
125ml/4 fl oz ($\frac{1}{2}$ cup) thick cream
75ml/3 fl oz ($\frac{1}{3}$ cup) milk
salt
freshly ground black pepper
pinch of cayenne
beaten egg to glaze

Heat the oven to 190°C (375°F) gas mark 5. Roll out the pastry and line a 20cm (8 in) flan ring (tart or layer cake pan).

Sauté the mushrooms in the butter for 2 minutes so that they absorb the butter. Arrange them in the pastry case and sprinkle the cheese on top. Beat together the eggs, yolk, cream and milk and season with salt, pepper and cayenne to taste. Pour over the mushrooms.

Roll out the trimmings and cut strips to make a lattice over the top of the quiche, sticking it to the pastry rim with water. Brush with salted, beaten egg. Bake for 35 minutes until set. Serve hot and puffy.
Cooking time: 45 minutes

Chicken and Ham Quiche

SERVES 6
$\frac{3}{4}$ × shortcrust pastry *(page 240)*
50g/2 oz ($\frac{1}{4}$ cup) butter
22ml (1$\frac{1}{2}$ tablespoons) plain flour
175ml/6 fl oz ($\frac{3}{4}$ cup) chicken stock
2 egg yolks
salt
freshly ground black pepper
5ml (1 teaspoon) dried marjoram
100g ($\frac{1}{4}$ lb) cooked French (green) beans, cut into 12mm ($\frac{1}{2}$ in) pieces
225g/$\frac{1}{2}$ lb (1 cup) cooked chicken, skinned and diced
100g/$\frac{1}{4}$ lb ($\frac{1}{2}$ cup) cooked ham, diced
parsley sprigs

Quiche Lorraine

This is the classic quiche from Lorraine, which contains no cheese; it is less well known than the cheese variation which is given at the end of the recipe.

SERVES 4–6
$\frac{3}{4}$ × shortcrust pastry *(page 241)*
100g ($\frac{1}{4}$ lb) bacon, chopped
2 medium-sized eggs, lightly beaten
150ml/$\frac{1}{4}$ pt ($\frac{2}{3}$ cup) thin cream
salt
freshly ground black pepper
pinch of nutmeg

Position shelf above centre of oven and heat oven to 200°C (400°F) gas mark 6. Line a 20cm (8 in) flan tin (layer cake pan) with the pastry and bake blind *(page 61)* for 15 minutes.

Meanwhile heat a frying-pan over a low heat. Sweat the bacon until the fat runs out, but do not brown. Drain and reserve.

Mix the eggs and the cream. Add salt, bearing in mind the saltiness of the bacon. Mix in the pepper and nutmeg. Arrange the bacon in pastry case. Pour over the egg mixture. Bake for 25 minutes. When cooked, a skewer pushed into the centre should come out clean.

Serve warm or leave to cool completely.
Cooking time: 45 minutes

● For a cheese quiche, sprinkle over 40g/1$\frac{1}{2}$ oz ($\frac{1}{3}$ cup) grated Gruyère (Swiss) cheese before baking.
● For a bacon and sweet corn flan, line a 23cm (9 in) flan ring and replace the cream in the filling with plain yogurt. Add 200g (7 oz) canned sweetcorn and flavour with 15ml (1 tablespoon) parsley and 2.5ml ($\frac{1}{2}$ teaspoon) dry mustard.

Heat oven to 200°C (400°F) gas mark 6. Roll out pastry and line a 23cm (9 in) flan ring (layer cake pan). Stand on a baking sheet and bake the pastry blind (*page 61*) for 20 minutes.

Meanwhile, in a small saucepan over medium heat, melt the butter. Remove from heat and stir in the flour. Return to heat and cook for 1–2 minutes, stirring. Remove from heat and gradually mix in the stock. When smooth return to the heat and bring to the boil. Cook for 2–3 minutes stirring constantly. Add a few spoonfuls of the sauce to the egg yolks and mix well. Beat the yolks into the sauce. Add seasoning and marjoram. Cook over low heat for 2 minutes, stirring. Add the green beans, chicken and ham.

Remove the cooked pastry from oven. Reduce heat to 180°C (350°F) gas mark 4. Spoon the filling into pastry case. Bake for 10–15 minutes. Transfer the quiche to a serving plate if serving warm or leave until completely cold. Garnish with parsley just before serving.

Cooking time: 35 minutes if serving hot

Kipper Quiche

This fish quiche will serve 8 as an appetizer, 6 as a light lunch or as few as 4 for a picnic.

SERVES 6
$\frac{3}{4}$ × **shortcrust pastry** (*page 240*)
250g (9 oz) kipper or herring fillets, cooked, or canned kippers
225ml/8 fl oz (1 cup) thin cream
3 medium-sized eggs, lightly beaten
15ml (1 tablespoon) prepared mustard
salt
freshly ground black pepper
2 lemons cut into wedges
parsley

Heat the oven to 200°C (400°F) gas mark 6. Line a 23cm (9 in) flan tin (layer cake pan) with the pastry and bake it blind (*page 61*) for 20 minutes. Meanwhile flake the fish with a fork. Mix the cream and eggs together. Add the mustard. Stir in the flaked fish with its juices and mix well. Season to taste.

Remove the pastry case from oven. Reduce heat to 180°C (350°F) gas mark 4. Pile the filling into the pastry. Bake for 20–25 minutes until filling has set. Remove from the oven and leave to cool.

To serve, garnish the flan with lemon wedges and parsley sprigs.
Cooking time: 1 hour

●Smoked haddock makes an excellent alternative: use $\frac{3}{4}$ × cream-cheese shortcrust pastry (*page 241*) and the same weight of fish. Combine it with 2 sliced onions, softened in butter, and 3 large tomatoes, skinned and chopped. Pour over 150ml/ $\frac{1}{4}$ pt ($\frac{2}{3}$ cup) thin cream combined with 2 beaten eggs. Sprinkle over 30ml (2 tablespoons) grated Parmesan before baking.

Prawn (Shrimp) and Chicory (Endive) Quiche

This tart uses small quantities of two expensive ingredients.

The pastry case is not baked before filling, but is painted inside with a spare egg white, to prevent the liquid filling from making the pastry soggy. This method is effective when you want to cut 20 minutes off the baking time of a flan or quiche: it is only suitable when the filling needs over 30 minutes to bake.

SERVES 4–6
$\frac{3}{4}$ × **shortcrust pastry** (*page 240*)
3 medium-sized eggs, separated
50g/2 oz ($\frac{1}{4}$ cup) butter
1 medium-sized onion, finely chopped
2 medium-sized heads of chicory (endive), chopped into rings
225g ($\frac{1}{2}$ lb) boiled prawns (small shrimp), peeled and deveined
1.5ml ($\frac{1}{4}$ teaspoon) cayenne pepper
1.5ml ($\frac{1}{4}$ teaspoon) grated nutmeg
salt and ground black pepper
150ml/$\frac{1}{4}$ pt ($\frac{2}{3}$ cup) thin cream
25g/1 oz ($\frac{1}{4}$ cup) Gruyère (Swiss) cheese, grated

Heat the oven to 200°C (400°F) gas mark 6. Heat a baking sheet in the oven if using a ceramic dish. Roll out the pastry and line a 23cm (9 in) flan tin (layer cake pan) or dish. Paint the inside with 1 lightly-beaten egg white. Melt the butter in a saucepan and fry the onion until soft. Stir in the chicory (endive) rings and cook for 10 minutes or until softened. Arrange the chicory (endive) inside the pastry shell and sprinkle over the prawns (shrimp).

Beat together 2 eggs and 1 yolk, the cream and cheese and stir in the cayenne, nutmeg and seasonings. Pour into the case and bake for 20–40 minutes or until the filling is set and golden brown. Serve hot.
Cooking time: 55 minutes

●For a chicory (endive) flan, the prawns (shrimp) may be omitted and 450g (1 lb) chicory (endive) used.

Fresh Herb Quiche

SERVES 6
23cm (9 in) fully-baked shortcrust pastry case
15ml (1 tablespoon) butter
4 spring onions (scallions) or 1 small onion, chopped
1 small (head of Boston) lettuce, washed and finely shredded
3 medium-sized eggs
5ml (1 teaspoon) Dijon mustard
150ml/$\frac{1}{4}$ pt ($\frac{2}{3}$ cup) thick cream
150ml/$\frac{1}{4}$ pt ($\frac{2}{3}$ cup) milk
60ml/4 tablespoons ($\frac{1}{4}$ cup) mixed, freshly chopped herbs
2.5ml ($\frac{1}{2}$ teaspoon) nutmeg
salt
freshly ground black pepper

Heat the oven to 200°C (400°F) gas mark 6. Melt the butter in a heavy-bottomed pan. Fry the onions for 5 minutes, stirring all the time. Stir in the lettuce and remove the pan from the heat.

Beat the eggs lightly and add the mustard. Stir in the cream and the milk. Add the cooked onions with the pan juices. Stir in the mixed herbs and the nutmeg. Add seasoning. Spoon filling into pastry case and bake for 25–30 minutes until the filling is set. Serve hot or cold.
Cooking time: 45 minutes minimum

●A cream cheese filling can be used for this flan. Substitute 250g/9 oz (1$\frac{1}{2}$ cups) cream cheese plus 125ml/4 fl oz ($\frac{1}{2}$ cup) thick cream for the cream and milk in the recipe and 6 spring onions (scallions) and 15ml (1 tablespoon) chopped parsley for the flavouring.

Onion Quiche

Serve this flan hot. Make the filling in advance if necessary.

SERVES 6
23cm (9 in) fully-baked shortcrust pastry case
15ml (1 tablespoon) olive oil
50g/2 oz (4 tablespoons) butter
900g (2 lb) onions, peeled and finely chopped
2 bacon slices
3 large egg yolks
150ml/$\frac{1}{4}$ pt ($\frac{2}{3}$ cup) thick cream
salt
freshly ground black pepper

Heat the oven to 200°C (400°F) gas mark 6. In a large frying-pan heat the oil and butter. Add the onions and cook, stirring occasionally, until they are soft. Keep the heat low as the onions must not turn brown—simply cook slowly for about 25–30 minutes

Meanwhile grill (broil) the bacon slices until crisp. Crumble and sprinkle the bacon on the pastry base. Beat the egg yolks with a fork and mix with the cream.

Remove the cooked onions from the heat and season with salt, pepper and nutmeg. Stir in egg yolks and cream and transfer to pastry case. Bake for 25–30 minutes and serve immediately.
Cooking time: 1 hour

● Leeks can be substituted as an alternative; use 450g (1 lb) leeks with 275ml/$\frac{1}{2}$ pt (1$\frac{1}{4}$ cups) béchamel sauce plus 50ml/ 2 fl oz ($\frac{1}{4}$ cup) cream, omitting the eggs entirely. Sprinkle over 50g/2 oz ($\frac{1}{2}$ cup) grated Cheddar or Gruyère cheese.
● The bacon may be omitted from this quiche and the custard made with 2 eggs and 150ml/$\frac{1}{4}$ pt ($\frac{2}{3}$ cup) sour cream.

Midsummer Pies

A baked pastry case, as every good housewife knows, is half way to a meal. Little, individual tarts are easy to serve for fine weather meals, while a variety of salads can be made more substantial by serving them in a pastry case instead of a lettuce leaf. Use any of the flavoured shortcrusts on pages 240–241.

These 10cm (4 in) tarts can be made by lining Yorkshire pudding moulds. The filling will also fill an 18cm (7 in) pastry case. Smaller tarts can also be made with the same quantity of pastry by lining 8 deep bun-hole tins or muffin pans. Grease generously, as they can be difficult to remove after baking, and allow 2 per person.

SERVES 4
4 × 10cm (4 in) fully-baked pastry cases OR an 18cm (7 in) baked case, made with $\frac{1}{2}$ × **cream-cheese shortcrust** (*page 241*)
4 good lettuce leaves, shredded
225g/1 pt ($\frac{1}{2}$ lb) boiled prawns (shrimp), peeled and cleaned
125ml/4 fl oz ($\frac{1}{2}$ cup) mayonnaise (*page 250*)
125ml/4 fl oz ($\frac{1}{2}$ cup) thick cream, whipped
10ml (2 teaspoons) tomato paste
paprika

Make a chiffonade (bed) of lettuce in the bottom of each tart. Reserve 4 prawns (shrimp) and divide the rest between the tarts.

To make dawn-coloured mayonnaise aurore, combine the mayonnaise, whipped cream and tomato paste. Spoon over the prawns and garnish each tart with a reserve prawn. Dust the top with paprika and chill until needed.
Preparation time: 5–10 minutes

● For crab tarts, substitute 175g (6 oz) crabmeat for the prawns, mixing this into the mayonnaise. Give these tarts a classic crab garnish, with straight lines. Two stripes are most suitable for a 10cm (4 in) tart, but a diamond is elegant for a larger one. Choose from among the following, all finely chopped: $\frac{1}{2}$ green (bell) pepper or 30ml (4 tablespoons) parsley, separated white and yolk of 1 hard-boiled egg or paprika powder. Hold a knife in place across the tart, bedding it into the mayonnaise, and sprinkle the garnish close to the blade, about 6mm ($\frac{1}{4}$ in) wide. Move the knife to the next position and sprinkle again. Though simple these coloured lines are very striking.
● For cottage cheese and herring tarts, mix together 100g/$\frac{1}{4}$ lb ($\frac{2}{3}$ cup) cottage cheese with 125ml/4 fl oz ($\frac{1}{2}$ cup) sour cream, 2 finely-chopped, pickled herrings, 2 finely-chopped dessert apples. Top each tart with a half shelled walnut.

● Salmon or tuna mousse provides a pleasant contrast to crisp rich shortcrust pastry. Drain and remove the bones from 200g (7 oz) canned fish. Flake in a bowl and stir in 75g/3 oz ($\frac{1}{4}$ cup) finely chopped cucumber, 4 finely chopped spring onions (scallions) and 75ml (5 tablespoons) mayonnaise. Soak 10ml (2 teaspoons) gelatin in 45ml (3 tablespoons) hot water, then dissolve over low heat. Cool slightly, then mix into the fish. Leave for 20 minutes, stirring occasionally, until starting to set, then pour into the pastry cases. Garnish each tart with 3 thin slices of cucumber.
● For egg tarts, made with rich shortcrust (*page 241*), mash 4 hard-boiled egg yolks with 60ml (4 tablespoons) mayonnaise and 20ml (4 teaspoons) anchovy essence (paste). Line the tarts with this purée. Chop the hard-boiled egg whites finely and arrange in a ring around the tarts. Decorate the centre of each tart with one of the following: either an anchovy fillet, split lengthwise, a pimento-stuffed green olive sliced in 4 and arranged in an overlapping line, or $\frac{1}{2}$ finely-chopped celery stalk between the 4, each topped with a pinch of chopped parsley.

Koulibiak is a celebrated hot Russian fish pie. It is made here with puff pastry and hard eggs, rice, mushrooms and fish make a succulent filling.

Koulibiak

Serve this Russian fish pie hot. Pass a cold sour cream and cucumber sauce separately.

SERVES 8
100g/¼ lb (⅔ cup) long-grain rice
275ml/½ pt (1¼ cups) chicken stock
salt
75g/3 oz (5 tablespoons) butter
freshly ground black pepper
450g (1 lb) cod or haddock
100g (¼ lb) shallots, finely chopped
100g (¼ lb) button mushrooms, sliced
30ml (2 tablespoons) chopped parsley
juice of a lemon
pinch of grated nutmeg
800g (1 lb 12 oz) made weight frozen puff pastry, thawed (pastry for a 2-crust pie)
2 hard-boiled eggs, sliced
1 small egg, lightly beaten

Put the rice, stock and salt into a saucepan and bring to the boil. Reduce heat, cover and simmer for 15–20 minutes until stock is absorbed and the rice is tender.

Meanwhile melt half the butter in a frying-pan and season the fish. When the foam subsides, fry the fish on each side for 2–3 minutes. Lift out and set aside. Add the remaining butter to the pan and fry the onions gently for about 8 minutes until soft. Add the mushrooms and cook for 4–5 minutes.

Remove the skin and flake the fish with a fork, discarding any bones. Add the cooked rice, fish and parsley to the onions. Season with lemon juice, nutmeg and salt and pepper. Set aside to cool.

Heat the oven to 200°C (400°F) gas mark 6. Divide the pastry in half. On a lightly-floured surface, roll each piece to a rectangle 30 × 15cm (12 × 6 in). Trim the edges with a sharp knife. Transfer one piece of pastry to a baking sheet. Arrange the fish on the pastry leaving 12mm (½ in) clear around the edge. Arrange the egg on the fish.

Dampen the pastry edge and place the other piece of pastry on top. Turn up the edges of the pastry to make a shallow rim around the filling. Pinch the rim to seal the edges. With a sharp knife, cut two slits in the middle of the top to allow steam to escape. Roll out the trimmings and make a decoration, sticking it to the pie with beaten egg. Brush the pastry with beaten egg to glaze. Bake for 30–40 minutes until the pastry is cooked and golden brown. Serve hot.
Cooking time: 1½ hours

Artichoke, Ham and Egg Pie

This type of pie makes good use of a corner of boiled gammon or a cheap bacon cut. If using ham stock in this recipe do not add salt. Cooking the artichokes unpeeled avoids the risk of discolouring.

SERVES 6
900g (2 lb) Jerusalem artichokes, scrubbed
salt
freshly ground black pepper
40g/1½ oz (3 tablespoons) butter
30ml (2 tablespoons) plain flour
30ml (2 tablespoons) fresh parsley, chopped
juice of ½ lemon
2.5ml (½ teaspoon) dry mustard powder
450g (1 lb) cooked ham, diced
1½ × shortcrust pastry (page 240)
6 medium-sized eggs, hard-boiled
125g (¼ lb) sage Derby or Cheddar cheese
1 small egg, lightly beaten

Cook the artichokes in boiling, salted water for 10 minutes. Meanwhile, melt the butter in a saucepan over low heat. Remove

A pie is a much more interesting way of serving vegetables when they form the main dish. For this artichoke pie, chopped ham, eggs and cheese add interest and also additional protein.

from heat and stir in the flour to make a smooth roux. Cook for 1–2 minutes, stirring all the time. Off the heat add the stock gradually, stirring until evenly blended. Bring to the boil, stirring, then cover and simmer for 5 minutes. Remove from the heat.

Drain the artichokes and allow them to cool slightly. Peel and dice the artichokes. Stir the parsley, lemon juice and mustard into the sauce. Fold in the artichokes and the ham. Set aside to cool.

Heat the oven to 200°C (400°F) gas mark 6. Divide the pastry into 2 pieces, one slightly larger than the other. Lightly grease a 25cm (10 in) pie dish. Roll out the larger piece of pastry until it is 4cm (1½ in) larger all around than the pie dish top. Trim the edges. Roll the pastry round the rolling pin to transfer it to the pie dish. Press it into the dish to fit neatly.

Topping a Single-crust Pie

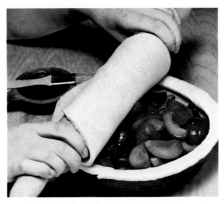

1. Roll out the pastry, using the empty inverted pie dish as a guide. Cut around the dish, then cut a strip from the outer edge of pastry for the rim.

2. Dampen the rim of the dish and fit the pastry strip round it, joining it with water. Dampen this and fill the pie. Lift over the lid, around the pin.

3. Unroll the pastry without stretching it. Press the lid to the rim to seal. Trim the edge with a knife against the pie dish. Flute the edges (see below).

Lining and Topping a Double-crust Pie

1. Cut the pastry into 2 unequal pieces and reserve the smaller. Roll out the larger piece to about 4cm (1½ in) larger than the top of the dish.

2. Lift the pastry on the rolling pin and ease into the dish. Press in place, working from the centre outwards and fitting the sides without folds.

3. Spoon in the filling, heaping it slightly in the centre. Roll out the pastry lid. Dampen the rim of the pastry lining and the lid underside.

4. Using the rolling pin, lift the lid. Line it up with the dish and unroll to cover the filling. Press gently to seal the two pastry layers together.

5. Trim away excess pastry by holding up the pie in one hand and cutting downwards with a knife. Cut decorations from the trimmings and dampen these.

6. Raise up the pie rim, cutting horizontally 2–3 times with the knife back, holding a bent finger on top. Flute with a vertical knife then stick on trimmings.

Put a third of the filling in the pie dish. Arrange the hard eggs around the side on the filling. Sprinkle the cheese over the eggs then add the remaining filling.

Roll out the remaining piece of pastry 12mm ($\frac{1}{2}$ in) larger all round than the pie dish. Brush the edge of the pastry in the pie dish with a little of the beaten egg. Cover with the lid. Seal the edge, trim away the pastry edges and raise the rim (*page 66*). Use the trimmings to make a decoration. Pierce a small hole in the pastry to let the steam escape and glaze the pie with the beaten egg.

Bake for 35 minutes until pastry is light brown. Serve hot.

Cooking time: 1 hour

● Leeks may be substituted for artichokes. Wash and cut into 5cm (2 in) lengths.

Egg and Cabbage Pie

SERVES 4

50g/2 oz ($\frac{1}{4}$ cup) butter
2 small onions, finely sliced
1 large white cabbage, coarse outer leaves removed, washed and finely shredded
salt and freshly ground black pepper
2.5ml ($\frac{1}{2}$ teaspoon) grated nutmeg
10ml (2 teaspoons) paprika
15ml (1 tablespoon) lemon juice
4 slices bacon, diced
4 medium-sized hard-boiled eggs, sliced
shortcrust pastry *(page 240)*
1 small egg, lightly beaten

In a large heavy-based saucepan melt the butter over medium heat. Fry the onions, stirring, for 5 minutes or until soft but not brown. Stir in the cabbage, salt and pepper, nutmeg, paprika, lemon juice and bacon. Reduce heat, cover and cook for 30 minutes until the cabbage is tender. Remove pan from heat and leave to cool.

Heat the oven to 200°C (400°F) gas mark 6. Arrange the cabbage in a medium-sized baking dish, arranging slices of egg between each layer. Roll out the pastry to a thickness of 6mm ($\frac{1}{4}$ in) and larger all around than the pie rim. Damp the edge of baking dish. Trim a strip from the edge of the pastry and use to line the rim of the dish. Dampen, then transfer the lid to cover the pie. Press to seal and use the trimmings for decoration. Make a small hole to allow steam to escape. Brush with beaten egg and bake for 30 minutes. Serve hot.

Cooking time: 1$\frac{1}{4}$ hours

Steak and Kidney Pie

SERVES 6

900g (2 lb) chuck steak, trimmed and cubed
225g ($\frac{1}{2}$ lb) ox (beef) kidney, prepared and cubed
30ml (2 tablespoons) flour
salt
freshly ground black pepper
10ml (2 teaspoons) mixed dried herbs
50g/2 oz ($\frac{1}{4}$ cup) butter
1 medium-sized onion, thinly sliced
275ml/10 fl oz (1$\frac{1}{4}$ cups) stock
15ml (1 tablespoon) Worcestershire sauce
300g (11 oz) made weight frozen flaky pastry, thawed (pastry for 1-crust pie)
1 small egg, lightly beaten

In a large mixing bowl, combine the steak, kidney, flour, salt and pepper and dried herbs. Stir to coat the meat with the flour.

In a large frying-pan melt half the butter over moderate heat. Fry the onions, stirring, for 5–7 minutes until soft but not brown. Add the remaining butter to the pan. When melted add the meat and cook for 10 minutes stirring frequently. Add the stock, Worcestershire sauce and salt and pepper. Bring to the boil, cover and simmer for 1$\frac{1}{2}$–2 hours until the meat is tender. Remove from heat and leave to cool.

Heat the oven to 230°C (450°F) gas mark 8. Transfer the meat to a pie dish.

Steak and kidney pie, rich and black under flaky pastry, makes use of one very economical ingredient.

On a floured surface roll out the pastry so that it is 2.5cm (1 in) larger all around than the pie dish. With a knife trim the edges and cut a 12mm ($\frac{1}{2}$ in) strip from around the dough.

Damp the edge of the pie dish with water and press the pastry strip to the edge of the pie dish. Brush the pastry strip with water. Using the rolling pin transfer the pastry onto the pie dish. Press to seal and crimp the edges. With a sharp knife make a small hole in the centre of the pie to allow steam to escape.

Use the trimmings to make a decoration for the top of the pie brushing underneath with beaten egg. Brush the pie top and decorations with the beaten egg to glaze. Bake the pie for 10 minutes then brush again with egg. Reduce the heat to 180°C (350°F) gas mark 4 and bake for a further 20 minutes until the pastry is a deep golden brown.

Cooking time: 3$\frac{1}{2}$ hours

● Shortcrust can also be used to cover the pie; you will need $\frac{3}{4}$ × shortcrust on *page 240.*

● For a beef and mushroom pie, substitute 100g ($\frac{1}{4}$ lb) mushrooms for the kidney. Fry after the onions and remove from the pan before frying the meat.

English Pub Pie

Standing pies are easier to make than you would imagine from their impressive appearance. Make the pie a day or so before needed. The pie only requires about 1 hour's work from the cook, but it is as well to allow yourself plenty of time the first time you do it, particularly if unmoulding the pastry. If you own a 19 × 6.5cm (7½ × 2¼ in) spring-form cake tin (pan), the pastry can be modelled and cooked inside the greased tin (pan). This makes the process quite simple (see steps 4–5 on page 242).

The cheapest way to get the chicken meat needed for this recipe is to take the breasts, plus thighs if necessary, off a roasting chicken. Put the rest of the chicken with an onion, carrot, bay leaf and a chicken stock cube into a pan and simmer until the meat falls off the bones. This will give you both the stock needed for finishing the pie and the basis of a quick supper on pie-making day.

SERVES 6–8
hot-water crust pastry *(page 242)*
100g (¼ lb) cooked ham, finely chopped
275g (10 oz) pork sausagemeat
350g (¾ lb) chicken meat, sliced in 2.5cm (1 in) strips
175g (6 oz) button mushrooms, quartered
1 hard-boiled egg, chopped
5ml (1 teaspoon) grated lemon rind
pinch of cayenne pepper
salt
freshly ground black pepper
50ml/2 fl oz (¼ cup) dry white wine or vermouth
425ml/¾ pt (2 cups) chicken stock
1 egg, lightly beaten with salt

Make and rest the pastry. Grease the outsides of a deep 15cm (6 in) cake tin (pan). Grease a baking sheet and put the tin on it, bottom upwards.

Cut off one-third of the pastry and wrap it in plastic wrap and then a damp towel until needed. Roll out the remaining pastry to a circle with a diameter of about 25cm (10 in). Lift the pastry over the cake tin. Gently mould the pastry with your fingers to fit the tin, pressing out any pleats. Then pick up the tin and work around the sides of the tin, pressing the pastry with your fingers, making sure that there are no thin patches of pastry and that the pastry reaches the rim all around to form a solid rim. Stand upside-down on the baking sheet.

Cut a double strip of greaseproof or waxed paper the height of the mould. Wrap this around the sides of the pie, to

cover the pastry completely. This will support the sides while they are cooking. Tie at the top and bottom with string. Cover the pie, still upside-down, with a damp cloth and rest it in the refrigerator for 2 hours.

Meanwhile prepare the filling. Mix together in a bowl all the ingredients except the stock and second egg.

Heat the oven to 200°C (400°F) gas mark 6. Remove the mould from the refrigerator and gently work a knife round between the pastry and the mould until loosened. Stand the pastry case right way up on the baking sheet and remove the mould. Check for holes: small cracks can be plastered up with a thick flour-and-water paste. Pile in the filling. Roll out the pastry for the lid about 2cm (½ in) bigger all around than the pie. Dampen the standing pie rim, then cover and seal, pressing the pastry over the rim, against the paper collar and crimping to make a decorative edge. Cut a 5cm (2 in) slit in the centre of the pie.

Brush with beaten egg and bake for 1 hour. Reduce the heat to 180°C (350°F) gas mark 4. Remove the pie from the oven. Cut the strings and pull off the paper collar. Cut off a small piece of the paper. Roll this into a cigarette and push it into the vent at the top of the pie to keep this open. With beaten egg brush the top of the pie again plus the sides. Return to the oven for a further hour. (If using a spring-form tin (pan), remove the ring only for the last 10 minutes, glaze and return to the oven.)

Remove the pie from the oven and pour the chicken stock through a funnel into the vent of the warm pie. If, however, the pie has leaked during cooking, wait until it is cold before adding the stock, and use the chicken jelly on the point of setting. Chill 5 hours before cutting.

Cooking time: 30 minutes plus 2 hours resting, then about 2½ hours plus chilling

● For pigeon pie, substitute the breasts of 4 pigeons for the chicken, use red wine instead of white and use the pigeon carcasses to make the stock for finishing.
● For rabbit pie, use the flesh of 1 rabbit and omit the hard-boiled egg. Use red wine.
● For game pie, 350–400g (12–14 oz) game can be substituted for the chicken; use red wine. If using stewing venison, it is wise to precook it, or it could be tough.

A raised pie uses hot-water crust, the most economical type of pastry.

Cheshire Pork and Apple Pies

These individual pies make excellent school lunches, picnic food and nourishing snacks for hungry teenagers who have missed out on meals.

SERVES 6
hot-water crust pastry *(page 242)*
900g (2 lb) sparerib (country style) pork
3 slices smoked, fatty bacon
2 onions, chopped
salt
freshly ground black pepper
175ml/6 fl oz (¾ cup) cider
1 large dessert apple, peeled and sliced
30ml (2 tablespoons) brown sugar
beaten egg
425ml/¾ pt (2 cups) jellied stock

Reserve one-third of the pastry for the lids, wrapped in plastic film and a damp towel. Divide the remaining pastry into 6. Invert 6 empty jars on to a baking sheet and grease the bottoms and sides. Flour them lightly. Roll out the pastry into circles about 15cm (6 in) in diameter.

Place the pastry circle over a jam jar and press this over the jar bottom. With your fingers work the pleats flat and model the pastry around the jar, so that the pastry rim is at the same height all around (see steps 6–7 on *page 242*). Repeat with the other jars. Cover with a damp cloth and put in the refrigerator for 2 hours while the pastry firms up.

Meanwhile, prepare the filling. Mince (grind) or finely chop the meat and put with the onion in a bowl. Season generously, stir in the cider and leave to marinate.

Heat the oven to 200°C (400°F) gas mark 6. Remove the jars from the refrigerator and invert on to a greased baking sheet. Gently remove the jars from the pastry cases. Half fill the pie cases with the meat mixture. Toss the apple slices in the sugar in a bowl and cover the meat in each pie with apple slices. Fill with the remaining meat.

Roll out the pastry reserved for the lids. Choose a pastry cutter of the right size for the top of the pies and stamp out the lids. Dampen the standing pie rim and cover each pie. Pinch the lids on to the dampened rim to seal. Make a hole in the centre of each pie and cut the trimmings into little apples and leaves to decorate the pies if desired. Do not, however, cover the centre hole.

Brush the pies, both top and sides, with the beaten egg and bake for 30 minutes. Reduce the heat to 160°C (325°F) gas mark 3 and cook for a further hour.

Remove from the oven. Warm the jellied stock until liquid then pour through a funnel into the holes in the pies, until you can see the liquid level through the pie slit. Leave 3 hours to set.

Cooking time: 30 minutes plus 2 hours resting, then about 2 hours plus chilling

● For small Melton Mowbray pies, omit the apples, onions and sugar. Pork fillet (tenderloin) may be used for the meat. Increase the quantity of bacon to 6 slices and flavour with 5ml (1 teaspoon) freshly chopped sage, 2.5ml (½ teaspoon) each cinnamon and allspice and 10ml (2 teaspoons) anchovy essence (paste). Moisten with stock, instead of cider.

Bacon and Egg Pies

These little pies can be made in Yorkshire pudding moulds.

SERVES 4
shortcrust pastry *(page 240)*
225g (½ lb) bacon, chopped
4 small eggs
30ml (2 tablespoons) chopped onion, spring onions (scallions) or chives
milk or beaten egg to glaze

Heat the oven to 200°C (400°F) gas mark 6. Grease 4 × 10cm (4 in) tart tins (pans) or a 4-hole Yorkshire pudding tin.

Cut off one-third of the pastry and roll out to 3mm (⅛ in) thickness. Cut 4 circles the size of the tops of the pies. Incorporate the pastry trimmings then reroll. Cut 4 circles about 15cm (6 in) in diameter and use to line the tins. Press well into position. Fill the tarts with the chopped bacon. Carefully break an egg into each nest. Sprinkle with the onion or chives. Dampen the edges of the pastry lids underneath. Cover the pies and press to seal.

Divide the pastry trimmings into 4. To make tassel decorations reroll into strips, then make parallel cuts all the way down the stripes, almost through it. Roll up and open out the top to make a tassel. Stock onto the pie with water or beaten egg and glaze the pie with egg or milk.

Bake for 25 minutes. Leave to cool in the tins (pans) for 5 minutes, then remove with a spoon on to a wire rack and leave until cold.

Preparation time: 40 minutes plus cooling

Salads and Salad Dressings

Spring is notoriously unpunctual but by the time it arrives the sustaining stews and steamed puddings of winter have lost their novelty. A change is called for and what better way of achieving this than enjoying the colourful new-season vegetables? With the prospect of summer and holidays, most people feel the urge for a slimmer and healthier way of life.

With the coming of warmer weather it is easier to eat less and to vary the diet: salads become more appealing. Imports from warmer areas mean summer's vegetables start to appear. Spring vegetables also give the cook the opportunity to be inventive and original, to present satisfying meals regardless of inclement weather. The crispness of raw vegetables is appreciated at the end of winter, but many excellent salads are made of cooked vegetables often cooled in the dressing. Spring can be temperamental, sometimes unpredictably cold and sometimes warm. What was planned for a hot meal can be adapted to become part of a salad or a cold dish. Bear this in mind when shopping. Potatoes, courgettes (zucchini), beans, globe artichokes and beetroot (beets) are all vegetables that can be cooked to become part of a hot or cold meal. Potatoes, green beans and courgettes (zucchini) positively benefit by being dressed with French dressing while warm: do this immediately after draining the vegetables and include whatever fresh herbs you have at hand. Although spring is too early for basil (unless you have an indoor pot) other herbs such as tarragon, chives, rosemary and parsley are to be found.

If winter has been hard and long, spring vegetables may be late in appearing. The art of salad making, as in other cooking, is to adapt what is readily available, rather than to pay a high price for scarce vegetables. Tomatoes and cucumbers and lettuce tend to be small and not of the best quality when out of season; they are better left for summer, when they come into their own. Cabbages are usually readily available in spring and leeks, carrots, and red and green (bell) peppers, celery, mushrooms and spinach may be plentiful: and cauliflower, small perhaps, is always useful.

Salads can be made more interesting with fruit, and in the cold months this is a great standby. Apple and celery is a good combination. Fruit also complements cheese; apple, pears and pineapple can be included with cottage cheese as part of a salad: citrus fruit on their own or with beetroot (beets) and watercress or onion also make successful salads. They are a good source of vitamin C. To serve raw vegetables at their best, wash, prepare and dry them, crisp them in the refrigerator for an hour.

To make the most of available vegetables, clever blending of salad dressings is called for. By serving the same vegetable with a vinaigrette one day, an egg-based emulsion sauce (*see page 250*) on another and a creamy dressing on the third, it can be transformed into a new dish each time. Experiment with different spices before the fresh herbs come, then try chopped herbs in different combinations as these become available in summer.

Make the salads substantial for main course meals with a fresh texture. Use red and green (bell) peppers, cauliflower and cabbage, to make healthy, filling meals adding eggs, cheese, fish or small quantities of ham for extra protein and leave the lighter, greener salads for summer.

Tricks with Vegetables

Correct preparation can make the difference between a successful salad and a dull one. Some more ideas are given in the pictures.

When adding tomatoes to a mixed salad, do not just slice or quarter them. Pour boiling water over the whole tomato first and leave 1 minute. Refresh in cold water than peel off the skin. Quarter and remove the seeds and juice (keep these for a tomato sauce). Use only the flesh—juice dilutes the dressing.

Remember the inexpensive onion can be used in moderation in salads. For the prettiest effect, slice it across thinly and push into separate rings. Coarsely shredded raw spinach and finely shredded raw cabbage can fill the salad bowl in cold weather, as can grated root vegetables and sliced fruit. Raw mushrooms should be left for 1 hour to soak up the dressing. Many cooked vegetables are attractive when cooled, diced and dressed.

1. Grate raw root vegetables, apples and cucumbers. Blot if necessary.

2. Use a melon baller to extract the flesh of fruit such as melons and avocados.

3. Use citrus fruit for winter salads, peeling away white pith and membranes.

Tomato and Green Bean Salad

Red and green is an attractive combination. The tomatoes are best skinned and seeded if you have the time. Make the salad ahead so that the vegetables have time to marinate.

SERVES 6
450g (1 lb) tomatoes, thinly sliced
450g (1 lb) French (green) beans, trimmed, cooked and drained
150ml/¼ pt (⅔ cup) French dressing (*page 76*)

Place the tomatoes and beans in a large serving dish and pour the dressing over. Using two large spoons, toss the salad until the vegetables are thoroughly coated with the dressing. Chill the salad before serving.

Preparation time: 10 minutes plus chilling

Chicory (Endive) and Orange Salad

SERVES 4
3 heads of chicory (endive), thinly sliced crosswise into rings
3 oranges
8 black olives, stoned (pitted)
125ml/4 fl oz (½ cup) French dressing (*page 76*)
salt
freshly ground black pepper

Peel all pith and rind from the oranges, then slice in rings. Combine with the chicory (endive) and olives in a salad bowl. Pour in any orange juice and the dressing and toss.

Preparation time: up to 10 minutes

Tomatoes and green beans make a colourful and inviting salad. Marinate the vegetables in the vinaigrette.

● An unusual orange salad can be made by substituting a large Spanish onion, cut into rings, for the chicory (endive). Add a few black olives if you have them. This is good with fatty meat.

● Fennel can also be used; chop the bulb and sprinkle the chopped leaves on top.

Carrot Salad

SERVES 4
225g (½ lb) young carrots
150ml/¼ pt (⅔ cup) yogurt
30ml (2 tablespoons) orange juice

Grate or shred the carrots. Stir in the yogurt and orange juice and season if desired.

Preparation time: 5 minutes

4. Cut down on either side of the segment and remove it whole without membrane.

5. Crush chopped garlic with a knife blade into salt to make a paste.

6. For a milder garlic flavour, wipe a cut clove round inside the salad bowl.

Three Bean Salad

SERVES 4–6

75g/3 oz (⅓ cup) dried red kidney beans, soaked overnight

75g/3 oz (⅓ cup) dried chick peas, soaked overnight

75g/3 oz (½ cup) dried white haricot (navy) beans, soaked overnight

2.5ml (½ teaspoon) dry mustard

2.5ml (½ teaspoon) fine sugar

30ml (2 tablespoons) wine vinegar

90ml (6 tablespoons) olive oil

30–45ml (2–3 tablespoons) chopped fresh herbs

salt and freshly ground black pepper

Drain the beans. Put the kidney beans in a saucepan, and the chick peas in another pan. Cover both with water and bring to the boil. Simmer the kidney beans for 1–1¼ hours or until tender. Simmer the chick peas for 30 minutes, then add the haricot (navy) beans and simmer for 1½ hours or until tender. Drain all the beans and cool.

Turn the beans into a salad bowl. Combine the remaining ingredients. Add to the beans and mix well. Cover and chill.
Cooking time: 2 hours plus cooling

Cucumber and Cheese Salad

This makes a slimming lunch for 3–4 or an appetizer for 4–6.

SERVES 4

1 large cucumber, peeled and coarsely shredded

225g/½ lb (1¼ cups) cottage, curd or cream cheese

45ml (3 tablespoons) lemon juice

30ml (2 tablespoons) chives, chopped

15ml (1 tablespoon) fresh herbs (parsley, mint etc as available), chopped

30ml (2 tablespoons) corn oil

salt

freshly ground black pepper

½ small cucumber to garnish (optional)

Drain the cucumber in a colander then blot inside absorbent paper wrapped in a towel. Mash the cheese with the lemon juice in a bowl, until smooth. Stir in the cucumber, herbs and oil and season to taste. Arrange the lettuce leaves on a serving plate and pile the cheese mixture in the middle. Arrange thin slices of unpeeled cucumber around the cheese mixture.
Preparation time: 15 minutes

Potato Salad with Herbs

SERVES 4

450g (1 lb) new potatoes, boiled in their skins

8 spring onions (scallions) trimmed and chopped

30ml (2 tablespoons) mixed fresh herbs, chopped

90ml (6 tablespoons) olive oil

30ml (2 tablespoons) wine vinegar

salt

freshly ground black pepper

Peel the hot potatoes, holding them in a cloth, then cut into 12mm (½ in) cubes. Put into a serving dish. Combine the oil, vinegar and seasoning. Pour the mixture over the warm potatoes and garnish with onions and herbs. Chill before serving.
Preparation time: 25 minutes, plus chilling

● Potato salad dressed with mayonnaise is also well liked. Potatoes should be dressed when hot, but they absorb a good deal of expensive olive oil. If the salad is to be dressed with mayonnaise, pour over 75ml/ 3 fl oz (⅓ cup) yogurt while they are still hot, and then dress with mayonnaise when absolutely cold.

Courgette (Zucchini) Salad

This salad can be served as a first course on lettuce leaves and garnished with fingers of wholewheat bread to mop up the dressing.

Fresh herbs are essential for this recipe; choose from parsley, chives, tarragon and a touch of mint—basil is particularly good when available. If you do not have a vegetable steamer, simply put a colander over a pan of boiling water and put a lid on the colander.

If you make the salad in advance the fresh green colour turns dark but the flavour does improve.

SERVES 4
450g (1 lb) courgettes (zucchini) washed and trimmed
salt
45ml (3 tablespoons) mixed, freshly chopped herbs
half a garlic clove
125ml/4 fl oz ($\frac{1}{2}$ cup) French dressing *(page 76)*
freshly ground black pepper

Slice the courgettes (zucchini) into rings about 6mm ($\frac{1}{4}$ in) thick. Place in a colander and sprinkle with salt. Leave for 60 minutes.

Rinse the courgettes (zucchini) under cold running water. Steam for 8 minutes, or until beginning to soften; do not overcook them, they should still be slightly firm when you remove them from the steamer.

Meanwhile, add herbs and the garlic to the vinaigrette. Shake the steamer to remove moisture from the courgettes (zucchini) and tip them into a serving dish. Give the vinaigrette a quick stir and pour it over the courgettes. Tilt the dish and spoon the dressing over until the vegetables are well coated. Leave until cool. Grind pepper over. Cover and chill until required.

Cooking time: 1 hour draining, then 10 minutes plus chilling time

● Coriander seeds can be used instead of the herbs; crush 6–8 seeds in a mortar with a pestle and add to the hot cooked vegetable.

At times of the year when vegetables are dull and traditional salads are scarce, fruit can fill the salad bowl. The sweet/sharp taste of grapefruit and orange salad goes well with cold meat at any time of the year. Add cucumber and mint in summer.

Leeks in Red Wine

Cooked and served cold, this leek dish makes an excellent first course. Use young leeks, all of a similar size: eight medium-sized leeks weigh about 1 kg (2$\frac{1}{2}$ lb) before cleaning.

SERVES 4
8 medium-sized leeks, trimmed and washed
30ml (2 tablespoons) olive oil
15ml (1 tablespoon) butter
75ml/3 fl oz (5 tablespoons) red wine
75ml/3 fl oz (5 tablespoons) light stock
salt

Heat the butter and the oil over a medium heat. Add the leeks and cook and turn them so they colour lightly all around— about 5 minutes.

Off the heat add the wine and the stock. Return to heat, cover the pan and cook gently for 10–15 minutes until the leeks are tender. Season to taste. Transfer the leeks to a serving dish and spoon the pan juices over. Leave until cold before serving.
Cooking time: 20 minutes plus chilling

● An alternative—equally good—is leeks provençale. Add 4 blanched and peeled tomatoes, 2 chopped garlic cloves, a pinch of fine sugar and the juice of $\frac{1}{2}$ lemon to the pan instead of wine and stock. Decorate with chopped parsley to serve.

Grapefruit and Orange Salad

Serve this refreshing dish as a side salad with lamb or glazed ham.

SERVES 4
2 medium-sized grapefruit, peeled
1 large orange, peeled
$\frac{1}{2}$ cucumber
fresh mint leaves
50ml/2 fl oz ($\frac{1}{4}$ cup) French dressing *(page 76)*

Using a sharp knife, separate the grapefruit and orange into segments and place them in a serving bowl. Cut the cucumber into slices and arrange them around the orange and grapefruit segments.

Pour the dressing over the salad and chill briefly before serving.
Preparation time: 15 minutes, plus chilling

● Dress the citrus fruits with 60ml (4 tablespoons) tahini and some lemon juice.

Spinach and Bacon Salad

SERVES 4
225g ($\frac{1}{2}$ lb) button mushrooms, sliced
juice of $\frac{1}{2}$ lemon
225g ($\frac{1}{2}$ lb) spinach, washed and drained
125ml/4 fl oz ($\frac{1}{2}$ cup) French dressing *(page 76)*
black pepper
100g ($\frac{1}{4}$ lb) bacon, cooked until crisp and well drained

Pour the lemon juice and half the dressing over the mushrooms, turn them, then leave to marinate. Pull off and discard the spinach stalks.

Combine the spinach and mushrooms, with their liquid in a salad bowl. Pour over the remaining dressing, season generously and toss. Crumble the bacon and sprinkle on top.
Preparation time: 45 minutes

Potato Salad with Kippers

Start the salad well in advance, as the fish must be marinated for 3 days before the salad is made.

SERVES 6
225g ($\frac{1}{2}$ lb) kipper or herring fillets, skinned and flaked
700g (1$\frac{1}{2}$ lb) potatoes
FOR THE MARINADE
125ml/4 fl oz ($\frac{1}{2}$ cup) olive oil
50ml/2 fl oz ($\frac{1}{4}$ cup) white wine vinegar
7.5ml ($\frac{1}{2}$ tablespoon) brown sugar
5ml (1 teaspoon) Dijon mustard
1 small onion, chopped
30ml (2 tablespoons) mixed fresh herbs, chopped
freshly chopped parsley or chives to garnish

Combine the oil, vinegar, sugar and mustard for the marinade. Add the onion and chopped herbs. Put the fish in a glass or earthenware dish and pour the marinade over. Cover the dish with foil and keep in the refrigerator for 3 days.

On the fourth day cook the potatoes. Drain them and chop roughly while still hot. Add immediately to the fish and spoon the marinade over to coat the potatoes. Leave until cold.

Garnish with the chopped parsley or chives to serve.
Cooking time: 3 days marinating, then 20 minutes plus chilling time

Cabbage Salad

Do not despise cabbage salad—coleslaw alone is world famous.

SERVES 8
1 cucmber, cubed
½ white cabbage, coarse outer leaves removed, washed and finely shredded
1 red (bell) pepper, seeded and sliced
1 green (bell) pepper, seeded and sliced
6 spring onions (scallions), finely chopped
450g (1 lb) tomatoes, blanched, skinned seeded and the flesh cut into strips
150ml/¼ pt (⅔ cup) sweet and sour salad dressing *(page 76)*

Put the cucumber in a colander, sprinkle over salt and leave for ½ hour. Then wash under running water and dry on absorbent paper. Combine all the vegetables in a bowl, pour over the dressing and toss thoroughly before serving.
Preparation time: 35 minutes

● Omit the other vegetables and mix into the shredded cabbage 2 celery stalks, chopped, 50g/2 oz (⅓ cup) sultanas (or raisins), 1 small onion, chopped, and dress with 75ml (5 tablespoons) mayonnaise mixed with 30ml (2 tablespoons) yogurt and seasoning. This is coleslaw.
● Another version uses ½ shredded green (bell) pepper instead of the celery and 15ml (1 tablespoon) caraway seeds instead of the raisins.
● For a main course salad for 4, omit the cucumber. Mound the cabbage salad in the centre of a dish and arrange round it in rings 4 tomatoes, blanched, skinned, seeded and sliced into strips and then 8 frankfurters, cooked and sliced. Chop 2 hard-boiled eggs and arrange the yolks on the outside of the tomatoes and the whites around the rim of the dish.

Caesar Salad

SERVES 4
50ml/2 fl oz (¼ cup) cooking oil
4 thick slices white bread, crusts removed and cut into cubes
2 heads cos (romaine) lettuce, washed and dried
6 anchovy fillets, cut into small pieces
125ml/4 fl oz (½ cup) French dressing *(page 76)*
1 egg, cooked in boiling water for 1 minute
50g/2 oz (½ cup) grated Parmesan cheese

Heat the oil in a frying-pan over medium heat. Fry the bread cubes in the oil until crisp, about 10 minutes. Remove the croûtons from the pan and leave to drain

A classic coleslaw salad from cabbage.

on absorbent paper.

Tear the lettuce into bite-sized pieces and put into a salad bowl. Add the anchovies and French dressing and toss. Break the egg over the top of the salad and scoop out the egg from the shell. Sprinkle the croûtons and Parmesan cheese on top. Serve immediately.
Cooking time: 15 minutes

Courgette (Zucchini), Tomato and Fennel Salad

SERVES 4
4 large courgettes (zucchini), peeled and sliced
4 large tomatoes, blanched, skinned and cut into wedges
1 large fennel bulb, sliced into rings
125ml/4 fl oz (½ cup) French dressing *(page 76)*

Steam or boil the courgettes (zucchini) until they are just tender. Drain if necessary and cool.

Combine all the ingredients in a salad bowl and chill for 15 minutes before serving.
Cooking time: 1½ hours including chilling

Salade Niçoise

There are many variations of this classic green bean, tomato and anchovy salad.

SERVES 3–6

1 small lettuce, outer leaves removed, washed and separated into leaves
6 medium-sized potatoes, cooked, cooled and diced
275g (10 oz) French (green) beans, cooked and cut into 12mm ($\frac{1}{2}$ in) lengths
6 tomatoes, blanched, skinned, seeded and quartered
125ml/4 fl oz ($\frac{1}{2}$ cup) French dressing (page 76)
6 anchovy fillets, halved
50g/2 oz (12) black olives, stoned (pitted)
30ml (2 tablespoons) capers

Arrange the lettuce leaves on a large serving plate. In a large bowl combine the potatoes, beans and tomatoes. Pour the French dressing over the vegetables and toss thoroughly. Spoon the vegetables on to the lettuce leaves and pour over any remaining dressing.

Garnish the salad with a lattice of anchovies. Arrange the olives in between and add the capers. Serve immediately.
Preparation time: 10 minutes

● Tuna fish—use a 200g (7 oz) can—is sometimes included, in which case the salad becomes a meal in itself and only needs some French bread to round it off.
● The potatoes are often omitted.

Tomato and Egg Salad

This attractive-looking summer appetizer needs big Mediterranean-type (beef steak) tomatoes. If they are not fully ripe, stand them on a sunny windowsill for a day.

SERVES 4

4 big ripe Mediterranean-type (beef steak) tomatoes
4 hard-boiled eggs
salt
120ml/8 tablespoons ($\frac{1}{2}$ cup) mayonnaise (page 250)
4 pinches chopped parsley

Blanch and skin the tomatoes. Cut off the tops and remove the cores, seeds and juice with a spoon. (Reserve these for making tomato sauce.) Sprinkle the insides of the tomatoes with salt, turn upside-down on a plate and leave for 30 minutes.

Slice each egg across into 6 rings. Slit each tomato from the rim almost to the base in 6 places equally around the rim. Stand an egg slice in each slit, so that it peeps through to the outside. Put a good dollop of mayonnaise into each tomato and sprinkle parsley on top. Chill until needed.
Preparation time: 40 minutes including resting, plus chilling

● If only smaller tomatoes are available, make a salad in a ring. Start with skinned tomato slices, arranging these in a rosette from the outside of the dish towards the middle, overlapping the slices. Top each slice with a slice of hard-boiled egg—you will need as many eggs as there are people—tucking the rim of the egg slice neatly under the inner ring if necessary.

Chop the round tips of hard egg white and pile neatly in the middle. Put a tomato cut like a cup (see recipe) in the centre, with a sprig of parsley in it. Dress before serving with a mild vinaigrette and a sprinkling of herbs.
● For a party make the ring salad and put 1.5ml ($\frac{1}{4}$ teaspoon) black lumpfish caviar on each egg slice.
● For a summer main course, pile canned, drained tuna fish in the middle of the ring salad and garnish with parsley and the finely-chopped egg white ends.

Salade niçoise from southern France will make the perfect main course, with French bread, for a summer lunch.

Three Green Salad

SERVES 6

1 Cos (Boston) lettuce
1 head of chicory (endive)
½ bunch of watercress, tough stalks removed

FOR THE DRESSING

pinch of salt
5ml (1 teaspoon) fine sugar
freshly ground black pepper
30ml (2 tablespoons) tarragon vinegar
150ml/¼ pt (⅔ cup) thin cream

Pull the leaves off the lettuce and chicory (endive) and wash both of these and the watercress. Dry, preferably in a salad spinner. Put in plastic bags in the bottom of a refrigerator for 1 hour to crisp.

Put the salt, sugar and plenty of pepper into a bowl and stir in the vinegar. Stir in the cream and check the taste. Add more vinegar if desired. Just before serving turn the salad into a large bowl, pour over the dressing and toss well.

Preparation time: total 10 minutes, plus 1 hour crisping

● Try lettuce with the fronds and chopped slices of a fennel bulb. The inner and outer lettuce leaves are often 2 different greens.
● Webb's (Iceberg) lettuce goes well with a selection of chopped mixed herbs and cucumber or spring onions (scallions).
● Use curly endive (chicory) or escarole with chopped mustard and cress; dress with a vinaigrette made with lemon juice.
● Serve lettuce with 100g (¼ lb) cold, cooked, petit pois (baby peas) or baby lima beans; skin the latter if you have time.
● If the salad contains watercress or chicory (endive), make the dressing slightly sweet. Add 5ml (1 teaspoon) Dijon mustard and another of sugar to a basic vinaigrette.

Waldorf Salad

This is an excellent winter salad.

SERVES 6

1 head (bunch) celery, washed and thinly sliced
1 large red dessert apple, cored and thinly sliced
2 bananas, thinly sliced
50g/2 oz (½ cup) shelled walnuts, chopped
8 pressed dates, stoned (pitted) and chopped
10ml (2 teaspoons) lemon juice
10ml (2 teaspoons) sugar
30ml (2 tablespoons) mayonnaise (*page 250*)

Put the first 5 ingredients in a salad bowl. Mix the dressing, pour over then toss the salad.
Preparation time: 10 minutes

Cauliflower and Walnut Salad

SERVES 4

1 medium-sized cauliflower, broken in florets
50g/2 oz (½ cup) shelled walnuts, chopped
15ml (1 tablespoon) parsley, chopped
25g/1 oz (2 tablespoons) blue cheese
150ml/¼ pt (⅔ cup) French dressing

Remove any hard base stems from the cauliflower florets and put them to soak in cold, salted water for 10 minutes. Dry, preferably in a salad spinner. Put the cauliflower in the salad bowl and add the walnuts.

Crumble the blue cheese and stir into the French dressing. Pour this well over the cauliflower florets and toss to mix thoroughly. Chill for at least 30 minutes before serving.
Preparation time: 40 minutes

Combine different shades of green for an eye-appealing summer salad.

French Dressing (Vinaigrette)

This dressing is worth making in quantity. Multiply the recipe ingredients and keep a bottle ready-made in your cupboard or refrigerator. Be sure to shake it well each time you use it. There are many variations to this dressing and these are given after the recipe itself. Vary the dressing according to the vegetables with which you are serving it.

MAKES 150ML/$\frac{1}{4}$ PT ($\frac{2}{3}$ CUP)
30ml (2 tablespoons) white wine vinegar
5ml (1 teaspoon) salt
5ml (1 teaspoon) ground black pepper
125ml/4 fl oz ($\frac{1}{2}$ cup) olive oil

Combine the vinegar, salt and pepper. Mix with a fork to dissolve the salt. Add the oil and mix again. Stir or shake before pouring over a salad.
Preparation time: 5 minutes

● Olive oil can be used half and half with corn oil to make the basic dressing for economy.
● Crushed garlic is sometimes added, or chopped fresh herbs.
● Mustard and/or sugar appear in some recipes.
● You can use a herb-flavoured vinegar or lemon juice.

Green Goddess Sauce

A mayonnaise-based sauce, this is best with fish and shellfish but can also add interest to a potato salad.

MAKES ABOUT 425ML/$\frac{3}{4}$ PT (1$\frac{1}{2}$ CUPS)
275ml/$\frac{1}{2}$ pt (1$\frac{1}{4}$ cups) mayonnaise (page 250)
3 anchovy fillets, drained and chopped
3 small spring onions (scallions), finely chopped
30ml (2 tablespoons) parsley, chopped
10ml (2 teaspoons) tarragon or chives, chopped
15ml (1 tablespoon) tarragon vinegar
150ml/$\frac{1}{4}$ pt ($\frac{2}{3}$ cup) sour cream
salt
freshly ground black pepper

Stir all the ingredients together except the sour cream and seasoning. When thoroughly blended, add the cream. Check seasoning and chill. The dressing will keep for up to a week.
Preparation time: 10 minutes plus chilling

Thousand Island Dressing

Whipped cream can be substituted for the French dressing in this recipe. The dressing can be served with hamburgers, salads and seafood cocktails.

MAKES 575ML/1 PT (2$\frac{1}{2}$ CUPS)
450ml/16 fl oz (2 cups) mayonnaise (page 250)
5ml (1 teaspoon) Tabasco sauce
30ml (2 tablespoons) pimentos, chopped
10 green olives, finely chopped
2 hard-boiled eggs, finely chopped
1 shallot, finely chopped
50ml/2 fl oz ($\frac{1}{4}$ cup) French dressing

In a large bowl beat all the ingredients together with a wooden spoon until they are thoroughly combined. Pour the dressing into a serving bowl and chill for at least 1 hour before serving.
Preparation time: 5 minutes plus 1 hour chilling

Sweet and Sour Salad Dressing

This unusual dressing combines well with cabbage.

MAKES ABOUT 150ML/$\frac{1}{4}$ PT ($\frac{2}{3}$ CUP)
125ml/4 fl oz ($\frac{1}{2}$ cup) oil
30ml (2 tablespoons) white wine vinegar
10ml (2 teaspoons) salt
5ml (1 teaspoon) black pepper
30ml (2 tablespoons) honey
juice of 1 lemon

Combine all the ingredients in a screw-top jar and shake to mix.
Preparation time: 2 minutes

Sour Cream and Cucumber Sauce

This sauce is good with fish dishes and salads containing fruit.

SERVES 4
1 large cucumber, peeled and seeded
150ml/$\frac{1}{4}$ pt ($\frac{2}{3}$ cup) thick cream
30ml (2 tablespoons) white wine vinegar
15ml (1 tablespoon) chives, tarragon or parsley, chopped

Grate the cucumber flesh then place in a colander and sprinkle generously with salt. Leave for 30 minutes to drain. Rinse the cucumber under cold running water and dry thoroughly on absorbent paper inside a towel.

Whisk the cream until thick. Add the vinegar gradually to sour the cream. Stir in the herbs and mix the cucumber then chill.
Preparation time: 45 minutes plus chilling

Yogurt Dressing

This refreshing dressing is particularly good with cucumber, grated root vegetables and tomato salads.

MAKES 150ML/$\frac{1}{4}$ PT ($\frac{2}{3}$ CUP)
juice $\frac{1}{2}$ lemon
5ml (1 teaspoon) clear honey
150ml/$\frac{1}{2}$ pt ($\frac{2}{3}$ cup) plain yogurt
1 garlic clove, chopped
salt
freshly ground black pepper
15ml (1 tablespoon) fresh mint, chopped

Combine the lemon juice and honey in a small bowl and blend in the yogurt. Crush the garlic on a plate with the salt, pressing with a round bladed knife until a paste is formed. Blend with the seasoning into the yogurt and stir in the mint.
Preparation time: 5 minutes plus chilling

Blue Cheese Dressing

Cottage cheese and buttermilk are used in this recipe. The dressing is particularly good with green salads and salads contining fruit.

MAKES 150ML/$\frac{1}{4}$ PT ($\frac{2}{3}$ CUP)
100g/$\frac{1}{4}$ lb ($\frac{2}{3}$ cup) cottage cheese
60ml/4 tablespoons ($\frac{1}{4}$ cup) buttermilk
30ml (2 tablespoons) wine vinegar
50g/2 oz blue cheese
freshly ground black pepper

Press the cottage cheese through a strainer into a bowl with the back of a wooden spoon. Stir in the buttermilk and then the wine vinegar. Mash the blue cheese and add to the cottage cheese mixture. Mix until well blended. Add black pepper to taste.
Preparation time: 10 minutes

● Blue cheese is also sometimes added to French dressing to make a simpler version of this dressing.

Summer

Soups and Starters

Shrimp Soup

Tiny shrimps are very tedious to peel. In this iced soup, for blender owners, they are not peeled at all. A chilled soup is always made ahead, so try to serve poached fish the day before and reserve the poaching liquid and the small amount of fish needed for this recipe.

SERVES 4
275ml/½ pt (1¼ cups) milk
50g/2 oz (¼ cup) onion, chopped
2 large tomatoes, blanched, skinned, seeded and chopped
1 bay leaf
50g/2 oz (¼ cup) cooked white fish
15ml (1 tablespoon) tomato paste
250g/1 pt (½ lb) boiled shrimps
225ml/8 fl oz (1 cup) fish stock or water
15ml (1 tablespoon) lemon juice
50ml/2 fl oz (¼ cup) white wine or vermouth
salt
freshly ground black pepper
100ml/4 fl oz (½ cup) thin cream

Put the chopped onion, tomatoes, and bay leaf in a small pan with the milk and simmer for 10 minutes until the onion is cooked. Remove the bay leaf and stir in the tomato paste.

Use a slotted spoon to transfer the solid contents of the saucepan to a blender. Add the fish and a little milk and blend. Transfer the purée to a medium-sized bowl and set aside. Add a handful of shrimps to the blender and cover with milk. Blend until smooth. Add the rest of the shrimps in batches with more milk or fish stock. Pour the purée into a strainer over the bowl and press through with a wooden spoon.

Add the wine or vermouth and the lemon juice and season to taste. Stir in half the cream and chill. Serve with a swirl of cream in each bowl, garnishing with a few shrimps.
Cooking time: 25 minutes plus chilling time

●Hot shrimp chowder is made with larger prawns (shrimp). Served with salad and French bread, it will make a modest lunch for 3. Peel 350g/1½ pt (¾ lb) boiled prawns and simmer the heads and shells with 275ml/½ pt (1¼ cups) water. Strain, then reserve the liquid. In 15ml (1 tablespoon) butter, sauté 1 large chopped onion and 225g (½ lb) chopped potatoes for 3 minutes. Add the fish stock, bring to the boil and add 225g/½ lb (1 cup) sweetcorn kernels. Simmer for 15 minutes then add 575ml/1 pt (2½ cups) milk and the prawns (shrimp). Simmer 5 minutes, spoon into bowls, sprinkle with 30ml (2 tablespoons) chopped parsley and serve.

Egg and Basil Tartlets

SERVES 6
¾ × shortcrust pastry *(page 240)*
225ml/8 fl oz (1 cup) mayonnaise *(page 250)*
1 large garlic clove, crushed
60ml (4 tablespoons) fresh basil, chopped
4 hard-boiled eggs, finely chopped
FOR THE GARNISH
6 slices hard-boiled egg
6 small basil sprigs

Heat the oven to 200°C (400°F) gas mark 6. Roll out the dough and use to line 6 × 7.5cm (3 in) fluted tartlet tins (pans). Bake blind (*see page 61*) for 15 minutes, then allow to cool.

Combine the mayonnaise, garlic and chopped basil. Carefully remove the pastry cases from the tins. Divide the chopped hard-boiled eggs between the pastry cases and cover with the mayonnaise mixture. Garnish each tartlet with an egg slice and a sprig of basil. Serve cold.
Cooking time: 35 minutes plus 1 hour cooling

Cucumber and Beer Soup

SERVES 6
350ml (12 fl oz) light ale (beer)
125ml/4 fl oz (½ cup) sour cream
1 medium-sized cucumber, peeled and finely chopped
1 garlic clove, crushed
2.5ml (½ teaspoon) fine sugar
salt
freshly ground black pepper
5ml (1 teaspoon) paprika

These egg and basil tartlets are filled with chopped egg and topped with a garlic and basil mayonnaise. Make the tarts ahead, then they are quick to finish.

Beat the beer and sour cream together until well mixed. Stir in the cucumber, garlic, sugar and seasoning to taste. Chill the soup for at least 1 hour before serving, sprinkled with the paprika.

Preparation time: 5 minutes plus 1 hour chilling

Finnish Vegetable Soup

SERVES 6–8
1 small cauliflower, broken into florets
225g ($\frac{1}{2}$ lb) green beans, trimmed and quartered
225g ($\frac{1}{2}$ lb) peas, weighed after shelling
6 baby carrots, sliced
6 small new potatoes, halved
3 small courgettes (zucchini), sliced
125g ($\frac{1}{4}$ lb) spinach, chopped
2 egg yolks
225ml/8 fl oz (1 cup) milk
salt
freshly ground black pepper
60ml/4 tablespoons ($\frac{1}{4}$ cup) thick cream
chopped parsley to garnish

Put the cauliflower, beans, peas, carrots, potatoes and courgettes (zucchini) in a saucepan and just cover with water. Bring to the boil, then simmer for 10 minutes or until the vegetables are nearly tender. Add the spinach and simmer for additional 5 minutes. Remove the vegetables from the pan with a slotted spoon and set aside.

Beat the egg yolks and milk together. Add a little of the hot liquid from the pan, then stir this mixture into the remaining liquid. Stir in the reserved vegetables, season to taste and heat very gently. Stir in the cream and serve garnished with parsley.

Cooking time: 30 minutes

Apricot and Soured Cream Salad

SERVES 4
700–900g ($1\frac{1}{2}$–2 lb) ripe apricots, peeled, halved and stoned (reserve the stones)
6 almonds (optional)
60ml/4 tablespoons ($\frac{1}{4}$ cup) sour cream
45ml (3 tablespoons) tarragon vinegar
15ml (1 tablespoon) sugar
salt
freshly ground black pepper
30ml (2 tablespoons) chopped fresh tarragon

Crack the apricot stones with a nutcracker or hammer and take out the kernels. Chop them and reserve. Alternatively, chop 6 almonds and set aside. Arrange the apricot halves in a glass serving bowl, cut side up.

Combine the sour cream, vinegar, sugar and seasoning to taste. Pour over the apricots and sprinkle with the apricot kernels or almonds and tarragon.

Preparation time: 10 minutes

With crusty bread, Finnish vegetable soup makes an ideal summer lunch.

Potted Bloaters

MAKES ABOUT 700G ($1\frac{1}{2}$ LB)
4 × 275g (10 oz) bloaters or herring, cleaned
225g/$\frac{1}{2}$ lb (1 cup) butter
pinch of ground mace
salt
freshly ground black pepper
pinch of cayenne pepper

Arrange the bloaters, side by side, in a shallow heatproof dish and pour boiling water over them. Leave for 15 minutes.

Drain the bloaters, then remove the heads and skin and fillet them. Blend the fish to a purée with 150g/5 oz ($\frac{5}{8}$ cup) of the butter, the mace, seasoning and cayenne. Alternatively, press the fish through a strainer and pound in a mortar with the butter and seasonings. Fill a pot or pots with the paste, leaving about 1.5cm ($\frac{1}{2}$ in) headroom. Smooth the surfaces.

To clarify the butter, heat it in a heavy-based pan over low heat. Leave it until it is foaming slightly, then pour it through a strainer lined with cheesecloth. Cover the pots with a thin layer of clarified butter and allow to set. Cover with the rest of the butter, then store in the refrigerator.

Cooking time: 40 minutes plus chilling time

Marinated Mackerel Fillets

An inexpensive fish is marinated to give the impression of a luxurious first course in Mexican style. Garnish the fish with seasonal salad vegetables and serve with thin slices of brown bread and butter is desired.

Reserve the marinade and use it, diluted in the proportion of 1:2 with water, as a court bouillon for poaching fish. It can also be used, diluted, to make a fish-based Greek egg and lemon soup (page 26).

SERVES 6
425ml/ $\frac{3}{4}$ pt (1$\frac{2}{3}$ cups) lemon juice
1 dried red chilli, stalk and seeds removed
2 large onions, thinly sliced in rings
$\frac{1}{2}$ garlic clove, finely chopped
salt
freshly ground black pepper
3 large mackerel, filleted and cut into 2.5cm (1 in) wide strips
lettuce leaves
1 fresh red chilli, seeded and cut into strips

Pound the dried chilli in a mortar with a pestle. Mix it together with the lemon juice, onion rings, garlic and seasonings in a shallow dish. Add the mackerel pieces and turn to coat them in the marinade. Cover the dish and marinate for about 6 hours.

Drain the fish and divide between six serving plates. Garnish with lettuce, the onion rings from the marinade and the strips of red chilli. Add seasonal vegetables, if liked.

Preparation time: 5 minutes plus 6 hours marinating.

Tomato Water Ice with Cucumber Salad

SERVES 6
700g (1$\frac{1}{2}$ lb) ripe tomatoes, sliced
grated rind and juice of 1 lemon
1 garlic clove, crushed
30ml (2 tablespoons) sugar
30ml (2 tablespoons) tomato paste
salt
freshly ground black pepper
1 egg white
1 cucumber, thinly sliced
30ml (2 tablespoons) French dressing
basil sprigs to garnish

Put the tomatoes, lemon rind and juice, garlic, sugar, tomato paste and seasoning in a saucepan and mix well. Cover the pan and cook for 15 minutes or until the mixture is pulpy. Press the tomato mixture through a strainer to remove skins and seeds and cool.

Pour the tomato purée into freezer trays and freeze for 30 minutes or until slushy. Beat the egg white until stiff. Stir the tomato mixture to break down the ice crystals, then beat in the egg white. Return to the freezer tray and freeze until firm (about 1$\frac{1}{2}$ hours).

Stir the tomato ice again and turn into a 575ml (1 pt) ring mould. Cover and freeze for 2 hours.

Turn the tomato ice out of the mould on to a serving platter. Combine the cucumber and dressing and pile in the centre of the ice ring. Garnish with basil sprigs.

Cooking time: 2$\frac{1}{2}$ hours plus 2 hours freezing

Summer Avocado Salad

SERVES 4
450g (1 lb) courgettes (zucchini), cut into 12mm ($\frac{1}{2}$ in) slices
90ml/6 tablespoons ($\frac{1}{3}$ cup) olive oil
30ml (2 tablespoons) wine vinegar
1 garlic clove, crushed
2.5ml ($\frac{1}{2}$ teaspoon) sugar
salt
freshly ground black pepper
1 large avocado, peeled, halved, stoned and sliced
lettuce leaves
12 stuffed green olives, halved
watercress

Blanch the courgette (zucchini) slices in boiling water for 3 minutes. Drain and refresh under cold running water. Drain thoroughly.

Combine the oil, vinegar, garlic, sugar and seasoning to taste in a bowl. Add the courgette (zucchini) and avocado slices and turn to coat with the dressing. Cover and marinate in the refrigerator for 6 hours.

Arrange lettuce leaves on six individual plates. Drain the courgette and avocado slices and divide between the plates. Garnish with the olives and watercress.

Preparation time: 15 minutes plus 6 hours marinating

Quick Liver Pâté

This is a quick starter to make in an emergency.

SERVES 4
175g (6 oz) liver sausage (liverwurst)
1 small onion, finely chopped
60ml (4 tablespoons) thin cream
1 small garlic clove, crushed
15ml (1 tablespoon) dry sherry or brandy (optional)
salt
freshly ground black pepper
chopped parsley to garnish

Mash together the liver sausage (liverwurst), onion, cream, garlic and sherry or brandy if using. Season to taste, then pile into a bowl. Garnish with parsley.

Preparation time: 2 minutes

Start a meal the Mexican way with spicy chilli and lemon marinated mackerel fillets. Garnish the dish with seasonal vegetables.

Economical Chicken Liver Pâté

With salad and French bread, this will make a light lunch for 4; with toast it makes an appetizer for 6.

SERVES 6
225g (½ lb) chicken livers, trimmed of green patches and membrane, then chopped
1 medium-sized onion, chopped
1 garlic clove, chopped
75g/3 oz (6 tablespoons) butter
small bouquet garni
15ml (1 tablespoon) medium sherry
salt and freshly ground black pepper
50g/2 oz (¼ cup) butter (optional)
4 pimento-stuffed green olives and/or watercress for garnish (optional)

Sauté the onions and garlic in 25g (2 tablespoons) of the butter for 3 minutes. Add the livers and bouquet garni and cook for an additional 3 minutes, then remove the bouquet garni.

Mince or chop the mixture finely. Cream the remaining butter and beat it, with the sherry, into the livers. Season to taste and pack into a small dish. Either melt the 50g/2 oz (¼ cup) butter and pour it over the top or garnish with sliced olives and/or watercress before serving. Chill.

Cooking time: 15 minutes plus 2 hours chilling time

Curried Apple Soup

Yogurt is used in this creamy soup to economize on cream. Curry spice (page 254) can be substituted for the spices.

SERVES 6
700g (1½ lb) dessert apples, peeled, cored and chopped
1 small onion, chopped
850ml/1½ pt (3¾ cups) chicken stock
salt
freshly ground black pepper
2.5ml (½ teaspoon) lemon juice
2.5ml (½ teaspoon) turmeric
2.5ml (½ teaspoon) ground cumin
2.5ml (½ teaspoon) ground coriander
pinch of chilli powder
pinch of ground cloves
150ml/¼ pt (⅔ cup) thin cream (or half and half)
90ml/6 tablespoons (⅓ cup) plain yogurt

Put the apples, onion, half the stock, the seasoning, lemon juice and spices in a saucepan and bring to the boil. Cover the pan and simmer for 10 minutes or until the vegetables are tender. Purée in a blender or through a food mill. Stir in the remaining stock and cool.

Stir in the cream and yogurt and chill for at least 30 minutes before serving.

Cooking time: 30 minutes plus 1½ hours cooling time

Invariably popular, yet quick and economical to make, chicken liver pâté can be dressed up for a party or eaten plain.

Ensaladilla

This classic Spanish starter can also be made from cold, left-over vegetables. Provided you are judicious in your selection—a good colour contrast and not too many of one type is essential—this is an attractive way of disguising them.

SERVES 4–6
100g (¼ lb) new potatoes, quartered
100g (¼ lb) broad (baby lima) beans, weighed after podding
100g (¼ lb) young carrots, quartered
100g (¼ lb) peas, weighed after shelling
100g (¼ lb) French (green) beans
150ml/¼ pt (⅔ cup) aioli *(page 250)*

Steam the potatoes for 10 minutes. Add the broad (lima) beans, carrots and peas to the steamer and steam for an additional 5 minutes. Add the French (green) beans and continue steaming for 10 minutes or until all the vegetables are tender. Cool.

Dice all the vegetables to the size of the broad (lima) beans, then fold in the aioli. Chill for 20 minutes before serving.

Cooking time: 25 minutes plus 1 hour cooling time

Iced Asparagus Soup

Soup is the best way to use asparagus that is very thin, or the trimmings from a bunch of asparagus. Reserve the tips for a showy garnish to fish or meat, or to lend excitement to a salad. Cook the tips first in a minimum of water. Reserve the water for soup and one tip each to garnish the soup.

SERVES 4
25g/1 oz (2 tablespoons) butter
50g/2 oz (¼ cup) onion, finely chopped
half garlic clove
15ml (1 tablespoon) flour
700ml/1¼ pt (3 cups) asparagus cooking liquid, made up with extra if necessary
2.5ml (½ teaspoon) celery salt
1.5ml (¼ teaspoon) grated nutmeg
1 chicken stock cube
salt
freshly ground black pepper
450g (1 lb) asparagus trimmings
60ml (4 tablespoons) thin cream (or half and half)
4 asparagus tips to garnish

Melt the butter in a saucepan. Add the onion and garlic and fry until soft. Stir in

No need to wait for a dinner party to eat this cheaply-made iced asaparagus soup.

the flour and cook for 1 minute. Gradually stir in the asparagus cooking liquid and simmer until thickened.

Trim and discard any heavy wooden bases from the asparagus stalks and chop the rest into 4cm (1½ in) lengths. Add these, with the celery salt, nutmeg and stock cube, to the pan. Cover and simmer for 30–40 minutes.

Purée the soup through a food mill to remove the fibres, or in a blender and then press through a strainer with a wooden spoon. Cool the soup, then chill for 3 hours.

To serve, ladle into individual bowls then swirl a little cream into each and garnish with an asparagus tip.

Cooking time: 50 minutes plus 3 hours chilling.

Cream of Lettuce Soup

Use the outside leaves of several lettuces for this soup, keeping the crisp, tender inner leaves for salads.

SERVES 4
75g/3 oz (⅓ cup) butter
25g/1 oz (¼ cup) flour
575ml/1 pt (2½ cups) chicken stock
salt and freshly ground black pepper
2 lettuces, core removed
1 small onion, finely chopped
90ml/6 tablespoons (⅓ cup) thick cream

Melt 25g (1 oz) of the butter in a saucepan. Add the flour and cook, stirring, for 2 minutes. Gradually stir in the stock and bring to the boil, stirring. Simmer until slightly thickened. Season to taste, then cover and cook gently for 10 minutes.

Meanwhile, melt another 25g (1 oz) of the butter in another saucepan. Separate the lettuce leaves and place them with the onion in the saucepan. Cover and cook gently for 10 minutes or until the vegetables are softened but not browned.

Transfer the onion and lettuce mixture to the other pan and simmer, covered, for a further 10 minutes.

Purée the lettuce mixture in a blender or with a food mill and return to the pan. Stir in the cream and heat through gently. Add the remaining butter, piece by piece, stirring well. Season and serve.

Cooking time: 40 minutes

84

Gazpacho
Spanish Iced Tomato Soup

A perfect party soup for a hot summer evening; serve it with finely chopped black olives, hard-boiled eggs, onion and cucumber and croûtons, each in a small bowl.

SERVES 4
3 slices of brown bread, cut into small cubes
275ml/½ pt (1¼ cups) tomato juice
2 garlic cloves, finely chopped
½ cucumber, peeled and finely chopped
1 green (bell) pepper, cored, seeded and finely chopped
1 red (bell) pepper, cored, seeded and finely chopped
1 large onion, finely chopped
700g (1½ lb) tomatoes, blanched, skinned, seeded and chopped
90ml/6 tablespoons (⅓ cup) oil
30ml (2 tablespoons) red wine vinegar
1.5ml (¼ teaspoon) dried marjoram
1.5ml (¼ teaspoon) dried basil
salt
freshly ground black pepper

Soak the bread cubes in the tomato juice for 5 minutes, then reserve the juice and mix the cubes with the garlic, cucumber, peppers, onion and tomatoes. Purée the mixture in a blender or food mill. Add the remaining ingredients and the reserved tomato juice to the purée and mix well. Chill for at least 2 hours.

Preparation time: 30 minutes plus 2 hours chilling

Mushroom and Mint Soup

SERVES 6
4 large potatoes, chopped
1 small onion, chopped
850ml/1½ pt (3¾ cups) chicken stock
grated rind and juice of 1 lemon
15ml (1 tablespoon) chopped fresh rosemary
salt and freshly ground black pepper
50g/2 oz (¼ cup) butter
225g (½ lb) mushrooms, sliced
15ml (1 tablespoon) flour
30ml (2 tablespoons) chopped fresh mint
150ml/¼ pt (⅔ cup) thick cream

Put the potatoes, onion, stock, lemon rind and juice, and rosemary in a pan, season to taste and bring to the boil. Cover and simmer for 25 minutes or until the vegetables are very tender.

Meanwhile, melt the butter in another saucepan. Add the mushrooms and cook gently for 10 minutes. Sprinkle over the flour and cook, stirring, for 1 minute. Remove from the heat.

Purée the potato and onion mixture and return to the saucepan. Stir in the mushroom mixture. Bring to the boil, stirring. Stir in the mint and adjust the seasoning. Stir in the cream and serve.

Cooking time: 55 minutes

● For iced mushroom soup, omit all other vegetables and herbs. Thicken the soup with arrowroot instead of flour. Purée, then add 2 egg yolks and 125ml/4 fl oz (½ cup) thick cream. Heat gently, stirring all the time. Then cool and chill. Sprinkle chopped chives over to serve.

Make gazpacho—Spain's most refreshing iced soup—when tomatoes are cheap.

Eggs and Cheese

Huevos Rancheros
Ranchers' Eggs

This vegetable supper dish from Mexico has plenty of protein.

SERVES 6

50g (2 oz) red (bell) pepper, cored, seeded and thinly sliced
15ml (1 tablespoon) oil
2 medium-sized onions, finely chopped
2 garlic cloves, crushed
6 large tomatoes, blanched, skinned, seeded and chopped
1 green chilli, seeded and finely chopped
5ml (1 teaspoon) sugar
2.5ml ($\frac{1}{2}$ teaspoon) ground coriander
salt
freshly ground black pepper
12 eggs
175g/6 oz (1$\frac{1}{2}$ cups) Cheddar cheese, grated
15g/$\frac{1}{2}$ oz (1 tablespoon) butter
1.5ml ($\frac{1}{4}$ teaspoon) chilli powder

Heat the oven to 230°C (450°F) gas mark 8. Blanch the red pepper for 2 minutes in boiling water, drain and set aside to cool a little. Heat the oil in a frying-pan. Add the onions and garlic and fry over low heat until softened. Stir in the tomatoes, red pepper, chilli, sugar, coriander. Season to taste. Simmer for 15 minutes.

Pour the tomato mixture into a baking dish. Make 12 hollows with the back of a spoon and break an egg into each. Sprinkle the cheese over the eggs, then dot with the butter and sprinkle over the chilli powder. Bake for 6–8 minutes or until the eggs are set and the top is golden brown.
Cooking time: 50 minutes

Pipérade Basque

SERVES 6–8

30ml (2 tablespoons) oil
1 onion, finely chopped
1 garlic clove, crushed
4 medium-sized green (bell) peppers, cored, seeded and thinly sliced
900g (2 lb) tomatoes, blanched, skinned and chopped
pinch of sugar
pinch of dried basil
salt and freshly ground black pepper
4 eggs

Heat the oil in a frying pan. Add the onion and garlic and fry until softened. Add the peppers and cook gently for 10 minutes. Stir in the tomatoes, sugar and basil, season to taste and cook for 5 minutes.

Beat the eggs and add to the mixture in the pan. Cook gently, stirring, until the eggs are set and lightly scrambled.
Cooking time: 30–40 minutes

Cheese Soufflé Tarts

SERVES 4

$\frac{1}{2}$ × hard-cheese shortcrust pastry (page 241)
4 slices fatty bacon, chopped
2 medium-sized onions, chopped
25g/1 oz (2 tablespoons) butter
20ml (4 teaspoons) flour
150ml/$\frac{1}{4}$ pt ($\frac{2}{3}$ cup) milk
2 medium-sized eggs, separated
salt
freshly ground black pepper
50g/2 oz ($\frac{1}{2}$ cup) Cheddar cheese, grated

Heat the oven to 200°C (400°F) gas mark 6. Roll out the pastry and line 4 × 10cm (4 in) tart tins (pans) or Yorkshire pudding moulds or an 18cm (7 in) tin or pan. Bake blind (*page 61*) for 15 minutes.

Meanwhile, fry the bacon in the butter over low heat until it sweats. Add the onions and fry, stirring gently, until soft but not coloured. Divide the mixture between the tarts.

Make a paste with the flour and some of the milk. Heat the remaining milk and pour on to the paste. Beat in the egg yolks and cheese and season well with pepper.

Whisk the egg whites with a pinch of salt until stiff, then fold in the milk mixture. Divide between the tarts and bake for a further 10–12 minutes until golden and puffy.
Cooking time: 25 minutes

●Leeks, ham and cream make delicious tarts. Divide 100g/$\frac{1}{4}$ lb ($\frac{2}{3}$ cup) chopped ham between the tarts. Sweat the white part of 225g ($\frac{1}{2}$ lb) chopped leeks in 25g/1 oz (2 tablespoons) butter and top the ham with the leeks. Beat 1 egg, 2.5ml ($\frac{1}{2}$ teaspoon) nutmeg, with salt and pepper, into 150ml/$\frac{1}{4}$ pt ($\frac{2}{3}$ cup) thin cream and pour over the tarts. Bake for 20 minutes.
●If desired, the bacon and onion can be omitted and 75g/3 oz ($\frac{3}{4}$ cup) grated Cheddar cheese, plus 45ml (3 tablespoons) grated Parmesan, used instead.

Ranchers' eggs, baked with vegetables and cheese, are easy to make and delicious for a simple supper, or even breakfast!

Anchovy Eggs Mornay

SERVES 4

| 6 hard-boiled eggs |
| 60ml/4 tablespoons ($\frac{1}{4}$ cup) thin cream |
| 50g (2 oz) canned anchovy fillets, drained and very finely chopped |
| black pepper |
| white sauce *(page 252)* |
| 175g/6 oz (1$\frac{1}{2}$ cups) Cheddar cheese, grated |
| 2.5ml ($\frac{1}{2}$ teaspoon) prepared mustard |
| 4 slices toast, cut into quarters |

Heat the oven to 200°C (400°F) gas mark 6. Halve the eggs lengthwise and carefully remove the yolks, keeping the whites intact. Mash the yolks with the cream, then beat in the anchovies and pepper to taste. Fill the egg whites with the yolk mixture and arrange them in one layer, cut side down, in an oven-proof serving dish.

Mix the white sauce with the mustard and 150g/5 oz (1$\frac{1}{4}$ cups) of the cheese and heat, stirring, until the cheese has melted

Anchovy eggs mornay are an interesting new way of serving eggs in cheese sauce.

and the sauce is piping hot. Pour it over the eggs and cover with cheese.

Bake for 15 minutes or until the top is golden brown. Serve decorated with triangles of toast.

Cooking time: 25 minutes

Soufflé Omelet Arnold Bennett

SERVES 2

| 100g ($\frac{1}{4}$ lb) smoked haddock |
| salt |
| freshly ground black pepper |
| 30ml (2 tablespoons) grated Parmesan cheese |
| 30ml (2 tablespoons) thick cream |
| 15ml (1 tablespoon) cold water |
| 3 eggs, separated |
| 20g/$\frac{3}{4}$ oz (5 teaspoons) butter |

Poach the fish for 10 minutes or until it flakes easily. Turn into a bowl, remove any skin and bone and flake. Season and add half the Parmesan cheese. Heat the grill (broiler) to hot.

Add half the cream and the cold water to the yolks. Mix well with a fork, then stir in the fish mixture. Add a pinch of salt to the egg whites then beat until they form soft peaks. Fold in the fish mixture carefully with a metal spoon.

Melt the butter in a 20cm (8 in) omelet pan. When it has stopped foaming, swirl the butter around the pan and then pour in the egg and fish mixture. Allow this to find its own level. Cook for 90 seconds without stirring, until the bottom has set.

Sprinkle over the remaining cream and cheese. Place the pan under the hot grill, about 5cm (2 in) from the heat. Leave for 30 seconds until golden and puffy. Either slip out the omelet on to a warmed serving plate or fold in half and turn out. Divide into two to serve.

Cooking time: 15 minutes

Cheese Aigrettes

These fluffy little aigrettes can be served as a first course for 6. With a spicy tomato sauce they will make a light lunch for 4.

SERVES 6
choux pastry *(page 244)*
50g/2 oz ($\frac{1}{2}$ cup) strong Cheddar cheese, grated
pinch of mustard
freshly ground black pepper
50g/2 oz ($\frac{1}{2}$ cup) Parmesan cheese, grated
paprika

Heat the oil in a deep fat fryer to 190°C (350°F) or until it will brown a cube of bread in 40 seconds. Make the choux, adding the cheese, mustard powder and pepper with the eggs. Dot on to a baking sheet with a tablespoon. Flick the balls on to a slotted spoon with a spatula and lower into the fat. Cook for 6–7 minutes. Lift out on to a dish lined with absorbent paper and keep warm until all are fried. Transfer to a warmed serving dish and sprinkle with the grated Parmesan and paprika to serve.
Cooking time: 30 minutes

● For deep-fried peanut balls, sprinkle the balls with 50g/2 oz ($\frac{1}{2}$ cup) finely chopped peanuts and turn them with your fingers to coat with nuts before frying.
● Deep-fried cheese balls are similar but have a melted cheese centre. Cut 100g ($\frac{1}{4}$ lb) Cheddar cheese into 12mm ($\frac{1}{2}$ in) cubes and coat with egg white batter *(page 245)*. Deep-fry for 5 minutes and serve with a mustard sauce.

Crisp cheese aigrettes can be served as a snack with drinks before dinner or with tomato sauce as a first course.

Egg and Tomato Mousse

This inexpensive egg mousse will make an appetizer for 8–9 people or a summer lunch for 6.

275ml/$\frac{1}{2}$ pt (1$\frac{1}{4}$ cups) chicken stock
225g ($\frac{1}{2}$ lb) mixed vegetables, diced
20g/$\frac{3}{4}$ oz (1 tablespoon) gelatin
450g (1 lb) ripe tomatoes, blanched, skinned, seeded and chopped
small bunch of parsley, finely chopped
6 large hard-boiled eggs
225ml/8 fl oz (1 cup) mayonnaise *(page 250)*
20ml (4 teaspoons) lemon juice
salt
paprika
FOR THE GARNISH
2 hard-boiled eggs, thinly sliced
2–3 tomatoes, thinly sliced
350ml/12 fl oz (1$\frac{1}{2}$ cups) canned chicken consommé
5ml (1 teaspoon) gelatin

Put 120ml (8 tablespoons) of the stock in a small pan and sprinkle over the gelatin. Leave to soften for 5 minutes. Cook the vegetables in the remaining stock. Drain the vegetables and reserve the stock, putting the vegetables aside to cool completely. Add the gelatin to the hot stock and stir until dissolved. Cool then chill in the refrigerator, stirring occasionally, until it thickens to the consistency of unbeaten egg white or a medium-thick syrup.

Sieve the egg yolks and chop the whites finely. Mix the mayonnaise and lemon juice with the jellied stock then fold in the eggs, tomatoes, parsley and cold mixed vegetables. Season to taste with salt and paprika. Turn the egg mixture into a lightly-oiled 1.1L/2 pt (1 US qt) soufflé dish and smooth the surface with the back of a spoon. Cover and chill until set— about 2 hours.

To garnish, arrange overlapping slices of egg and tomato around the rim. Melt the consommé and sprinkle in the gelatin. Let it stand 1 minute, then heat gently to dissolve, then allow to cool to room temperature. Spoon over just enough to give a thin glaze to the mousse top and the decorations. Cover with plastic wrap and return to the refrigerator to set completely.
Cooking time: about 1 hour, plus 2 hours setting, then 5 minutes plus chilling

Italian Vegetable and Ham Omelet

SERVES 4
25g/1 oz (2 tablespoons) butter
15ml (1 tablespoon) oil
1 medium-sized onion, finely chopped
2 courgettes (zucchini), sliced
2 large tomatoes, blanched, skinned, seeded and finely chopped
175g (6 oz) cooked ham, diced
6 eggs
10ml (2 teaspoons) fresh oregano, chopped
10ml (2 teaspoons) fresh marjoram, chopped
salt
freshly ground black pepper
50g/2 oz ($\frac{1}{2}$ cup) Parmesan or Provolone cheese, grated

Melt the butter with the oil in a large omelet pan. Add the onion and fry over low heat until golden. Add the courgettes (zucchini) and fry for 4 minutes. Stir in the tomatoes and ham and fry for a further 4 minutes.

Heat the grill (broiler) to high. Lightly beat together the eggs, herbs and seasoning. Pour the egg mixture into the pan. Cook until the bottom of the omelet is set and the top is still creamy.

Sprinkle over the cheese and transfer the pan to the grill. Cook for 2 minutes or until the cheese has melted.
Cooking time: 4 minutes

Meat and Poultry

Baked Chicken with Herbs

SERVES 6
40g/1½ oz (3 tablespoons) butter
6 chicken portions
150ml/¼ pt (⅔ cup) white wine
150ml/¼ pt (⅔ cup) water
1 chicken stock cube
2 garlic cloves, crushed
30ml (2 tablespoons) parsley, chopped
30ml (2 tablespoons) fresh tarragon, chopped
10ml (2 teaspoons) marjoram, chopped
30ml (2 tablespoons) chopped spring onions (scallions)
100g (¼ lb) mushrooms, sliced
juice of 1 lemon
salt
freshly ground black pepper

Heat the oven to 160°C (325°F) gas mark 3. Melt the butter in a frying-pan. Add the chicken pieces in batches and brown on all sides. Transfer the pieces to an ovenproof dish and season generously. Drain off most of the fat from the pan and reserve for another dish.

Put the mushrooms, onions and garlic in the frying-pan and sauté for 2–3 minutes. Stir in the wine, stock, herbs and lemon juice and pour over the chicken in the casserole.

Cover the casserole tightly and cook in the oven for 1½ hours or until the chicken is tender.
Cooking time: 2 hours

Orange Rosemary Chicken

SERVES 4
4 chicken quarters
salt
freshly ground black pepper
75g/3 oz (⅓ cup) butter
2 large onions, thinly sliced
450ml/16 fl oz (2 cups) orange juice
15ml (1 tablespoon) fresh rosemary, chopped
15ml (1 tablespoon) grated orange rind
22.5ml (1½ tablespoons) cornflour (cornstarch) dissolved in 15ml (1 tablespoon) water

Rub the chicken quarters all over with salt and pepper. Melt 50g/2 oz (¼ cup) of the butter in a deep frying pan with a lid. Add the chicken quarters and brown on all sides. Remove them from the pan.

Add the remaining butter to the pan. When it has melted add the onions. Fry until softened, then stir in the orange juice, rosemary and orange rind. Bring to the boil.

Return the chicken quarters to the pan. Cover the pan and simmer for 30–35 minutes or until the chicken quarters are cooked through. Transfer them to a warmed serving dish and keep hot.

Boil the liquid in the pan for 3 minutes. Stir in the cornflour (cornstarch) and cook, stirring, until thickened. Pour this sauce over the chicken and serve.
Cooking time: 1 hour

Baked chicken with herbs is economical and easy to prepare: gently cooked in a blend of lemon, marjoram, tarragon and wine, it is popular with children and can be served from the cooking pot.

Breast of Lamb Riblets

Grilling (broiling) before stewing removes much of the fat and crisps this rather fatty meat.

SERVES 4
2 breasts of lamb, divided into 1-rib pieces
1 small onion, chopped
150ml/¼ pt (⅔ cup) tomato juice
150ml/¼ pt (⅔ cup) water
30ml (2 tablespoons) brown sugar
30ml (2 tablespoons) Worcestershire sauce
15ml (1 tablespoon) vinegar
salt and freshly ground black pepper

Heat the grill (broiler) to high. Grill (broil) the rib pieces until browned on both sides.

Meanwhile, put the remaining ingredients in a large saucepan and bring to the boil. Transfer the riblets to the saucepan and mix into the sauce. Cover the pan and simmer gently for 1½ hours.
Cooking time: 1 hour 50 minutes

Kidney and Liver Brochettes

Vermouth is a practical substitute for wine when small quantities are demanded in a recipe, because the bottle can be capped and will keep for up to a month without the contents souring. Vermouth also compares quite well with wine in price and alcohol content.

SERVES 4
60ml/4 tablespoons ($\frac{1}{4}$ cup) olive oil
90ml/6 tablespoons ($\frac{1}{3}$ cup) red vermouth
5ml (1 teaspoon) dried thyme
salt
freshly ground black pepper
450g (1 lb) veal kidneys, cubed or lambs' kidneys, skinned, cored and halved
450g (1 lb) lamb's liver, cut into 2.5cm (1 in) cubes
chopped parsley to garnish

Combine the oil, wine, thyme and seasoning to taste in a shallow dish. Add the kidney and liver cubes and turn to coat. Leave to marinate for at least 4 hours, turning occasionally.

Thread the kidney and liver cubes alternately on to 4 skewers. Grill (broil) for about 4 minutes on each side, basting with the marinade. Serve on a bed of rice, garnished with parsley.

Cooking time: 4 hours marinating time plus 15 minutes

Lamb Meatballs in Spinach

Spinach leaves are used instead of vine leaves in this adaptation of a traditional Turkish recipe.

SERVES 4
20 large spinach leaves, stalks removed
900g (2 lb) minced (ground) lamb
1 large onion, finely chopped
salt
freshly ground black pepper
5ml (1 teaspoon) paprika
50g/2 oz ($\frac{1}{4}$ cup) butter
425ml/$\frac{3}{4}$ pt (1$\frac{2}{3}$ cups) tomato juice
60ml/4 tablespoons ($\frac{1}{4}$ cup) lemon juice

Blanch the spinach leaves for 2 minutes in boiling water. Then spread them out on a clean glass towel or absorbent paper to drain until needed.

Combine the lamb, onion, seasonings and paprika. Shape into 20 balls and wrap each one in a spinach leaf, folding the leaf sides over the filling and then roll up.

Melt the butter in a large saucepan, then remove from the heat. Pack in the spinach parcels neatly with the seams underneath, in one layer if possible. Pour over the tomato and lemon juices and bring to the boil. Cover the pan and simmer gently for 1$\frac{1}{2}$ hours or until the meatballs are cooked through.

Cooking time: 1 hour 40 minutes

Spiced Bacon Chops (Ham Steaks)

SERVES 4
275ml/$\frac{1}{2}$ pt (1$\frac{1}{4}$ cups) cider
2 cloves
4 mild-cure lean bacon chops (700g/1$\frac{1}{2}$ lb ham steak)
15ml (1 tablespoon) cornflour (cornstarch)
75g/3 oz ($\frac{1}{3}$ cup) Demerara (brown) sugar
2.5ml ($\frac{1}{2}$ teaspoon) dry mustard
1.5ml ($\frac{1}{4}$ teaspoon) ground ginger
1.5ml ($\frac{1}{4}$ teaspoon) grated nutmeg
50g (2 oz) button mushrooms, thinly sliced
4 canned pineapple rings

Heat the oven to 180°C (350°F) gas mark 4. Put the cider and cloves into a saucepan and boil briskly until reduced to 150ml/$\frac{1}{4}$ pt ($\frac{2}{3}$ cup). Cool slightly.

Place the meat in a single layer in a greased baking dish. Combine the cornflour (cornstarch), sugar, mustard, ginger and nutmeg and sprinkle over the top. Surround with the mushrooms and place the pineapple rings on top. Pour in the cider. Cover the dish and bake for 25–30 minutes.

Cooking time: 30–35 minutes

Kebabs or brochettes are always popular: for an inexpensive meal, use kidney and liver instead of beef steak or lamb.

Lamb chops cooked in foil with mushrooms and vegetables become tender and absorb all the vegetable flavours.

Lamb Chops in a Parcel

SERVES 4
2 small courgettes (zucchini), thinly sliced
100g ($\frac{1}{4}$ lb) button mushrooms, thinly sliced
1 small onion, finely chopped
2 ripe tomatoes, blanched, skinned and chopped
1 garlic clove, crushed
5ml (1 teaspoon) dried oregano
30ml (2 tablespoons) tomato paste
15ml (1 tablespoon) hot water
salt
freshly ground black pepper
4 butterfly (shoulder) lamb chops
100g/$\frac{1}{4}$ lb ($\frac{1}{2}$ cup) butter

Heat the oven to 200°C (400°F) gas mark 6. Heat the grill (broiler) to high. Combine the courgettes (zucchini), mushrooms, onion, tomatoes, garlic, oregano, tomato paste and hot water. Season to taste.

Grill (broil) the chops until browned on both sides. Remove from the heat. Place each chop on a square of foil large enough to enclose it comfortably. Cover with the vegetable mixture, then dot each chop with 25g/1 oz (2 tablespoons) of the butter.

Bring up the sides of the foil over the chops and vegetables and fold to seal. Place the parcels on a baking sheet and bake for 25–30 minutes or until the chops are cooked through.
Cooking time : about 1 hour

Breast of Lamb with Mushroom and Watercress Stuffing

Vinegar and water are used as an inexpensive substitute for wine to cook this lamb roll. Use 150ml/$\frac{1}{4}$ pt ($\frac{2}{3}$ cup) white wine if desired. The meat can also be served cold.

SERVES 4
15g/$\frac{1}{2}$ oz (1 tablespoon) butter
100g ($\frac{1}{4}$ lb) mushrooms, finely chopped
1 garlic clove, crushed
1 bunch of watercress
50g (2 oz) cooked ham, cut into strips
30ml (2 tablespoons) fresh white breadcrumbs
salt
freshly ground black pepper
1 large, meaty breast of lamb, trimmed of excess fat and boned
23ml (1$\frac{1}{2}$ tablespoons) white wine vinegar
125ml/4 fl oz ($\frac{1}{2}$ cup) water
1 bayleaf
TO SERVE HOT
white sauce *(page 254)*
5ml (1 teaspoon) mustard
5ml (1 teaspoon) white wine vinegar
5ml (1 teaspoon) fine sugar

Melt the butter in a frying-pan. Add the mushrooms and garlic and cook until most of the moisture has evaporated. Remove from the heat.

Snip the watercress leaves from the stems—reserving the latter—then blanch the leaves in boiling water for 30 seconds. Drain and squeeze dry. Chop the leaves finely and add to the mushrooms. Stir in the ham and breadcrumbs. Season.

Lay the meat flat, fat side down, and spread with the mushroom stuffing. Roll up and tie with string.

Place the lamb roll in a saucepan which is a good fit with 6 watercress stems and the bayleaf. Add the vinegar and just enough hot water to cover the meat and bring to the boil. Skim off the scum that rises to the surface, then cover the pan and simmer very gently for 1–1$\frac{1}{2}$ hours or until the meat is tender.

Heat all the ingredients for the sauce, pour it into a gravy boat to pass.
Cooking time : about 1$\frac{1}{2}$ hours

Sausages with Apples and Grapes

SERVES 4
8 pork sausages
25g/1 oz (2 tablespoons) butter
2 dessert apples, peeled, cored and quartered
2.5ml ($\frac{1}{2}$ teaspoon) sugar
salt and freshly ground black pepper
175g (6 oz) seedless green grapes

Fry the sausages until they are browned on all sides and cooked through. Drain on absorbent paper and keep warm.

Wipe out the frying-pan and melt the butter in it. Add the apples and sprinkle with the sugar and seasoning to taste. Cook, stirring frequently, until the apples are tender. Add the grapes, mix well and cook for an additional 3 minutes.

Spread the apple mixture on the warmed serving platter and arrange the sausages on top.
Cooking time : 15 minutes

Chicken Sauté with Basil

SERVES 2

2 chicken breast portions
salt
freshly ground black pepper
50g/2 oz ($\frac{1}{4}$ cup) butter
125ml/4 fl oz ($\frac{1}{2}$ cup) dry white wine
125ml/4 fl oz ($\frac{1}{2}$ cup) chicken stock
15ml (1 tablespoon) fresh basil, chopped
5ml (1 teaspoon) flour

Rub the chicken breasts all over with salt and pepper. Melt all but 5ml (1 teaspoon) of the butter in a frying-pan. Add the chicken breasts and brown on both sides. Cover the pan and cook gently for a further 30–35 minutes or until the chicken breasts are cooked through. Transfer them to a warmed serving dish and keep hot.

Add the wine, stock and basil to the pan and bring to the boil, stirring well. Boil for 10 minutes or until the liquid has reduced by about half.

Mash together the remaining butter and the flour. Add a little of the hot liquid, then stir this mixture into the rest of the liquid in the pan. Simmer, stirring, until thickened. Pour this sauce over the chicken.
Cooking time: 55–60 minutes

● Try this dish also with tarragon.

Avgolemono Chicken

SERVES 6

1.8kg (4 lb) roasting chicken
grated rind and juice of 1 large lemon
1 large onion, sliced
1 large carrot, sliced
1 bouquet garni
2.5ml ($\frac{1}{2}$ teaspoon) black peppercorns
250g/9 oz ($1\frac{1}{2}$ cups) long-grain rice
salt
freshly ground black pepper
25g/1 oz (2 tablespoons) butter
30ml (2 tablespoons) flour
75g/3 oz ($\frac{3}{4}$ cup) walnuts, chopped
60ml/4 tablespoons ($\frac{1}{4}$ cup) chopped chives
30ml (2 tablespoons) chopped parsley
1 large egg yolk
150ml/$\frac{1}{4}$ pt ($\frac{2}{3}$ cup) thick cream
$\frac{1}{2}$ head of lettuce, shredded

Put the chicken in a saucepan which is a good fit and add the lemon rind, onion, carrot, peppercorns and bouquet garni. Pour in enough warm water to cover the chicken thighs and bring to the boil. Cover the pan and simmer gently for $1\frac{1}{2}$ hours or until the chicken is tender.

Remove the chicken from the pan and keep warm. Strain and measure the cooking liquid and return 575ml/1 pt ($2\frac{1}{2}$ cups) of it to the pan. Boil briskly until reduced to 425ml/$1\frac{3}{4}$ pt ($1\frac{2}{3}$ cups). Set this aside for the sauce.

To cook the rice, you will need twice its volume in unreduced cooking liquid, that is, 700ml/$1\frac{1}{4}$ pt (3 cups). Add water if necessary to make up the amount and salt to taste. Bring to the boil, add the rice, stir once, cover the pan and simmer very gently for 25 minutes or until the rice is tender and the liquid has been absorbed.

Meanwhile, melt the butter in another saucepan. Add the flour and cook, stirring, for 1 minute. Gradually stir in the reduced cooking liquid and the lemon juice and bring to the boil, stirring. Simmer, stirring, until thickened.

Fold most of the nuts, chives and parsley into the rice, season with pepper and spread out on a warmed serving platter. Joint and skin the chicken and arrange the pieces on the rice.

Combine the egg yolk and cream. Add a little of the hot sauce, then stir this mixture into the rest of the sauce. Heat through gently without boiling. Season.

Pour the sauce over the chicken and sprinkle with the rest of the nuts and parsley. Arrange the lettuce around the chicken and sprinkle with the remaining chives.
Cooking time: $2\frac{1}{4}$ hours

For a sophisticated but simple dinner at home for two, there is nothing to beat the delicate flavour of chicken sauté with an aromatic basil sauce.

Beef Olives

SERVES 4

8 slices of lean braising steak (top or
bottom round), 6mm ($\frac{1}{4}$ in) thick and
12.5cm (5 in) square

30ml (2 tablespoons) oil

2 onions, finely chopped

2 carrots, diced

425ml/$\frac{3}{4}$ pt (1$\frac{2}{3}$ cups) beef stock

225g ($\frac{1}{2}$ lb) tomatoes, blanched, skinned,
seeded and chopped

1 garlic clove, crushed

1 bay leaf

salt

freshly ground black pepper

FOR THE STUFFING

175g (6 oz) minced (ground) pork

1 small onion, finely chopped

25g/1 oz (2 tablespoons) butter, softened

25g/1 oz ($\frac{1}{2}$ cup) fresh breadcrumbs

15ml (1 tablespoon) fresh parsley,
chopped

5ml (1 teaspoon) dried sage

grated rind of 1 lemon

1 egg, beaten

6 green olives, stoned and chopped

salt

freshly ground black pepper

*Beef olives make a wonderful party dish,
but are not too expensive to serve to the
family as only 600g (1$\frac{1}{4}$ lb) beef topside
(beef round) is needed to make them.*

Heat the oven to 180°C (350°F) gas mark 4.
Mix together the ingredients for the stuffing, seasoning to taste. Divide the mixture
between the slices of beef. Fold the sides
slightly over the stuffing and then roll up
each beef olive so that the stuffing is
contained neatly inside the meat. Tie each
end with string.

Heat the oil in a frying-pan and brown
the olives on all sides. Transfer them to a
casserole.

Add the onions and carrots to the frying-
pan and cook until softened. Stir in the
stock, tomatoes, garlic, bay leaf and
seasoning to taste and bring to the boil.
Pour this mixture over the beef olives.
Cover the dish tightly and cook in the
oven for 1$\frac{1}{2}$ hours or until the beef is
tender.

Remove the beef olives from the casserole, remove the strings and arrange in a
warmed serving dish. Strain the cooking
liquid and pour over the beef olives.
Cooking time: about 2$\frac{1}{2}$ hours

Baked Spicy Chicken

*A family recipe that demands the minimum
attention from the cook, this dish is made
with chicken thighs. You can substitute
15g/$\frac{1}{2}$ oz (2 tablespoons) broken cornflakes
from the bottom of a packet (box) for part
of the breadcrumbs.*

SERVES 4

8 chicken thighs

50ml/2 fl oz ($\frac{1}{4}$ cup) milk

50g/2 oz ($\frac{2}{3}$ cup) browned dry
breadcrumbs

5ml (1 teaspoon) mixed herbs

5ml (1 teaspoon) salt

5ml (1 teaspoon) paprika

freshly ground black pepper

40g/1$\frac{1}{2}$ oz (3 tablespoons) margarine

Heat the oven to 200°C (400°F) gas mark 6.
Generously grease a gratin dish (baking
pan). Put the crumbs and all the flavourings into a plastic bag. Turn the chicken
thighs in the milk on a plate, then shake
them one by one in the crumbs. Arrange in
the dish, dot with the margarine and bake
for 45 minutes.
Cooking time: 50 minutes

93

Dijon Kidneys

SERVES 3

9 lambs' kidneys, skinned and cored

30ml (2 tablespoons) margarine

50g/2 oz (¼ cup) onion, finely chopped

50ml/2 fl oz (¼ cup) white vermouth

30g (2 tablespoons) flour

150ml/¼ pt (⅝ cup) milk

15ml (1 tablespoon) Dijon mustard

5ml (1 teaspoon) anchovy essence

15ml (1 tablespoon) Worcestershire sauce

pinch cayenne

45ml (3 tablespoons) thick cream

Fry the onion in the margarine in a frying-pan over moderate heat for 5 minutes. Chop the kidneys roughly and add. Cook them over high heat to seal the surfaces, stirring, for 5 minutes.

Sprinkle over the flour and cook again at moderate heat for 12 minutes, stirring the flour into the onions. Add the vermouth and milk and scrape around the pan. Add the mustard and flavourings and cook for 5 minutes. Check the seasonings and add the cream before serving in a ring of boiled rice or noodles.

Cooking time: 20 minutes

French mustard, anchovy essence and Worcestershire sauce give piquancy to the creamy sauce of Dijon kidneys, served in a ring of fluffy boiled rice.

Coronation Chicken

This curry-flavoured mayonnaise is one of the great sauces of the 20th century. Devised for the Jubilee of George V, it was recreated for the coronation banquet for Queen Elizabeth II, which gives its name. It turns cold, boiled chicken into a feast and this is a dish easily multiplied for a bigger party.

SERVES 6

1.8kg (4 lb) chicken, dressed weight

1 carrot

1 celery stalk

1 bouquet garni

5ml (1 teaspoon) peppercorns

1 chicken stock cube

FOR THE MAYONNAISE

15ml (1 tablespoon) olive oil

25g/1 oz (1 tablespoon) onion, chopped

15ml (1 tablespoon) curry powder

5ml (1 teaspoon) tomato paste

175ml/6 oz (¾ cup) red wine

1 bay leaf

pinch of salt

5ml (1 teaspoon) fine sugar

freshly ground black pepper

1 slice of lemon

5ml (1 teaspoon) lemon juice

400ml/14 fl oz (1¾ cups) mayonnaise
(page 252)

15ml (1 tablespoon) apricot jam

50ml/2 fl oz (¼ cup) lightly whipped cream

bunch of watercress to garnish

Put the chicken into a pan that fits it well and add the carrot, celery, peppercorns, bouquet garni and stock cube. Bring to the boil, skimming off any scum, then lower the heat, cover and simmer for 1½ hours. Cool the chicken overnight in the stock.

To make the mayonnaise, pour the oil into a small saucepan and fry the onion for 3 minutes, stirring. Add the curry powder and cook for an additional 2 minutes. Add the tomato paste, wine and bay leaf. Bring to the boil. Add salt, sugar, pepper, lemon slice and juice, then reduce the heat and simmer uncovered for 10 minutes, stirring occasionally. Remove the bay leaf and lemon slice and cool the sauce.

Add the cold onion sauce a little at a time to the mayonnaise, then stir in the jam. Lightly fold the whipped cream into the mayonnaise. Check the seasonings, adding more lemon juice if desired.

Skin the cold chicken and remove all bones and any fat. Cut the flesh into cubes or pull into small strips. Put in a dish and mix with the curry mayonnaise. Leave covered in the refrigerator for 1–2 hours for the flavours to blend. Transfer to a serving dish and garnish with seasonal salad vegetables.

Cooking time: 1½ hours plus chilling, then 1¼ hours plus 2 hours chilling

● This cold curry mayonnaise makes an excellent sauce for leftover turkey, a wonderful dressing for cold potatoes and an interesting sandwich filling.

Lamb Korma

Serve korma with boiled rice and your own home-made pickles.

SERVES 4
450g (1 lb) boned shoulder of lamb, cut in 2.5cm (1 in) cubes
FOR THE MARINADE
275ml/$\frac{1}{2}$ pt (1$\frac{1}{4}$ cups) plain yogurt
15ml (1 tablespoon) ground coriander
45ml (3 tablespoons) ground almonds
10ml (2 teaspoons) ground cumin
5ml (1 teaspoon) ground turmeric
5ml (1 teaspoon) ground chilli
2.5ml ($\frac{1}{2}$ teaspoon) ground black pepper
FOR THE DISH
50g/2 oz ($\frac{1}{4}$ cup) butter
1 small onion, finely chopped
2 garlic cloves, crushed
12mm ($\frac{1}{2}$ in) piece fresh ginger, finely chopped
5ml (1 teaspoon) ground cloves
5ml (1 teaspoon) ground cardamom
piece of cinnamon 5cm (2 in) long
100g ($\frac{1}{4}$ lb) creamed coconut (optional)
150ml/$\frac{1}{4}$ pt ($\frac{2}{3}$ cup) boiling water
150ml/$\frac{1}{4}$ pt ($\frac{2}{3}$ cup) thickened yogurt (*page 249*)

Stir the coriander, 15ml (1 tablespoon) almonds and cumin, turmeric, chilli and pepper into the yogurt. Add the lamb and leave to marinate for 1$\frac{1}{2}$ hours.

Clarify the butter by heating in a small pan and then pouring through a cheese-cloth inside a strainer or a coffee filter-paper. Put the clarified butter in a large pan and add the onions and garlic. Cook, stirring, for 4 minutes. Add the ginger, cloves, cardamom and cinnamon and cook another 4 minutes.

Add the meat and marinade. Simmer, covered, for 5 minutes then stir in the remaining almonds. Cover and cook over low heat for 1$\frac{1}{4}$ hours until the meat is tender. Stir occasionally to prevent sticking. Add a little extra water if necessary.

Just before the end of cooking time, make the coconut milk, if using, by putting the creamed coconut in a bowl and pouring on the boiling water. Mix with a spoon until smooth. Five minutes before the end of cooking time stir into the pot and heat through. Alternatively, stir in the thickened yogurt. Remove the cinnamon stick and serve.

Cooking time: 1$\frac{1}{2}$ hours marinating then 2 hours 10 minutes

● This dish can be made with pork.

Beef and Sausage Ring

SERVES 8
50g/2 oz ($\frac{1}{4}$ cup) dripping
175g/6 oz ($\frac{3}{4}$ cup) onion, finely chopped
2 garlic cloves, finely chopped
700g (1$\frac{1}{2}$ lb) minced (ground) beef
225g ($\frac{1}{2}$ lb) pork sausagemeat
400g (14 oz) canned tomatoes
15ml (1 tablespoon) Worcestershire sauce
5ml (1 teaspoon) dried thyme
5ml (1 teaspoon) paprika
salt and freshly ground black pepper
dash of Tabasco
75g/3 oz (1 cup) fine, dry breadcrumbs
2 medium-sized eggs, beaten

Heat the oven to 180°C (350°F) gas mark 4. Melt the dripping in a large saucepan. Fry the onions and garlic over medium heat until softened. Add the beef and sausagemeat and mix them up.

Add the tomatoes with their juice, Worcestershire sauce, thyme, paprika and Tabasco. Stir to mix and then taste for seasoning. Add the breadcrumbs and stir again. Remove from the heat and stir in the beaten eggs, mixing well.

Pack the mixture firmly into a greased 22.5cm (9 in) ring mould. Bake for 1$\frac{1}{4}$–1$\frac{1}{2}$ hours or until cooked and set. Turn out.

Cooking time: 1$\frac{1}{2}$–1$\frac{3}{4}$ hours

Devilled Country Style Pork Ribs

SERVES 4
15g/$\frac{1}{2}$ oz (1 tablespoon) butter
30ml (2 tablespoons) oil
4 thick pork spare rib chops (country-style pork ribs)
15ml (1 tablespoon) chilli sauce
30ml (2 tablespoons) lemon juice
1 small onion, finely chopped
10ml (2 teaspoons) prepared mustard
15ml (1 tablespoon) Worcestershire sauce
125ml/4 fl oz ($\frac{1}{2}$ cup) water
30ml (2 tablespoons) black treacle (molasses)
2.5ml ($\frac{1}{2}$ teaspoon) salt

Melt the butter with the oil in a frying-pan. Add the meat and brown on both sides. Combine the remaining ingredients and pour into the pan. Bring to the boil, then cover the pan and cook gently, stirring occasionally, for 40 minutes or until the meat is cooked through.

Cooking time: 50 minutes

Duck Pie

This open flan is an unusual way of making one duck serve 8 people. The sweet fruit combines excellently with the rather fat duck meat. Use the duck bones for aspic.

SERVES 8
$\frac{3}{4}$ × rich shortcrust (*page 241*)
1 duck, 1.8kg (4 lb) oven-ready weight
grated juice and rind of 1 orange
700g (1$\frac{1}{2}$ lb) cooking apples, peeled, cored and thinly sliced
25g/1 oz (2 tablespoons) butter
45ml (3 tablespoons) fine sugar
1 onion, chopped finely
150ml/$\frac{1}{4}$ pt ($\frac{2}{3}$ cup) thick cream
15ml (1 tablespoon) fresh sage, chopped
salt and freshly ground black pepper
275ml/$\frac{1}{2}$ pt (1$\frac{1}{4}$ cups) aspic (*page 253*)

Heat the oven to 200°C (400°F) gas mark 6. Prick the duck skin all over with a fork to help the fat to flow out. Season inside and out with salt and pepper and put the orange rind inside. Put the duck in a roasting tin (pan) and pour the orange juice over it. Roast for 1$\frac{1}{2}$ hours, basting occasionally.

While the duck is cooking, line a 25cm (10 in) flan case or pie plate with the pastry. Bake blind in the oven with the duck for 15–20 minutes. Set the pastry aside to cool.

Melt the butter in a pan and add the apples without any water. Cook over a low heat until reduced to a dry pulp. Stir the sugar into the apples and remove from the heat.

Put the onion into a pan with the cream and simmer for 15 minutes. Stir into the apples with the sage and seasoning. Put the apple and onion mixture into the cold pastry shell.

Remove the duck from the oven and leave until cold. Cut the breast fillets away from the duck, running the knife close to the carcass. Peel off the skin and then slice each fillet into large thin slices.

Remove the remaining meat from the duck, discarding skin and bone. Chop the meat roughly and spread it over the apples. Arrange the breast slices, overlapping, on top of the chopped duck, so that the inside of the pie is hidden. Press down slightly all over with the back of a spoon so that the flan is compact.

Pour over the aspic to glaze the flan and leave to set for about 2 hours.

Cooking time: 2 hours with 2 cooling periods of 2 hours

Fish and Shellfish

Stuffed Whiting Rolls

SERVES 4

2 × 450g (1 lb) whiting, filleted and skinned

75g/3 oz (⅓ cup) butter

30ml (2 tablespoons) chopped fresh herbs, such as chives, mint, parsley, balm

salt

freshly ground black pepper

grated rind and juice of 1 lemon

40g/1½ oz (¾ cup) fresh white breadcrumbs

Heat the grill (broiler) to moderate. Cut each fillet in half lengthwise, so you have 8.

Cream the butter with the herbs, seasoning, lemon rind and a few drops of thr lemon juice. Beat in the breadcrumbs. Divide this mixture into 8 portions and spread over the fish pieces. Roll them up and tie with string or secure with wooden cocktail sticks (picks).

These whiting rolls are stuffed with herbs, butter, lemon and breadcrumbs.

Place the fish rolls in one layer in a flame-proof gratin dish and sprinkle over the remaining lemon juice. Grill (broil) for 5–8 minutes on each side or until the fish flakes easily.

Cooking time: 25 minutes

Fish Fillets with Artichoke Sauce

SERVES 6

900g (2 lb) fillets of plaice or sole

salt

freshly ground black pepper

1 small onion, thinly sliced into rings

1 celery stalk, chopped

1 mace blade

1 bouquet garni

6 white peppercorns, bruised

275ml/½ pt (1¼ cups) fish stock

175ml/6 fl oz (¾ cup) dry white wine

15ml (1 tablespoon) lemon juice

15ml (1 tablespoon) fresh parsley, chopped

FOR THE SAUCE

25g/1 oz (2 tablespoons) butter

25g/1 oz (¼ cup) flour

salt

freshly ground black pepper

pinch of cayenne pepper

60ml/4 tablespoons (¼ cup) thick cream

3 globe artichoke hearts, cooked, drained and chopped

Season the fillets and place them in an even layer over the bottom of a deep frying-pan. Sprinkle over the onion rings, celery, mace, bouquet garni and peppercorns, then pour in the stock, wine and lemon juice. Bring to the boil, then cover the pan and simmer for 8–12 minutes.

Transfer the fillets to a warmed serving dish and keep hot. Strain the cooking liquid and reserve.

Melt the butter for the sauce in a saucepan. Add the flour and cook, stirring, for 2 minutes. Gradually stir in the reserved cooking liquid and bring to the boil, stirring. Adjust the seasoning and stir in the cayenne, cream and artichoke hearts. Heat through gently. Pour this sauce over the fillets and sprinkle with the parsley.

Cooking time: 25–30 minutes

Crabmeat Pie

Crabs can be cheap in summer and even canned crab is not expensive when shared among a number of people. If you use a pottery gratin dish, heat a baking sheet in the oven and stand the dish on it. Allow 5 extra minutes to bake the pastry blind and up to 10 extra minutes to set the custard.

You will probably have to buy a bulb of fennel to get the fennel leaves, so serve a fennel and orange or fennel and cucumber salad with the flan.

SERVES 6
900g (2 lb) boiled crab or 450g (1 lb) crabmeat
5ml (1 teaspoon) lemon juice
15ml (1 tablespoon) fresh fennel leaves, chopped
1 small onion, finely chopped
30ml (2 tablespoons) parsley, chopped
30ml (2 tablespoons) dry sherry
$\frac{5}{8}$ × rich shortcrust pastry *(page 241)*
4 eggs, beaten
350ml/12 fl oz (1$\frac{1}{2}$ cups) thin cream
1.5ml ($\frac{1}{4}$ teaspoon) ground cinnamon
salt and freshly ground black pepper

Clean the crab, removing the white gills and the green-brown stomach bag which lies just behind the head. All the rest of the shell contents—meat and creamy curd—are eatable. Scrape the meat out of the shell and break the claws, legs and body with a hammer. Scrape the meat out of the crevices, working in sections, with a grapefruit knife. Discard all bits of shell and flake the meat. Mix the meat, lemon juice, fennel leaves, onion, parsley and sherry, cover and leave to marinate.

Heat the oven to 200°C (400°F) gas mark 6. Roll out the pastry and use to line a 28cm (11 in) flan tin (pie dish) or an oval gratin dish 28cm (11 in) long. Bake blind for 15 minutes.

Reduce the oven heat to 180°C (350°F) gas mark 4. Spoon the crab mixture into the pastry shell and spread it out evenly. Combine the eggs, cream and seasonings and pour over the crab mixture. Return to the oven for 40–45 minutes or until the custard is set and an inserted skewer comes out clean. Serve warm or cold.

Cooking time: 20 minutes to clean a crab, then 70 minutes, plus chilling time

●For prawn pie, spread the cold, cooked pastry case with 15ml (1 tablespoon) Dijon mustard. Scatter over 221g ($\frac{1}{2}$ lb) peeled prawns. Blanch, skin and deseed 450g (1 lb) tomatoes. Chop roughly and add. Mix 2 eggs, 1 yolk, pinch garlic salt, plenty of pepper, 175ml/6 fl oz ($\frac{3}{4}$ cup) cream and 150ml/$\frac{1}{4}$ pt ($\frac{2}{3}$ cup) milk, pour over and bake as in recipe.

This rich crabmeat pie is flavoured with fennel and is delicious hot or cold.

Cod Balls

SERVES 6
4 medium-sized potatoes, chopped
900g (2 lb) cod fillets, skinned and chopped
100g/$\frac{1}{4}$ lb ($\frac{1}{2}$ cup) butter
15ml (1 tablespoon) fresh parsley, chopped
pinch of cayenne pepper
salt
freshly ground black pepper
1 egg, beaten
flour for coating

Put the potatoes and cod into a saucepan, just cover with water and bring to the boil. Cover and simmer for 15–20 minutes or until the potatoes are soft but not mushy. Drain the fish and potatoes and return them to the saucepan. Heat gently for about 2 minutes to dry the fish and potatoes. Remove from the heat.

Add 25g/1 oz (2 tablespoons) of the butter, the parsley, cayenne and seasoning to taste and mix well, mashing the potatoes and flaking the fish to combine. Add the egg. With floured hands, shape the mixture into small balls.

Melt the remaining butter in a frying-pan. Add the cod balls and fry for about 4 minutes or until crisp and brown all over. Serve very hot. Pass a parsley or mornay sauce separately if desired.

Cooking time: about 30 minutes

97

Cod and Parsley Pie

SERVES 4
450g (1 lb) cod fillets, cooked, skinned and flaked
120ml/8 tablespoons ($\frac{1}{2}$ cup) fresh parsley, chopped
275ml/$\frac{1}{2}$ pt (1$\frac{1}{4}$ cups) béchamel sauce (page 252)
5ml (1 teaspoon) lemon juice
700g (1$\frac{1}{2}$ lb) made-weight of frozen, flaky pastry, thawed (pastry for 2-crust pie)
1 egg yolk, lightly beaten

Heat the oven to 190°C (375°F) gas mark 5. Combine the cod, parsley, sauce and lemon juice in a large mixing bowl.

Roll out the pastry to a square about 6mm ($\frac{1}{4}$ in) thick. Trim the edges, then roll the pastry round the pin and lift it on to a baking sheet, so that it lies like a diamond. Brush all the edges with water. Spoon the fish filling into the centre. Lift the four corners of the pastry square up over the filling to meet in the centre. Pinch the seams together. Brush the pie top with the egg yolk.

Bake for 30–40 minutes, or until the pastry is risen and golden brown. Serve hot.
Cooking time: 1 hour

The fish filling of cod and parsley pie is wrapped in golden-brown flaky pastry.

Baked Fish Provençale

SERVES 4
4 cod steaks
4 tomatoes, skinned and sliced
100g ($\frac{1}{4}$ lb) mushrooms, sliced
1 green (bell) pepper, cored, seeded and sliced
15ml (1 tablespoon) fresh parsley, chopped
salt
freshly ground black pepper

Heat the oven to 200°C (400°F) gas mark 6. Put each cod steak on a square of foil large enough to enclose it. Cover it with tomato, mushroom and green pepper slices, then sprinkle with parsley and seasoning. Bring up the foil and fold it over to enclose the fish.

Place the parcels on a baking sheet and bake for 40 minutes or until the fish flakes easily.
Cooking time: 50 minutes

● Omit the mushrooms and add 5ml (1 teaspoon) curry powder.

Roll Mops

No need to buy pickled herrings from a delicatessen when you can make them at home. They will keep for 5–6 weeks and will provide a ready salad when you do not feel like cooking.

SERVES 8
8 fresh herrings, cleaned, boned and without heads
50g/2 oz ($\frac{1}{4}$ cup) coarse salt
575 ml/1 pt (2$\frac{1}{2}$ cups) cold water
575ml/1 pt (2$\frac{1}{2}$ cups) white wine vinegar or cider
1 large mild onion, sliced in rings
4 small pickled gherkins, halved lengthwise
2 bay leaves
6 white peppercorns
15ml (1 tablespoon) mixed pickling spice

Dissolve the salt in the cold water. Bone the herrings and lay them open in a dish. Cover with the brine and leave for 2 hours. Bring the vinegar and spices to the boil. Set aside to cool for 1 hour.

Drain the fish and lay open, skin side downward. Put some onion and gherkin on each herring and roll up towards the tail.

Pack the herrings into 2 × 350ml (12 fl oz) jars. Divide the bay leaves and peppercorn between the jars and add any remaining onion. Cover the fish with the stirred vinegar. Top up with more vinegar if the fish are not covered. Cover with a non-corrosive airtight lid. Keep refrigerated and eat within 6 weeks.
Cooking time: 2 hours 20 minutes including marinating time

Jellied Fish Mould

SERVES 6
900g (2 lb) white fish fillets, cooked, skinned and flaked
30ml (2 tablespoons) chives, chopped
150ml/$\frac{1}{4}$ pt ($\frac{2}{3}$ cup) mayonnaise *(page 250)*
150ml/$\frac{1}{4}$ pt ($\frac{2}{3}$ cup) sour cream
salt
freshly ground black pepper
25g/1 oz (1 tablespoon) gelatin
125ml/4 fl oz ($\frac{1}{2}$ cup) fish stock
1 head lettuce, shredded
8 stuffed green olives, sliced

Combine the fish, chives, mayonnaise, sour cream and seasoning. Sprinkle the gelatin over the fish stock in a heat-proof cup and let it stand 5 minutes to soften. Place the cup in a pan of hot water, stirring gently until the gelatin is dissolved. Stir the dissolved gelatin into the fish mixture. Pour into a dampened decorative mould and chill for 2 hours or until firmly set.

Turn out on to a serving platter and surround with the shredded lettuce. Garnish with the olive slices.

Cooking time: 10 minutes plus 2 hours setting time

Kedgeree

This classic combination of fish and rice, brought home by the British from India, has long been associated with a substantial breakfast. Some people may prefer to omit the curry powder and onions at this time of day. It makes a filling family supper.

SERVES 4
350g ($\frac{3}{4}$ lb) smoked haddock fillets
1 medium-sized onion, finely chopped
75g/3 oz (5 tablespoons) butter
175g/6 oz (1 cup) Basmati or long-grain rice
5ml (1 teaspoon) curry paste *(page 254)* or powder
25g/1 oz (3 tablespoons) raisins
575ml/1 pt (2$\frac{1}{2}$ cups) water
2 hard-boiled eggs
30ml (2 tablespoons) parsley, chopped

Pour boiling water over the smoked haddock fillets. Leave for 5 minutes and then drain. Remove the skin and flake the fish.

Melt $\frac{1}{3}$ of the butter in a heavy-bottomed pan over moderate heat. Cook the onion for 2 minutes, stirring, then lower the heat and add the remaining butter, the rice and the curry paste or powder. Turn the rice in the butter and cook for about 3 minutes.

Pour in the water and add the raisins. Bring to the boil then cover and simmer for 10 minutes. Add the fish and simmer a further 5 minutes until all the liquid has gone. Stir to prevent the rice sticking. Turn into a warmed serving dish and mix in the chopped eggs. Sprinkle with parsley and serve immediately.

Cooking time: 30 minutes

● The proportion of fish to rice, and the type of fish used, will vary according to how rich or poor you are feeling. When it is a question of stretching a small piece of fish to feed many mouths, use an equal weight of uncooked rice to the weight of fish, but never exceed this.

● For a party dish for 6, 450g (1 lb) cooked salmon from a salmon tail can be combined with 225g/$\frac{1}{2}$ lb (1$\frac{1}{3}$ cups) rice, 1 onion, 3 hard-boiled eggs and 50g/2 oz ($\frac{1}{2}$ cup) flaked almonds. Use 100g/$\frac{1}{4}$ lb ($\frac{1}{2}$ cup) melted butter with 45ml (3 tablespoons) thick cream and 4 drops of cayenne or hot pepper sauce instead of the curry. Garnish with chopped chives.

Seafood Crêpes

SERVES 4–6
crêpe batter *(page 245)*
30ml (2 tablespoons) oil
30ml (2 heaped tablespoons) bean sprouts
30ml (2 tablespoons) finely chopped spring onions (scallions)
90ml/6 tablespoons ($\frac{1}{3}$ cup) dry white vermouth
30ml (2 tablespoons) fresh parsley, chopped
5ml (1 teaspoon) fresh chervil, chopped
175g ($\frac{1}{2}$ lb) crab meat, flaked
175g ($\frac{1}{2}$ lb) boiled, peeled prawns (shrimp)
salt and freshly ground black pepper
25g/1 oz (2 tablespoons) butter
15g/$\frac{1}{2}$ oz (2 tablespoons) flour
575ml/1 pt (2$\frac{1}{2}$ cups) milk

Make the crêpes and keep them warm, layered with greaseproof or waxed paper, on a plate over a saucepan of hot water.

Heat the oil in a saucepan. Add the bean sprouts and spring onions (scallions) and turn them for 1 minute. Add the vermouth, bring to the boil and boil briskly until reduced by half. Remove from the heat and stir in half the parsley, the chervil, crab meat, prawns and seasoning. Return to a very low heat and heat through.

Meanwhile, melt the butter in another saucepan. Add the flour and cook, stirring, for 2 minutes. Gradually stir in the milk, then bring to the boil, stirring. Simmer until thickened. Stir in the seafood mixture and adjust the seasoning.

Divide the seafood mixture between the pancakes and roll them up. Arrange on a warmed serving dish and sprinkle with the rest of the parsley.

Cooking time: about 45 minutes

● Up to one-third cooked white fish can be used for this stuffing.

● If desired, 50g (2 oz) mushrooms can be substituted for the beansprouts.

● In winter use mussels or clams for half the quantity. You will need 1kg/2 pt (2 lb) mussels to get 100g ($\frac{1}{4}$ lb) flesh. Open the cleaned mussels in a dry pan, covered, over low heat. Use the strained mussel liquor to make the sauce, making it up to 575ml/1 pt (2$\frac{1}{2}$ cups) with milk.

To make these tempting seafood crêpes, you will need a 450g (1 lb) crab and $\frac{1}{2}$ kg/2 pt (1 lb) prawns in their shells. Other seafoods can also be used in season.

with the lid of the pan and steam for 10–15 minutes, depending on the thickness of the fillets.

Meanwhile, melt 25g/1 oz (2 tablespoons) of the butter in a saucepan. Add the cucumber, cover the pan and cook gently for 5 minutes.

Melt the remaining butter in another pan. Add the flour and cook, stirring, for 1 minute. Gradually stir in the milk and bring to the boil, stirring. Simmer until thickened. Add the cucumber, chives and seasoning and heat through gently.

Transfer the fish to a warmed serving platter. Pour the fish juices into the sauce, stir well, then pour the sauce over the fish.
Cooking time: 20 minutes

Smoked Salmon and Sour Cream Quiche

A flan makes the most of this luxurious fish, spreading it among several diners. Trimmings of salmon can be used, which are usually sold at a reduced price. The quiche will serve 6 as an appetizer or 4 for a main course.

SERVES 4–6
$\frac{5}{8}$ × **rich shortcrust** *(page 241)*
175g (6 oz) smoked salmon trimmings
4 medium-sized eggs
275ml/$\frac{1}{2}$ pt (1$\frac{1}{4}$ cups) milk
150ml/$\frac{1}{4}$ pt ($\frac{2}{3}$ cup) sour cream
salt
freshly ground black pepper
25g/1 oz (2 tablespoons) butter

Heat the oven to 200°C (400°F) gas mark 6. Line a 20cm (8 in) flan ring or pie dish with the pastry. Blind bake for 20 minutes.

Beat together in a bowl the eggs, milk, cream, salt and pepper. Cut the salmon into 5 × 1.2cm (2 × $\frac{1}{2}$ in) strips.

Remove the pastry case from the oven and reduce the oven temperature to 160°C (325°F) gas mark 3. Pour the egg mixture into the pastry and carefully arrange the smoked salmon strips over the surface. Cut the butter into small pieces and dot over the salmon. Return the quiche to the centre of the oven and bake for 40 minutes or until the filling is set. Serve cold.
Cooking time: 70 minutes plus 2–3 hours chilling time

● For a family dish, substitute 175g (6 oz) drained canned tuna, putting this into the flan (pie case) before the custard.

Sardines with Watercress

SERVES 4
12 fresh sardines, cleaned
30ml (2 tablespoons) oil
1 bunch of watercress, finely chopped
15ml (1 tablespoon) chopped parsley
225ml/8 fl oz (1 cup) mayonnaise *(page 250)*
salt
freshly ground black pepper

Heat the grill (broiler) to high. Arrange the sardines in one layer in the grill pan and brush with half the oil. Grill (broil) for 3–5 minutes or until lightly browned, then turn the sardines over, brush with the rest of the oil and cook for a further 3–5 minutes.

Meanwhile, combine the watercress, parsley, mayonnaise and seasoning in a serving bowl. Serve the sardines hot accompanied by the watercress sauce.
Cooking time: 7–10 minutes

Fresh or frozen sardines are delicious freshly grilled (broiled) and served with mayonnaise-based watercress sauce.

Steamed Fillets with Chive and Cucumber Sauce

SERVES 4
4 fillets of plaice (or flounder), skinned
salt
freshly ground black pepper
juice of $\frac{1}{2}$ a lemon
50g/2 oz ($\frac{1}{4}$ cup) butter
$\frac{1}{2}$ small cucumber, diced small
25g/1 oz ($\frac{1}{4}$ cup) flour
275ml/$\frac{1}{2}$ pt (1$\frac{1}{4}$ cups) milk
30ml (2 tablespoons) chives, chopped

Season the fillets and sprinkle them with lemon juice. Fold each fillet in three and place on a greased, heatproof plate. Cover with greased foil. Place the plate over a saucepan of boiling water, cover the plate

Fish Steaks in Sweet and Sour Sauce

Use reconstituted pineapple juice for this recipe and drink the rest, or use for a dessert.

SERVES 4
4 large cod, haddock or halibut steaks
50g/2 oz ($\frac{1}{2}$ cup) seasoned flour
1 egg, beaten
75g/3 oz (1 cup) rolled oats
60ml/4 tablespoons ($\frac{1}{4}$ cup) oil
FOR THE SAUCE
45ml (3 tablespoons) tomato paste
45ml (3 tablespoons) soft brown sugar
1.5ml ($\frac{1}{4}$ teaspoon) ground ginger
1 small garlic clove, crushed
15ml (1 tablespoon) soy sauce
30ml (2 tablespoons) white wine vinegar
275ml/$\frac{1}{2}$ pt (1$\frac{1}{4}$ cups) pineapple juice
salt and freshly ground black pepper
10ml (2 teaspoons) cornflour (cornstarch) dissolved in 30ml (2 tablespoons) of the pineapple juice

Coat the fish steaks first with the flour, then with egg and finally with the oats. Heat the oil in a frying-pan. Add the fish steaks and brown on both sides. Remove the steaks from the pan.

Add the sauce ingredients, except the cornflour (cornstarch), to the pan and bring to the boil, stirring. Stir in the cornflour and simmer for 2 minutes.

Return the fish steaks to the pan. Cover the pan and simmer for 10 minutes or until the fish is cooked through.

Cooking time: about 30 minutes

Scottish Crumble

SERVES 4
450g (1 lb) smoked haddock fillets
65g/2$\frac{1}{2}$ oz (5 tablespoons) butter
6 hard-boiled eggs, sliced
30ml (2 tablespoons) chives, chopped
60ml/4 tablespoons ($\frac{1}{4}$ cup) fresh parsley, chopped
salt
freshly ground black pepper
6 tomatoes, sliced
75g (3 oz) fresh wholewheat breadcrumbs
2.5ml ($\frac{1}{2}$ teaspoon) dried thyme
2.5ml ($\frac{1}{2}$ teaspoon) dried marjoram

Heat the oven to 190°C (375°F) gas mark 5. Poach the haddock for 10 minutes or until it is cooked and flakes easily. With a slotted spoon lift the fillets into a bowl.

When it has cooled slightly, discard all skin and flake the fish, adding 40g/1$\frac{1}{2}$ oz (3 tablespoons) of the butter. Add the eggs, chives and parsley. Season the fish and mix together gently.

Cover the bottom of a greased baking dish with half the tomato slices. Spoon over the fish mixture and cover with the rest of the tomato slices. Combine the breadcrumbs and dried herbs. Press half this mixture on top of the tomato slices and dot with 15g/$\frac{1}{2}$ oz (1 tablespoon) butter. Bake for 10 minutes.

Sprinkle over the rest of the breadcrumb mixture and dot with the remaining butter. Bake for a further 15–20 minutes and serve hot.

Cooking time: 45 minutes

Egg and Cucumber Ring

This very economical jellied ring stretches a small quantity of prawns (shrimp) for 6 people. You will need to buy 240g ($\frac{1}{2}$ lb) in the shell, plus extra if you would like a shellfish garnish for a party.

SERVES 6
15g/$\frac{1}{2}$ oz (3$\frac{1}{2}$ teaspoons) gelatin
60ml (4 tablespoons) cold water
400ml/14 fl oz (1$\frac{3}{4}$ cups) chicken stock
22.5ml (1$\frac{1}{2}$ tablespoons) lemon juice
5ml (1 teaspoon) paprika
salt
freshly ground black pepper
60ml/4 tablespoons ($\frac{1}{2}$ cup) medium-dry sherry
100g ($\frac{1}{4}$ lb) peeled prawns (shrimp)
$\frac{1}{2}$ medium-sized cucumber, peeled and thinly sliced
2 hard-boiled eggs, sliced
1 small lettuce, shredded

Soften the gelatin in the water then dissolve over low heat. Stir in the stock, lemon juice, paprika, seasoning and sherry. Chill in a bowl until the mixture begins to thicken.

Pour a little of the stock mixture into a rinsed out 1.1L (2 pt) ring mould to cover the bottom in a thin layer. Put in the freezer briefly to set.

Arrange the prawns on the jelly layer, then dribble over a little more stock. Return to the freezer to set.

Arrange the cucumber and egg slices, alternately, in the mould, reserving a few cucumber slices for the garnish. Pour over the remaining stock mixture. Chill until set.

Unmould the ring on to a serving plate. Arrange the shredded lettuce and reserved cucumber slices around the ring and serve.

Cooking time: about 1$\frac{1}{4}$ hours plus chilling time

● A pretty garnish for this ring, for a party, is made from slices of hard-boiled egg with false caviar—black lumpfish roe—piled on the yolk. Arrange a sprig of parsley between each slice.
● Alternatively, set the lumpfish roe in the bottom of the mould. Garnish the ring with prawns (shrimp) on tomato slices.

Coated with rolled oats, these fish steaks in sweet and sour sauce make an excellent supper dish for all the family.

101

Rice and Pasta

Italian Prawn (Shrimp) Risotto

SERVES 4

50g/2 oz (¼ cup) butter

30ml (2 tablespoons) oil

1 large onion, finely chopped

1 garlic clove, finely chopped

1 medium-sized red (bell) pepper, cored, seeded and diced

100g (¼ lb) button mushrooms, chopped

10ml (2 teaspoons) fresh basil, chopped

salt

freshly ground black pepper

350g (¾ lb) Italian rice (1¾ cups long-grain rice)

350g (¾ lb) boiled, peeled prawns (shrimp)

850ml/1½ pt (3¾ cups) boiling fish stock or light chicken stock

50g/2 oz (½ cup) grated Parmesan cheese

Melt half the butter with the oil in a saucepan. Fry the onion, garlic and red (bell) pepper until softened. Stir in the mushrooms, basil and seasoning and cook for a further 2 minutes.

Add the rice and cook, stirring frequently, for 5 minutes. Stir in the prawns (shrimp), then add about one-third of the fish or chicken stock. Keep the mixture bubbling and stir occasionally. When the liquid has been absorbed, add another third of the stock, then the remainder when that has been absorbed.

Stir in the cheese and the rest of the butter and serve hot.

Cooking time: about 35 minutes

Fettucine alla Romana

SERVES 6

65g/2½ oz (5 tablespoons) butter

1 large onion, chopped

1 garlic clove, chopped

400g (14 oz) canned tomatoes

60ml/4 tablespoons (¼ cup) red wine or vermouth

100g (¼ lb) mushrooms, sliced

5ml (1 teaspoon) sugar

salt

freshly ground black pepper

450g (1 lb) fettucine noodles

15ml (1 tablespoon) vegetable oil

30ml (2 tablespoons) grated Parmesan cheese

Melt 50g/2 oz (¼ cup) of the butter in a saucepan. Fry the onion and garlic until softened. Stir in the tomatoes with their liquid, wine or vermouth, mushrooms, sugar and seasoning. Cover and cook gently for 20 minutes.

Meanwhile, cook the fettucine in boiling salted water with the added oil for 5–7 minutes or until just tender. Drain well and put in a warmed serving dish. Add the remaining butter and toss to coat the noodles. Pour over the tomato sauce and sprinkle with the cheese.

Cooking time: 30 minutes

Risi e Bisi (Rice with Peas)

This classic Venetian risotto combines rice with pulses for a perfect protein balance. It will serve 3–4 as a main course and up to 6 as an appetizer or side dish.

SERVES 4

50g/2 oz (⅓ cup) ham, chopped

1 small onion, chopped

350g (¾ lb) peas, shelled weight

75g/3 oz (6 tablespoons) butter

850ml/1½ pt (3¾ cups) warm chicken stock

175g/6 oz Italian rice (1 cup long-grain rice)

25g/1 oz (¼ cup) grated Parmesan cheese

Put 50g (4 tablespoons) butter in a large pan. Add the onion, peas and ham and cook for 1 minute, stirring to coat with butter.

Add about 150ml/¼ pt (⅔ cup) stock, bring to the boil and add the rice. Add about 550ml/1 pt (1¼ cups) more stock, cover and cook gently without stirring until the stock is absorbed—about 20 minutes. Add the remaining stock in two batches. When the rice is soft and creamy, stir in the remaining butter and cheese.

This dish is more liquid than other risottos and is traditionally eaten with a spoon.

Cooking time: about 45 minutes

Italian prawn risotto makes good use of a small quantity of boiled prawns.

● For zucchini risotto to serve 6, fry 2 chopped garlic cloves and 450g (1 lb) sliced courgettes (zucchini) in the butter. Add 400g (14 oz) canned tomatoes with their juice and 75ml/3 fl oz ($\frac{3}{8}$ cup) white vermouth and bring to the boil. Add the rice as above, in batches, with 900ml 1 pt 12 fl oz (4 cups) hot chicken stock and serve with grated Parmesan.

Pan Pizza

SERVES 4–6

225g/$\frac{1}{2}$ lb (2 cups) self-raising flour
pinch of salt
60ml/4 tablespoons ($\frac{1}{4}$ cup) oil
45–60ml (3–4 tablespoons) water
400g (14 oz) canned tomatoes, drained and chopped
175g/6 oz (1$\frac{1}{2}$ cups) Cheddar cheese, grated
5ml (1 teaspoon) garlic powder
5ml (1 teaspoon) dried oregano
50g (2 oz) canned anchovy fillets, drained
10 pimiento-stuffed green olives

A flash in the pan pizza—this professional pizza is produced in half an hour from your reserve stock of ingredients.

Sift the flour and salt into a bowl. Make a well in the centre and pour in half the oil and 45ml (3 tablespoons) of water. Mix together to make a soft dough, adding the rest of the water if necessary. Knead the dough until smooth, then roll out to a round to fit the bottom of a 23cm (9 in) frying-pan.

Heat the remaining oil in the frying-pan. Place the dough circle in the pan and fry gently for 5 minutes or until the under-side is lightly browned. Turn the dough over and fry for an additional 5 minutes.

Heat the grill (broiler) to moderate. Spread the tomatoes over the dough and sprinkle with the cheese, garlic powder and herbs. Make a lattice of anchovies on top and place a stuffed olive in the centre of each anchovy square.

Grill (broil) the pizza top until the cheese is melted and golden brown.
Cooking time: 30 minutes

Spaghetti with Pesto Sauce

SERVES 6

50g/2 oz ($\frac{1}{2}$ cup) fresh basil, finely chopped
3 garlic cloves, chopped
25g/1 oz ($\frac{1}{4}$ cup) pine kernels (Indian nuts) or blanched almonds
50g/2 oz ($\frac{1}{2}$ cup) Parmesan cheese, grated
salt
freshly ground black pepper
150ml/$\frac{1}{4}$ pt ($\frac{2}{3}$ cup) olive oil
350g ($\frac{3}{4}$ lb) spaghetti
15ml (1 tablespoon) oil

Put the basil, garlic and nuts in a mortar and pound with a pestle to a smooth paste. Alternatively, process in a blender. Work in the cheese and seasoning. Gradually mix in the olive oil, adding just enough to make a sauce consistency.

Meanwhile, cook the spaghetti in boiling salted water with the spoonful of oil until just tender—about 10 minutes. Drain well and turn into a warmed serving dish. Add the pesto sauce and toss well together.
Cooking time: 10 minutes

103

Macaroni with Green Pea Sauce

SERVES 4

30ml (2 tablespoons) oil
1 medium-sized onion, chopped
4 lean bacon slices, diced
700g (1½ lb) peas, weighed after shelling
225ml/8 fl oz (1 cup) water
5ml (1 teaspoon) fresh basil, chopped
2.5ml (½ teaspoon) fresh dill, chopped
salt and freshly ground black pepper
350g (¾ lb) macaroni
15ml (1 tablespoon) vegetable oil
125ml/4 fl oz (½ cup) thin cream
25g/1 oz (2 tablespoons) butter
50g/2 oz (½ cup) grated Parmesan cheese

Heat the oil in a saucepan. Fry the onion and bacon until the onion is softened. Stir in the peas, water, herbs and seasoning and bring to the boil. Simmer for 10–12 minutes or until the peas are tender.

Meanwhile, cook the macaroni in boiling salted water with the oil for 15 minutes or until it is tender. Drain and keep hot.

Purée the pea sauce and return to the saucepan. Stir in the cream and heat through gently.

Add the butter to the macaroni and stir until well coated. Pile the macaroni in a warmed serving dish and pour over the pea sauce. Serve with the cheese.
Cooking time: 20 minutes

Noodle and Spinach Bake

SERVES 4–6

100g/¼ lb (½ cup) butter
2 onions, finely chopped
1.4kg (3 lb) spinach, washed and stripped of its stalks
salt and freshly ground black pepper
2 eggs, beaten
350g (¾ lb) noodles, cooked
75g/3 oz (¾ cup) grated Parmesan cheese
425ml/¾ pt (1⅔ cups) white sauce (page 254)
75g/3 oz (1½ cups) fresh breadcrumbs

Heat the oven to 190°C (375°F) gas mark 5. Melt half the butter in a large pan. Fry the onions until golden. Put in the spinach and cook until reduced—about 10 minutes. Season. Add the eggs and cook, stirring, until they are just beginning to set. Remove from the heat.

Spread half the noodles over the bottom of a greased baking dish. Sprinkle with half the cheese and cover with half the spinach mixture. Repeat the layers, then pour the sauce over the top.

Melt the remaining butter in a clean pan. Add the breadcrumbs and stir well. Scatter this mixture over the sauce layer. Bake for 20 minutes or until the breadcrumbs are golden brown.
Cooking time: about 35 minutes

● For noodle and tomato bake, fry 225g (½ lb) chopped bacon and 2 chopped onions in 50g (4 tablespoons) butter. Add 550g (1¼ lb) chopped tomatoes, season well and layer with the noodles. Top with 425ml/ ¾ pt (1½ cups) béchamel sauce (*page 252*) and 175g (6 oz) sliced Mozzarella. Bake for ½ hour.

Below: for a new way with peas, make a bacon-flavoured sauce for macaroni.

Turkish Chicken Pilau

Noodle and spinach bake is layered with eggs and cheese—and has a crisp topping.

Noodles with Herbs

Well-flavoured rice stretches the chicken in this traditional Middle-Eastern dish.

SERVES 4–6
175g/6 oz (1 cup) long-grain rice
45ml (3 tablespoons) oil
1 large onion, finely chopped
4 chicken breasts, skinned, boned and cut into cubes
salt
freshly ground black pepper
2.5ml (½ teaspoon) ground cinnamon
30ml (2 tablespoons) tomato paste
45ml (3 tablespoons) cold water
2 ripe tomatoes, skinned, seeded and chopped
1 small red (bell) pepper, cored, seeded and diced (optional)
45ml (3 tablespoons) fresh parsley, chopped
275ml/½ pt (1¼ cups) boiling water

Cook the rice for 8 minutes in boiling salted water, then drain, rinse and fluff it.

Meanwhile, heat the oil in a heavy-bottomed saucepan. Fry the onion until softened. Add the chicken pieces and brown on all sides. Season and sprinkle with cinnamon.

Mix the tomato paste with the cold water and stir in with the tomatoes, pepper and parsley. Add enough water just to cover and bring to the boil. Cover the pan and simmer for 1 hour.

Stir in the rice and boiling water and return to the boil. Recover the pan and simmer for an additional 30 minutes or until the rice is tender and the pilau is thick.

Cooking time: 2 hours

● For lamb pilau, fry the onion and then 450g (1 lb) cubed lamb. Add the rice, 50g/2 oz (⅓ cup) raisins, 575ml/1 pt (2½ cups) stock and 30ml (2 tablespoons) tomato paste. Top with 45ml (3 tablespoons) chopped parsley and celery leaves.

SERVES 6
450g (1 lb) noodles
15ml (1 tablespoon) oil
75g/3 oz (6 tablespoons) butter
3 garlic cloves, crushed
45ml (3 tablespoons) parsley, chopped
15ml (1 tablespoon) fresh basil, chopped
10ml (2 teaspoons) fresh oregano or marjoram, chopped
salt
freshly ground black pepper
100g/¼ lb (⅔ cup) Romano or Parmesan cheese, grated

Cook the noodles in boiling salted water with the oil for 8–10 minutes or until just tender. Meanwhile, melt the butter in another saucepan. Add the garlic and fry for 1 minute. Stir in the herbs and seasoning.

Drain the noodles and return to the saucepan. Stir in the herb mixture and cheese and toss well together. Serve hot.

Cooking time: 10 minutes

Vegetables and Salads

Eggplant au Gratin

4 medium-sized aubergines (eggplants),
sliced 6mm ($\frac{1}{4}$ in) thick

salt

freshly ground black pepper

flour for coating

75ml/3 fl oz ($\frac{1}{3}$ cup) oil

150g/5 oz ($1\frac{1}{4}$ cups) cheese, grated

25g/1 oz ($\frac{1}{2}$ cup) fresh breadcrumbs

25g/1 oz (2 tablespoons) butter

FOR THE SAUCE

40g/$1\frac{1}{2}$ oz (3 tablespoons) butter

1 small onion, finely chopped

45ml (3 tablespoons) flour

400g (14 oz) canned tomatoes

10ml (2 teaspoons) tomato paste

5ml (1 teaspoon) fresh basil, chopped

Put the aubergine (eggplant) slices in a colander, sprinkle with salt and leave to drain for 30 minutes.

Meanwhile, make the sauce. Melt the butter in a saucepan. Fry the onion until softened. Stir in the flour and cook, stirring, for 1 minute. Add the tomatoes with

Serve spinach leaves stuffed with mushrooms and lemon sauce for an appetizer.

their liquid, tomato paste, basil and seasoning to taste and bring to the boil, stirring well. Cover and simmer gently for 15 minutes.

Heat the oven to 180°C (350°F) gas mark 4. Rinse the aubergine slices and pat dry with absorbent paper. Coat the slices with flour. Heat half the oil in a frying-pan and fry the aubergine slices in batches until browned on both sides. Add more of the oil as needed.

Make a layer of the tomato sauce on the bottom of a baking dish. Sprinkle with some of the cheese, then cover with a layer of aubergine slices. Continue making layers in this way, ending with sauce sprinkled with cheese. Scatter over the breadcrumbs and dot with the butter. Bake for 25 minutes or until the top is golden brown and the aubergines are tender.

Cooking time: $1\frac{1}{2}$ hours

Spinach Leaves with Mushroom Stuffing

These stuffed spinach leaves are an adaptation of Greek dolmades—stuffed vineleaves. They contain no meat; serve them as an appetizer or side dish. If sausage forcemeat (stuffing) on page 255 is used instead, they could make a light main course.

16 large spinach leaves, trimmed of stalk

40g/$1\frac{1}{2}$ oz (3 tablespoons) butter

2 medium-sized onions, thinly sliced

225g ($\frac{1}{2}$ lb) mushrooms, sliced

225g/$\frac{1}{2}$ lb (4 cups) fresh breadcrumbs

1 egg, beaten

1 garlic clove, crushed

pinch of grated nutmeg

salt

freshly ground black pepper

275ml/$\frac{1}{2}$ pt ($1\frac{1}{4}$ cups) chicken stock

1 egg yolk

juice of $\frac{1}{2}$ lemon

Blanch the spinach leaves in boiling water for 2 minutes. Lay them out on a clean glass towel to drain.

Melt the butter in a frying pan. Fry the onions until softened. Stir in the mushrooms and fry for a further 3 minutes. Remove from the heat and add the breadcrumbs, beaten egg, garlic, nutmeg and seasoning. Mix well.

Set aside 4–6 spinach leaves. Divide the stuffing between the rest of the leaves and roll them up securely, folding the sides of the loaf over the filling and then rolling each one up. Line a greased flame-proof saucepan with the reserved spinach leaves. Arrange the rolls on top, in one layer with the seams underneath. Pour over the stock.

Bring to the boil, then cover the pot and simmer for 30 minutes.

Transfer the spinach rolls to a warmed serving dish. Keep warm. Strain the cooking liquid back into the saucepan. Combine the egg yolk and lemon juice. Add a little of the hot cooking liquid, then stir this mixture into the rest of the liquid. Cook gently, stirring, until thickened. Serve this sauce with the spinach rolls.

Cooking time: 1 hour

Stuffed Green Peppers

The possible variations for stuffing this versatile vegetable are numerous.

SERVES 6
6 large green (bell) peppers
25g/1 oz (2 tablespoons) butter
1 onion, chopped
100g ($\frac{1}{4}$ lb) mushrooms, sliced
4 tomatoes, blanched, skinned and chopped
175g/6 oz (1 cup) cooked brown rice
10ml (2 teaspoons) fresh thyme, chopped
15ml (1 tablespoon) fresh parsley, chopped
salt
freshly ground black pepper
275ml/$\frac{1}{2}$ pt (1$\frac{1}{4}$ cups) beef stock

Heat the oven to 180°C (350°F) gas mark 4. Cut a slice from the stem end of each pepper. Scoop out the core and seeds. Blanch the peppers in boiling water for 5 minutes, then drain and refresh under cold running water.

Melt the butter in a saucepan. Add the onion and fry until softened. Chop the trimmings from the pepper stalks and add to the pan. Add the mushrooms and fry for an additional 3 minutes. Remove from the heat and stir in the tomatoes, rice, herbs and seasoning.

Stuff the peppers with the rice mixture and stand them in a baking dish. Pour over the stock. Bake for 20 minutes, basting frequently with the stock.

Cooking time: 35 minutes

●Minced (ground) meat or cheese can replace the rice—or a combination of breadcrumbs and nuts. Allow 45 minutes baking time if the pepper is to contain raw meat.

●Canned sardines, mashed, go well with long-grain rice; chopped, fried bacon is another standby.

●Use tomato juice as the poaching liquid.

Make a change in the family menu and save a little money by serving marrow or squash with nutty stuffing as a meatless main dish.

Baked Courgettes (Zucchini) with Dill

SERVES 4
8 medium-sized courgettes (zucchini), peeled and sliced in half lengthwise
1 garlic clove, finely chopped
10ml (2 teaspoons) sugar
5ml (1 teaspoon) salt
15ml (1 tablespoon) fresh dill, chopped
1 medium-sized onion, sliced into rings
75g/3 oz ($\frac{3}{4}$ cup) grated Parmesan cheese

Heat the oven to 180°C (350°F) gas mark 4. Arrange the courgettes (zucchini) in a baking dish, cut sides up. Sprinkle with the garlic, sugar, salt and dill, then arrange the onions over the top. Scatter with the cheese. Bake for 20 minutes.

Transfer the dish to the grill (broiler) and grill (broil) for 4 minutes or until the top is lightly browned.

Cooking time: about 35 minutes

Marrow (Squash) with Nutty Stuffing

With roast potatoes and a tomato sauce, this would make a modest family main course.

SERVES 4–6
1 medium-sized marrow (squash)
100g/$\frac{1}{4}$ lb (2 cups) fresh breadcrumbs
100g/$\frac{1}{4}$ lb (1 cup) nuts, finely chopped
60ml/4 tablespoons ($\frac{1}{4}$ cup) oil
45ml (3 tablespoons) fresh parsley, chopped
1 small onion, grated
grated rind and juice of $\frac{1}{2}$ lemon
1 medium-sized egg

Heat the oven to 200°C (400°F) gas mark 6. Cut a lid from the length of the marrow (squash) and scoop out the seeds. Parboil the marrow in boiling water for 5 minutes. Drain and pat dry with absorbent paper.

Combine the remaining ingredients and use to stuff the marrow. Replace the lid. Put the marrow in a greased baking dish and cover with foil. Bake for $\frac{3}{4}$–1 hour or until tender.

Cooking time: about 70 minutes

New Potatoes with Mange-tout (Snow Peas) and Mint

SERVES 8
900g (2 lb) new potatoes
700g (1½ lb) mange-tout (snow peas)
salt
freshly ground black pepper
30ml (2 tablespoons) chopped fresh mint
50g/2 oz (¼ cup) butter

Steam the potatoes for 20 minutes. Add the mange-tout (snow peas) to the steamer and steam for a further 5–10 minutes or until the vegetables are just tender. Melt the butter in a small saucepan.

Turn half the vegetables into a warmed serving bowl, season, add a little mint and toss in half the butter. Add the rest of the vegetables and sprinkle over the remaining butter. Season once more and add the remaining mint.

Cooking time : 35 minutes

Peas with Onions

SERVES 6
700g (1½ lb) peas, weighed after shelling
10ml (2 teaspoons) sugar
salt
freshly ground black pepper
50g/2 oz (¼ cup) butter
4 small white onions, halved
2 shallots, thinly sliced
4 spring onions (scallions), cut into 6mm (¼ in) pieces

Put the peas in a saucepan with the sugar and salt. Pour over enough hot water to cover and bring to the boil. Cook for 4 minutes, or until nearly tender then drain.

Melt the butter in another saucepan. Add the onions, shallots and spring onions (scallions) and fry until golden brown. Season to taste, then stir in the peas. Cook for an additional 3–4 minutes or until the peas are hot and tender.

Cooking time : 20 minutes

Fresh Corn Fritters

This will make an appetizer or a filling side dish. With golden or maple syrup it will make a dessert.

SERVES 4
225g/½ lb (½ cup) fresh sweetcorn kernels, cut from the cob
50g/2 oz (½ cup) flour
2.5ml (½ teaspoon) baking powder
30ml (2 tablespoons) sugar
salt
freshly ground black pepper
1 egg, beaten
30ml (2 tablespoons) grated Parmesan cheese
oil for deep frying

Combine the corn, flour, baking powder, sugar, seasoning, egg and cheese. Heat

Peas with onions is a classic and simple-to-make vegetable dish from France.

the oil to 185°C (360°F) or until a small cube of bread dropped in will turn golden in 60 seconds.

Drop spoonfuls of the corn mixture into the oil and fry for 3–4 minutes or until golden brown. Drain on absorbent paper. Serve hot.

Cooking time : 15–30 minutes

Dhal Curry

SERVES 4
25g/1 oz (2 tablespoons) butter
1 onion, sliced
1 garlic clove, crushed
1 green chilli, chopped
5ml (1 teaspoon) ground cumin
5ml (1 teaspoon) turmeric
2.5ml (½ teaspoon) chilli powder
225g (½ lb) lentils
700ml/1¼ pt (2¾ cups) water
2.5ml (½ teaspoon) salt
50g/2 oz (¼ cup) creamed coconut dissolved in 50ml/2 fl oz (¼ cup) water

Melt the butter in a saucepan. Fry the onion until soft and golden. Add the garlic and green chilli and fry for 2 minutes. Stir in the cumin, turmeric and chilli powder and fry for an additional 5 minutes. If the mixture becomes too dry, add a spoonful or two of water.

Gradually stir in the lentils and fry for 2 minutes. Add the water and salt, stir well and bring to the boil. Half cover the pan and simmer for 1 hour. Stir and mash the dhal occasionally.

Purée the dhal in a food mill or blender or by rubbing through a sieve. Return to the saucepan and stir in the coconut mix-mixture. Bring to the boil and simmer for 10 minutes, stirring occasionally. Serve hot, with rice.

Cooking time : 1½ hours

Cucumber and Radish Salad

SERVES 4–6
1 large cucumber (2 cucumbers)
6–12 large radishes, trimmed
½ bunch watercress or mint
45ml (3 tablespoons) olive oil
15ml (1 tablespoon) lemon juice
1 garlic clove, crushed
salt and freshly ground black pepper

For the radish decorations, sometimes called Van Dyck roses, cut the radish

round the middle with a sharp knife in a zig-zag, piercing it through almost to the middle. Then take hold of the ends and give it a sharp twist. The two halves will separate giving you two attractive cups. Cut all the radishes in this way.

Score the cucumber from end to end with a fork to make ridges. Then slice as thinly as you can and layer with salt in a colander. Leave for $\frac{1}{2}$ hour to drain. Wash the slices under running water, then drain on absorbent paper.

Combine the last 5 ingredients to make the dressing and turn the cucumber slices in it. Arrange the cucumber in the centre of a shallow glass plate. Arrange the radishes around and put a small sprig of watercress or mint between each one. Chill for 30 minutes.

Preparation time: 30 minutes, plus chilling time

●Realistic radish roses can only be made with really crisp radishes. Test one by cutting it 48 hours before a party. Soak it for 24 hours in ice-cold water and if it opens up, cut and soak the rest in the same way.

With a sharp knife start about half way up the radish and cut a strip, towards the stalk, to form a petal. Work around the radish, cutting more strips to form a ring of petals. Cut the next ring of petals between the first and the tip. Each cut should fall inside the middle of the petal on the row below. Make a final row of petals next to the tip on the same principle. Put the radish roses into cold, salted water and leave in the refrigerator for 24 hours. They should open up like flowers.

●Combine the cucumber with a fennel bulb, thinly sliced into strips and 3 spring onions (scallions) finely chopped. Garnish with parsley before serving.

●As an accompaniment to curries and hot spiced dishes make raita. Combine 150ml/ $\frac{1}{4}$ pt ($\frac{5}{8}$ cup) yogurt, $\frac{1}{4}$ cucumber salted and drained, 1 spring onion (scallion) finely chopped, $\frac{1}{2}$ green chilli, chopped (optional) and chopped mint leaves.

●Include the radishes in the salad, rather than using them as a decoration. Combine 100g ($\frac{1}{4}$ lb) sliced radishes with $\frac{1}{2}$ cucumber, 3 spring onions (scallions) chopped and dress with 65ml/2$\frac{1}{2}$ fl oz ($\frac{1}{3}$ cup) yogurt and the same amount of thin cream, 30ml (2 tablespoons) lemon juice and a pinch of sugar and seasoning.

●If fresh radishes are not available, make the salad without them, adding 15ml (1 tablespoon) creamed horseradish sauce to the dressing.

An ususual and striking contrast of colours and flavour, this beetroot (beet) and orange salad goes well with cold meat and would look attractive on a buffet table.

Potato and Egg Salad

Yogurt is used to extend the mayonnaise for a creamy dressing for this salad.

SERVES 4–6
12 new potatoes
15ml (1 tablespoon) oil
30ml (2 tablespoons) wine vinegar
1 small onion, thinly sliced
45ml (3 tablespoons) very finely chopped celery
salt
freshly ground black pepper
150ml/$\frac{1}{4}$ pt ($\frac{2}{3}$ cup) plain yogurt
125ml/4 fl oz ($\frac{1}{2}$ cup) mayonnaise (page 250)
2 hard-boiled eggs, quartered
FOR THE GARNISH
grapefruit or orange segments
watercress

Cook the potatoes in boiling water until tender. Drain, peel and slice. Add the oil and vinegar to the potatoes and mix gently. Leave for 1 hour.

Add the onion, celery and seasoning to the potatoes and fold together. Mix the yogurt with the mayonnaise and stir into the potato mixture. Gently fold in the egg quarters.

Garnish the salad with the fruit segments and watercress.

Cooking time: 1$\frac{1}{2}$ hours including chilling time

Beetroot (Beet) and Orange Salad

SERVES 4
2 large oranges
1 bunch of watercress to garnish
450g (1 lb) beet, cooked, peeled and sliced
FOR THE DRESSING
60ml/4 tablespoons ($\frac{1}{4}$ cup) olive oil
22.5ml (1$\frac{1}{2}$ tablespoons) wine vinegar
5ml (1 teaspoon) prepared mustard
5ml (1 teaspoon) fresh tarragon, chopped
2.5ml ($\frac{1}{2}$ teaspoon) sugar
salt
freshly ground black pepper

Grate the rind from one of the oranges and reserve. Peel both oranges, removing all the white pith, and slice them into rings.

Make a bed of watercress on a serving plate and arrange alternate slices of orange and beetroot, overlapping, on top.

Combine the dressing ingredients with seasoning to taste and stir in the orange rind. Pour the dressing over the salad just before serving.

Preparation time: 15 minutes

●The oranges can be replaced by 450g (1 lb) cooked, diced potato. Dress additionally with 1–2 chopped, hard-boiled eggs, parsley and chives.

●Alternatively, replace the oranges with 2–3 sliced dessert apples.

●For a main course salad for 4, combine both variations—use potatoes, eggs and apples—plus 4 pickled herring fillets. If using a jar of roll mops, include the onion rings from the jar and use the vinegar to make the dressing.

Desserts

Pears Cardinal

SERVES 4

100g/$\frac{1}{4}$ lb ($\frac{1}{2}$ cup) sugar
275ml/$\frac{1}{2}$ pt (1$\frac{1}{2}$ cups) water
1 vanilla pod
a squeeze of lemon juice
4 large cooking pears, peeled
450g (1 lb) raspberries
60ml/4 tablespoons ($\frac{1}{4}$ cup) icing
(confectioners') sugar

Put the sugar and water in a saucepan and heat, stirring to dissolve the sugar. Bring to the boil and boil for 2 minutes. Add the vanilla pod and lemon juice, then place the pears in the syrup. Cover the pan and poach gently for 30 minutes or until the pears are tender. Spoon the syrup over the pears from time to time.

Remove the pears from the pan and continue boiling the syrup until it has reduced by half. Remove from the heat and replace the pears in the pan. Cover and cool, turning the pears after $\frac{1}{2}$ hour.

Meanwhile, sieve the raspberries to make a purée. Stir in the icing (confectioners') sugar. Lift the cold pears out of the syrup and place in individual serving dishes. Pour a spoonful or two of syrup over each pear, then coat with the raspberry purée.

Cooking time: 40 minutes plus 1 hour chilling time

Fruit Nests

SERVES 8

Italian meringue (*page 247*)
275ml/$\frac{1}{2}$ pt (1$\frac{1}{4}$ cups) thick cream
4 peaches
100g ($\frac{1}{4}$ lb) strawberries
45ml (3 tablespoons) redcurrant jelly

Heat the oven to 110°C (225°F) gas mark $\frac{1}{4}$. Line 2 baking sheets with oiled greaseproof or waxed or silicone paper. Fit a piping bag with 12mm ($\frac{1}{2}$ in) éclair nozzle. Spoon the cooked meringue into the bag.

Pipe a circle on a baking sheet working from the centre outward until it is 10cm (4 in) in diameter. Pipe 7 more in the same way. Pipe a ring on the rim of each circle to make the sides of the nest. Bake below the centre of the oven for about 2 hours until dry and crisp.

Whip the cream until stiff and divide between the nests. Slice each peach into 8 sections, putting 4 into each nest. Divide the strawberries between the nests. Melt the redcurrant jelly in a small pan over low heat; brush over the fruit, then chill.
Cooking time: 2$\frac{3}{4}$ hours.

Cheap but hugely popular, fruit nests can be filled with a variety of fruits.

Meringue Pancakes with Raspberry Sauce

SERVES 4

225g (½ lb) raspberries
icing (confectioners') sugar
2 egg yolks
pinch of salt
1.5ml (¼ teaspoon) vanilla extract
15ml (1 tablespoon) flour
4 egg whites
50g/2 oz (¼ cup) fine sugar
25g/1 oz (2 tablespoons) butter

First make the sauce. Sieve the raspberries, then sweeten the purée to taste with icing (confectioners') sugar.

Beat the egg yolks in a bowl until they are creamy. Add the vanilla and flour and beat again. Beat the egg whites with the salt until stiff, fold in the sugar, a little at a time, then fold into the yolks.

Melt the butter in a frying-pan. Drop heaped spoonfuls of the meringue mixture into the pan and cook for 2–3 minutes on each side or until golden brown. Serve hot with the raspberry sauce.

Cooking time: 30–40 minutes

Beating the egg whites separately makes these tiny meringue pancakes particularly light and fluffy. With raspberry sauce, they are perfect for hungry children.

Gooseberry and Geranium Ice-cream

Fruit juice or purée mixed with thick cream makes the perfect ice-cream. Here are two unusual, inexpensive ice-creams.

For other home-made ice-creams, see the variations under lemon water ice, page 115.

SERVES 4–6

350g (¾ lb) gooseberries
90g/3½ oz (7 tablespoons) sugar
45–60ml (3–4 tablespoons) water
6 sweet geranium leaves
150ml/¼ pt (⅔ cup) thick cream

Put the gooseberries in a pan with the sugar, water and half the geranium leaves. Cover the pan and cook gently until the fruit is tender and pulpy. Purée in a blender or through a strainer with 3 geranium leaves. Leave until cold.

Turn into a freezer tray, cover with foil and freeze for ½ hour or until slushy.

Whip the cream then stir the ice well to break down the ice crystals. Stir in the cream, cover and return to the freezer. Beat again after ½ hour, then cover the top with the remaining geranium leaves. Freeze a further 2 hours. Allow 20 minutes in the refrigerator before serving.

Cooking time: total 15 minutes plus 2 hours freezing

● If geranium leaves are not available, a head of elderflower can be used instead. Cook this with the berries and remove before puréeing.

● Use apples to make ice-cream before the summer red berries arrive. Cook 350g (¾ lb) cooking apples with 25g (2 tablespoons) butter, 50g/2 oz (¼ cup) sugar and the rind of 1 orange. Purée then cool and freeze for ½ hour. Add 150 ml/¼ pt (⅔ cup) whipped, thick cream and then, ½ hour later, 2 stiffly-beaten egg whites. Freeze in a 450g (1 lb) loaf tin (pan). Turn out to serve. Mix 25g/1 oz (⅓ cup) fine brown breadcrumbs with an equal amount of brown sugar and press this over the outside. Serve in slices for 8.

Bread dough makes an interesting variant on pastry in this apricot galette.

Apricot Galette

A filling dessert is often a good idea after a light salad main course. This sweet yeast cake makes excellent picnic fare. If fresh yeast is not available, use 5ml (1 teaspoon) dried yeast and soak it in the water.

SERVES 6–8
7g/¼ oz fresh yeast (½ × ⅗ oz cake compressed yeast)
60ml/4 tablespoons (¼ cup) lukewarm water
150g/5 oz (⅔ cup) fine sugar
175g/6 oz (1½ cups) flour
2.5ml (½ teaspoon) salt
25g/1 oz (2 tablespoons) butter, melted
1 egg
450g (1 lb) fresh apricots, halved and stoned
grated rind of ½ lemon

Mash the yeast with the water and 1.5ml (¼ teaspoon) of the sugar, then leave in a warm place until the mixture is frothy.

Sift the flour and salt into a mixing bowl. Make a well in the centre and put in the yeast mixture, melted butter and egg. Gradually draw the dry ingredients into the liquid and mix until the dough comes away from the sides of the bowl. Knead the dough like bread dough until it is smooth and elastic. Leave the dough in an oiled plastic bag to rise, in a warm place, for 1½–2 hours or until it has almost doubled in bulk.

Put the apricots in a saucepan with 50g/2 oz (¼ cup) of the sugar and the lemon rind. Just cover the bottom of the pan with water, then poach the apricots gently until they are tender. Drain, reserving the liquid.

Heat the oven to 190°C (375°F) gas mark 5. Knead the dough for 3 minutes, then pat it out to fit a 20cm (8 in) flan ring or pie dish, on a baking sheet. Gently press the dough to hollow the centre slightly. Leave to rise for 15 minutes.

Arrange the apricot halves on the dough circle, cut sides down. Sprinkle over 50g/ 2 oz (¼ cup) of the remaining sugar and 15ml (1 tablespoon) of reserved liquid.

Bake for 20 minutes. Remove the flan ring, then sprinkle the apricots with the remaining sugar and another 15ml (1 tablespoon) of the cooking liquid. Bake for a further 10 minutes. Serve warm or cold.
Cooking time: 1½ hours plus rising period of 2 hours

Red Summer Tart

Broken biscuits (graham crackers) make a popular substitute for a pastry case.

SERVES 4–5
175g/6 oz (1¼ cups) digestive biscuits (graham crackers), finely crushed
grated rind of 1 orange
75g/3 oz (6 tablespoons) butter, melted
25g/1 oz (2 tablespoons) fine sugar
350g (¾ lb) mixed strawberries, raspberries and ripe blackberries
45ml (3 tablespoons) redcurrant jelly
30ml (2 tablespoons) fruit juice or water

Heat the oven to 180°C (350°F) gas mark 4. Combine the biscuit (graham cracker) crumbs, orange rind, butter and sugar. Turn into a greased 18cm (7 in) tart tin or pie plate and make an even layer on the bottom and sides by smoothing with a glass jar. Bake for 10 minutes, then cool.

Hull and halve the strawberries. Gently remove the crust from the tart tin (if using). Arrange the fruit decoratively in it.

Melt the jelly in the fruit juice or water, then brush this glaze over the fruit. Leave to set for 30 minutes before serving.
Cooking time: about ½ hour plus cooling

Red Fruit Compote

SERVES 6–8
450g (1 lb) redcurrants
225g (½ lb) cooking plums, halved and stoned
225g (½ lb) cooking cherries, halved and stoned
450g (1 lb) sugar
175ml/6 fl oz (¾ cup) water
450g (1 lb) raspberries
30ml (2 tablespoons) medium-sweet sherry

Put the redcurrants, plums, cherries, sugar and water in a saucepan. Heat, stirring to dissolve the sugar, then cook gently for 20–25 minutes or until the mixture is soft and pulpy. Stir in the raspberries and cook for an additional 5 minutes. Cool.

Stir in the sherry, then chill the compote for at least 1 hour before serving.
Cooking time: 25–30 minutes plus 1 hour chilling time

Swedish Gooseberry Pie

SERVES 6

275g/10 oz (2½ cups) flour
2.5ml (½ teaspoon) grated nutmeg
175g/6 oz (¾ cup) butter
75g/3 oz (½ cup) sugar
450g (1 lb) gooseberries

Heat the oven to 200°C (400°F) gas mark 6. Sift the flour and nutmeg into a bowl. Add the butter and rub in until the mixture resembles breadcrumbs. Stir in half the sugar.

Press the mixture into the bottom of a greased 28cm (11 in) oval baking dish. Cover with the gooseberries and sprinkle over the remaining sugar.

Bake for 40 minutes or until the gooseberries are tender and the bottom crust is cooked. Serve hot.
Cooking time: 50 minutes

The butter-crumble base beneath the fruit soaks up the gooseberry juice in this hot Swedish gooseberry pie.

Raspberry Sherbet

SERVES 8

225g/½ lb (1 cup) sugar

450ml/16 fl oz (2 cups) water

7g/¼ oz (½ teaspoon) gelatin, softened in 30ml (2 tablespoons) water

700g (1½ lb) raspberries

125ml/4 fl oz (½ cup) thick cream

1 egg white

Dissolve the sugar in the water in a saucepan, then bring to the boil. Boil briskly until the temperature reaches 106°C (220°F) on a sugar thermometer (at this stage a short thread pulled out between two forks will snap). Remove from the heat and cool the syrup for 5 minutes, then stir in the gelatin.

Press the raspberries through a strainer to make a purée. Stir in the syrup mixture and chill for 1 hour. Pour into a freezer tray, cover with foil and freeze for 1 hour or until slushy.

Whip the cream until thick. Beat the egg white until stiff and fold it into the cream. Beat the raspberry mixture to break up any ice crystals, then fold in the cream mixture. Return to the freezer tray and freeze for an additional 6 hours.

Allow the sherbet to soften for about 30 minutes in the refrigerator before serving.

Cooking time: 30 minutes in total, plus 8 hours freezing

The perfect summer dessert, dark, fruity raspberry sherbet is a refreshing way to round off any meal. Serve langue de chat biscuits (page 119) with the ice-cream.

Summer Pudding

SERVES 6

225g (½ lb) redcurrants

225g (½ lb) blackberries

225g (½ lb) raspberries

225g (½ lb) strawberries

225g/½ lb (1 cup) fine sugar

10 slices of stale white bread, crusts removed

whipped cream

Combine the fruit in a bowl and sprinkle with the sugar. Leave for 1 hour to draw out the juices.

Line a greased 1.1L/2 pt (5-cup) pudding bowl with the bread slices, cutting them to fit nicely and reserving two for the top. Spoon in the fruit and juice, then arrange the reserved bread slices on top to cover completely. Stand the bowl on a plate to catch any drips and put a plate and a weight on top. Chill for at least 8 hours or overnight.

Turn out the pudding on to a serving plate and serve with whipped cream.

Preparation time: 1½ hours plus 8 hours chilling time

● Use one type of fruit only or a selection. Always include some firm fruit with very soft berries. Rhubarb, cherries and blackcurrants should all be stewed and sweetened. Cherries should be stoned. This is the perfect recipe for garden owners who have a little of every red fruit ripe at one time.

Summer pudding has a crust saturated with the red juices of a variety of summer fruit.

Melon Surprise

SERVES 4

1 medium-sized cantaloup melon
275g (10 oz) strawberries, hulled
75ml/5 tablespoons ($\frac{1}{3}$ cup) sugar
60ml/4 tablespoons ($\frac{1}{4}$ cup) sweet sherry

Cut the top 1.2cm ($\frac{1}{2}$ in) off the melon and scoop out the seeds. Remove the melon flesh and chop it, or cut it into balls. Keep the melon shell intact. Cut a thin slice from the bottom of the melon shell to make it flat.

Combine the melon flesh, strawberries, sugar and sherry. Spoon the mixture into the melon shell. (If there is too much fruit, serve the extra in a separate bowl.) Chill for at least 30 minutes before serving.
Preparation time: 20 minutes plus 30 minutes chilling

Lemon Water Ice

If your children spend a fortune on bought lollies (popsicles), try giving them half a glassful of water ice, with a spoon to eat it, when they complain of being hot. For a change from peach melba for a party, serve a fresh peach enclosed in a wineglass of lemon water ice.

Home-made fruit ices are simplicity itself to make: they cost very little and you can be confident that they contain real fruit.

SERVES 6–8

3 large juicy lemons
850ml/1$\frac{1}{2}$ pt (3$\frac{3}{4}$ cups) water
200g/7 oz (1 cup) fine sugar
2 egg whites

If you have no freezer and are using the freezing compartment of a refrigerator, turn the setting to maximum. Peel the rind from the lemons with a potato peeler and squeeze the juice. Put 850ml/1$\frac{1}{2}$ pt (3$\frac{3}{4}$ cups) water, the lemon rind, juice and 200g/7 oz (1 cup) fine sugar into a saucepan.

Bring to the boil over medium heat, stirring until the sugar has dissolved. Lower the heat and simmer for 5 minutes.

Pour the syrup, through a strainer to remove the rind, into a cold bowl. Allow to cool: stand in a sink of cold water if desired. Then chill in the refrigerator.

Pour the mixture into ice-cube freezer trays (without the divisions) for maximum freezing speed. Cover with foil and freeze

for 30 minutes, or until slushy.

Just before removing from the freezer, beat the egg whites until stiff. Turn the ice into a bowl and beat well with a wire whisk. Fold in the egg whites, using a figure-of-eight motion of the spoon. When ice and white are amalgamated, turn into a plastic box, cover and freeze.

Allow the ice to stand up to $\frac{1}{2}$ hour at room temperature before serving. If using water ices for dessert, spoon into individual glasses and put in the refrigerator 15 minutes before needed.
Cooking time: 35 minutes plus 1 hour cooling and 2 hours freezing

● For a party, serve water ices in the scooped out shell of the fruit; replace the lid if desired.
● For orange ice, use the juice and grated rind of 3 large oranges, plus half a lemon, with 575ml/1 pt (2$\frac{1}{2}$ cups) water and 175g/ 6 oz ($\frac{3}{4}$ cup) sugar. Use 2 egg whites.
● For grapefruit ice, squeeze 2 grapefruit and make the juice up to 1L/1$\frac{3}{4}$ pt (4 cups)

A melon shell makes an attractive container for fruit. Chop the flesh or use a melon baller to make neat shapes. In this recipe the flesh is marinated in sherry before mixing with strawberries.

with water. Use the grated rind plus 150–175g/6–7 oz ($\frac{3}{4}$–1 cup) sugar. Use 2 egg whites.

With fruit purées, make the syrup just from the sugar and water and then add it to the cold fruit purée when cold.
● For strawberry or raspberry ice, use 425ml/$\frac{3}{4}$ pt (1$\frac{2}{3}$ cups) purée, plus the juice of half a lemon and half an orange, with 150ml/$\frac{1}{4}$ pt ($\frac{2}{3}$ cup) water and 175g/6 oz ($\frac{3}{4}$ cup) sugar. Use 2 egg whites.
● For blackberry ice, use 425ml/$\frac{3}{4}$ pt (1$\frac{2}{3}$ cups) purée sweetened to taste, with 150ml/$\frac{1}{4}$ pt ($\frac{2}{3}$ cup) water, 30ml (2 tablespoons) lemon juice and 100g/$\frac{1}{4}$ lb ($\frac{1}{2}$ cup) sugar. Use 2 egg whites.
● For a cream ice, add 275ml/$\frac{1}{2}$ pt (1$\frac{1}{4}$ cups) stiffly whipped, thick cream to the above.

Glazed orange and lemon slices top a cake mixture above rich shortcrust pastry for an unfamiliar summer tart.

Divide the plum mixture between the crêpes and roll them up. Arrange, in one layer if possible, in a gratin dish. Sprinkle over the brown sugar, then grill (broil) until caramelized.
Cooking time: 35 minutes

Strawberry Baked Alaska

SERVES 6
25cm (10 in) sponge base *(page 246)*
15ml (1 tablespoon) medium-sweet sherry
350g ($\frac{3}{4}$ lb) strawberries, sliced
4 egg whites
pinch of salt
225g ($\frac{1}{2}$ lb) fine sugar
575ml (1 pt) strawberry ice-cream

Heat the oven to 220°C (425°F) gas mark 7. Place the flan case on an oven-proof serving dish and sprinkle with the sherry. Cover with the strawberries.

Beat the egg whites with the salt until stiff. Gradually beat in up to one half of the sugar, then carefully fold in the rest of the sugar.

Turn out the ice-cream and arrange over the strawberries. Spread with the meringue, covering the ice-cream and cake completely, right down to the dish.

Bake for 4 minutes or until the meringue is lightly browned. Serve immediately.
Cooking time: 20 minutes

Orange and Lemon Tart

SERVES 6–8
rich shortcrust pastry *(page 241)*
2 eggs
75g/3 oz ($\frac{1}{3}$ cup) fine sugar
125ml/4 fl oz ($\frac{1}{2}$ cup) thin cream (or half and half)
100g/$\frac{1}{4}$ lb (1$\frac{1}{3}$ cups) stale cake crumbs
grated rind and juice of 1 small orange
few drops of almond extract
FOR THE TOPPING
75g/3 oz ($\frac{1}{3}$ cup) sugar
150ml/$\frac{1}{4}$ pt ($\frac{2}{3}$ cup) water
2 large thin-skinned lemons, very thinly sliced
2 small thin-skinned oranges, very thinly sliced
60ml/4 tablespoons ($\frac{1}{4}$ cup) sieved marmalade or orange jelly

Heat the oven to 200°C (400°F) gas mark 6. Roll out the dough and use to line a 23cm (9 in) tart tin or dish. Bake blind *(page 61)* for 15 minutes. Reduce the oven heat to 190°C (375°F) gas mark 5 and allow the tart to cool briefly.

Beat the eggs and sugar together until pale and thick. Beat in the cream, cake crumbs, orange rind and juice and almond extract. Pour into the tart case and spread out. Bake for 30–40 minutes or until golden and firm.

Meanwhile, for the topping, put the sugar and water in a saucepan and heat, stirring to dissolve the sugar. Bring to the boil. Put the lemon and orange slices in the pan, one at a time, and simmer for 3 minutes. Remove the fruit slices with a slotted spoon and drain. Continue to boil the syrup until it has reduced by half. Add the marmalade or jelly and stir until melted.

Heat the grill (broiler) to moderate. Arrange the orange and lemon slices on top of the filling in the tart case and brush generously with the syrup. Grill (broil) for 3–4 minutes or until the glaze has caramelized. Serve warm or cold.
Cooking time: 55–65 minutes

Plum Crêpes

SERVES 6
sweet crêpe batter *(page 245)*
700g (1$\frac{1}{2}$ lb) sweet dark plums, stoned and chopped
25g/1 oz (2 tablespoons) butter
30ml (2 tablespoons) fine sugar
1.5ml ($\frac{1}{4}$ teaspoon) ground allspice
10ml (2 teaspoons) arrowroot (or 20ml (4 teaspoons) cornstarch) dissolved in 15ml (1 tablespoon) water
75ml (5 tablespoons) soft brown sugar

Make the crêpes and keep warm. Put the plums, butter, sugar and allspice in a saucepan. Cover and cook gently for 8–10 minutes or until the plums are beginning to pulp. Stir in the dissolved arrowroot and simmer, stirring, until thickened.

Heat the grill (broiler) to moderate.

Summer Foam

SERVES 4
225g ($\frac{1}{2}$ lb) redcurrants
225g ($\frac{1}{2}$ lb) raspberries
100g/$\frac{1}{4}$ lb (1 cup) icing (confectioners') sugar
2 medium-sized egg whites
pinch of salt

Pass all the fruit through a strainer to make a purée. Stir in the sugar until dissolved. Beat the egg whites with the salt until stiff. Fold into the fruit purée, then turn into a saucepan. Beat over gentle heat until the mixture starts to thicken and rise like a soufflé. Serve hot or cold.
Cooking time: about 20 minutes

Cakes, Biscuits and Cookies

Butterfly Cup Cakes

MAKES 12

100g/¼ lb (½ cup) butter or margarine

100g/¼ lb (½ cup) fine sugar

2 medium-sized eggs, beaten

100g/¼ lb (1 cup) self-raising flour

FOR THE BUTTERCREAM

50g/2 oz (¼ cup) butter, softened

100g/¼ lb (1 cup) icing (confectioners')
sugar

few drops of red food colouring

Heat the oven to 190°C (375°F) gas mark 5. Cream the fat and sugar together until light and fluffy. Beat in the eggs, then sift in the flour and fold in.

Divide the mixture between 15 paper cases placed on a baking sheet or in deep bun-hole (muffin) pan. Bake for 15 minutes or until the cakes are golden brown. Cool on a wire rack.

To make the buttercream, cream the butter and gradually work in the sifted sugar. Beat in the food colouring.

Cut a thin slice from the top of each cake, then cut each slice in half. Put a generous swirl of buttercream on top of each cake and replace the two halves of each slice at an angle to represent butterfly wings. Pipe the remaining cream between the wings.

Cooking time: 40 minutes plus ¾ hour cooling time

French Apple Cheesecake

SERVES 4–6

¾ × sweet rich shortcrust pastry
(page 241) flavoured with 2.5ml
(½ teaspoon) each ground cloves and

cinnamon and the grated rind of ½ lemon

450g (1 lb) curd (cottage) cheese

100g/¼ lb (½ cup) fine sugar

1 large egg, beaten

25g/1 oz (3 tablespoons) sultanas or
raisins

15ml (1 tablespoon) grated lemon rind

juice of ½ lemon

2 dessert apples, peeled, cored and sliced

30ml (2 tablespoons) apricot jam

30ml (2 tablespoons) brandy or water

Heat the oven to 190°C (375°F) gas mark 5. Roll out the dough and line a 20cm (8 in) flan tin (quiche pan).

For the filling, combine the cheese, sugar, egg, sultanas or raisins and lemon rind. Put the lemon juice in a bowl and turn the apple slices in it so they are thoroughly coated.

Spread the cheese filling in the pastry case, then arrange the apple slices decoratively on top. Bake for 40–45 minutes.

Cool the flan for 10 minutes, then remove it from the tin, if using, and place on a serving plate.

Sieve the jam into a saucepan and stir in the brandy or water. Heat until the mixture is bubbling. Brush the apples with this glaze and leave until completely cold.

Cooking time: about 70 minutes plus cooling time

Hazelnut Bars

MAKES 8–10

50g/2 oz (¼ cup) butter

100g/¼ lb (½ cup) fine sugar

1 small egg, beaten

100g/¼ lb (1 cup) self-raising flour

50g/2 oz (½ cup) ground hazelnuts

Heat the oven to 180°C (350°F) gas mark 4. Cream the butter with the sugar until light and fluffy. Beat in the egg. Sift in the flour and add the hazelnuts. Mix all together well. Press the mixture into a greased 18cm (7 in) square cake tin (pan). Bake for 25 minutes.

Cool in the tin for 5 minutes, then cut into bars and cool on a wire rack.

Cooking time: 35 minutes plus cooling time

Decorate these butterfly cup cakes with buttercream, using a piping bag with star nozzle. Stand the bag in a jar to fill it.

All-in-one Lemon Cake

SERVES 6–8
175g/6 oz (1½ cups) self-raising flour
5ml (1 teaspoon) baking powder
175g/6 oz (¾ cup) fine sugar
175g/6 oz (¾ cup) soft margarine
3 medium-sized eggs
grated rind of 1 lemon
15ml (1 tablespoon) lemon juice
FOR SIMPLE GLACÉ ICING
125g/¼ lb (1 cup) icing (confectioners') sugar, sifted
30ml (2 tablespoons) lemon juice
candied lemon slices to decorate

Heat the oven to 170°C (325°F) gas mark 3. Grease a deep 18cm (7 in) round cake tin (pan), line with greaseproof or waxed paper and grease again.

Sift the flour and baking powder into a bowl. Add the remaining ingredients and beat until glossy and light. Pour into the tin and bake for 1¼–1½ hours or until a skewer inserted into the centre comes out clean. Rest for 3 minutes in the tin, then turn out on to a wire rack to cool.

To make the icing, beat together the sugar and lemon juice until smooth. Cover the cold cake. Decorate with lemon slices.
Cooking time: 1¾ hours plus 1½ hours cooling time

This easy-to-make all-in-one sponge cake is flavoured with lemon and topped with lemon glacé icing and lemon slices. On the left are shown small apple cakes. The recipe for these is given on page 221.

● For two deep 20cm (8 in) sandwich tins double the mixture and bake for 1–1¼ hours. Sandwich the cold cakes with 120ml (8 tablespoons) lemon curd and increase the icing by one third.

Oatmeal Cookies

MAKES ABOUT 4 DOZEN
75g/3 oz (6 tablespoons) butter
250g/9 oz (1⅓ cups) soft brown sugar
2 eggs, beaten
1 egg yolk
5ml (1 teaspoon) vanilla extract
175g/6 oz (1½ cups) flour
2.5ml (½ teaspoon) baking powder
175g (6 oz) rolled oats soaked in 60ml/4 tablespoons (¼ cup) milk

Heat the oven to 180°C (350°F) gas mark 4. Cream the butter with 225g/½ lb (1¼ cups) of the sugar until fluffy. Beat in the eggs, egg yolk and vanilla. Sift together the flour, salt and baking powder and fold into the creamed mixture, followed by the soaked oats.

Drop small spoonfuls of the mixture on to greased baking sheets, keeping them spaced about 5cm (2 in) apart. Sprinkle with the remaining sugar. Bake for 10–12 minutes or until golden brown. Transfer immediately to a wire rack to cool.
Cooking time: 35 minutes

Chocolate Fork Biscuits (Cookies)

MAKES ABOUT 2 DOZEN
100g/¼ lb (½ cup) butter
100g/¼ lb (½ cup) fine sugar
150g/5 oz (1¼ cups) self-raising flour
pinch of salt
37.5ml (2½ tablespoons) cocoa

Heat the oven to 190°C (375°F) gas mark 5. Cream the butter and sugar together until light and fluffy. Sift in the flour, salt and cocoa and mix well. Form the mixture into walnut-sized balls and place on greased baking sheets. Squash each ball slightly with a fork.

Bake for 8 minutes. Cool on a wire rack.
Cooking time: 20 minutes plus cooling time

Chocolate Munchies

MAKES 10

50g/2 oz ($\frac{1}{4}$ cup) butter or margarine
30ml (2 tablespoons) clear honey
50g/2 oz ($\frac{1}{4}$ cup) fine sugar
30ml (2 tablespoons) cocoa
25g/1 oz ($\frac{1}{2}$ cup) puffed rice

Put the butter, honey and sugar in a saucepan and heat gently, stirring to melt the fat and dissolve the sugar. Remove from the heat and stir in the cocoa.

Carefully fold in the puffed rice. Divide the mixture between 10 small paper cases and chill until set.
Cooking time : 5 minutes plus chilling time

● Add 30ml (2 tablespoons) raisins or 25g/ 1 oz ($\frac{1}{4}$ cup) chopped walnuts.

Tuiles

Home-made wafers with summer ice-cream or fruit purées are more delicious than shop-bought ones and save a lot of money. These curved wafers were called 'tiles' because they resembled the curved, terracotta roof tiles of the French villages where they were invented. The wafer is limp when hot and can be shaped ; when cooled and stiff it will hold the shape.

MAKES ABOUT 4 DOZEN

2 large egg whites
100g/$\frac{1}{4}$ lb ($\frac{1}{2}$ cup) fine sugar
50g/2 oz ($\frac{1}{2}$ cup) plain flour, sifted
25g/1 oz ($\frac{1}{4}$ cup) ground almonds
2-3 drops vanilla extract
50g/2 oz ($\frac{1}{4}$ cup) butter

Tuiles and langue de chat biscuits (cookies).

Heat the oven to 180 C (350 F) gas mark 4. Generously grease 2–3 baking sheets.

Put the egg whites and sugar in a large bowl and beat until combined and smooth. Gradually mix in the flour, ground almonds and vanilla. Melt the butter, which should be quite hot and stir in to make a thin batter.

Spread out the mixture in small spoonfuls leaving 5cm (2 in) between them. Bake one tray at a time, for 6–7 minutes or until golden-brown around the edges.

Remove from the oven and allow to cool on the baking sheet for a few seconds. Then speed is essential. Remove them from the baking sheet with a spatula and lay them in rows over a rolling pin, one layer on top of the other.

If the wafers will not come off the baking sheet, or become crisp before being shaped, return the sheet to the oven for a few minutes. When the wafers are set, remove to a wire rack. Store in an airtight container where they will keep for a week.
Cooking time : 25 minutes

● For a party, make cigarettes russe. Rolled up like cigarettes, these are a more ornamental shape than tuiles and consequently take slightly longer to do. Use exactly the same quantities, but omit the ground almonds. Use several baking sheets and spread out the mixture 15ml (1 tablespoon) at a time into oblongs and only about 4 to a baking sheet. Bake one sheet at a time for 7–8 minutes. Remove from the oven and leave to cool on the tray for just a few seconds. Then quickly remove and roll around the greased handle of a wooden spoon. Cool until rigid. If desired, the ends can be dipped into melted chocolate. This gives them the black tips which earned them the name of 'Russian cigarettes'. The cigarettes will keep for up to 2 days; the recipe makes 1$\frac{1}{2}$–2 dozen.
● For 2$\frac{1}{2}$–3 dozen langues de chat 'cat's tongues', use the same mixture as for cigarettes russe, or halve the amount of sugar in it. Cook in thin oblongs. Dip the tips in melted chocolate if desired.

To make a cigarette russe, roll the hot biscuit (cookie) round a spoon handle.

Jams and Jellies

Preserving summer fruit by making it into jams, jellies, curds and cheeses is the best way of capturing its luscious flavours. The process is so simple that you will find it no chore to fill your cupboard with jars of home-made preserves. Home-made jams make good winter snacks with bread and also make wonderful cakes and desserts. Jellies can also be served with cold meat and are useful for glazing fruit desserts. Jams keep for a year or more, but it is sensible to finish them before making the new season's jam.

The fruit used for jam and jelly making must be fresh, firm and underripe. (Overripe fruit will not set successfully.) A natural substance in many fruit, called pectin, enables a jam or jelly to set. Some fruits are richer in pectin than others, so to ensure a good set, you must choose—or mix—fruit, to reach the required pectin level. Citrus fruit, cooking apples, cranberries, damsons, gooseberries, plums and quinces are high in pectin. When jam-making with low-pectin fruit—cherries, figs, grapes, pears, pineapple, rhubarb, strawberries—you should include some of the former group to ensure a good set. Alternatively, pectin in liquid or powder form can be added. If in doubt about the pectin content of fruit, do the simple test shown on *page 122*, then follow the directions supplied with the pectin.

You need very little special equipment for making a jam: a large, wide saucepan of about 4L (1 gal) capacity; a funnel for potting the jam; a long-handled wooden spoon; a sugar thermometer to test for setting point is useful but not essential; a good supply of jars which must be free of chips, cracks or any flaws and completely clean; and waxed discs, cellophane covers, rubber bands and labels (in the US, paraffin wax, metal or plastic lids). For jelly, you also need a jelly bag.

To make jam, cook the washed fruit, with or without water as specified in the recipe, with additional pectin if required, until it is completely softened and broken down. In Britain preserving or lump sugar is preferred, but granulated sugar works effectively. Warm the sugar in a very low oven to help it to dissolve quickly. Add the sugar to the pan, raise the heat and boil briskly without stirring until setting point is reached. Test the set with either a thermometer or on a saucer, as shown in the steps.

Skim off any scum or stones. If the jam has whole or half fruits, cool it then stir to suspend the fruit (see steps). Fill the warmed jars with the hot jam. Wipe the jars and cover with waxed paper discs. Cook, then add the cellophane covers and secure with rubber bands. (The American method is to leave a 1.5cm ($\frac{1}{2}$ in) space at the top, pour melted paraffin wax up to half this depth and then cover with clean lids.) Label and store in a cool, dark place.

For jelly, pour the softened fruit into the jelly bag and leave to drain for 6–12 hours or overnight. Do not squeeze the bag, as this will make the finished jelly cloudy. Measure the juice and return it to the pan. Bring to the boil, then add sugar in proportion. Stir to dissolve, then boil briskly until setting point is reached. Test and pot as for jam.

Fruit cheeses—so called because they have the consistency of soft cheese—are made from stiff purées of fruit. The fruit is cooked and puréed before sugar is added in the proportion of 450g (1 lb) sugar to 450g (1 lb) fruit purée. Fruit cheeses keep like jams. Fruit curds—orange and lemon—contain butter and eggs which are beaten to an emulsion over hot water. They are poor storers but can be frozen.

Peach Jam

MAKES ABOUT 2.3KG (5 LB)
1 medium-sized cooking apple, chopped
thinly pared rind of 2 lemons
2 cloves
1.4kg (3 lb) peaches, stoned and sliced
275ml/$\frac{1}{2}$ pt (1$\frac{1}{4}$ cups) water
5ml (1 teaspoon) ground allspice
1.4kg (3 lb) sugar

Put the apple, lemon rind and cloves in a cheesecloth bag and put into the preserving pan with the peaches and water. Bring to the boil, then simmer, stirring frequently, until the peaches are soft.

Remove the cheesecloth bag, pressing it against the side of the pan to squeeze out the liquid. Add the allspice and sugar to the peaches and stir until dissolved. Bring back to the boil and boil rapidly until setting point is reached.

Remove from the heat. Allow to stand for 10 minutes. Stir, then ladle into jars and seal.
Cooking time: 1 hour

Easy to make peach jam is delicious eaten as the French do—with warm croissants.

Rhubarb and Ginger Jam

MAKES ABOUT 2.7KG (6 LB)
1.8kg (4 lb) rhubarb, cut into 2.5cm (1 in) pieces
225ml/8 fl oz (1 cup) water
juice of 1 lemon
5cm (2 in) piece ginger root, peeled and crushed
1.4kg (3 lb) sugar
60ml/4 tablespoons ($\frac{1}{2}$ cup) crystallized ginger, finely chopped

Put the rhubarb, water and lemon juice in the preserving pan and bring to the boil. Add the root ginger and simmer, stirring frequently, until the rhubarb is soft. Remove the ginger.

Add the sugar and stir until dissolved. Bring back to the boil and boil rapidly until setting point is reached. Stir in the crystallized ginger, then pot.
Cooking time: 45 minutes

●Vegetable marrow (baking squash) is usually cheaper than fruit. For marrow and ginger jam, sprinkle 1.8kg (4 lb) prepared marrow with 450g (1 lb) sugar and allow to stand 24 hours. Tie up 50g (2 oz) sliced green ginger with the rind of

Rhubarb and ginger jam is delicately flavoured with crystallized ginger.

3 lemons in a cheesecloth and simmer, with the marrow, 1.4kg (3 lb) sugar and juice of the lemons for 30 minutes.

Damson (Plum) Cheese

MAKES ABOUT 1.1KG (2$\frac{1}{2}$ LB)
2.7kg (6 lb) damsons (purple plums)
275ml/$\frac{1}{2}$ pt (1$\frac{1}{4}$ cups) water
sugar
10ml (2 teaspoons) ground allspice

Put the fruit in the preserving pan with the water. Cover and simmer gently until soft. Purée the fruit, removing stones (pits). For each 225ml/8 fl oz (1 cup) purée, you will need 22g/$\frac{1}{2}$ lb (1 cup) sugar.

Return the purée to the pan and add the sugar and allspice, stirring to dissolve. Continue cooking gently, stirring, until very thick, then pot.
Cooking time: 1$\frac{1}{4}$ hours

●Make 'cheese' from greengages and other plums in the same way.

Making Jam

1. To test for set, cook some of the fruit and put a spoonful in a glass. Leave till cold. Add 15ml (1 tablespoon) methylated spirit (grain alcohol) and shake. Leave 1 minute. Turn out onto a saucer.

2. If the mixture forms a jelly-like lump, the fruit is high in pectin. If the clot breaks into 2–3 pieces, the jam will still set. If the jelly breaks in small pieces, extra pectin must be added to the fruit.

3. Prepare the fruit and put the sugar in the oven on baking sheets to warm. Put the fruit in a pan with water. Simmer until tender. Scald the jam jars and put them in the oven to dry.

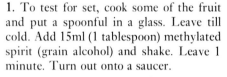

4. If the fruit failed the pectin test, add extra pectin at this point, in liquid or powder form, to ensure a satisfactory set. Use lemon juice, tartaric acid or pectin, or a fruit rich in pectin.

5. Add the warmed sugar to the cooked fruit stirring until it has dissolved. Attach the sugar thermometer, if using, to the side of the preserving pan. Bring the mixture to the boil.

6. Boil at a rolling boil for several minutes, stirring all the time. If using a sugar thermometer, the setting point is 108–109°C (220–222°F), depending on the type of fruit.

7. Remove the pan from the heat to test for set. Put a spoonful of jam on a saucer, leave $\frac{1}{2}$ minute, then stroke the surface with your finger. If the surface of the jam wrinkles, the jam will set.

8. Remove the pan from the heat and skim off any scum with a slotted spoon. Allow all whole fruit jams and marmalades to cool for 15–20 minutes to suspend the fruit. Then stir them before potting.

9. Pour more liquid jams into the warmed jars, using a funnel or jug. Fill right to the top. Cover with waxed paper discs (or in the US, melted paraffin wax) then seal and label with type and date.

Making Jellies

1. Prepare fruit and test for pectin. Add liquid, filling the pan half full. Simmer gently until the fruit is pulpy.

2. Pour the fruit pulp into the jelly bag and allow to drip 6 hours or overnight. Do not press fruit through the bag.

3. Measure the juice and then the sugar to match. Heat the juice, add sugar and boil. Test for set then strain and pot.

Making Fruit Butters

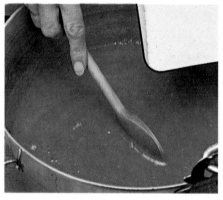

1. Cook the fruit with water then purée. Return the purée to the pan and cook over low heat until purée is thick and stiff.

2. Measure the purée and add 450g (1 lb) sugar to the same weight of purée (1 cup of sugar to 1 cup of purée).

3. Return to the boil and boil for 1 hour, stirring to prevent burning. Test for set, then pot as for jams.

Making Citrus Fruit Curds

1. Grate the rind and squeeze the juice. Prepare a double boiler and melt the butter in the top.

2. Beat the eggs and add, with the lemon juice to the butter. Add the sugar and heat, stirring until dissolved.

3. Cook gently, stirring all the time, until the curd thickens. Strain and pour into jars. Cool and cover as jam.

Lemon Curd

Double the quantities if you have a large freezer; lemon curd freezes well and will keep for 3 months. Otherwise eat in 1 month.

MAKES ABOUT 700G (1½ LB)

175g/6 oz (¾ cup) butter, cut into small pieces

450g (1 lb) sugar

thinly pared rind and juice of 3 large lemons

4 eggs, beaten

Put all the ingredients in a heatproof bowl placed over a saucepan of boiling water, or in the top of a double boiler. Cook gently, stirring, until the butter has melted and the sugar dissolved. Strain the mixture and discard the lemon rind.

Return the mixture to the heatproof bowl and cook, over the boiling water, stirring frequently, until thickened. Pot. *Cooking time:* 45 minutes

Fresh lemon curd has twice the appeal and flavour of the shop-bought curd.

Redcurrant Jelly

The most useful of all jellies to have in the house, this can be served with venison (or lamb), used in sauces and to glaze fruit.

MAKES ABOUT 1.8KG (4 LB)

1.8kg (4 lb) redcurrants

575ml/1 pt (2½ cups) water

sugar

Put the redcurrants and water in a preserving pan and bring to the boil. Simmer

for $\frac{3}{4}$–1 hour or until the fruit is very soft. Mash well, then strain through a jelly bag.

Measure the juice and add 450g (1 lb) sugar to each 575ml/1 pt ($2\frac{1}{2}$ cups) juice. Return to the pan and stir until the sugar has dissolved. Bring back to the boil and boil briskly until setting point is reached, then pot.

Cooking time: $1\frac{1}{2}$ hours plus overnight straining

● Blackcurrants are sourer than red and need more sugar. Add 550g/$1\frac{1}{4}$ lb ($2\frac{1}{2}$ cups) for each 575ml/1 pt ($2\frac{1}{2}$ cups) purée.

Apple and Berry Jelly

Something for nothing is always an attractive proposition: jellies from fruit growing wild provide just this.

MAKES ABOUT 3.6KG (8 LB)
2.7kg (6 lb) cooking apples, chopped, but not peeled or cored
900g (2 lb) elderberries or blueberries
15ml (1 tablespoon) lemon juice (for blueberries)
sugar

Put the apples in the preserving pan. Remove the stems from the elderberries or blueberries and add the berries to the pan with water to cover. Bring to the boil, then simmer for 45 minutes or until the fruit is very soft and pulpy.

Strain through a jelly bag. Measure the juice and add 450g (1 lb) sugar to each 575ml/1 pt ($2\frac{1}{2}$ cups) juice. Add the lemon juice if using blueberries, to help the set.

Return to the pan and stir until the sugar has dissolved. Bring back to the boil and boil briskly until setting point is reached. Pot in the usual way.

Cooking time: $1\frac{1}{2}$ hours plus overnight straining

● For sloe jelly, prick 900g (2 lb) sloes all over and simmer for 1 hour with 900g (2 lb) apples.
● Wild blackberries are low in pectin so, for bramble jelly, add 30ml (2 tablespoons) lemon juice to 1.8kg (4 lb) blackberries and 275ml/$\frac{1}{2}$ pt ($1\frac{1}{4}$ cups) water.
● For crabapple jelly, use 1.8kg (4 lb) apples with the rind of 2 lemons.
● From your flower garden use japonica (listed in garden catalogues as *Chaenomeles*); simmer 1.3kg (3 lb) quartered fruit with 450g (1 lb) apples and the juice of 1 lemon.

Mint Jelly

Mint jelly is the American accompaniment to lamb, while the British eat mint sauce.

MAKES ABOUT 2.3KG (5 LB)
2.3kg (5 lb) cooking apples, sliced
575ml/1 pt ($2\frac{1}{2}$ cups) water
75ml (5 tablespoons) fresh mint leaves
225ml/8 fl oz (1 cup) malt vinegar
sugar
6 drops of green food colouring

Put the apples and water in the preserving pan. Stir in half the mint leaves and bring to the boil. Simmer for 40–45 minutes or until the fruit is soft and pulpy. Add the vinegar and boil for a further 5 minutes.

Strain through a jelly bag, allowing about 12 hours. Measure the juice and add 450g (1 lb) sugar to each 575ml/1 pt ($2\frac{1}{2}$ cups) juice. Return to the pan and stir until the sugar has dissolved. Bring back to the boil and boil briskly until setting point is reached. Skim any foam off the surface, then add the remaining mint and food colouring. Stir well, then pot.

Cooking time: $1\frac{1}{2}$ hours plus overnight straining

● Rosemary jelly can be made in the same way, using 60ml (4 tablespoons) fresh rosemary leaves.
● For mint sauce, chop a large handful of mint leaves, then pound with 15ml (1 tablespoon) sugar. Add 60ml (4 tablespoons) boiling water and more sugar. Dissolve, then add 60ml (4 tablespoons) vinegar.

Fresh and green, rosemary jelly goes well with hot or cold lamb, and is a change from the more familiar mint jelly.

Barbecues and Picnics

On a sunny summer's day what could be better than a day out in a park, on a beach or in the country with a picnic? Fresh air and some exercise will sharpen your appetite. If you want to enjoy your own garden or know a picnic spot that permits it, try a barbecue. You can cook outdoors—not in a hot kitchen—and everyone will enjoy the new flavours. Barbecues are an ideal way of entertaining, too, since almost all the preparation is done ahead of time—and men enjoy doing the cooking when it is over an open fire!

Picnics call for a little thought because not all food is suitable for travelling on a warm day, unless you have an insulated box or a styrofoam chest or a bag with a cold brick. Mayonnaise, for example, is not always successful, and some sandwich fillings make the bread soggy after a while. There is a great range of picnic equipment available, from elaborate—and expensive—hampers to an assortment of unbreakable cups, plates and cutlery in a canvas bag. Whichever you choose, remember you will be sitting on the ground and take easy to handle food.

A barbecue is also an informal affair. If you have a patio with an outside table, then you can sit down to your meal. Provide paper napkins if you are serving hamburgers or finger food. Plenty of relishes, ketchup (recipe on *page 254*) and a variety of sliced salads and buns are traditional for this type of barbecue.

If you do not already have a purpose-built barbecue, they are easily made with a few spare bricks and an old oven shelf. Light the charcoal briquettes at least one hour before you start cooking. The fire must be hot and without flames or the food will dry out and cook unevenly. Hold your hand about 7.5cm (3 in) above it. If you can stand the heat for only 2–3 seconds, it is a hot fire.

If possible, use the long-handled fish slice and tongs specially made for barbecuing; an oven glove is also useful. Very useful impromptu skewers can be made from wire coat hangers. Remove the hook and straighten the wire to make a U-shape. Sausages can be threaded on, and up to a dozen can be cooked at one time.

If the charcoal is not completely burnt out at the end of cooking, dowse it with a little water and use it for your next fire.

Traveller's Tomato Soup

Picnics are not inevitably in summer; sometimes a family picnic is demanded by a winter journey. Hot soup is the answer.

SERVES 5
25g/1 oz (2 tablespoons) butter
3 fatty bacon slices, cut into matchsticks
2 carrots, diced
2 celery stalks, chopped
1 small onion, chopped
800g (1¾ lb) canned tomatoes, drained and juice reserved
1 garlic clove, crushed
2 cloves
1 bouquet garni
25g/1 oz (¼ cup) flour
45ml (3 tablespoons) milk
salt
freshly ground black pepper
5ml (1 teaspoon) sugar

Melt the butter in a saucepan. Add the bacon and fry for 2 minutes. Stir in the carrots, celery and onion and continue frying until the onion is softened.

Stir in the tomatoes, garlic, cloves and bouquet garni. Make up the juice from the tomato can to 850ml/1½ pts (3¾ cups) with water and add to the pan. Bring to the boil, then cover the pan and simmer for 20 minutes.

Discard the bouquet garni and cloves, then blend the soup to a purée or pass through a food mill or strainer. Return to the pan.

Mix the flour with the milk and add to the pan. Simmer, stirring, until thickened. Season and add the sugar. Pour into a vacuum flask (bottle) to take to the picnic. *Cooking time: 40 minutes*

Picnic Meat Loaf

SERVES 8
1.4kg (3 lb) lean minced (ground) beef
4 lean bacon slices, diced
1 garlic clove, crushed
60ml/4 tablespoons (¼ cup) red wine
15ml (1 tablespoon) wine vinegar
5ml (1 teaspoon) Dijon mustard
10ml (2 teaspoons) fresh thyme, chopped
salt
freshly ground black pepper

Heat the oven to 160°C (325°F) gas mark 3. Combine all the ingredients with seasoning to taste. Pack into a greased 900g (2 lb) loaf tin (pan). Place the tin in a deep baking dish and pour boiling water around to come half way up the sides. Bake for 1½ hours. Cover the meat loaf with foil if it is browning too much.

Cool the meat loaf in the tin, then turn out and wrap in foil to take to the picnic. Serve with crisp salad vegetables. *Preparation time: 1¾ hours plus 3 hours cooling time*

Grosvenor Pie

SERVES 8–10
700g (1½ lb) pie or stewing veal, chopped
350g (¾ lb) smoked corner gammon or boiling bacon (bacon)
salt
freshly ground black pepper
grated rind of ½ lemon
15ml (1 tablespoon) fresh parsley, chopped
5ml (1 teaspoon) fresh sage, chopped
hot-water crust pastry (*page 242*)
4 large hard-boiled eggs
beaten egg to glaze
425ml/¾ pt (1⅔ cups) jellied stock

Heat the oven to 200°C (400°F) gas mark 6. Coarsely mince (grind) or finely chop the two meats then mix together with the lemon rind, parsley, sage and seasoning.

Roll out two-thirds of the pastry and use to line a 900g (2 lb) loaf tin (pan),

leaving the pastry hanging over the edge of the tin by 6mm ($\frac{1}{4}$ in) (*page 242*). Put half the meat mixture into the tin and arrange the eggs in a row on top. Cover with the rest of the meat mixture.

Roll out the remaining dough and use to cover the pie. Dampen all the edges, then press together to seal. Make holes along the centre length of the pie and decorate with the pastry trimmings if you like. Brush with beaten egg.

Bake for 30 minutes, then reduce the temperature to 160°C (325°F) gas mark 3. Cover the top with foil if overbrowning.

Ten minutes before the baking time is up, remove the pie from the oven. Work a spatula between the tin and the sides of the pie to loosen. Then turn the pie out of the tin, rolling it on to a wire rack covered with a cloth, so that the decorations are not damaged. Place, right side up, on a baking sheet. Brush the sides with beaten egg and

Barbecues—whether home-built or bought —make summer eating easy and fun.

return to the oven.

Remove from the oven and pour the stock down a funnel through the holes in the crust. Leave to cool and set for 3 hours.

Take to the picnic wrapped in foil or return to the loaf tin.

Cooking time: 3 hours plus 3 hours cooling

127

Chicken and Mushroom Scallops

These portable little pies are ideal for a picnic. However, they also make excellent buffet party food. Arrange them on a platter with their attractive scalloped bottoms uppermost, surrounded by watercress.

SERVES 5
75g/3 oz ($\frac{1}{3}$ cup) butter
1 medium-sized onion, chopped
100g ($\frac{1}{4}$ lb) button mushrooms, quartered
30ml (2 tablespoons) flour
150ml/$\frac{1}{4}$ pt ($\frac{2}{3}$ cup) milk
275g/10 oz (1$\frac{1}{4}$ cups) chicken meat, diced
15ml (1 tablespoon) parsley, chopped
15ml (1 tablespoon) lemon juice
salt
freshly ground black pepper
2 × shortcrust pastry *(page 240)*
beaten egg to glaze

Melt the butter in a saucepan. Add the onion and fry until softened. Add the mushrooms and fry for a further 3 minutes. Stir in the flour and cook for 2 minutes. Gradually stir in the milk and bring to the boil, stirring. Simmer until thickened. Add the chicken, parsley, lemon juice and seasoning and mix well. Cool.

Heat the oven to 220°C (425°F) gas mark 7. Divide the pastry into 2 portions, one larger than the other. Divide the larger portion into 5 balls. Roll out each ball and use to line 5 greased scallop shells. Prick each lined shell with a fork.

Divide the chicken and mushroom filling between the shells. Divide the remaining dough into 5 and roll out each portion. Use to make the lids and press the edges together to seal. Brush with the beaten egg. Place the scallops on a baking sheet and bake for 25 minutes.

Turn the pastry scallops out of the shells, curved side upward, on to the baking sheet and glaze generously with beaten egg. Bake for a further 10 minutes. Cool on a wire rack. Replace the scallops in the shells to take to the picnic.

Cooking time : 10 minutes for the filling plus cooling time, 45 minutes for the pies plus cooling time

Chicken Drumsticks en Croûte

SERVES 6
30ml (2 tablespoons) oil
6 chicken drumsticks, skinned
30ml (2 tablespoons) Dijon mustard
salt
freshly ground black pepper
225g ($\frac{1}{2}$ lb) made weight frozen rough puff or flaky pastry, thawed (pastry for 1-crust pie)
beaten egg to glaze

Heat the oil in a frying pan. Add the drumsticks and brown on all sides. Drain and cool. Make cuts in the meat of the drumsticks at 1.2cm ($\frac{1}{2}$ in) intervals and spread the mustard in these cuts, then season.

Heat the oven to 220°C (425°F) gas mark 7. Roll out the dough to a rectangle 25 × 33cm (10 × 13 in) about 3mm ($\frac{1}{8}$ in) thick. Trim the edges and cut into strips 2.5cm (1 in) wide and 30cm (12 in) long. Brush the edges of the dough strips with beaten egg. Wrap one end of a pastry strip round the bone of one drumstick. Then wind the pastry round the chicken, just overlapping the pastry below. Continue until the meat is entirely covered, pressing to seal the pastry strips together. Repeat with the other drumsticks. Place on a baking sheet and leave to rest for 30 minutes.

Brush all over with beaten egg, then bake for 25 minutes. Allow to cool. Take to the picnic wrapped in foil.

Cooking time : 2$\frac{1}{2}$ hours plus chilling time

Frankfurter Kebabs

SERVES 4
8 medium-sized frankfurters, each cut into 4 pieces
400g (14 oz) canned pineapple chunks, drained
8 lean bacon slices, rolled up
8 small onions
2 green (bell) peppers, cored, seeded and cut into squares
60ml/4 tablespoons ($\frac{1}{4}$ cup) oil

Thread the frankfurter pieces, pineapple chunks, bacon rolls, onions and green pepper squares on to eight skewers, alternating the ingredients. Brush the kebabs all over with oil and place on the grill, about 10cm (4 in) above the coals. Cook for 15 minutes, turning frequently and brushing with more oil as necessary.
Cooking time: 20 minutes

Chicken Tikka

SERVES 4–6
150ml/¼ pt (⅔ cup) plain yogurt
4 garlic cloves, crushed
2.5cm (1 in) piece root ginger, peeled and grated
1 small onion, grated
7.5ml (1½ teaspoons) hot chilli powder
15ml (1 tablespoon) ground coriander
5ml (1 teaspoon) salt
6 chicken breasts, skinned, boned and cut into 2.5cm (1 in) cubes
TO SERVE
1 large onion, thinly sliced into rings
2 large tomatoes, thinly sliced
30ml (2 tablespoons) fresh coriander leaves, chopped
6 pitta bread (optional)

Combine the yogurt, garlic, ginger, onion, chilli powder, coriander and salt in a mixing bowl. Add the chicken cubes and stir well. Cover and marinate in the refrigerator for at least 6 hours, stirring occasionally.

Thread the chicken cubes on to skewers. Place on the grill about 12.5cm (5 in) above the coals and cook for 5–6 minutes, turning occasionally.

For patio eating, slide the chicken cubes off the skewers on to a warmed serving platter and garnish with the onion rings, tomato slices and coriander. For finger food, warm 6 pitta bread, cut open the pockets and divide the chicken mixture and garnishes between them.
Cooking time: 6 hours marinating then 10 minutes

● For meat tikka, use 700g (1½ lb) lean, cubed shoulder of lamb.
● If pitta bread is not available, use a split French loaf or a long crusty roll to hold your meat and salad fillings.

Arabian Kofta

SERVES 4
550g (1¼ lb) minced (ground) lamb
1 medium-sized onion, grated
1 small egg
5ml (1 teaspoon) ground cinnamon or allspice
salt
freshly ground black pepper

Combine all the ingredients, using your fingers to knead them well. Divide the mixture into 12 portions and shape into balls with dampened hands. Slide three meatballs on to each of four skewers.

Place the skewers on the grill, about 10cm (4 in) above the coals, and cook for 8–12 minutes, turning frequently. For a patio meal, serve on a bed of noodles. For finger food use French or pitta bread to hold the meat and a selection of salads.
Cooking time: 25 minutes

Marinated Steak

SERVES 4
90ml/6 tablespoons (⅓ cup) soy sauce
90ml/6 tablespoons (⅓ cup) medium-dry sherry
90ml/6 tablespoons (⅓ cup) oil
1 garlic clove, crushed
salt
freshly ground black pepper
900g (2 lb) skirt (flank) steak, well beaten

Combine the soy sauce, sherry, oil, garlic and seasoning in a shallow dish. Add the steak and leave to marinate for at least 8 hours, turning occasionally.

Drain the steak and place it on the grill, about 10cm (4 in) above the coals. Cook for about 5 minutes on each side, depending on how well done you like your meat. Slice at a slanted angle to serve.
Cooking time: about 8 hours marinating, then 10 minutes

Grilling a kebab on a barbecue is the easiest form of cooking there is and one of the most enjoyable. Meat tikka is marinated for extra flavour. Serve it with salads in French bread or Greek pitta.

Hamburgers

SERVES 12

1.4kg (3 lb) lean minced beef (ground chuck)

1 large onion, finely chopped

6 slices white bread, crumbed

5ml (1 teaspoon) dried thyme

15ml (1 tablespoon) fresh herbs, chopped

10ml (2 teaspoons) salt

freshly ground black pepper

3 medium-sized eggs

12 baps or hamburger rolls

Combine all ingredients except the rolls, using your hands to mix thoroughly. Shape into 12 patties. Store in a plastic box in the refrigerator until needed, then take to the barbecue in their box.

Place the burgers on the grill, about 10cm (4 in) from the coals, and cook for 5–7 minutes on each side.

Serve the hamburgers in the buns with all the traditional relishes and salads.

Cooking time: 20 minutes plus 20 minutes' barbecuing

Whether a pure beef hamburger or the more economical one with added onion here, serve it with relishes on a sesame bun.

Barbecue Sauce

SERVES 8

100g/$\frac{1}{4}$ lb ($\frac{1}{2}$ cup) margarine

250ml/$\frac{1}{2}$ pt (1$\frac{1}{4}$ cups) red wine vinegar

2.5ml ($\frac{1}{2}$ teaspoon) English mustard powder

5ml (1 teaspoon) onion, finely chopped

30ml (2 tablespoons) Worcestershire sauce

15ml (1 tablespoon) chilli sauce

10ml (2 teaspoons) lemon juice

5ml (1 teaspoon) brown sugar

Put all ingredients in a heavy-bottomed pan over low heat. Stir until the fat has melted. Use for basting hamburgers, steaks, chicken or spareribs (pork ribs).

Cooking time: 2 minutes

Burger Relishes

EACH RELISH SERVES 6–8

FOR MID-WEST RELISH

175g/6 oz ($\frac{3}{4}$ cup) cooked sweetcorn kernels

$\frac{1}{2}$ red (bell) pepper, finely chopped

30ml (2 tablespoons) Dijon or German mustard

60ml/4 tablespoons ($\frac{1}{4}$ cup) mayonnaise (*page 250*)

FOR RUSSIAN RELISH

1 cucumber, diced

1 onion, finely chopped

250ml/$\frac{1}{2}$ pt (1$\frac{1}{4}$ cups) sour cream or plain yogurt

FOR HORSERADISH RELISH

20ml (4 teaspoons) freshly grated horse-radish or 30ml (2 tablespoons) prepared horseradish sauce

250ml/$\frac{1}{2}$ pt (1$\frac{1}{4}$ cups) mayonnaise

Combine the ingredients for each relish and store in plastic containers, covered, ready to take out-of-doors.

Preparation time: a few minutes each

Barbecued Mackerel with Fennel

SERVES 4

4 large mackerel, cleaned
3 dozen dried fennel stalks
25g/1 oz (2 tablespoons) butter
a squeeze of lemon juice
15ml (1 tablespoon) fresh parsley, chopped
salt
freshly ground black pepper
30ml (2 tablespoons) oil
15ml (1 tablespoon) brandy

Stuff each fish with 6 fennel stalks. Melt the butter in a saucepan on the side of the barbecue. Stir in the lemon juice, parsley, seasoning and oil, then score the fish lightly, making 3 cuts on each side. Arrange the remaining fennel stalks on a serving platter.

Place the fish on the barbecue grill, about 15cm (6 in) above the coals. Enclose the fish in a wire basket if you have one; it will make it much easier to turn the fish without their breaking up. Baste with the butter mixture and cook for about 7 minutes on each side or until the fish flakes easily, basting frequently.

Transfer the fish to the serving dish. Pour the brandy into a warm spoon then sprinkle it over the fish. Set alight and serve with the smoking fennel stalks.
Cooking time: about 25 minutes

Barbecued Fish Steaks

SERVES 4

4 cod or haddock steaks, about 225g (½ lb) each
225ml/8 fl oz (1 cup) dry red wine
pinch of cayenne pepper
5ml (1 teaspoon) prepared mustard
10ml (2 teaspoons) chilli sauce
30ml (2 tablespoons) lemon juice
5ml (1 teaspoon) brown sugar
salt
freshly ground black pepper
60ml/4 tablespoons (¼ cup) oil
15ml (1 tablespoons) capers

Grilled mackerel is flavoured with the smoke of burning fennel stalks.

Put the fish steaks in a shallow dish. Combine the wine, cayenne, mustard, chilli sauce, lemon juice, sugar, salt, pepper and oil in a saucepan and heat, stirring to dissolve the sugar. Pour this mixture over the fish steaks and leave to marinate for 1 hour, turning occasionally.

Drain the fish steaks, reserving the marinade, and arrange on the grill about 10cm (4 in) above the coals. Put the marinade in a saucepan on the side of the grill to heat.

Cook the fish steaks for about 5 minutes on each side, basting frequently with the marinade. Stir the capers into the marinade and serve as a sauce with the fish. Eat this dish at a patio table.
Cooking time: after 1 hour marinating, about 10 minutes

●Omit the wine for a more economical version, substitute 30ml (2 tablespoons) red wine vinegar and tomato juice.

Autumn

Soups and Starters

Stuffed Marinated Mushrooms

SERVES 3

6 large mushrooms
pinch of mustard powder
pinch of fine sugar
salt and pepper
30ml (2 tablespoons) wine vinegar
60ml (4 tablespoons) corn or olive oil
75ml/3 fl oz ($\frac{1}{3}$ cup) thick or whipping cream
15ml (1 tablespoon) lemon juice
1 celery stalk, chopped
30ml (2 tablespoons) chopped fresh chives
30ml (2 tablespoons) chopped fresh parsley
50g (2 oz) ham
finely chopped parsley sprigs

Wipe mushrooms and trim off stalks level with caps. Place mushrooms in a single layer, gills facing upward, in a shallow dish. Put mustard, sugar and seasoning in a bowl. Add vinegar and oil and blend with a fork. Pour the marinade over the mushrooms. Cover the dish with foil and leave in a cold place for 4–8 hours. Spoon the marinade over mushrooms 2–3 times.

Whip the cream until it stands in stiff peaks. Stir in the lemon juice. Stir the celery and ham into the cream with the chopped herbs and season to taste.

Transfer the mushrooms from the marinade into a serving dish. Stir any left-over marinade into the cream mixture. Using a small spoon, divide the stuffing between the mushrooms, mounding it in the centre of each. Garnish with parsley.

Preparation time: 30 minutes plus 4–8 hours marinating

Celery with Anchovies

SERVES 4

50g (2 oz) anchovy fillets in oil
freshly ground black pepper
15ml (1 tablespoon) olive oil
15ml (1 tablespoon) white wine vinegar
2 heads (bunches) of celery
30ml (2 tablespoons) chopped parsley

Pound the anchovies with their oil in a mortar with a pestle or in a bowl, using the rounded end of a rolling pin. Continue until the anchovies are reduced to a completely smooth paste: this may take as long as 10 minutes. Stir in the black pepper and gradually add oil and vinegar. Cover and place in refrigerator to chill.

Add ice cubes to a bowl of water. Remove the tough outer stalks from the celery and set aside for use in other dishes. When you reach the heart section, trim off any top leaves and scrub the stalks. Cut the celery hearts into four and place in the ice-cold water for at least 30 minutes to crisp. (You can leave them for up to 2 hours.)

When ready to serve, drain the celery hearts and pat dry. Arrange in a shallow dish. Pour the sauce over. Sprinkle with parsley and serve.

Preparation time: 1 hour

This anchovy sauce lends French elegance to crisp celery stalks; a widely-available vegetable is turned into a quick starter.

Minorcan Vegetable Soup

Vary the vegetables for this soup according to the season.

SERVES 4
45ml (3 tablespoons) olive oil
4 garlic cloves, chopped
2 large onions, coarsely chopped
2 leeks, white part only, chopped
2 celery stalks, trimmed and chopped
225g ($\frac{1}{2}$ lb) tomatoes, blanched, peeled and chopped
1 large red (bell) pepper, white pith removed, seeded and cut into strips
1.1L/2 pt (5 cups) water
1 small cabbage, outer leaves removed and shredded
5ml (1 teaspoon) dried thyme
1 bay leaf
5ml (1 teaspoon) salt
2.5ml ($\frac{1}{2}$ teaspoon) black pepper
4 slices of brown bread
2 garlic cloves, crushed
30ml (2 tablespoons) olive oil

This substantial vegetable soup, from the island of Minorca in the Mediterranean, has bread as its base. It makes a meal in its self—perhaps a Saturday lunch.

In a large saucepan, heat the oil over moderate heat. Add the garlic and fry it, stirring constantly, for 2–3 minutes. Add the onions, leeks and celery. Fry, stirring occasionally, for 5–7 minutes, or until the onions are soft and translucent but not brown. Add the tomatoes and the red pepper and cook, stirring occasionally, for a further 15 minutes. Add the water, increase the heat to high and bring the mixture to the boil, stirring constantly. Add the cabbage, thyme, bay leaf, salt and pepper. Cover the pan and simmer the soup for 2 hours.

Spread the slices of bread with the garlic and oil mixed. Place the bread in a warmed large soup tureen, or in individual soup bowls. Pour the soup over the bread and serve immediately.

Cooking time: 2$\frac{3}{4}$ hours

Savoury Pears

SERVES 8
100g/$\frac{1}{4}$ lb (4) fatty bacon slices, rinded
225g/$\frac{1}{2}$ lb (1 cup) curd cheese
10ml (2 teaspoons) lemon juice
5ml (1 teaspoon) oil
5ml (1 teaspoon) Worcestershire sauce
salt
4 large ripe dessert pears, peeled, halved and cored
watercress sprigs to garnish

Heat the grill (broiler) to moderate. Lay the bacon slices on the rack and cook until crisp. Drain on absorbent paper and crumble. Mix together the cheese, half the lemon juice, oil, Worcestershire sauce and seasoning, then fold in the bacon.

Place the pear halves on serving plates and brush over with the remaining lemon juice. Fill the hollow in each with a generous spoonful of the cheese and bacon. Garnish with watercress and chill.

Cooking time: 40 minutes

Cotriade

This is the original fish chowder from Brittany. The fish that goes into it is largely a matter of what is available and what is cheap, but it is a good idea to include a little shellfish (usually prawns or clams, shrimps or mussels) to give variety. When buying mussels, remember 450g (1 lb) gives you about 100g ($\frac{1}{4}$ lb) flesh.

SERVES 6
900g (2 lb) mixed filleted fish (cod, haddock, mackerel, mullet, John Dory etc) with some shellfish (prawns, clams, shrimps or mussels)
25g/1 oz (1 tablespoon) butter
1 large onion, chopped
1 garlic clove, crushed
2 carrots, chopped
2 celery stalks, chopped
1 large potato, diced
bouquet garni
salt
freshly ground black pepper
10ml (2 teaspoons) tomato paste
juice of half a lemon
TO SERVE
1 small loaf French bread
2 plump garlic cloves, crushed
30ml (2 tablespoons) olive oil

If using shellfish, peel prawns or shrimps. Clean clams or mussels thoroughly, discarding broken or open ones. Shake them in a heavy-bottomed pan over low heat until the shells open. Remove the fish from the shells. Reserve the liquid to add to the soup. Cut all other fish into chunks.

Melt the butter in a heavy-bottomed pan over low heat and sauté the onion and garlic until soft. Add 1.1L/2 pt (5 cups) cold water. Add carrots, celery, potato and the bouquet garni and bring to the boil. Simmer for 15 minutes.

Add the fish, seasoning, tomato paste and lemon juice. Pour the mussel stock through a cheesecloth-lined strainer into the pan. Simmer for 15 minutes until the fish is cooked but still firm. Adjust seasoning if necessary.

Meanwhile, cut the French bread into thick slices. Put half the oil and half the garlic in a frying pan over medium heat. Fry the slices of French bread until golden on both sides, frying in batches and adding more oil and garlic as needed. Float the slices of bread on top of the soup and serve.
Cooking time: 1$\frac{1}{4}$ hours

Jerusalem Artichoke and Tomato Soup

Tomatoes add colour to this soup.

SERVES 4
700g (1$\frac{1}{2}$ lb) Jerusalem artichokes
225g ($\frac{1}{2}$ lb) onions, chopped
25g/1 oz (2 tablespoons) butter
225g ($\frac{1}{2}$ lb) tomatoes
salt
freshly ground black pepper
1 garlic clove, crushed
850ml/1$\frac{1}{2}$ pt (3$\frac{3}{4}$ cups) chicken or white stock

Cotriade is the original fish chowder.

Peel and thinly slice Jerusalem artichokes. Melt the butter in a heavy-bottomed saucepan over low heat. Add the onions and artichokes. Cover the pan and sweat, shaking the pan occasionally, for about 5 minutes.

Meanwhile, pour boiling water over the tomatoes, then skin and halve them and remove seeds. Add the tomato flesh to the pan, cover and sweat for 3 minutes more.

Add crushed garlic, salt and pepper. Pour on stock. Bring to a simmering point, and cover and simmer for 15 minutes. Reduce the contents of the pan to a purée, using a vegetable mill, blender or strainer. Reheat for serving.
Cooking time: 30 minutes

Oatmeal and Carrot Soup

SERVES 4
25g/1 oz (2 tablespoons) butter
2 leeks, white part only, sliced
450g (1 lb) carrots, thinly sliced
1.1L/2 pt (5 cups) chicken stock
2.5ml ($\frac{1}{2}$ teaspoon) salt
2.5ml ($\frac{1}{2}$ teaspoon) black pepper
bouquet garni
2.5ml ($\frac{1}{2}$ teaspoon) grated orange rind
25g/1 oz (2 tablespoons) fine oatmeal
75ml/3 fl oz ($\frac{1}{3}$ cup) milk
75ml/3 fl oz ($\frac{1}{3}$ cup) thick cream
30ml (2 tablespoons) chopped fresh watercress

In a large saucepan, melt the butter over moderate heat. Fry the leeks, stirring occasionally with a wooden spoon, for 5–7 minutes or until they are soft and translucent but not brown.

Add the carrots and fry for 5 minutes, stirring occasionally. Add the chicken stock, salt, pepper, bouquet garni and orange rind. Bring the soup to the boil then simmer for 30–40 minutes or until the carrots are tender.

Mix the oatmeal and milk together, then stir into the soup, a little at a time. Cook, stirring frequently, for a further 15–20 minutes, or until the soup has thickened slightly. Remove and discard the bouquet garni.

Stir the cream into the soup and cook for a further 1 minute. Do not allow the soup to boil. Remove the pan from the heat. Ladle the soup into warmed soup bowls. Sprinkle with the watercress. Serve immediately.
Cooking time: 1½ hours

Eggplant hors d'oeuvre

Serve this Persian hors d'oeuvre on thin triangles of black bread, garnished with lemon slices.

SERVES 4

2 medium-sized aubergines (eggplants)
30ml (2 tablespoons) vegetable oil
1 medium-sized onion, finely chopped
2.5ml (½ teaspoon) salt
1.5ml (¼ teaspoon) black pepper
15ml (1 tablespoon) tomato paste
10ml (2 teaspoons) wine vinegar
15ml (1 tablespoon) lemon juice
30ml (2 tablespoons) chopped fresh parsley

Half fill a large saucepan with water. Add the aubergines (eggplants) and set the pan over high heat. When the water boils, reduce the heat, cover the pan and simmer for 15 minutes.

Drain the aubergines in a colander. Place them on a chopping board and carefully peel off and discard the skins. Using a kitchen fork, mash the aubergine flesh. Set aside.

In a large frying-pan, heat the oil over moderate heat. Fry the onion and garlic, stirring occasionally, for 5–7 minutes or until the onion is soft and translucent but not brown.

Add the aubergine flesh, the salt, pepper, tomato paste and vinegar. Reduce the heat to low and, stirring constantly, simmer the mixture for 5 minutes. Stir in the lemon juice and parsley.

Transfer the mixture to a serving bowl and leave to cool. Place the bowl in the refrigerator to chill for 1 hour before serving.
Cooking time: 1 hour plus 2 hours chilling time

Oxtail Consommé

This well-flavoured consommé is a by-product of cooking oxtails. Add a little meat to the soup. The remainder can be served with a savoury sauce of your choice for a main course.

SERVES 4

2 small oxtails about 1.8kg (4 lb) cut into pieces
2 carrots, chopped
2 small turnips, chopped
4 celery stalks, chopped
1 medium-sized onion, quartered
5ml (1 teaspoon) sugar
bouquet garni
5ml (1 teaspoon) white peppercorns
shell and white of 1 large egg
175ml/6 fl oz (¾ cup) port
salt and pepper

Place the oxtails in a large pan over low heat. Allow them to brown in their own fat. Add the vegetables. Stir until just coated with fat. Add sugar and allow to caramelize slightly.

Pack the oxtails down to fit the pan and pour on enough water to cover. Add the bouquet garni and simmer gently. When a thick scum has risen to the surface, skim this off. Add the peppercorns. Half cover the pan and simmer for about 3½ hours, topping up with extra water as necessary.

Pour through a strainer double-lined with cheesecloth. Discard the vegetables but reserve the oxtail. Leave the stock until cold and then lift fat from the surface.

Place the stock in a large pan. Pour in the port and add the egg white and shell to clarify the soup. Whisk over low heat until almost boiling. Reduce heat and simmer uncovered for 60 minutes.

Pour through a strainer double-lined with cheesecloth. Season and strain as before. Reheat and serve garnished with about 100g (¼ lb) of the oxtail cut into dice.
Cooking time: 5 hours plus cooling time in the middle

Philadelphia Pepper Pot

This warming soup uses tripe.

SERVES 6–8

1 veal knuckle, sawn into 3 pieces
bouquet garni
6 black peppercorns
4.5L/4 qt (5 qt) water
450g (1 lb) blanched tripe, cut into 2.5cm (1 in) pieces
1 medium-sized onion, finely chopped
2 large carrots, cut into 2.5cm (1 in) pieces
2 celery stalks, trimmed and cut into 2.5cm (1 in) pieces
5ml (1 teaspoon) salt
5ml (1 teaspoon) black pepper
2.5ml (½ teaspoon) red pepper flakes
2 medium-sized potatoes, peeled and diced
15g/½ oz (1 tablespoon) butter
15g/½ oz (1 tablespoon) flour
30ml (2 tablespoons) chopped fresh parsley

In a very large saucepan, combine the veal knuckle, bouquet garni, peppercorns and water. Place the pan over moderate heat and bring the liquid to the boil, skimming any scum from the surface with a slotted spoon. Cover the pan and simmer for 2½ hours.

Remove the pan from the heat and lift out the knuckle. Place the veal pieces on a chopping board and, with a sharp knife, remove the meat from the knuckle. Discard the bones and any fat or gristle. Chop the meat into 1.2 cm (½ in) cubes and set aside. Strain the stock through a wire strainer into a large mixing bowl.

Return the strained stock to the pan and add the tripe, onion, carrots, celery, salt, pepper and red pepper flakes. Return the pan to moderate heat and bring the soup to the boil. Reduce the heat to low, cover the pan and simmer for 1 hour. Add the potatoes and the reserved veal cubes and cook for a further 30 minutes or until the potatoes are tender.

Combine the butter and flour to make a beurre manié, then stir this, a small piece at a time, into the hot liquid. Continue stirring until the mixture thickens slightly. Taste the soup and add more salt and pepper if liked.

Remove the pan from the heat and stir in the chopped parsley. Ladle the soup into a soup tureen or warmed bowls and serve immediately.
Cooking time: 4½ hours

137

Eggs and Cheese

Eggs Stuffed with Ham and Herbs

Hard-boiled eggs stuffed with a delicious ham and herb mixture and then deep-fried, make a croquette with a surprise filling. Serve the eggs with a thick tomato and onion sauce (page 254).

SERVES 2
4 hard-boiled eggs
50g (2 oz) cooked ham, finely chopped
75g/3 oz (9 tablespoons) butter
5ml (1 teaspoon) dried thyme
5ml (1 teaspoon) Worcestershire sauce
2 eggs
2.5ml ($\frac{1}{2}$ teaspoon) salt
1.5ml ($\frac{1}{4}$ teaspoon) black pepper
60ml (4 tablespoons) dry white breadcrumbs

Cut the hard-boiled eggs in half, length-wise. Remove the yolks and place them in a medium-sized mixing bowl. Set the whites aside. Add the ham, one-third of the butter, thyme, Worcestershire sauce, one raw egg, salt and pepper. With a wooden spoon, cream the mixture thoroughly until it is smooth.

Spoon the mixture into the egg white halves. Sandwich the halves together to form a whole egg. The halves should not fit tightly together.

On a small plate, lightly beat the second egg with a fork. Roll the stuffed eggs in the beaten egg and then in the breadcrumbs.

In a medium-sized frying-pan, melt the remaining butter over moderate heat. Put in the stuffed eggs and fry them for 5 minutes, or until they are golden brown all over. With a slotted spoon, carefully transfer the stuffed eggs to a warmed serving dish and serve at once.

Cooking time: 30–45 minutes

● Stuff the eggs with 50g/2 oz ($\frac{1}{2}$ cup) grated cheese, 1 raw egg and the thyme.

These hard eggs are stuffed with ham and herbs, with a crisp golden coating.

Cheese Charlotte

This light charlotte can be topped with crisply-fried bacon and parsley.

SERVES 4
1 thick slice white bread, cut into cubes
200ml/7 fl oz ($\frac{7}{8}$ cup) milk
8 slices of white bread, crusts removed
40g/1$\frac{1}{2}$ oz (3 tablespoons) butter
3 eggs, separated
22.5ml (1$\frac{1}{2}$ tablespoons) flour
225g/$\frac{1}{2}$ lb (2 cups) cheddar cheese, grated
2.5ml ($\frac{1}{4}$ teaspoon) salt
1.5ml ($\frac{1}{4}$ teaspoon) grated nutmeg
125ml/4 fl oz ($\frac{1}{2}$ cup) thin cream

Heat the oven to moderate 180°C (350°F) gas mark 4. Put the bread cubes in a shallow dish and sprinkle over half the milk. In another dish, spread out the bread slices and sprinkle them with the remaining milk. Leave the cubes and slices to soak.

In a large bowl, cream the butter with a wooden spoon and mix in the egg yolks,

one at a time. Stir in the flour. Add the soaked bread cubes, cheese, salt and nutmeg. Blend well and stir in the cream. Beat the egg whites until they are stiff. Fold them into the cheese mixture.

Line a greased, straight-sided soufflé dish or casserole with the soaked bread slices. Pour the cheese mixture into the dish. Bake in the oven for 35–40 minutes. Serve immediately.
Cooking time: 1 hour

Essen Eggs

SERVES 4–6
60ml/4 tablespoons ($\frac{1}{4}$ cup) olive oil
1 medium-sized onion, finely chopped
2 medium-sized potatoes, diced
50g (2 oz) cooked ham, diced
1 small green (bell) pepper, white pith removed, seeded and finely chopped
225g ($\frac{1}{2}$ lb) canned tomatoes, drained and chopped
8 frankfurters, cut into 1.2cm ($\frac{1}{2}$ in) slices
1.5ml ($\frac{1}{4}$ teaspoon) dried basil
6 eggs
5ml (1 teaspoon) salt
2.5ml ($\frac{1}{2}$ teaspoon) black pepper

Heat the oven to 230°C (450°F) gas mark 8. In a large frying-pan, heat the oil over moderate heat. Add the onion and potatoes and cook, stirring occasionally, for 5 minutes. Add the ham, green pepper, tomatoes, frankfurters and basil. Cook, stirring occasionally, for 15 minutes.

Turn the mixture into a medium-sized oven-proof dish. Smooth the top with a knife. Break the eggs on top of the mixture and sprinkle them with the salt and pepper.

Place the dish in the upper part of the oven and bake for 8–10 minutes, or until the whites of the eggs are set. Serve at once.
Cooking time: 45 minutes

Cheese and Yogurt Moussaka

SERVES 4
700g ($1\frac{1}{2}$ lb) aubergines (eggplants)
30ml (2 tablespoons) salt
2 medium-sized green (bell) peppers
450g (1 lb) firm tomatoes
120ml/8 tablespoons ($\frac{1}{2}$ cup) olive oil or sunflower oil
1 large onion, thinly sliced
1 large garlic clove, finely chopped
225g ($\frac{1}{2}$ lb) Mozzarella cheese, thinly sliced
30ml (2 tablespoons) wholewheat flour
4 medium-sized eggs, beaten
75g (3 oz) cheddar cheese, grated
150ml/$\frac{1}{4}$ pt ($\frac{2}{3}$ cup) plain yogurt

Add a touch of sunshine to your autumn supper table with bright, tasty Essen eggs.

Cut the aubergines (eggplants) into 1.5cm ($\frac{1}{2}$ in) slices. Put them in a colander, sprinkle with the salt and leave to drain for 30 minutes. Wash them with running water and pat them dry with paper.

Heat the oven to 200°C (400°F) gas mark 6. Core and seed the peppers and cut them into pieces 25 × 6mm (1 × $\frac{1}{4}$ in). Scald and skin the tomatoes and cut them into rounds.

Heat 30ml (2 tablespoons) of the oil in a frying-pan on moderate heat. Put in as many aubergine slices as you can in one layer and cook them, until they turn a green colour, on each side. Set them aside and cook the rest in the same way, adding more oil as and when necessary.

Reduce the heat, put in the onion, garlic and peppers and cook them until they are soft. Beat the flour, eggs, yogurt and cheddar cheese together. Put half the aubergines in the bottom of a large, greased, oven-proof dish, then add half the onion and peppers and half the tomatoes. Cover them with all the Mozzarella and repeat the layers in reverse order, ending with the aubergines. Pour the yogurt mixture over the top. Cook in the oven for 30 minutes until the top is golden.
Cooking time: $1\frac{1}{4}$–$1\frac{1}{2}$ hours

Persian Onion Omelet

SERVES 2–3

1 medium-sized aubergine (eggplant) cut into 2cm ($\frac{3}{4}$ in) cubes
20ml (4 teaspoons) salt
45ml (3 tablespoons) vegetable oil
1 medium-sized onion, finely chopped
2.5ml ($\frac{1}{2}$ teaspoon) turmeric
1.5ml ($\frac{1}{4}$ teaspoon) ground cumin
2.5ml ($\frac{1}{2}$ teaspoon) black pepper
4 eggs
22.5ml ($1\frac{1}{2}$ tablespoons) cold water
15ml (1 tablespoon) butter

Put the aubergine (eggplant) cubes into a colander, scattering three-quarters of the salt between the layers. Weight with a plate. Leave for $\frac{1}{2}$ hour to drain to extract the bitter juices from the vegetable

In a medium-sized frying-pan, heat the oil over moderate heat. Fry the onion, stirring occasionally, for 8–10 minutes or until it is golden brown.

Rinse and dry the aubergine cubes and then add them to the pan. Cook them, stirring constantly, for 3 minutes. Stir in the turmeric, cumin, 2.5ml ($\frac{1}{2}$ teaspoon) of the salt and half the quantity of pepper. Reduce the heat and simmer the aubergine mixture for 10 minutes or until the cubes are tender when pierced. Remove the pan from the heat and set aside.

In a medium-sized mixing bowl, beat the eggs, the remaining salt, the remaining pepper and the water together with a fork. Add the aubergine mixture and beat until the ingredients are well mixed. Set aside.

In a medium-sized omelet pan, melt the butter over moderate heat. When the foam subsides, pour in the egg mixture. Stir the eggs, then leave them for a few seconds until the bottom sets. Reduce the heat to low. Using a flat knife or spatula, lift the edge of the omelet and, at the same time, tilt the pan away from you, so that the liquid egg escapes from the top and runs into the pan. Put the pan down flat over the heat and leave until the omelet begins to set.

Invert a medium-sized plate over the pan and reverse the two. The omelet should fall on to the plate. Slide the omelet back into the pan, browned side uppermost, and continue cooking for 1 minute or until completely set.

Slide the omelet on to a heated serving dish. Cut into wedges and serve immediately, with a tomato salad.
Cooking time: 1–1$\frac{1}{4}$ hours

Ricotta and Olive Scramble

SERVES 2–3

6 eggs
60ml/4 tablespoons ($\frac{1}{4}$ cup) milk
2.5ml ($\frac{1}{2}$ teaspoon) black pepper
2.5ml ($\frac{1}{2}$ teaspoon) dried basil
45ml (3 tablespoons) olive oil
100g ($\frac{1}{4}$ lb) green olives, stoned (pitted) and quartered
1 red (bell) pepper, white pith removed, seeded and chopped
100g/$\frac{1}{4}$ lb ($\frac{1}{2}$ cup) Ricotta or curd cheese
50g/2 oz ($\frac{1}{2}$ cup) grated Parmesan cheese

Heat the grill (broiler) to high. In a medium-sized mixing bowl, lightly beat the eggs, milk, pepper and basil together.

In a shallow pan, heat the olive oil over moderate heat. Add the olives and red pepper and cook, stirring frequently, for 3 minutes. Add the cheese and, stirring constantly, cook for a further 2 minutes.

Reduce the heat to low. Pour the egg mixture into the pan and cook, stirring constantly, until the eggs are nearly scrambled.

Remove the pan from the heat. Sprinkle over the Parmesan cheese and place the pan under the grill. Cook for 3 minutes or until the cheese has melted and the top is lightly browned. Serve at once.
Cooking time: 20–30 minutes

Ricotta and olive scramble livens up scrambled eggs to make a supper dish.

Sage and Cheese Bake

SERVES 4

450ml/16 fl oz (2 cups) milk
225g ($\frac{1}{2}$ lb) cheddar cheese, grated
175g/6 oz (3 cups) fresh white breadcrumbs
10ml (2 teaspoons) dried sage
$\frac{1}{2}$ small onion, finely chopped
2.5ml ($\frac{1}{2}$ teaspoon) salt
1.5ml ($\frac{1}{4}$ teaspoon) black pepper
4 eggs, separated

Heat the oven to 180°C (350°F) gas mark 4. Scald the milk (bring to just below boiling point) then set aside to cool to lukewarm.

In a large mixing bowl, place the cheese, breadcrumbs, sage, onion, salt, pepper and egg yolks. Combine well with a fork. Gradually stir in the milk, then set the mixture aside for 30 minutes.

Beat the egg whites until they form stiff peaks. Using a large metal spoon, carefully fold the egg whites into the cheese mixture then spoon it into a greased medium-sized oven-proof dish. Bake for 50–55 minutes or until the top is golden brown and the mixture has set. Serve at once.
Cooking time: 1$\frac{3}{4}$–2 hours

Meat and Poultry

Yugoslavian Lamb Chops with Paprika

SERVES 4

50g/2 oz ($\frac{1}{4}$ cup) butter
4 lamb chops
1 large leek, thoroughly washed and finely chopped
2.5ml ($\frac{1}{2}$ teaspoon) salt
1.5ml ($\frac{1}{4}$ teaspoon) black pepper
15ml (1 tablespoon) paprika
15ml (1 tablespoon) tomato paste
1 bay leaf
275ml/10 fl oz ($1\frac{1}{4}$ cups) brown stock

In a large frying-pan, melt the butter over moderate heat. When the foam subsides, add the chops to the pan and brown them, for 2–3 minutes on each side. Remove the chops from the pan and set them aside on a plate.

Add the chopped leek to the pan and fry it for 6–8 minutes. Add the salt, pepper, paprika, tomato paste, bay leaf and stock to the pan and stir well to mix the ingredients together.

Return the chops to the pan, cover and simmer gently over low heat for 15–20 minutes, or until the chops are tender. Transfer the chops to a warmed serving dish, pour the sauce over and serve at once.

Cooking time: 45 minutes

Chicken with Ginger

SERVES 4

4 chicken quarters
2.5ml ($\frac{1}{2}$ teaspoon) salt
2.5ml ($\frac{1}{2}$ teaspoon) black pepper
100g ($\frac{1}{4}$ lb) butter
1 garlic clove, finely chopped
275ml/$\frac{1}{2}$ pt ($1\frac{1}{4}$ cups) chicken stock
2 pieces preserved ginger, chopped
10ml (2 teaspoons) lemon juice
15ml (1 tablespoon) cornflour (cornstarch)
45ml (3 tablespoons) cold water
30ml (2 tablespoons) chopped parsley

Rub the chicken pieces with salt and pepper. In a large frying-pan with a lid, melt the butter over moderate heat. When the foam subsides add the chicken pieces. Cook them for 5–7 minutes on each side until golden brown.

Reduce the heat to low. Add the garlic to the pan and stir in the stock. Cover the pan and cook the chicken for about 30–35 minutes or until tender.

Transfer the chicken to a warmed serving dish and cover with foil to keep it warm. Mix the chopped ginger and lemon juice into the juices in the pan. Cook very gently for about 1 minute.

In a cup, mix together the cornflour and water to form a smooth paste. Add this to the pan, stirring until it dissolves and the sauce thickens. Add the parsley. Return the chicken to the sauce in the pan and cook for a further 5–8 minutes. Transfer the chicken to the warmed serving dish, spoon over the sauce and serve immediately.

Cooking time: 1 hour

Lamb chops are given a facelift the Yugoslavian way; gently simmered in tomato and paprika sauce with leek, they should be served with rice or noodles.

Holstein Stew

SERVES 4

900g (2 lb) lean stewing beef cut into 5cm (2 in) cubes
50g/2 oz ($\frac{1}{2}$ cup) flour
5ml (1 teaspoon) salt
2.5ml ($\frac{1}{2}$ teaspoon) black pepper
50ml/2 fl oz ($\frac{1}{4}$ cup) vegetable oil
2 medium-sized onions, thinly sliced
2 carrots, thinly sliced
2 celery stalks, trimmed and thinly sliced
275ml/$\frac{1}{2}$ pt ($1\frac{1}{4}$ cups) beef stock
2.5ml ($\frac{1}{2}$ teaspoon) Dijon mustard
2.5ml ($\frac{1}{2}$ teaspoon) sugar
10ml (2 teaspoons) lemon juice
2.5ml ($\frac{1}{2}$ teaspoon) dried dill
8 prunes, soaked overnight in cold water, drained, halved and stoned (pitted)
2 ripe pears, cored and sliced

Roll the beef cubes in seasoned flour, so that they are well coated on all sides. In a large pan, heat the oil over moderate heat. Add the beef cubes, and cook them, stirring and turning occasionally for 5 minutes, or until they are evenly browned all over. With a slotted spoon, remove the cubes from the pan and set them aside.

Fry the onions, carrots and celery, stirring occasionally, for 5–7 minutes, or until the onions are soft and translucent but not brown.

Meanwhile combine the beef stock, mustard, sugar, lemon juice and dill, and stir to mix well. Pour the stock mixture into the pan and return the beef cubes to the pan. Bring the mixture to the boil. Cover the pan and simmer the stew for $1\frac{1}{2}$ hours.

Add the prunes and pears to the mixture, re-cover the pan and simmer the stew for a further 15–20 minutes, or until the meat is tender when pierced with the point of a sharp knife.
Cooking time: $2\frac{1}{2}$–3 hours

Pork Chops with Plum Sauce

SERVES 4

450g (1 lb) plums, washed and stoned (pitted)
50g/2 oz ($\frac{1}{4}$ cup) sugar
1.5ml ($\frac{1}{4}$ teaspoon) ground cinnamon
225ml/8 fl oz (1 cup) red wine
4 thick pork chops, trimmed of excess fat
5ml (1 teaspoon) salt
2.5ml ($\frac{1}{2}$ teaspoon) black pepper

Heat the grill (broiler) to high. In a medium-sized saucepan, bring the plums, sugar, cinnamon and red wine to the boil over moderate heat. Reduce the heat to low and simmer for 10–15 minutes, or until the plums are soft.

Heat the oven to moderate, 180°C (350°F) gas mark 4. Rub the chops with the salt and pepper and place them on the grill (broiler) rack.

Reduce the heat to low and grill (broil) for 3 minutes on each side, or until they are lightly browned. Transfer the chops to an ovenproof serving dish and keep warm.

Purée the plums through a food mill or sieve then pour the purée over the chops. Cover the dish and bake for 1 hour.
Cooking time: $1\frac{1}{2}$ hours

Broiled Chicken with Lemon Barbecue Sauce

SERVES 4

4 chicken portions
watercress sprigs
1 lemon
FOR THE MARINADE
1 garlic clove, crushed
5ml (1 teaspoon) salt
2.5ml ($\frac{1}{2}$ teaspoon) ground black pepper
45ml (3 tablespoons) oil
45ml (3 tablespoons) lemon juice
bay leaf

Put the garlic into an earthenware or glass dish, add all the other ingredients for the marinade and stir well. Put the chicken

Holstein stew is beef with an exciting mixture of prunes, pears and vegetables.

pieces in the marinade and spoon the marinade over. Cover and leave in a cool place for at least 2 hours.

Heat the grill (broiler) to medium. Place the chicken pieces skin side down in the pan. Cook 12cm (5 in) away from the heat for 15 minutes, basting frequently with the lemon marinade.

Turn the chicken skin side up and cook for 10 minutes, basting frequently with the lemon marinade.

Test the chicken by piercing it with a fine skewer to see that the juices run clear. If the chicken shows signs of overbrowning, turn the heat down. The skin should be crisp when the chicken is cooked. Serve on a hot dish garnished with lemon quarters and watercress.
Cooking time: 2 hours marinating, then 30–40 minutes

Rabbit with Apricots

SERVES 4

1.8kg (4 lb) rabbit, cut into serving pieces and marinated *(page 255)*
2.5ml ($\frac{1}{2}$ teaspoon) salt
2.5ml ($\frac{1}{2}$ teaspoon) white pepper
1.5ml ($\frac{1}{4}$ teaspoon) ground cloves
50g/2 oz ($\frac{1}{4}$ cup) butter
25g/1 oz ($\frac{1}{4}$ cup) flour
425ml/$\frac{3}{4}$ pt ($1\frac{3}{4}$ cups) chicken stock
225g ($\frac{1}{2}$ lb) dried apricots, soaked overnight and drained

Remove the rabbit pieces from the marinade and dry them thoroughly on absorbent paper. Rub the rabbit pieces all over with the salt, pepper and cloves.

Heat the oven to moderate 180°C (350°F) gas mark 4. In a flameproof casserole (dutch oven), melt the butter over moderate heat. When the foam subsides, add the rabbit pieces and cook, turning them occasionally with tongs, for 8–10 minutes or until they are lightly and evenly browned. Remove the pan from the heat and, using the tongs, transfer the rabbit pieces to a plate. Keep warm.

With a wooden spoon, stir the flour into the butter in the casserole. Reduce the heat to low and return the pan to the heat. Cook the mixture for 1 minute, stirring constantly. Remove the pan from the heat.

Gradually pour the stock into the pan, stirring constantly to avoid lumps. Return the pan to the heat. Increase the heat to high and, stirring constantly, bring the liquid to the boil. Add the apricots and return the rabbit pieces to the pan. Stir to coat them with the sauce. Remove the pan from the heat, cover and place it in the oven. Cook for 1–1¼ hours or until the rabbit meat is very tender when pierced with the point of a sharp knife.

Lift the rabbit pieces out of the pan and arrange them on a warmed serving dish. Pour over the sauce and serve immediately.
Cooking time: overnight marinating then 2–2¼ hours

Devonshire Squab Pie

This pie does not actually contain squabs (pigeons) but is traditionally made with mutton (or lamb) and apples. It is made in a deep pie dish with a covering of shortcrust pastry and is usually served with clotted cream in Devon or with warmed cream poured over it.

SERVES 4

¾ × shortcrust pastry *(page 240)*
4 mutton chops (arm or blade lamb chops) or large best end of neck cutlets (neck slices)
3 medium-sized leeks or 1 large onion, sliced
4 dessert apples, peeled, cored and sliced
10ml (2 teaspoons) brown sugar
1.5ml (¼ teaspoon) grated nutmeg
275ml/½ pt (1¼ cups) cider or white wine
salt
freshly ground black pepper
beaten egg to glaze

Heat the oven to 200°C (400°F) gas mark 6. Roll out the pastry to fit the top of 850ml/1½ pt (4 cup) pie dish, cut out a strip and place in position on the rim of the dish.

Trim the excess fat from the meat. The bones can be removed if you prefer. Cut each chop in half lengthwise. Season with salt and pepper, and lay half in the base of the dish.

Sprinkle the apples with the brown sugar and place half of them, with half the leeks, in the dish. Repeat the layers with meat and the remaining leeks and apples, sprinkling with the nutmeg and some salt and pepper. Pour over the cider or wine.

Cover the dish with the pastry lid and use the trimming to decorate. Make a small hole in the top and brush with beaten egg. Bake for 15 minutes, then lower the heat to 150°C (300°F) gas mark 2, and bake for 1¼ hours. Cover with foil if the pastry begins to get too brown.
Cooking time: 2¼ hours

Spicy Beef Pie

This economical family pie has a topping made from 'yogurt crust'—a quickly-made and economical alternative to pastry. If desired, the filling may be made in advance.

SERVES 4

800g (1¾ lb) minced (ground) beef
1 medium-sized onion, finely chopped
1 large garlic clove, chopped
1 celery stalk, chopped
25g/1 oz (2 tablespoons) beef dripping
75g (3 oz) mushrooms, sliced
15ml (1 tablespoon) plain flour
125ml/¼ pt (½ cup) beef stock
30ml (2 tablespoons) tomato paste
10ml (2 teaspoons) curry paste *(page 254)*

FOR THE TOPPING

275ml/½ pt (1¼ cups) thickened plain yogurt *(page 249)*
2 large eggs, beaten
25g/1 oz (¼ cup) plain flour
30ml (2 tablespoons) grated cheddar cheese
freshly ground black pepper

Melt the dripping in a heavy-bottomed pan over low heat. Add the mince (ground beef) and brown gently. Add the chopped vegetables and cook, stirring, until soft but not coloured.

Heat the oven to 190°C (375°F) gas mark 5. Stir in the flour. Cook for 2 minutes and then stir in the stock, tomato purée and curry paste. Simmer gently for 5 minutes until slightly thickened. Add the mushrooms. Transfer to a 1.15L/2 pt (6 cup) ovenproof dish.

Stir the yogurt until smooth. Beat the flour into the eggs and add to the yogurt. Stir in the cheese. Season to taste. Pour the mixture over the filling. Place in the centre of the oven. Cook for 30 minutes until the topping has set and is golden.
Cooking time: 1–1¼ hours

Moroccan Kefta

After shaping, these meat balls are poached in water, drained, and allowed to cool. They can then be finished in various ways: grilled (broiled), cooked on skewers, fried or, as in this recipe, simmered in a rich, thick tomato sauce served with boiled rice.

SERVES 4

450g (1 lb) boneless shoulder of lamb, trimmed of fat and muscle
1 small onion, quartered
3 fresh mint leaves
4 fresh marjoram leaves
6 parsley sprigs
1.5ml (¼ teaspoon) ground cumin
1.5ml (¼ teaspoon) paprika
pinch each of cayenne pepper, ginger, cinnamon and nutmeg
salt
freshly ground black pepper
275ml/½ pt (1¼ cups) home-made tomato sauce *(page 256)*

Cut away any skin and gristle from the meat and cube the meat. Pass the meat, onion, mint, marjoram, and parsley through the fine blades of a mincer (meat grinder) 3 times, collecting the ingredients in a mixing bowl.

Add all the spices and the salt and pepper to the mixture and, with a wooden spoon, stir and pound until thoroughly blended and smooth. Check that the mixture is very well flavoured. Bring a large saucepan of water to simmering point.

With slightly wet hands, take a small spoon of meat at a time and roll into balls the size of walnuts.

Lower the balls into the pan of gently simmering water. Poach for 10 minutes. Lift out with a slotted spoon and leave on a plate until cold.

Shortly before serving, bring the tomato sauce to simmering point, lower the kefta balls into it, and simmer for 10 minutes until hot through. Serve in the sauce.
Cooking time: ¾–1 hour

Beef Stew with Chick-Peas

Canned chick-peas may be used for this dish, but are more expensive than dried ones: you will need a 425g (15 oz) can. If you have no basil or chervil, substitute thyme and marjoram. Serve with baked potatoes and braised celery. This stew can also be reheated.

SERVES 6
3 slices bacon, chopped
1.4kg (3 lb) lean stewing beef, cut into 2.5cm (1 in) cubes
30ml (2 tablespoons) vegetable oil
2 large onions, thinly sliced
2 garlic cloves, crushed
15ml (1 tablespoon) flour
1L/1¾ pt (4 cups) water
30ml (2 tablespoons) tomato paste
350g (¾ lb) tomatoes, blanched, peeled and quartered
5ml (1 teaspoon) dried basil or chervil
2.5ml (½ teaspoon) salt
2.5ml (½ teaspoon) black pepper
225g (½ lb) chick-peas, soaked overnight

Place the bacon in a large, deep frying-pan and set the pan over moderate heat. Fry the bacon for 6–8 minutes or until it is golden brown. Using a slotted spoon, remove the bacon from the pan and place it in a large ovenproof casserole.

Increase the heat to moderately high and fry the meat cubes a few at a time, turning occasionally, for 4–5 minutes or until they are lightly browned. Using a slotted spoon transfer the browned meat cubes to the casserole.

Heat the oven to 170°C (325°F) gas mark 3. Add the vegetable oil to the frying-pan. Fry the onion and garlic, stirring occasionally, for 8–10 minutes or until the onions are golden brown. Reduce the heat to low and sprinkle over the flour. Stir the flour until it has been absorbed by the onions and cook 1–2 minutes until well coloured.

Remove the pan from the heat and stir in the water. Bring the liquid to the boil, scraping the bottom of the pan to incorporate the brown flour mixture. Stir in the tomato paste, tomatoes, basil, chervil, salt and pepper and bring the liquid to the boil, stirring occasionally.

Add the drained chick-peas to the casserole and pour in the tomato sauce. Cover the casserole and cook in the oven for 2½ hours or until the beef is tender when pierced with the point of a sharp knife.
Cooking time: 3¾–4 hours

● To stretch the casserole, increase the quantity of chick-peas, bacon, onions, garlic, herbs and tomato purée by 50% and add 6 stalks of celery, chopped in chunks, a brown beef stock cube and a further 275ml/½ pt (1¼ cups) water.

Stuffed Breasts of Lamb

A tasty and extremely economical dish of Syrian origin, stuffed lambs' breasts are roasted and finished in an apricot sauce.

SERVES 6
2 large whole breasts of lamb, boned
5ml (1 teaspoon) salt
2.5ml (½ teaspoon) black pepper
30ml (2 tablespoons) olive oil
225g (½ lb) dried apricots, soaked in water overnight
30ml (2 tablespoons) sugar
FOR THE STUFFING
30ml (2 tablespoons) vegetable oil
1 large onion, finely chopped
225g (½ lb) minced (ground) beef
22.5ml (1½ tablespoons) long-grain rice
5ml (1 teaspoon) ground cumin
5ml (1 teaspoon) turmeric
175ml/6 fl oz (¾ cup) water
45ml (3 tablespoons) chopped parsley
5ml (1 teaspoon) salt
2.5ml (½ teaspoon) black pepper
50g/2 oz (⅓ cup) chopped almonds
50g/2 oz (¼ cup) seedless raisins

To prepare the stuffing, in a large saucepan, heat the oil over moderate heat. Fry the onion, stirring occasionally, for about 8 minutes or until lightly coloured. Stir in the minced beef and cook for 5–8 minutes, or until the meat is brown. Stir in the rice and cook, stirring constantly, for 4 minutes.

Mix in the cumin, turmeric, water, parsley, salt and pepper and blend well. Bring the mixture to the boil. Cover the pan and simmer the mixture for 15–20 minutes, or until the rice is cooked and the water is absorbed. Remove the pan from the heat, stir in the almonds and raisins and allow to cool.

Heat the oven to 180°C (350°F) gas mark 4. Spread out the breasts, skin side down, and rub with salt and pepper. Spread the stuffing mixture over the lamb and roll up each breast. Tie the rolls with string. Rub the meat with the salt and pepper and, with a pastry brush, brush over the outsides with oil. Place the

Extend your beef protein with crunchy chick-peas, flavoured with tomatoes and garlic.

breasts in a roasting pan. Roast them in the oven for 1½ hours or until the meat is well browned and tender.

After the meat has been roasting for 1 hour, prepare the glaze. Place the apricots in a small saucepan, with the water in which they were soaked and the sugar. Bring to the boil and simmer for 30 minutes, or until the apricots are pulpy.

Remove the roasting pan from the oven and pour off the cooking liquids in the pan. Increase the oven temperature to 230°C (450°F) gas mark 8. Pour the apricots and their liquid over the lamb breasts and return them to the oven.

Roast for 10 minutes, or until the lamb is glazed and golden brown. Remove from the oven and serve at once, carving in slices across the lamb.
Cooking time: 2¾–3 hours

Lemon and Parsley Pork Crumble

SERVES 4

8 slices belly of pork (thick bacon slices)
25g/1 oz (½ cup) stale white breadcrumbs
3-4 pimento-stuffed olives, sliced
grated rind of 1 lemon
15ml (1 tablespoon) chopped fresh parsley
salt and freshly ground black pepper
3 tomatoes

Heat the grill (broiler), with the pan and grid in position, until very hot. Mix the olives with the crumbs, lemon rind and parsley in a small bowl and season very generously.

Lay the pork (bacon) on the grid and grill (broil) under a fierce heat for 1 minute on each side, and then under a moderate to low heat for 6–9 minutes on each side until crisp and golden. Using tongs, transfer the meat to a gratin dish.

Slice the tomatoes and arrange them over the meat. Sprinkle the breadcrumb mixture on top and pour on a little fat from the grill pan.

Reduce the heat to low and grill until the crumb mixture turns golden brown. *Cooking time:* ¾–1 hour

German Roast Saddle of Hare

SERVES 6

1 hare, weighing 2-2.25kg (4½-5 lb) when skinned, paunched and marinated for 12 hours *(page 254)*
6 slices fat bacon
75g/3 oz (⅓ cup) dripping or bacon fat
275ml/½ pt (1¼ cups) red wine
225g (½ lb) mushrooms
150ml/¼ pt (⅔ cup) sour cream
15ml (1 tablespoon) cornflour (cornstarch) mixed with 30ml (2 tablespoons) water
salt and freshly ground black pepper

Heat the oven to 220°C (425°F) gas mark 7. Take the hare from the marinade and cut off the front legs to save for another day. Pat dry carefully with absorbent paper. Truss the hind legs by pulling them forward and securing them alongside the body with skewers. Place the hare on a rack in a roasting tin. Cover the back with

Apricot glaze and rice and nut stuffing turn breasts of lamb into an appealing dish.

the bacon slices and the hind legs with some greased foil if the bacon does not cover them.

Heat the dripping gently until melted. Pour it over the hare. Roast the hare for 15 minutes. Reduce the oven heat to 180°C (350°F) gas mark 4. Pour the wine into the roasting pan. Continue roasting for another 1¼ hours. Baste the hare with wine several times.

Place the mushrooms around the meat. Baste them well, remove the bacon and reserve. Roast the meat for another 10 minutes or until it is tender.

Put the hare, mushrooms and bacon on a heated serving dish and keep hot. Blend the cornflour (cornstarch) with water.

Tilt the roasting pan, and skim off as much fat as you can from the sauce. Scrape up the sediment from the bottom of the pan. Stir in the sour cream. Heat the sauce in the pan over low heat. Bring it to boiling point and add a little to the blended cornflour. Stir this mixture into the pan and boil for 1 minute. Season.

Portion the hare, making 2 portions from the saddle, 2 from the haunch and 1 each from the hind legs. Arrange these on a serving dish and pour a little of the sauce over. Cut up the bacon and arrange this and the mushrooms on the serving dish. Serve the remaining sauce separately.
Cooking time: 12 hours marinating, then 2½ hours
● Make a family stew with the front legs and forcemeat (stuffing) balls *(page 254)*.

145

Tongue with Hot Raisin Sauce

Hot tongue is ideal for an adventurous family meal, or to serve at a dinner party with a green vegetable and steamed new potatoes. If you prefer, the tongue may be divided—one half being served hot with half the amount of sauce and the other half being stored and served cold, with salad.

SERVES 8
1 salted ox (beef) tongue about 1.6kg (3½ lb), soaked for 24 hours
12 peppercorns
1 bay leaf
5 parsley stalks
peelings from 900g (2 lb) apples (optional)
FOR THE SAUCE
50g/2 oz (¼ cup) butter
25g/1 oz (¼ cup) flour
125ml/4 fl oz (½ cup) tongue stock
400ml/14 fl oz (1¾ cups) water
125g (¼ lb) raisins
2.5ml (½ teaspoon) salt
2.5ml (½ teaspoon) black pepper
juice of ½ lemon
5ml (1 teaspoon) soft brown sugar
1.5ml (¼ teaspoon) hot chilli powder
1.5ml (¼ teaspoon) ground cinnamon
1.5ml (¼ teaspoon) ground ginger
large pinch ground cloves
30ml (2 tablespoons) thin cream

Put the soaked tongue in a large pan with water to cover; add the peppercorns, bay leaf and parsley and apple peelings. (If the tongue is fresh, or frozen rather than salted, add salt to the water.) Bring to the boil and skim off any scum with a slotted spoon. Cover with a tight-fitting lid, reduce the heat and simmer for 3½ hours or until tender.

Turn off the heat but leave the tongue in the cooking liquor for ½ hour. Drain the tongue, remove the skin and any bones and gristle. Trim off any fat. Keep warm in the cooking liquor.

In a medium-sized saucepan, melt the butter over moderate heat. Remove the pan from the heat and, with a wooden spoon, stir in the flour to make a smooth paste. Gradually add the tongue stock and water, stirring constantly. Return the pan to the heat and cook, stirring constantly, for 2–3 minutes or until the mixture is fairly thick and smooth.

Stir in the raisins, salt, pepper, lemon juice, sugar, chilli powder, cinnamon, ginger and cloves. Reduce the heat to moderately low and cook the sauce for 8

minutes or until the raisins are plump.

Meanwhile, place the tongue on a board and cut it into 6mm (¼ in) thick slices. A hot tongue is cut across the grain into a series of rings. Arrange the tongue slices on a warmed serving dish.

Remove the pan from the heat. Stir in the cream and pour a little of the sauce over the tongue slices. Pour the remaining sauce into a warmed sauceboat. Serve immediately.
Cooking time: 4 hours then 30 minutes

●Cold tongue is very economical, as it is carved in thin slices. It is an excellent standby during a holiday and makes good buffet party food. It will keep in a refrigerator, loosely wrapped, for 10 days. Ends of tongue make excellent sandwiches.

To prepare a cold tongue, after skinning curl it round to fit into a deep cake tin (pan) 15cm (6 in) in diameter. Pour in a little tongue stock to cover. On top place a small plate that fits inside the rim of the cake tin (pan). Weight this and leave overnight to set. Keep chilled in the refrigerator.
●Tongue stock is useful for cooking vegetables and as a soup base. Do not use more than ⅓ tongue stock for soup as it can be very salty.

Lamb and Bean Casserole

SERVES 6–8
850ml/1½ pts (3¾ cups) water
225g (½ lb) dried broad (lima) beans, soaked overnight in cold water and drained
100g (¼ lb) dried or split peas, soaked overnight in cold water and drained
1.4kg (3 lb) lean, boned lamb shoulder, cut into 2.5cm (1 in) cubes
2 onions, quartered
1 small onion, finely chopped
10ml (2 teaspoons) salt
2.5ml (½ teaspoon) black pepper
575ml/1 pt (2½ cups) chicken stock
350g (¾ lb) canned tomatoes, roughly chopped
5ml (1 teaspoon) mustard powder
5ml (1 teaspoon) mixed dried herbs
30ml (2 tablespoons) brown sugar
30ml (2 tablespoons) red wine vinegar
22.5ml (1½ tablespoons) lemon juice
2.5ml (½ teaspoon) turmeric

In a large saucepan, bring the water to the boil over high heat. Add the beans and peas and boil for 2 minutes.

Remove the pan from the heat and allow

the beans and peas to soak for 1 hour. Drain them in a colander and set them aside.

Place the lamb in a large heavy-bottomed pan. Scatter the onion pieces on top and cover them with the peas and beans. Add the salt and pepper and pour in the chicken stock.

Put the mustard powder, turmeric, mixed herbs and brown sugar into a cup, add the vinegar and lemon juice and stir into a paste. Add a little stock to dilute, then add the contents of the cup, plus the remaining stock, to the pan. Season with salt and pepper, then add the tomatoes, plus their juice.

Bring to the boil, then lower the heat, cover, and simmer gently for 2½ hours, or until the peas and beans are tender.
Cooking time: 4 hours

Arabian Stewed Lamb

In this adaptation of a classic Arabian dish, the lamb is stewed with prunes and flavoured with cinnamon and turmeric. It is inexpensive, easy to make and unusual. Serve it with rice which has been boiled with a bay leaf.

SERVES 4–5
30ml (2 tablespoons) cooking oil
900g (2 lb) lamb shoulder, boned and cut into 4cm (1½ in) cubes
1 large onion, sliced
1 clove garlic, crushed
5ml (1 teaspoon) powdered turmeric
5cm (2 in) cinnamon stick
5ml (1 teaspoon) salt
freshly ground black pepper
15ml (1 tablespoon) flour
350ml/12 fl oz (1½ cups) beef stock
15ml (1 tablespoon) brown sugar
16 prunes, soaked in water for 2 hours and stoned

Heat the oil in a large saucepan over moderate heat. Sauté the lamb cubes, stirring occasionally, until they are brown on all sides. Using a slotted spoon, remove the pieces of lamb and set aside on a plate.

Fry the onion until it is golden brown, stirring occasionally. Add the garlic, turmeric, cinnamon, salt and 7 grindings of pepper; stir and sauté for 5 minutes. Add the flour, stir and cook for a few seconds before gradually adding the stock.

Raise the heat and continue stirring until the mixture comes to the boil. Return the meat to the pan, lower the heat and simmer for 40 minutes or until the lamb is tender. Ten minutes before the lamb is

cooked, add the sugar and the prunes. Serve hot.
Cooking time: 1 hour

Farshmak

An excellent way of using up leftover meat, this Russian recipe combines lamb or beef with pickled fish. Serve the farshmak hot or cold.

SERVES 4–6
450g (1 lb) cooked meat (beef or lamb)
2 pickled herrings or rollmops
1 large onion, very finely chopped
50g/2 oz (1 cup) fresh white breadcrumbs
2 eggs, lightly beaten
5ml (1 teaspoon) salt
2.5ml ($\frac{1}{2}$ teaspoon) black pepper
5ml (1 teaspoon) paprika
50ml/2 fl oz ($\frac{1}{4}$ cup) sour cream

Heat the grill (broiler) to high. Mince (grind) the meat and herrings or rollmops twice. Put the minced mixture into a large mixing bowl. Add the onion, breadcrumbs, eggs, salt, pepper and paprika and beat the ingredients with a fork. With your hands, form the mixture into flat patties.

Grill (broil) the patties for 8 minutes on each side, or until they are deeply and evenly browned. Serve with sour cream.
Cooking time: 45 minutes

Near Eastern Pork with Peanuts and Grapes

SERVES 6–8
30ml (2 tablespoons) peanut oil
900g (2 lb) pork fillet (tenderloin), cut into 2.5cm (1 in) cubes
5ml (1 teaspoon) salt
2.5ml ($\frac{1}{2}$ teaspoon) black pepper
65g/2$\frac{1}{2}$ oz ($\frac{1}{3}$ cup) unsalted peanuts, ground
30ml (2 tablespoons) soy sauce
1.5ml ($\frac{1}{4}$ teaspoon) mild chilli powder
450g (1 lb) seedless white grapes, halved
65g/2$\frac{1}{2}$ oz ($\frac{1}{3}$ cup) unsalted peanuts, finely chopped and toasted

Russian farshmak are unusual patties, combining leftover cooked lamb or beef with pickled fish. Serve with sour cream.

In a large frying-pan, heat the oil over moderate heat. Fry the pork cubes, stirring and turning occasionally, for 5–10 minutes or until lightly browned.

Add the salt, pepper, ground peanuts, soy sauce and chilli powder and mix well. Reduce the heat to low. Add the grapes and simmer the mixture for 15–20 minutes, or until the pork is very tender when pierced with the point of a sharp knife.

Transfer to a dish, sprinkle with the chopped peanuts and serve.
Cooking time: 45 minutes

●Use pork sparerib meat (country-style ribs); simmer 40 minutes in some stock.
●For a Turkish version fry the pork, then remove and fry 225g ($\frac{1}{2}$ lb) onions. Return the meat and add 6 stalks celery, chopped, 50g/2 oz ($\frac{1}{3}$ cup) each raisins and almonds, 5ml (1 teaspoon) cinnamon, seasoning and 275ml/$\frac{1}{2}$ pt (1$\frac{1}{4}$ cups) stock.

Creamed Chicken Livers

This savoury mixture is an unusual way of preparing chicken livers; serve it on toast for a brunch or supper snack, or with boiled rice and tomatoes for a main dish.

SERVES 4
50g/2 oz (¼ cup) butter
2 onions, thinly sliced and separated into rings
12 chicken livers, cut into 2.5cm (1 in) strips
225ml/8 fl oz (1 cup) thin cream
2 hard-boiled eggs, coarsely chopped
2.5ml (½ teaspoon) salt
2.5ml (½ teaspoon) white pepper
2.5ml (½ teaspoon) paprika

In a deep, medium-sized frying-pan, melt half of the butter over moderate heat. Fry the onion rings for 6–8 minutes, or until they are golden brown. With a slotted spoon, transfer the onions from the pan to a large plate and set aside.

Fry the chicken liver strips for 4–5 minutes, adding more butter if necessary. With a slotted spoon, transfer the livers from the pan and mix with the onions.

Add the remaining butter to the frying-pan and melt it over low heat. Add the cream, livers, onions, eggs, salt, pepper and paprika. Cook, stirring briskly, for 4–5 minutes but do not let the mixture boil. Turn the mixture into a warmed serving dish or spoon it on to hot toast.
Cooking time: 30 minutes

Greek Lamb Stew

Aubergines (eggplants) and lamb are a classic Greek combination.

SERVES 4
2 aubergines (eggplants)
15ml (1 tablespoon) plus 2.5ml (½ teaspoon) salt
75ml (5 tablespoons) olive oil
900g (2 lb) boned shoulder of lamb, cut into 2.5cm (1 in) cubes
10ml (2 teaspoons) coriander seeds, coarsely crushed in a mortar
1 large onion, sliced
1 garlic clove, crushed
30ml (2 tablespoons) chopped fresh mint
450g (1 lb) tomatoes, blanched, peeled and chopped or 400g (14 oz) canned tomatoes, drained
freshly ground black pepper

Cheap and widely available, chicken livers, eggs and onions in a creamy sauce can be served with toast as an appetizer for 8 or with fluffy rice as a main course.

Cut the aubergines (eggplants) into 2.5cm (1 in) cubes. Place the cubes in a colander, sprinkle with 15ml (1 tablespoon) of salt, put a plate with a weight on it on top of the aubergines and leave to drain for 30 minutes. Rinse the cubes and pat dry with absorbent paper before cooking.

Heat the oil in a large frying-pan. Add the lamb cubes, a few at a time, and the crushed coriander seeds. When all the lamb has been browned, remove the cubes with a slotted spoon, put on a plate and set aside. Add the onion to the pan and fry until golden. Add the garlic and all the mint and cook for 1 minute. Add the aubergine cubes and fry, stirring frequently, for 10 minutes.

Return the lamb to the pan with the tomatoes, 2.5ml (½ teaspoon) of salt and 6 grindings of black pepper. Cover and simmer for 1 hour. If the stew seems too liquid, simmer without a cover for the last 20 minutes. Serve with a yogurt and cucumber salad.
Cooking time: 2 hours 15 minutes

Pigs' Hearts à l'orange

In this recipe the rich texture of the pigs' hearts is emphasised by a full-bodied orange-flavoured sauce. The dish can be simmered on top of the stove, or casseroled in a low oven. Serve with buttered egg noodles and a watercress salad.

SERVES 4
4 pigs' hearts
225g ($\frac{1}{2}$ lb) onions, sliced
1 garlic clove, chopped
1 orange
25g/1 oz (2 tablespoons) butter
30ml (2 tablespoons) oil
30ml (2 tablespoons) flour
425ml/$\frac{3}{4}$ pt (1$\frac{2}{3}$ cups) meat stock
15ml (1 tablespoon) tomato paste
1 bay leaf
1 sprig of thyme
30ml (2 tablespoons) bitter marmalade
10ml (2 teaspoons) lemon juice
salt
freshly ground black pepper
15-30ml (1-2 tablespoons) orange liqueur (optional)

Wash the hearts under cold running water, removing any patches of congealed blood. Snip out the muscular artery walls to make a good pocket and trim away any skin. Wash again under running water, then soak in lightly salted water for 30 minutes.

Meanwhile, peel 2 strips of orange rind from the orange. Drain the hearts and dry thoroughly with absorbent paper.

Heat the butter and oil in a heavy pan over moderately high heat. Add the hearts and fry for several minutes until browned and sealed on all sides. Remove from the pan and reserve.

Reduce the heat, add the onions and garlic to the casserole and fry gently for about 5 minutes until they are slightly softened and beginning to brown. Remove from the heat, sprinkle on the flour, stir in. Cook gently, stirring continuously, until the flour turns fawn.

Remove the pan from the heat and stir in the stock, tomato purée, bay leaf, thyme, orange rind and marmalade. Bring slowly to the boil, stirring continuously. Season with salt and pepper to taste and replace the hearts in the pan. Cover and simmer very gently for 1$\frac{1}{2}$ hours or until the hearts are tender when pierced with a fork.

Lift out the hearts, cut in halves lengthwise, and arrange in a circle in a warm shallow serving dish. Keep warm.

Skim off the surface fat from the cooking liquid, add the lemon juice and boil rapidly, uncovered, until the liquid is reduced to a thick consistency. Check the seasoning, add the liqueur if used, and strain over the hearts. Serve immediately.
Cooking time: 3–3$\frac{1}{4}$ hours

Spiced Kidneys

This is an attractive way of cooking pig's kidneys, the least tasty of all the different types of kidney. The sauce can be made more spicy by adding extra chilli powder to taste: however, go cautiously! Serve the kidneys on a bed of plain boiled rice.

SERVES 4
4 pigs' kidneys
450g (1 lb) onions, sliced
1 garlic clove, crushed
45ml (3 tablespoons) oil
350g ($\frac{3}{4}$ lb) ripe tomatoes
15ml (1 tablespoon) coriander seeds, crushed
2.5ml ($\frac{1}{2}$ teaspoon) cumin seeds
10ml (2 teaspoons) turmeric
275ml/$\frac{1}{2}$ pt (1$\frac{1}{4}$ cups) plain yogurt
30ml (2 tablespoons) meat stock
salt
a good pinch of chilli powder (optional)

Skin the kidneys and snip out the white cores. Soak in lightly salted cold water— 5ml (1 teaspoon) salt to 575ml/1 pt (2$\frac{1}{2}$ cups) of water—for an hour, then drain and pat dry. Cut across into 6mm ($\frac{1}{4}$ in) slices.

Blanch, skin and chop the tomatoes. Heat the oil in a heavy pan over a moderately high heat. Fry the kidney slices quickly, stirring them until they are brown on both sides. With a slotted spoon lift them out and reserve.

Reduce the heat and fry the onions gently for 10 minutes until they are softened and lightly coloured, then add the garlic and cook for 1 minute.

Place the cumin seeds in a pan without fat. Heat the seeds over a medium heat for 1 minute to release their aroma. Remove the pan containing onions from the heat and stir in the croshed coriander, the cumin seeds and turmeric.

Add the tomatoes, yogurt and stock, and return the pan to the heat. Bring slowly to the boil, stirring constantly. Cover and simmer gently for 15–20 minutes.

Taste the sauce, add salt to taste and a small pinch of chilli powder, if you wish. Return the kidneys to the sauce, cover the pan and simmer very gently for 15–20 minutes, until the kidneys are just cooked. Serve immediately on a bed of rice.
Cooking time: 2–2$\frac{1}{2}$ hours

If you have never eaten pigs' hearts before, try this French way of cooking them.

Roast Birds with Orange and Wine Sauce

Pigeons are easy to prepare and, when they can be obtained cheaply, roast pigeons make an inexpensive dinner party dish. Baby poussins or Rock Cornish game hens may be substituted. Slightly increased quantities are given in the brackets for stuffing these birds as they are a little larger than pigeons.

SERVES 4

4 pigeons (small Rock Cornish game hens), oven-ready

6 (8) slices bacon, cut in half

100g/¼ lb (½ cup) butter, melted

2 oranges, all peel and pith removed and sliced into rings

FOR THE STUFFING

25g/1 oz (50g/2 oz/¼ cup) butter

1 medium-sized (large) onion, finely chopped

2 (4) celery stalks, trimmed and finely chopped

100g/¼ lb (225g/½ lb) white bread, cubed

juice and grated rind of 1 orange

juice and grated rind of 1 medium lemon

1 egg, lightly beaten

2.5ml (½ teaspoon) salt

1.5ml (¼ teaspoon) black pepper

2.5ml (½ teaspoon) dried thyme

FOR THE SAUCE

175ml/6 fl oz (¾ cup) chicken stock

225ml/8 fl oz (1 cup) red wine

125ml/4 fl oz (½ cup) orange juice

1.5ml (¼ teaspoon) salt

large pinch black pepper

15ml (1 tablespoon) beurre manié

(page 204)

Heat the oven to moderate, 180°C (350°F) gas mark 4. First make the stuffing. In a small frying-pan, melt the butter over moderate heat. When the foam subsides, add the onion and celery and fry, stirring occasionally for 5–7 minutes, or until the onion is soft and translucent but not brown. Remove the pan from the heat and, with a slotted spoon, transfer the onion and celery to a medium-sized mixing bowl.

Put the bread cubes in a small mixing bowl. Pour over the orange and lemon juice. When the bread is soft, add it to the onion and celery mixture. Add the grated orange and lemon rind, egg, salt, pepper and thyme. Using your hands, mix the ingredients well. Spoon the stuffing into the cavity of the birds. Transfer them to a medium-sized roasting pan. Cover the breasts with the bacon and pour over the melted butter.

Place the roasting pan in the oven and roast the pigeons, basting occasionally, for 50–60 minutes or until the breast is tender when pierced with the point of a sharp knife. Remove the bacon for the last 20 minutes to allow the breasts of the birds to brown. Transfer the birds to a warmed serving dish and keep hot while you prepare the sauce.

Pour away all but 30ml (2 tablespoons) of the fat in the roasting pan. Place the pan over high heat, pour in the chicken stock, wine and the orange juice and bring them to the boil, stirring constantly.

Boil for 5–6 minutes, or until the liquid has reduced by about one-third. Add the salt and pepper. Reduce the heat to low and stir in the beurre manié, a little at a time. Cook for a further 3 minutes, stirring constantly, or until the sauce in smooth and thick. Taste the sauce and add more seasoning if necessary. Strain the sauce over the birds. Garnish round the dish with orange slices and serve immediately.
Cooking time: 1¾–2 hours

Breast of Veal with Anchovy and Herb Stuffing

Stuffing helps to keep veal moist and extends the number of servings. The breast is not boned and rolled but a slit is cut along one side, above the bones, to form a pocket into which the stuffing is inserted. Ask the butcher to cut through the sternum bone.

SERVES 5–6

2kg (4½ lb) breast of veal, unboned

25g/1 oz (2 tablespoons) butter

15ml (1 tablespoon) oil

salt

freshly ground black pepper

25g/1 oz (2 tablespoons) flour

275ml/½ pt (1¼ cups) stock

FOR THE STUFFING

150g/5 oz (2 cups) fine white breadcrumbs

1 slice fat bacon, chopped

40g/1½ oz (3 tablespoons) shredded suet (lard)

3-4 shallots, chopped

15ml (1 tablespoon) each parsley and chives, chopped

5ml (1 teaspoon) lemon thyme

half a lemon

6 anchovy fillets, chopped

1 medium-sized egg, beaten

salt

freshly ground black pepper

stock to moisten

Heat the oven to 180°C (350°F) gas mark 4. To make the stuffing, mix breadcrumbs, bacon, suet (lard), shallots, anchovies and herbs thoroughly in a bowl and season well. Grate the rind from the lemon and squeeze half the juice. Combine the egg and lemon rind and juice with the dry ingredients. Moisten gradually with a little stock until the mixture holds together but do not allow it to become wet.

Wipe the meat with a clean damp cloth. Placing it with the meaty side uppermost and the breast bone towards your knife hand, cut a slit almost the length of the

Roast game birds with orange and wine sauce make an impressive dinner party dish.

Devilled Beef Rolls

Here is a way of serving 450g (1 lb) cold roast beef, left over from a meal, to make a rather special hot main course for 4 people. Add any left-over meat juice to the gravy.

SERVES 4
8 thin slices of cold roast beef
15ml/½ oz (1 tablespoon) butter
15ml/½ oz (2 tablespoons) flour
FOR THE STUFFING
50g/2 oz (¼ cup) shredded suet (lard)
50g/2 oz (2 slices) bacon, chopped and lightly fried
100g/¼ lb (2 cups) fresh white breadcrumbs
25g/1 oz (3 tablespoons) raisins, chopped
50g/2 oz (¼ cup) onion, chopped
15ml (1 tablespoon) chopped parsley
grated rind of 1 lemon
FOR THE SAUCE
15ml (1 tablespoon) Dijon mustard
275ml/½ pt (1¼ cups) stock
30ml (2 tablespoons) redcurrant or crabapple jelly
15ml (1 tablespoon) prepared horseradish sauce
60ml/4 tablespoons (¼ cup) red wine
salt
freshly ground black pepper
100g/¼ lb (1 cup) mushrooms, sliced
40g/1½ oz (3 tablespoons) butter

Heat the oven to 180°C (350°F) gas mark 4. Combine all the stuffing ingredients together in a mixing bowl. Divide the mixture equally and place a mound on each beef slice. Roll up and tie each one with string at both ends.

Melt the butter in a pan and sprinkle in the flour. Cook briefly, stirring. Add the mustard, stock, fruit jelly, horseradish and wine and bring to the boil. Stir until the jelly dissolves. Season to taste. Pack the rolls neatly with the seams underneath in one layer in a casserole dish. Pour over the sauce. Cover and cook in the oven for 45 minutes.

Fifteen minutes before the end of cooking time, melt the butter in a frying-pan and add the mushrooms. Sauté for 3 minutes over low heat, turning gently. Distribute the mushrooms over the beef rolls in the casserole. Cover and complete cooking. Remove string and serve.
Cooking time: 1 hour

breast bone. Working the knife under the meat above the bones, cut a pocket. Be careful not to pierce the upper covering of meat or to cut through the meat. Put the butter and oil in the roasting pan and heat in the oven.

Using a tablespoon, pack the stuffing into the pocket formed between the upper flesh and the rib. Push it well into the pocket so that it is not spilling out.

Weigh the stuffed meat and calculate cooking time at 30 minutes per 450g (1 lb). Season with salt and pepper and place the meat on a rack (with the pocket uppermost)

over the hot fat in the roasting pan. Baste immediately. Roast, basting at 20 minute intervals throughout cooking.

At the end of cooking time transfer to a warm carving dish. Pour off excess fat from the roasting pan. Off the heat stir in the flour then cook for one minute. Add the stock off the heat, bring to the boil and simmer for 2–3 minutes. Check seasoning and pour into a warm gravy boat.

Carve the breast in strips between the bones to give each person a bone and a portion of stuffing with meat above.
Cooking time: 3–3¼ hours

Fish and Shellfish

Carnival Fish Kebabs

Use thick fillets of firm white fish, such as gurnard, rock salmon, coley or cod (in the US halibut, swordfish or tuna). Thick fillets are needed to cut 2.5cm (1 in) cubes. A bed of boiled rice coloured with turmeric, or sweet corn topped with crumbled crispy bacon, goes well with this colourful dish. Serve the kebabs garnished with wedges of lemon.

SERVES 3
450g (1 lb) fish fillets
1 large green (bell) pepper, seeded and cut into 2.5cm (1 in) squares
100g ($\frac{1}{4}$ lb) fresh button mushrooms, stalks trimmed off
1 garlic clove
6 bay leaves
6 small firm tomatoes (cherry tomatoes)
FOR THE MARINADE
45ml (3 tablespoons) olive oil
30ml (2 tablespoons) lemon juice
salt
freshly ground black pepper
5ml (1 teaspoon) dried oregano

Remove the skin from the fillets by easing it away from the flesh with a knife, then pulling gently with your fingers. Cut the flesh into 2.5cm (1 in) cubes.

Mix all the marinade ingredients together in a bowl and add the fish, green pepper and mushroom caps. Stir to coat the ingredients thoroughly. Cover and refrigerate for 2 hours. Stir once or twice during this time.

Rub the kebab skewers with oil, then rub each skewer with a halved garlic clove to pick up the flavour. Drain the kebab ingredients, reserving the marinade. Thread pieces of fish, pepper and mushroom caps alternately on to the skewers. Continue until all the ingredients have been used; include two bay leaves on each skewer.

Heat the grill (broiler) pan with the grid in position to medium heat. Put the kebabs on the grid and cook for 12 minutes, turning the skewers and basting with the marinade several times. Slip the tomatoes on the ends of the skewer for the last 5 minutes of cooking time.

Heat any remaining marinade in a small pan. Transfer the fish to a warmed serving dish and pour the heated marinade and pan juices over the fish. Garnish and serve immediately.
Cooking time: 2 hours marinating, then 1–1$\frac{1}{4}$ hours

Seafood Pie

This is a lovely pie, using coley for economy, but cod can be used instead. A good fish stock is important and both stock and wine need to be reduced to strengthen the flavour.

SERVES 4
700g (1$\frac{1}{2}$ lb) coley or cod fillet, cut in 2.5cm (1 in) pieces
575ml/1 pt (2$\frac{1}{2}$ cups) fish stock (page 253)
150ml/$\frac{1}{4}$ pt ($\frac{2}{3}$ cup) dry white wine
50g/2 oz ($\frac{1}{4}$ cup) butter
1 medium-sized onion, chopped
4 celery stalks, finely sliced
100g/$\frac{1}{4}$ lb (1 cup) mushrooms, sliced
30ml (2 tablespoons) flour
freshly ground black pepper
salt
60ml/4 tablespoons ($\frac{1}{4}$ cup) thin cream
100g ($\frac{1}{4}$ lb) peeled prawns (shrimp)
225g ($\frac{1}{2}$ lb) made weight frozen flaky pastry, thawed (pastry for 1-crust pie)
1 small egg for glaze

Put the fish in a large saucepan, cover with the fish stock and poach for 5 minutes. Lift out with a slotted spoon and put into a 1.15L/2 pt (5 cup) pie or soufflé dish.

Strain the stock then put it in a pan with the wine and boil until it has reduced to 575ml/1 pt (2$\frac{1}{2}$ cups).

Melt the butter in another pan and add the onion. Cook until softened. Add the celery and cook for 5 minutes. Add the mushrooms to the pan and cook for 3 minutes.

Stir the flour into the vegetables, taking care not to break them. Remove from the heat and blend in the stock and the wine. Bring the sauce to the boil, then simmer for 2–3 minutes, season, and stir in the cream. Scatter the prawns (shrimp) over the fish, pour the sauce over the

surface and allow to cool for 15 minutes.

Meanwhile heat the oven to 200°C (400°F) gas mark 6. Roll out the pastry 6mm ($\frac{1}{4}$ in) thick, large enough to overlap the pie dish all around. Cut 2 strips each 12mm ($\frac{1}{2}$ in) wide from the outside of the pastry. Use these to line the dampened pie rim. Dampen the strips and cover the prepared pie with the pastry lid. Seal the edges and decorate with the trimmings. Brush with beaten egg and cook for 20–30 minutes until well risen and golden brown.
Cooking time: 2–2$\frac{1}{4}$ hours

Tenali Fish

A tasty but simple dish, this grilled (broiled) fish is traditionally served with a salad of thinly sliced onions, green chillis and mint leaves, dressed with lime juice.

SERVES 4
4 thick cod or haddock steaks
10ml (2 teaspoons) salt
30ml (2 tablespoons) lemon juice
5ml (1 teaspoon) cayenne pepper
2 garlic cloves, crushed
2.5cm (1 in) piece fresh ginger root, peeled and grated or very finely chopped
10ml (2 teaspoons) ground coriander
60ml (4 tablespoons) yogurt

Pat the fish dry with absorbent paper. In a saucer, mix the salt, lemon juice and cayenne pepper together and rub this mixture into the fish steaks. Put the fish in a shallow bowl and set aside to marinate at room temperature for 30 minutes.

Meanwhile, in a small bowl, mix together the remaining ingredients. Spoon the mixture over the fish, turning the steaks so that they are well coated with the marinade. Set aside for 1 hour.

Heat the grill (broiler) to moderately high. Line the pan with foil. Arrange the fish on the foil and grill (broil) for 10 minutes on each side or until the fish flakes easily when tested with a fork.

Transfer the fish to a warmed serving dish, pour over any pan juices and serve immediately.
Cooking time: 1$\frac{1}{2}$ hours marinating then 20 minutes

Cullen Skink

This is an old Scottish recipe which is a mixture of a soup and a stew. Smoked haddock is traditional for this dish, which originated in the fishing port of Findon, on the northeast coast of Scotland.

SERVES 4
450g (1 lb) smoked fish
275ml/½ pt (1¼ cups) water
2 onions, finely chopped
3 large potatoes, sliced
2.5ml (½ teaspoon) white pepper
425ml/¾ pt (scant 2 cups) milk
15ml (1 tablespoon) butter
1.5ml (¼ teaspoon) salt

Place the fish in a large saucepan with the water. Bring to the boil, lower the heat and gently poach for 15 minutes. With a slotted spoon lift the fish out of the liquid and set it aside on a plate.

Strain the cooking liquid into a bowl. Clean the pan and return the strained cooking liquid to it. Add the onions, potatoes and pepper. Cover the pan and simmer for 20 minutes or until the potatoes are soft.

Meanwhile, remove the skin and bones from the fish and discard them. With a fork, flake the fish into large pieces.

When the potatoes are cooked remove the pan from the heat. Mash the potatoes with the onion and cooking liquid, using fork or a potato masher. Gradually add the milk, stirring constantly until it is blended with the potatoes.

Return the pan to low heat. Add the flaked fish and butter and stir and cook the mixture until it is hot. Taste and add the salt if necessary. Serve at once.
Cooking time: 1 hour

Monte Carlo Cod Steaks

SERVES 4
4 cod steaks
30ml (2 tablespoons) oil
450g (1 lb) ripe tomatoes, blanched, skinned, seeded and roughly chopped
15ml (1 tablespoon) finely chopped onion
1 small garlic clove, crushed
salt and freshly ground black pepper
5ml (1 teaspoon) sugar
2.5ml (½ teaspoon) oregano or thyme
4 anchovy fillets

Tasty and warming cullen skink is an old Scottish dish of smoked fish and potatoes.

Heat half the oil in a small saucepan, add the onion, cover and sweat over a low heat for about 5 minutes. Stir in the garlic and cook for another minute.

Stir in the tomatoes, raise the heat and cook until the tomatoes are soft and most of their liquid has evaporated, about 5–10 minutes. Season to taste with salt, pepper and sugar.

Heat the grill (broiler) to medium heat. Choose a shallow pan or flameproof dish into which the fish will fit in a single layer. Heat the remaining oil in it. Season the fish fairly liberally with salt and pepper on each side, place in the pan and turn so that each side is lightly coated with oil.

Grill (broil) the fish on each side for 4 minutes. Meanwhile, cut each anchovy fillet in half lengthwise. Spread each portion of fish with the tomato mixture and sprinkle a little oregano or thyme on top. Add the anchovy fillets, arranging them criss-cross fashion on top.

Continue cooking for another 3–4 minutes until the fish is cooked through.
Cooking time: 45 minutes

Stargazey (Deep Dish) Pie

Stargazey pie is a famous English recipe from Cornwall, so-called because the heads of the fish gaze towards the stars! The heads of the fish were kept on so that the rich oil could drain back into the pie. Fresh pilchards are traditionally used, but herrings may be used instead.

SERVES 8
5ml (1 teaspoon) butter
8 medium-sized herrings, cleaned and boned and with the heads left on
5ml (1 teaspoon) salt
2.5ml ($\frac{1}{2}$ teaspoon) black pepper
37.5ml ($2\frac{1}{2}$ tablespoons) prepared mustard
shortcrust pastry *(page 240)*
4 hard-boiled eggs, sliced
2 medium-sized onions, finely chopped
4 slices fat bacon, rinded and very finely chopped
15ml (1 tablespoon) dried mixed herbs
125ml/4 fl oz ($\frac{1}{2}$ cup) thick cream
1 egg, lightly beaten

Heat the oven to 200°C (400°F) gas mark 6. Use the butter to grease a 25cm (10 in) pie dish. Set aside.

Place the fish on a work surface and season them, inside and out, with the salt and pepper. Spread a small spoonful of mustard over the inside of each fish. Set aside.

On a floured surface, roll out the pastry and cut a lid to fit the top of the pie. Cut a 1.2cm ($\frac{1}{2}$ in) strip from the trimmings and reserve the leftover pastry. Dampen the rim of the dish with water and press on the pastry strip.

Place the egg slices on the bottom of the prepared dish. Lay the fish over the eggs, with the tails pointing towards the middle and the heads overlapping the edge of the dish. Sprinkle over the onions, bacon and mixed herbs. Pour over the cream.

Lightly moisten the strip of dough around the pie dish. Lift the dough rolled around the rolling pin on to the dish. Unroll and carefully seal the pastry around the fish heads. With a sharp knife, cut a fairly large cross in the centre of the dough.

With a pastry brush, coat the surface of the dough with beaten egg. Roll out the dough trimmings and use them to make a star decoration for the top of the pie. Arrange them in a pattern, then glaze the decorations.

Bake the pie for 35–40 minutes or until the pastry is golden brown. Serve immediately.

Cooking time: $1\frac{1}{4}$–$1\frac{1}{2}$ hours

Mackerel Casserole

SERVES 4
2 mackerel, each weighing about 450-700g (1-1$\frac{1}{2}$ lb)
40g/1$\frac{1}{2}$ oz (3 tablespoons) butter
salt
2 leeks, white parts only, finely sliced
225g ($\frac{1}{2}$ lb) canned tomatoes
15ml (1 tablespoon) dill seeds
2.5ml ($\frac{1}{2}$ teaspoon) paprika
juice of half a lemon
150ml/$\frac{1}{4}$ pt ($\frac{2}{3}$ cup) sour cream

Wash and fillet the mackerel and skin if preferred. Heat the oven to 180°C (350°F) gas mark 4.

Use one-third of the butter to grease the inside of a casserole which will just hold the fillets in one layer and lay the fish in it.

Melt the remaining butter in a frying-pan and sauté the leeks until soft. Add the tomatoes, dill seeds and paprika, mix together and transfer to the casserole.

Sprinkle in the lemon juice and pour the sour cream over the top. Cover the dish. Put into the oven and bake for 20 minutes. Serve hot from the dish.
Cooking time: 45 minutes

Fish Croquettes

Croquettes are a classic way of presenting leftovers in a new and attractive form. Season generously for success.

SERVES 4
200ml/7 fl oz ($\frac{7}{8}$ cup) milk
2 bay leaves
40g/1$\frac{1}{2}$ oz (3 tablespoons) butter
45ml (3 tablespoons) flour
45ml (3 tablespoons) chopped onions
2.5ml ($\frac{1}{2}$ teaspoon) salt
2.5ml ($\frac{1}{2}$ teaspoon) black pepper
2.5ml ($\frac{1}{2}$ teaspoon) red (bell) pepper flakes
225g ($\frac{1}{2}$ lb) cooked fish, such as cod or haddock, skinned, boned and flaked
2 eggs
30ml (2 tablespoons) finely chopped fresh parsley
100g/$\frac{1}{4}$ lb (1$\frac{1}{3}$ cups) dry breadcrumbs
oil for deep frying

In a medium-sized saucepan, scald the milk with the bay leaves over moderate heat. Remove the pan from the heat and allow the milk to cool to lukewarm. Strain the milk.

In another pan, melt the butter over moderate heat. Off the heat stir in the flour to make a smooth paste. Gradually add the milk, stirring constantly. Add the onions, salt, black pepper and red pepper flakes and stir well to blend.

Bring the sauce to the boil, stirring constantly, then simmer for 2–3 minutes. Gradually stir in the fish. Add 1 egg, beaten, and the parsley and mix well.

The fish heads in this decorative Cornish stargazey pie are not intended to be eaten, but they add richness to the dish.

Pour the mixture into a medium-sized bowl; cover with plastic wrap. Allow the mixture to cool and then chill in the refrigerator for 1 hour or until completely cold.

Remove the bowl from the refrigerator. Divide the mixture into equal portions. On a floured board, roll and shape the portions into croquettes. Beat the remaining egg on a plate. Dip the croquettes in the egg and roll them in the breadcrumbs.

In a deep-frying pan, heat the oil over high heat until it registers 180°C (350°F) on a fat thermometer or a small cube of dry bread dropped into the pan turns golden in 60 seconds. Line a dish with absorbent paper and keep warm.

Place the croquettes, a few at a time, in a deep-frying basket and place the basket in the pan. Lower the heat to moderate and fry for 5–6 minutes, or until the croquettes are crisp and brown all over. Remove and drain the croquettes well on absorbent paper. Transfer to the serving dish. Serve at once.
Cooking time: 2$\frac{1}{2}$ hours including chilling

● For economy, or to feed more mouths, use half fish and half well-mashed, seasoned potato. Add a good dash of anchovy essence (sauce) or two mashed anchovy fillets.
● Substitute cheese for the fish. For cheesy potato balls, use 450g (1 lb) potatoes well-mashed with milk, butter and seasoning. Beat in 1 raw egg yolk and form into balls. Cube 50g (2 oz) cheese and push a cube into each ball before coating.

Marinated Whiting

Any firm-fleshed fish cut into small pieces can be used for this deep-fried, crisp fish dish.

SERVES 4
450g (1 lb) whiting fillets, cut into 5cm (2 in) strips
juice of 1 lemon
2.5ml ($\frac{1}{2}$ teaspoon) freshly ground black pepper
5ml (1 teaspoon) dry English mustard
2.5ml ($\frac{1}{2}$ teaspoon) dried oregano
10 anchovy fillets
45ml (3 tablespoons) olive oil
15ml (1 tablespoon) chopped parsley
45ml (3 tablespoons) plain flour
1 large egg
oil for deep frying

Put the lemon juice, pepper, mustard and oregano into a bowl and mix. Chop the

anchovy fillets finely and add with the olive oil and parsley. Mix well.

Put in the fish, stir gently for a few seconds to mix the marinade with the fish. Cover the dish loosely and leave in a cool place for at least 1–2 hours.

Lift the pieces of fish out of the marinade, letting surplus liquid drain back into the bowl. Reserve the marinade. Roll each piece of fish in flour to coat thoroughly. Beat the egg lightly in a shallow dish.

Heat the oil for frying to 190°C (375°F) or until a cube of dry bread turns golden in about 50 seconds. Dip the fish, piece by piece into the beaten egg to coat lightly, and immediately lower into the hot fat. Do not crowd the pan. Fry for 2–3 minutes, turning once or twice, until golden and crisp all over.

Lift out the fish with a slotted spoon, drain briefly on crumpled absorbent paper and pile up on a hot serving dish. Keep hot and repeat with the remaining fish. Immediately before serving sprinkle with a little of the marinade.
Cooking time: 2 hours marinating, then 30 minutes.

Jiffy Tuna Surprise

When you are short of time and ideas, this family supper can be made from store cupboard ingredients. Serve with rice or noodles.

SERVES 2–3
50g/2 oz ($\frac{1}{4}$ cup) butter
1 large onion, chopped
1 garlic clove, chopped
2.5ml ($\frac{1}{2}$ teaspoon) curry powder
225g ($\frac{1}{2}$ lb) canned tomatoes
225g ($\frac{1}{2}$ lb) canned tuna fish, flaked
5ml (1 teaspoon) dried basil
30ml (2 tablespoons) sultanas (white raisins)
2.5ml ($\frac{1}{2}$ teaspoon) salt
1.5ml ($\frac{1}{4}$ teaspoon) freshly ground black pepper

In a medium-sized saucepan, melt the butter over moderate heat. Fry the onion and garlic for 5 minutes, or until the onion is soft and translucent but not brown. Stir in the curry powder and add the tomatoes. with the can juice, tuna, basil, sultanas or white raisins, salt and pepper. Bring up to the boil then simmer gently for 10 minutes. Turn the mixture into a warmed serving dish. Serve at once.
Cooking time: 30–40 minutes

Rice and Pasta

Vegetable Rice

This appetizing vegetable rice dish from West Africa makes an ideal accompaniment to casseroled meat. The dish also makes an excellent stuffing for roasted meat or poultry.

SERVES 4

350g/¾ lb (2 cups) long-grain rice, washed, soaked in cold water for 30 minutes and drained

850ml/1½ pt (4 cups) water

10ml (2 teaspoons) salt

50g/2 oz (¼ cup) butter

1 onion, finely chopped

2 large tomatoes, blanched, skinned and chopped

1 red (bell) pepper, white pith removed, seeded and finely chopped

2 celery stalks, trimmed and finely chopped

100g (¼ lb) broccoli, chopped

100g (¼ lb) mushrooms, finely chopped

1.5ml (¼ teaspoon) cayenne pepper

Put the rice in a large saucepan. Pour over the water and add 7.5ml (1½ teaspoons) of the salt. Bring to the boil, then cover the pan, reduce the heat to very low and simmer the rice for 15–20 minutes or until all the liquid has been absorbed and the rice is tender. Remove the pan from the heat and set aside.

In a large frying-pan, melt the butter over moderate heat. Fry the onion, stirring occasionally, for 5–7 minutes or until it is soft and translucent but not brown. Add the tomatoes, red pepper, celery and broccoli. Fry, stirring frequently, for 10 minutes or until the vegetables begin to soften. Add the mushrooms to the pan and fry, stirring frequently, for a further 3 minutes. Season with the remaining salt and cayenne.

Add the rice to the pan and stir to combine. Cook, stirring frequently, for a further 10 minutes or until the mixture is thoroughly heated through. Serve at once.
Cooking time: 1½ hours

This colourful vegetable rice dish comes from West Africa where it is called puntzin. An exciting vegetable risotto, it can be an accompaniment or a main dish.

Tagliatelle with Walnut Sauce

This famous, beautifully creamy, cold purée or sauce, called 'salsa di noci' in Italy, is based on nuts.

Serve tagliatelle with walnut sauce as a first course for 4, reducing the quantity of tagliatelle to 225g (½ lb). The quantity in the recipe will make a light main course with salad.

SERVES 4

350g (¾ lb) tagliatelle

15ml (1 tablespoon) salt

65g/2½ oz (⅓ cup) butter

FOR THE SAUCE

grated Parmesan cheese

4-6 sprigs fresh marjoram or 6-8 sprigs fresh parsley

100g/¼ lb (1 cup) shelled walnuts

125ml/4 fl oz (½ cup) thick cream

15ml (1 tablespoon) olive oil

salt

freshly ground black pepper

Pick the leaves off the marjoram sprigs (or remove parsley heads from the stalks) and

Stuffed rice and cheese balls are known in Italy as 'suppli al telephono' (telephone wires) because the melted cheese forms threads when the balls are cut.

chop them finely or snip with scissors.

Grind the walnuts to a paste in a coffee mill or blender with the marjoram or parsley leaves. If you do not have a blender, chop the nuts, then pound them to a paste with a pestle in a mortar—the paste need not be completely smooth.

Add the cream slowly, blending it in thoroughly. The result should be a fairly soft, pale green paste. Work in just enough oil to make the sauce like a soft purée. Season the sauce and set aside.

Cook the tagliatelle in plenty of boiling salted water, adding $15g/\frac{1}{2}$ oz (1 tablespoon) of the butter, for 6–9 minutes until cooked but still firm. Toss the drained pasta in the remaining butter. Put the pasta on a heated serving dish, and spoon the sauce over it. Pass the cheese separately.
Cooking time: $\frac{1}{2}-\frac{3}{4}$ hour

● This beautiful, creamy sauce makes an excellent dressing for boiled turnips.
● Celery is attractive with salsa di noci; with the addition of hard-boiled eggs, this makes a supper dish.

Stuffed Rice and Cheese Balls

Cooked rice is rolled into little balls with cheese and ham inside, then deep fried.
Serve as a first course for 5 people, or as a main course, with tomato sauce, for 3–4.

SERVES 4–5
$225g/\frac{1}{2}$ lb ($1\frac{1}{3}$ cups) Italian (white) rice
salt
$50g/2$ oz (4 tablespoons) butter, melted
freshly ground black pepper
$100g$ ($\frac{1}{4}$ lb) ham, thinly sliced
$100g$ ($\frac{1}{4}$ lb) Mozzarella cheese
2 eggs, lightly beaten
$75g/3$ oz (1 cup) breadcrumbs
oil for deep frying

Cook the rice in boiling salted water for 15 minutes. Drain, rinse and fluff. Stir in the melted butter and leave to get completely cold.

Cut the ham into 2cm ($\frac{3}{4}$ in) squares. Cube the cheese into 2cm ($\frac{3}{4}$ in) dice. Beat the eggs, salt and pepper into the rice until thoroughly combined. Place 15ml (1 tablespoon) of the rice mixture in the palm of your hand and flatten it it into a small circle. Lay a slice of ham on top and then a cube of cheese.

Top with another 15ml (1 tablespoon) of rice. Gently roll the mixture between your hands, to make a neat ball. Make more balls in the same way until all the remaining ingredients have been used up. There will be about 20 balls. Spread out the breadcrumbs on a plate and roll each ball in the crumbs, coating them all over. Shake off any excess.

Heat the oil for deep frying until it reaches 190°C (375°F) on a deep-fat thermometer or until a small cube of stale bread dropped into the oil turns golden in 60 seconds. Lower the balls into the oil, a few at a time, and fry for 5 minutes or until they are golden brown. Remove the balls from the pan and drain on absorbent paper.

Keep them hot while you fry and drain the remaining balls in the same way. Serve at once.
Cooking time: 2 hours including resting period

● In Italy this dish is made with leftover risotto milanese, which gives a deliciously moist ball; you will need risotto made with $225g/\frac{1}{2}$ lb ($1\frac{1}{3}$ cups) raw rice. Omit the melted butter in the recipe.
● If using cold, cooked, leftover rice, you will need $700g/1\frac{1}{2}$ lb (4 cups). Add the melted butter given in the recipe and chill briefly before making the balls.

Special Fried Rice with Foo Yung

Foo Yung is a Chinese omelet. It is drier and firmer than the classic French omelet and is used to garnish a dish of rice or meat, or can be served by itself.

SERVES 4
225g/½ lb (1⅓ cups) long grain rice
5ml (1 teaspoon) salt
2 medium-sized onions, finely chopped
50g/2 oz (½ cup) button mushrooms, thinly sliced
75ml/5 tablespoons (⅓ cup) oil
60ml/4 tablespoons (¼ cup) cooked peas
100g (¼ lb) peeled prawns (shrimp)
50g (2 oz) cooked ham, cut in shreds

FOR THE FOO YUNG
2 large eggs
15ml (1 tablespoon) soy sauce
salt
freshly ground black pepper
15g/½ oz (1 tablespoon) unsalted butter

Put rice, salt and 575ml/1 pt (2½ cups) cold water into a large saucepan. Place over medium heat, bring to the boil and stir once. Cover and simmer for 15 minutes without removing the lid or stirring.

Test, and if it is not quite tender, or if the liquid is not quite absorbed, cook for a few minutes longer. Turn the rice into a dish, fluff with a fork and leave until cold.

Heat the oil in a heavy-bottomed frying-pan over medium heat. Add the onions, mushrooms, peas and shrimps and stir-fry for 1 minute, moving them about with a fork as they cook. Add the ham to the pan and stir-fry for 1 minute to mix ingredients.

Add the rice to the pan. Stir-fry for 2 minutes, mixing well with the vegetables. Mound the rice in a serving dish and place in a low oven to keep warm.

Break the eggs into a bowl. Add the soy sauce and seasonings. Beat with a fork until frothy. Heat the butter in a 25cm (10 in) omelet pan over high heat. When it has stopped foaming, add the eggs. Stir the eggs twice and then leave to set.

Heat the grill (broiler) to medium. When

Cook the rice ahead, then special fried rice with foo yung can be made in a flash.

the bottom of the foo yung has set (after about 2 minutes), remove from the heat and place under the grill for a minute to set the top.

Tip on to a warmed plate. Cut into strips and use to decorate the rice with a lattice pattern.

Cooking time: 1½ hours including cooling the rice

● If you wish to make a foo yung on its own, without the rice, it may be filled with beansprouts, chopped ham or mushrooms. Cook the filling in the pan before adding the eggs.

Tomato Pilav

This Persian dish is good as an accompaniment to a meat dish. When fresh tomatoes are cheap, use them in preference to canned; blanch, skin and seed before use.

SERVES 6
175g/6 oz (1 cup) rice
225g (½ lb) onions, finely chopped
45ml (3 tablespoons) cooking oil
1 garlic clove, chopped (optional)
700g (1½ lb) canned tomatoes
salt
freshly ground black pepper
5ml (1 teaspoon) fine sugar
1 bay leaf
5ml (1 teaspoon) dried thyme or oregano (optional)
60ml (4 tablespoons) chopped parsley

Put 575ml/1 pt (2½ cups) of water into a pan and add 5ml (1 teaspoon) salt and the rice. Cook for 8 minutes then drain and reserve.

Heat the oil in a large, heavy-bottomed pan and fry onions and garlic gently for 3 minutes. Add the tomatoes and season to taste. Stir in the sugar. Fry for a further 4 minutes, breaking up the tomatoes with a wooden spoon. Add the herbs and simmer for 10 minutes.

Add the rice and 275ml/½ pt (1¼ cups) of water. Bring to the boil, then simmer, covered, for 20 minutes. Sprinkle with freshly chopped herbs if wished.

Cooking time: ¾–1 hour

● If you add 225g (½ lb) mince (ground beef), it makes a main dish for 3. Add the meat after the onions and fry for 5–10 minutes before adding the tomatoes.
● Cubed pork can be used instead of the mince.

Noodles with Ham

Sprinkle this quick supper dish with grated Parmesan cheese just before serving. Use smoked bacon, cut into matchsticks and fried if you cannot get prosciutto. Serve the noodles with a dish of creamed spinach.

SERVES 4–6
450g (1 lb) noodles
15ml (1 tablespoon) vegetable oil
20ml (4 teaspoons) salt
50g/2 oz (¼ cup) butter, diced
2.5ml (½ teaspoon) black pepper
5ml (1 teaspoon) dried basil
50g (2 oz) prosciutto, cut into thin strips
175g (6 oz) cooked lean ham, cut into thin strips
125g (¼ lb) garlic sausage, cut into thin strips
2 large tomatoes, blanched, peeled, seeded and cut into strips

Put the noodles in boiling water, adding 15ml (1 tablespoon) salt and the vegetable oil to the water. Cook for 7–10 minutes until cooked but still firm, then drain.

In a large saucepan, heat the noodles and butter over very low heat. When the butter has melted, using two forks, toss the noodles until they are coated with the butter. Add the remaining salt, pepper, basil, prosciutto, ham, sausage and tomatoes. Increase the heat to moderate and cook the noodle mixture, stirring frequently with a wooden spoon, for 6–8 minutes or until it is very hot. Serve immediately.

Cooking time: 20 minutes

Brown Rice Savoury

Nutty and slightly chewy, brown rice makes a filling supper dish when combined with fish, fruit and nuts. Remember, brown rice takes longer to cook than white rice, because of the extra layer on the seed.

SERVES 4
175g/6 oz (1 cup) brown rice
500ml/18 fl oz (2¼ cups) chicken stock
25g/1 oz (2 tablespoons) butter
5ml (1 teaspoon) salt
175g (6 oz) smoked haddock fillets
50g/2 oz (¼ cup) salted peanuts
50g/2 oz (¼ cup) raisins
25g/1 oz (¼ cup) grated Parmesan cheese
2 hard-boiled eggs
15ml (1 tablespoon) finely chopped parsley

Wash and pick over the rice. Place in a pan with the stock, butter and salt. Bring to the boil, stir once and cover. Reduce heat to very low and leave the rice very gently simmering for 45 minutes.

About 10 minutes before the rice will be ready, place the haddock in a bowl of boiling water. Leave for 15 minutes.

Roughly chop the peanuts. Set aside. Remove the rice from the heat and rinse with hot water. Turn into hot dish and fluff with butter. Set aside in a warm place.

Drain and flake the haddock. Stir into the rice with the peanuts, raisins and cheese. Slice the hard-boiled eggs and arrange on top of the rice. Sprinkle with finely chopped fresh parsley and serve.

Cooking time: 1¼–1½ hours

Thin Pasta with Chicken Livers

SERVES 4–6
30ml (2 tablespoons) olive oil
450g (1 lb) chicken livers, cleaned and chopped
2 garlic cloves, crushed
450g (1 lb) canned tomatoes, drained and with 125ml/4 fl oz (½ cup) of the can juice reserved
20ml (4 teaspoons) salt
2.5ml (½ teaspoon) freshly ground black pepper
2.5ml (½ teaspoon) dried thyme
2.5ml (½ teaspoon) dried basil
175g/6 oz (¾ cup) fresh or frozen peas
450g (1 lb) tagliarini or spaghetti
15ml (1 tablespoon) vegetable oil

In a large, heavy-bottomed pan, heat the oil over moderate heat. Add the chicken livers and garlic and cook, stirring constantly, for 3–4 minutes or until the livers are lightly browned all over.

Add the tomatoes with the reserved can juice, 5ml (1 teaspoon) salt, pepper, thyme and basil and bring the mixture to the boil, stirring constantly. Simmer for 30 minutes, stirring occasionally. Add the peas and continue cooking, stirring occasionally, for a further 15 minutes.

Meanwhile prepare a large pan of boiling water, adding the remaining salt and 15ml (1 tablespoon) vegetable oil. Cook the tagliarini for 6–9 minutes until cooked but still firm. Drain and return to the pan. Pour over the sauce. Using two large spoons, toss the mixture until it is thoroughly coated with the sauce. Serve immediately.

Cooking time: 1 hour

Vegetables

Sugar-glazed Parsnips

When the oven is on, it makes sense to bake the vegetables that accompany the meal; otherwise simmer on the top of the stove. Carrots and turnips can be sugar-glazed by the same method.

SERVES 8
450g (1 lb) parsnips, peeled
75g/3 oz (6 tablespoons) margarine
275-575ml/$\frac{1}{2}$-1 pt (1$\frac{1}{4}$-2$\frac{1}{2}$ cups) water
salt
freshly ground black pepper
60ml (4 tablespoons) sugar

Cut the parsnips into bite-sized pieces. Melt the margarine in a heavy-bottomed pan and turn the parsnips in the fat for 5 minutes until they are thoroughly coated and beginning to take on colour. Add the water barely to cover, season and add the sugar. Cover and braise in the oven at 180°C (350°F) gas mark 4 or on the top of the stove for 30–40 minutes.

When the vegetables are tender, remove the lid and fast boil on the top of the stove to reduce the liquid to 30ml (2 tablespoons), stirring to prevent burning.
Cooking time: 50 minutes

Coriander Marrow

Marrow (squash) can be rather a bland vegetable; but here is an interesting way to serve it, flavoured with spices and bathed in a garlicky tomato sauce.

SERVES 4–6
2 medium-sized onions, finely sliced
2 large garlic cloves, crushed
900g (2 lb) marrow (squash)
30ml (2 tablespoons) oil
450g (1 lb) tomatoes, blanched, skinned and sliced
10ml (2 teaspoons) coriander seeds, crushed
1 bay leaf
salt
freshly ground black pepper
30ml (2 tablespoons) freshly chopped parsley

Peel off the marrow (squash) skin if tough, cut into dice and discard seeds if tough.

Heat the oil in a heavy-bottomed pan, then add the onions, cover and sweat over low heat for 5 minutes. Add the garlic and marrow to the pan, cook for 2–3 minutes, stirring occasionally, then add the tomatoes, bay leaf and crushed coriander seeds. Season with salt and pepper, cover and stew gently for about 30 minutes until the marrow is tender.

Remove the bay leaf and check seasoning. Serve sprinkled with chopped parsley.
Cooking time: $\frac{3}{4}$–1 hour

Onions Smothered with Walnuts

This original way of serving onions makes a hot crunchy dish to serve with roast meat or boiled chicken.

SERVES 4
5ml (1 teaspoon) butter
450g (1 lb) pickling (pearl) onions, peeled
75g/3 oz ($\frac{3}{4}$ cup) walnuts, chopped
25g/1 oz (2 tablespoons) butter, melted
30ml (2 tablespoons) clear honey
15ml (1 tablespoon) chilli sauce
125ml/4 fl oz ($\frac{1}{2}$ cup) chicken stock
2.5ml ($\frac{1}{2}$ teaspoon) salt
1.5ml ($\frac{1}{4}$ teaspoon) freshly ground black pepper
1.5ml ($\frac{1}{4}$ teaspoon) ground cinnamon
1.5ml ($\frac{1}{4}$ teaspoon) Worcestershire sauce

Heat the oven to 170°C (325°F) gas mark 3. Use the butter to grease a medium-sized ovenproof dish. Set aside.

In a medium-sized mixing bowl, combine the whole onions, walnuts, melted butter, honey, chilli sauce, chicken stock, salt, pepper, cinnamon and Worcestershire sauce.

Pour the onion mixture into the ovenproof dish. Cover the dish with foil and place it in the oven. Bake the onions for 1$\frac{1}{4}$ hours or until they are tender when pierced with the point of a sharp knife, and well browned. Turn them in the sauce once or twice during the cooking period. Remove the dish from the oven and serve.
Cooking time: 1$\frac{1}{2}$–1$\frac{3}{4}$ hours

Barley and Mushroom Casserole

This is an excellent example of how a vegetable casserole is turned into a complete meal with the addition of pearl barley. It takes a little longer than the usual time for a vegetable casserole to cook, to allow the pearl barley to expand and absorb the liquid during cooking. The finished dish has a delicious chewy texture and is invitingly colourful to serve.

SERVES 6
3 large onions, sliced
350g ($\frac{3}{4}$ lb) small mushrooms, sliced
2 green (bell) peppers, seeded and sliced
30ml (2 tablespoons) vegetable oil
350g/$\frac{3}{4}$ lb (1$\frac{1}{2}$ cups) pearl barley
850g (1 lb 14 oz) canned tomatoes
175ml/6 fl oz ($\frac{3}{4}$ cup) chicken stock
10ml (2 teaspoons) freshly chopped thyme
salt
freshly ground black pepper
30ml (2 tablespoons) freshly chopped parsley

Heat oven to 180°C (350°F) gas mark 4. Heat the oil in a frying-pan, add onions, cover and sweat. Add the mushrooms to the pan and cook for a further 2 minutes, stirring occasionally.

Put the pearl barley in a casserole dish. Add the onions and mushrooms. Pour over the tomatoes, stock, green peppers and thyme. Season with salt and pepper and stir well. Cover the dish and cook in the oven for 1 hour until the barley is just tender and most of the liquid is absorbed.

Just before serving, uncover and sprinkle over the chopped parsley.
Cooking time: 1$\frac{1}{2}$ hours

Aniseed Carrots

SERVES 4
700g (1$\frac{1}{2}$ lb) carrots
15ml (1 tablespoon) soft brown sugar
50g/2 oz ($\frac{1}{4}$ cup) butter
6.5ml (1 heaped teaspoon) aniseed
5ml (1 teaspoon) salt
freshly ground black pepper

Tasty and economical barley and mushroom casserole is filling enough to be a complete meal. Even meat-eaters will find this vegetarian dish a pleasant change.

Wash and scrape the carrots. If you are using small carrots leave them whole; large carrots should be cut in quarters lengthways.

Put the sugar, butter, aniseed, salt and pepper into a pan. When the mixture begins to bubble, add the carrots. Stir well, cover, lower the heat and simmer for about 15 minutes or until the carrots are tender when pierced with a fork. Serve hot.
Cooking time: 25 minutes

Potato Croquettes

Double the amount of mashed potato you normally make and reserve half for this dish.

SERVES 6
450g (1 lb) potato, cooked and mashed with 25g/1 oz (2 tablespoons) margarine and 30ml (2 tablespoons) milk
flour
1 egg yolk
25g/1 oz ($\frac{1}{4}$ cup) Cheddar cheese, grated
salt and freshly ground black pepper
1 medium-sized egg, beaten
dried brown breadcrumbs
oil for deep frying

Beat the egg yolk and cheese into the mashed potato and season well.

Roll out the potato on a lightly-floured surface into a long sausage and cut into fairly large bullet shapes. Dip in beaten egg and roll in the bread crumbs.

Heat the oil in a deep-fat frier to 180°C (350°F) or until a bread cube will brown in 60 seconds. Deep-fry in batches for 4 minutes. Drain on kitchen paper.
Cooking time: 30 minutes

● In the recipe the croquettes are deep-fried, but if the oven is already hot, bake them. Dot with 50g/2 oz ($\frac{1}{4}$ cup) margarine and bake for 20 minutes at 200°C (400°F) gas mark 6, 30 minutes in a cooler oven.

Brussels Sprouts Creole

SERVES 4

700g (1½ lb) Brussels sprouts
40g/1½ oz (3 tablespoons) butter
1 large onion, finely chopped
1 garlic clove, crushed
1 green (bell) pepper, white pith removed, seeded and chopped
450g (1 lb) tomatoes, blanched, peeled and chopped
2.5ml (½ teaspoon) freshly ground black pepper
1.5ml (¼ teaspoon) dried basil
5ml (1 teaspoon) salt

Trim any tough or discoloured outer leaves from the sprouts, and wash them thoroughly. Cut a cross in the base of each sprout.

Melt the butter in a heavy, medium-sized saucepan over moderate heat. Fry the onion, garlic and green pepper, stirring occasionally, for 8 minutes. Add the tomatoes, sprouts, black pepper, basil and salt. Taste the mixture and add more salt and pepper if necessary.

Reduce the heat, cover the pan and cook for 15–20 minutes, or until the sprouts are tender. Turn the mixture into a warmed serving dish. Serve at once.

Cooking time: 35 minutes

Arabian Eggplant

SERVES 4

4 medium- to large-sized aubergines (eggplants)
75g/3 oz (½ cup) rice
75g/3 oz (½ cup) raisins
2 large tomatoes, blanched, skinned and seeded
1 medium-sized onion, finely chopped
15ml (1 tablespoon) oil
175g (6 oz) mince (ground beef)
2.5ml (½ teaspoon) ground cumin
2.5ml (½ teaspoon) ground coriander
salt and freshly ground black pepper
575ml/1 pt (2½ cups) beef stock
30-45ml (2-3 tablespoons) freshly chopped parsley

Halve the aubergines (eggplants) lengthwise and scoop out the flesh. Place the flesh in a colander and sprinkle salt over. Salt the shells and leave upside down for 30 minutes.

Meanwhile, place the rice in a pan with 275ml/½ pt (1¼ cups) of water. Bring to the boil over high heat, stir once, cover and simmer gently for about 15minutes. Five minutes before the end of cooking time, add the raisins.

Fry the onion in the oil over a low heat until soft. Place the mince (ground beef) in a bowl and stir in the rest of the ingredients except the stock and parsley.

Rinse the aubergine flesh and shells under cold water. Pat the shells with absorbent paper and squeeze the flesh dry. Roughly chop the flesh and add it to the stuffing in the bowl. Arrange the aubergines in a casserole (dutch oven) and spoon in the stuffing, packing fairly loosely to allow the raw ingredients to expand during

Simple to make, Brussels sprouts creole is a colourful dish to serve with meat.

cooking. Make more than one layer if necessary.

Pour into the pan enough stock to come half way up the bottom layer of aubergines. Simmer, covered, on top of the stove, for $\frac{3}{4}$–1 hour or until tender. Garnish with parsley before serving.
Cooking time: 2 hours

Scandinavian Potato Cakes

SERVES 2–4
450g (1 lb) potatoes, peeled and grated
4 small spring onions (scallions), trimmed and finely chopped
5ml (1 teaspoon) salt
5ml (1 teaspoon) black pepper
15ml (1 tablespoon) butter
45ml (3 tablespoons) vegetable oil

Place the grated potatoes in a large mixing bowl. With a kitchen fork, stir in the spring onions (scallions), salt and pepper. Set aside for 10 minutes. Drain off the liquid and pat the surface of the mixture dry with absorbent paper.

In a medium-sized frying-pan, melt the butter with the oil over moderate heat. When the foam subsides, place 30ml (2 tablespoons) of the potato mixture in the pan, flattening it slightly with the back of the spoon. Add two or three similar amounts to the pan. Fry the fritters for 2 to 3 minutes, until they are golden brown on both sides, turning once. Using a slotted spoon, transfer the potato cakes to absorbent paper to drain. Cook and drain the remaining potato mixture in the same way. Serve immediately.
Cooking time: 30–45 minutes

Stir-Braised Cauliflower with Parsley

Cauliflower florets have maximum flavour cooked this way; the braising at the end ensures that the stalks are tender.

SERVES 4
1 medium-sized cauliflower, trimmed into florets
1 medium-sized onion, thinly sliced
1 garlic clove, chopped
45ml (3 tablespoons) oil
150ml/$\frac{1}{4}$ pt ($\frac{2}{3}$ cup) stock
30ml (2 tablespoons) dry white wine
60ml/4 tablespoons ($\frac{1}{4}$ cup) chopped parsley

Heat the oil in a pan over moderate heat, then add the vegetables. Stir-fry for a minute, using a fork to keep turning over the vegetables, then pour in the stock and wine and add the parsley.

Bring to the boil, cover the pan and cook over moderate heat for 7 minutes. Serve immediately.
Cooking time: 15 minutes

Stuffed Celeriac

A rather different way of serving this vegetable, slices are stuffed with a mixture of other vegetables. Serve as a garnish to roast meat. Make salad from the trimmings.

SERVES 4
75g/3 oz (6 tablespoons) butter
225g ($\frac{1}{2}$ lb) carrots, finely chopped
1 large onion, finely chopped
2.5ml ($\frac{1}{2}$ teaspoon) salt
2.5ml ($\frac{1}{2}$ teaspoon) black pepper
2.5ml ($\frac{1}{2}$ teaspoon) sugar
60ml (4 tablespoons) vegetable stock, or stock made with a chicken stock cube
1 large or 2 small celeriacs (celery roots)
100g/$\frac{1}{4}$ lb (1 cup) cheese, grated

Stuff slices of celeriac (celery root) with vegetables to garnish roast meat.

In a small pan melt 50g/2 oz ($\frac{1}{4}$ cup) of the butter over moderate heat. Add the carrots, onion, salt, pepper, sugar and stock. Cook for 5 minutes, stirring so that the mixture does not stick to the pan. Cover tightly and simmer for about 15 minutes or until the mixture is soft and all the liquid has been absorbed.

Heat the oven to 170°C (325°F) gas mark 3. Peel the celeriac and cut it into slices 2.5–4cm (1–1$\frac{1}{2}$ in) thick then trim.

Bring a pan of water to the boil. Drop in the slices of celeriac and boil for 10 minutes. Drain the celeriac in a colander and rinse with cold water. Scoop out the centre of each slice to about half its depth. Chop the spare flesh and stir into the carrot mixture. Fill the hollows with the mixture.

Place the stuffed celeriac slices in a shallow ovenproof dish and cover with the grated cheese. Dot the remaining butter over the cheese and place the dish in the centre of the oven. Bake for about 20 minutes, or until the celeriac is soft and the cheese is golden brown. Serve immediately.
Cooking time: 1$\frac{1}{4}$ hours

163

Desserts

Tudor Pears

Careful poaching makes even the most wooden cooking pears tender and a lovely ruby red. If the oven is already heated, cook for 50–70 minutes at a moderate heat.

SERVES 4
4 large, whole cooking pears
175g/6 oz ($\frac{3}{4}$ cup) fine sugar or (2 tablespoons) honey
5ml (1 teaspoon) lemon juice
200ml/7 fl oz (1 cup) red wine or cider
4 whole cloves
5cm (2 in) cinnamon stick

Thinly peel the pears, keeping them whole, with the stalk and the core intact. Lay the pears on their sides in a shallow pan which is a good fit. Laying them top to tail will take up less room.

To make the syrup, put the sweetener, 5ml/3 fl oz ($\frac{1}{3}$ cup) water and the lemon juice in a small pan. Bring to the boil, stirring, over low heat. Boil the syrup for 2 minutes. Remove from heat, stir in the wine and spices and pour over the pears.

Cover the pan with a lid. Cook over low heat on the stove top for 40 minutes. Carefully turn the pears half-way through cooking time, using a slotted spoon.

When cooked, lift the pears out of the syrup on to serving dishes. Strain the syrup, discarding the spices, and pour over the pears. When cold, cover and chill in the refrigerator for 1 hour before serving.
Cooking time: $1\frac{1}{4}$–$1\frac{3}{4}$ hours plus chilling time

Pears with Ginger Syrup

Fresh ginger can be stored in a jar, covered in sherry, for at least 6 months if you have left-over ginger from this recipe.

SERVES 4
4 pears, peeled, cored and thickly sliced
juice of 1 lemon
50g/2 oz ($\frac{1}{4}$ cup) sugar
2.5cm (1 in) piece of fresh ginger root, peeled and thinly sliced
175ml/6 fl oz ($\frac{3}{4}$ cup) water

Place the pears in a serving dish and pour over half the lemon juice. Put the dish in the refrigerator while you make the syrup.

Put the sugar, ginger, the remaining lemon juice and the water into a small pan. Set the pan over low heat and cook the mixture, stirring constantly, until the sugar has dissolved. Increase the heat to moderate and boil the syrup for 2 minutes.

Remove the dish from the refrigerator and pour the syrup over the pears; set aside to cool. Chill the dish in the refrigerator for 1 hour or until ready to serve.
Cooking time: $1\frac{1}{4}$–$1\frac{1}{2}$ hours plus chilling time

Festive Layer Pudding

SERVES 6
FOR THE FILLING
350g/$\frac{3}{4}$ lb (1 cup) mincemeat *(page 255)*
15ml (1 tablespoon) brandy or rum (optional)
FOR THE SPONGE
100g/$\frac{1}{4}$ lb (1 cup) wholewheat flour
5ml (1 teaspoon) baking powder
50g/2 oz ($\frac{2}{3}$ cup) wholewheat breadcrumbs
100g/$\frac{1}{4}$ lb ($\frac{1}{2}$ cup) butter or margarine
100g/$\frac{1}{4}$ lb ($\frac{2}{3}$ cup firmly packed) soft brown sugar
2 medium-sized eggs, beaten
about 65ml/$\frac{1}{8}$ pt ($\frac{1}{4}$ cup) milk

Heat the oven to 180°C (350°F) gas mark 4. Generously grease a 1.1L/2 pt (6 cup) pie or baking dish. Put the mincemeat in a bowl together with the brandy or rum (if used). Stir well with a fork so the filling is easy to spread.

Sift the flour and baking powder into a bowl and reserve. Tip any remaining bran left in the sieve into the bowl and stir lightly to mix. Stir in the breadcrumbs.

Cream the butter and sugar until light and fluffy. Beat the eggs into the creamed mixture, a little at a time, beating well after each addition. Lightly fold in the flour and breadcrumbs. Add just enough milk to give a soft dropping consistency.

Spread a scant one-third of the sponge mixture over the bottom of the dish and top with half the mincemeat. Cover this with another scant third of sponge. Spread over the rest of the mincemeat and cover with the remaining sponge. Smooth the top with a spatula and bake for about 1–1½ hours or until cooked.
Cooking time: $1\frac{1}{4}$–$1\frac{3}{4}$ hours

Bread Pudding

This is often confused with bread and butter pudding but is in fact very different. It is an economical way of using up stale bread. It can be eaten hot with custard or cold, sprinkled with sugar and served in slices as a cake. It makes filling picnic food! Make the pudding in either a 450g (1 lb) loaf tin (pan) or a slab cake tin (pan) about 10cm (4 in) deep and about 20 × 15cm (8 × 6 in).

SERVES 8
8 slices white or brown stale bread
275ml/$\frac{1}{2}$ pt (1$\frac{1}{4}$ cups) milk
350g ($\frac{3}{4}$ lb) mixed dried fruit
50g/2 oz ($\frac{1}{3}$ cup) mixed candied peel
1 medium-sized cooking apple, peeled, cored and grated
25g/1 oz (3 tablespoons) soft brown sugar
45ml (3 tablespoons) thick-cut orange marmalade
2 medium-sized eggs
5ml (1 teaspoon) lemon juice
5ml (1 teaspoon) ground cinnamon
100g/$\frac{1}{4}$ lb ($\frac{1}{2}$ cup) butter or margarine

Cut the crusts off the bread and break it into small pieces. Place in a bowl, pour the milk over and leave for about 45 minutes, until the bread has absorbed all the milk.

When the bread is soft, add the dried fruit and grated apple to the bowl with the remaining ingredients, except the butter. Mix well.

Heat the oven to 150°C (300°F) gas mark 2. Melt the butter and use a little to grease the mould lightly. Pour half the remainder into the bread mixture and mix together. Turn the mixture into the mould and smooth the top with a spatula or the back of a spoon. Pour on the remaining butter. Leave for 5 minutes to allow it to soak into the mixture.

Bake in the centre of the oven for 1½ hours. Increase the temperature to 180°C

(350°F) gas mark 4 and bake for a further 30 minutes. If the top of the pudding over-browns, cover with foil.
Cooking time: 3–3¼ hours

Frosted Plum Tricorns

Crisp pastry encasing a surprise filling of plums and cream makes these decorative parcels an impressive dessert. Yet they are economical to make, as only one plum is needed for each parcel. Choose firm, good-sized plums.

SERVES 4
¾ × **shortcrust pastry** *(page 240)*
8 plums
40ml (8 teaspoons) fine sugar
150ml/¼ pt (⅔ cup) cream
milk to glaze
fine sugar to decorate

Heat the oven to 200°C (400°F) gas mark 6. Split each plum in half and remove the stone. Fill the cavity of each plum with 5ml (1 teaspoon) fine sugar. Sandwich the halves together and set aside.

Roll out the pastry on a lightly-floured board to 30 × 26cm (12 × 10 in). Cut in half lengthwise. To help in cutting, first mark some guidelines. Fold the pastry in half to mark the centre and then fold in each end in turn to mark the quarters.

Arrange one strip with the long side next to you. Cut from the bottom corner up to the quarter mark, then back to the base at half way. Cut again up to the second quarter mark, then back to the final base corner. You will now have 3 equal-sided triangles. Join the two spare corners together, dampening, overlapping slightly and pressing, to make the fourth triangle. Cut the second strip in the same way.

Brush around each triangle with cold

These decorative frosted plum tricorns, filled with cream are the sort of parcels all your family will be only too pleased to unwrap. Economical and not difficult to make, they look very luxurious.

water and stand a plum upright in the centre. Bring the three corners of pastry up to meet at the top of the plum. Pinch the seams firmly together to seal.

Fold back the tips of the pastry at the top, making a hole for the steam to escape. Carefully transfer the tricorns on to an ungreased baking sheet. Brush the sides with milk and sprinkle with sugar to give the pastry a sweet glaze. Bake above the centre of the oven for 30 minutes.

Just before serving, dribble a little cream into the steam vent to fill the tricorns and sprinkle lavishly with fine sugar.
Cooking time: 1–1½ hours

Apple and Cheese Crêpes

Grated apple added to crêpe batter makes the crêpes more substantial. Apple and cheese traditionally go well together. Cream cheese is layered between the crêpes to make this delightful dessert. Sprinkle a little sugar over the top for a final flourish.

SERVES 4
sweet crêpe batter *(page 245)*
60ml/4 tablespoons ($\frac{1}{4}$ cup) clarified butter or oil
100g ($\frac{1}{4}$ lb) cream cheese
45ml (3 tablespoons) thick cream
25g/1 oz (2 tablespoons) fine sugar
75g/3 oz ($\frac{1}{2}$ cup) sultanas or raisins
1 large cooking apple

Place the cream cheese in a bowl and beat with a wooden spoon until light and fluffy. Gradually beat the cream into the cream cheese mixture. Stir in the sugar and dried fruit and set aside.

Peel, core and grate the apple. Stir into the batter. Use the clarified butter or oil to grease the pan and use the batter to make 12 crêpes. Keep them warm, layered with greaseproof or waxed paper, over a pan of water.

Place one of the crêpes on a plate. Spread with 15–30ml (1–2 tablespoons) of the cream cheese mixture. Top with another crêpe and spread it with cream cheese mixture. Continue layering in this way until all cheese mixture and crêpes have been used. Serve at once.
Cooking time: 1 hour

Golden Oranges

Yogurt makes a refreshing contrast to this sweet dish of golden oranges topped with candied peel. The candied peel can be replaced with julienne strips of orange rind. Blanch the peeled rind of half an orange, cut it into thin slivers and add to the pan with the golden syrup or honey.

SERVES 4
6 large oranges
40g/1$\frac{1}{2}$ oz (3 tablespoons) butter
30ml (2 tablespoons) golden syrup or honey
15ml (1 tablespoon) chopped candied peel
150ml/$\frac{1}{4}$ pt ($\frac{2}{3}$ cup) plain yogurt

Cut the rind and pith from four of the oranges. Cut the flesh into 1.2cm ($\frac{1}{2}$ in) slices and pick out the seeds and centre pith. Squeeze the juice from the remaining oranges and set aside.

Melt 25g/1 oz (2 tablespoons) of the butter in a large frying-pan over high heat. Put in as many orange slices as the pan will take in single layer and brown them on both sides, turning carefully. Remove and keep warm. Add more butter to the pan if necessary and cook the remaining orange slices.

Return all the oranges to the pan and spoon in the honey. Pour the orange juice over and allow to bubble for 1 minute. Transfer everything to a warmed serving dish.

Scatter the candied peel over the top and serve the yogurt separately in a small bowl.
Cooking time: $\frac{3}{4}$ hour

Bananas in Orange Juice

SERVES 4
4 firm bananas
25g/1 oz (2 tablespoons) butter
15ml (1 tablespoon) Barbados or dark brown sugar
pinch of nutmeg
120ml/8 tablespoons ($\frac{1}{2}$ cup) freshly squeezed orange juice
50g/2 oz ($\frac{1}{2}$ cup) chopped walnuts (optional)

Peel the bananas and cut them in half lengthwise. Melt the butter in a large frying-pan over moderate heat. Lay the bananas in the pan, cut side up, and brown the underside—this will take about 1$\frac{1}{2}$ minutes.

Sprinkle them with half the sugar and turn them over. Sprinkle them with the remaining sugar and the nutmeg. Pour the orange juice over and cook for 2 minutes more. Transfer to a warm serving dish and scatter the walnuts over if used.
Cooking time: 20 minutes

Pennywise Apricot Cream

A strongly flavoured fruit is used in this poor man's cream to mask the distinctive sweet taste of the evaporated milk.

SERVES 6
225g (½ lb) dried apricots
275ml/½ pt (1¼ cups) evaporated milk
50g (2 oz) flaked almonds

Boil the unopened can of evaporated milk in water for 15 minutes. Refrigerate overnight. Soak the apricots overnight in tepid water.

Drain the apricots and rub the flesh through a sieve. Turn out the evaporated milk into a bowl and whisk it until thick. Then fold into it the purée. Turn the mixture into 1 large or 6 individual serving dishes. Chill in the refrigerator for 1 hour. Just before serving, decorate the top with flaked almonds.
Cooking time: overnight preparation, then 1½ hours, plus 1 hour chilling

Exciting contrasts of colours, tastes and textures give prune and apple meringue its wide appeal. It is an ideal autumn (fall) dessert: elegant, unusual and satisfying.

Prune and Apple Meringue

Meringue is a wonderfully quick and economical way of producing a glamorous-looking dessert. If your numbers increase unexpectedly, it is also an excellent way of eking out a small quantity of fruit.

SERVES 6–8
23cm (9 in) pastry case made with shortcrust pastry *(page 240)*, uncooked
FOR THE FILLING
175g/6 oz (1 cup) prunes, soaked overnight, drained, stoned and halved
225g (½ lb) cooking apples, weighed after peeling, coring and slicing
5ml (1 teaspoon) lemon juice
50g/2 oz (⅓ cup) sultanas or seedless raisins
2.5ml (½ teaspoon) ground cinnamon
30ml (2 tablespoons) sugar
FOR THE MERINGUE
3 egg whites
175g (6 oz) fine sugar (for a less sweet American chiffon topping, use ⅓ cup sugar)
1.5ml (¼ teaspoon) cream of tartar

Heat the oven to 200°C (400°F) gas mark 6. Place the container of the pastry case on a baking sheet.

Combine the prunes, apples, lemon juice, sultanas or seedless raisins, cinnamon and 15ml (1 tablespoon) of the sugar in a mixing bowl. Transfer the mixture to the pastry case, smoothing it out evenly with a spatula. Sprinkle over the remaining sugar. Place the baking sheet in the centre of the oven and bake for 15 minutes.

Meanwhile, in a large mixing bowl, beat the egg whites until they form stiff peaks. Beat in 15ml (1 tablespoon) fine sugar and the cream of tartar and continue beating until the meringue is stiff and glossy. With a metal spoon, fold in the remaining sugar.

Remove the baking sheet from the oven. Reduce the oven temperature to moderate, 180°C (350°F) gas mark 4. Spoon the meringue over the filling to cover it completely. Using the back of the spoon, flick up the meringue into decorative peaks.

Return the tart to the oven and continue baking for 20–25 minutes or until the meringue has set and is golden brown. Transfer to a dish and serve immediately.

Cooking time: overnight soaking, then ¾–1 hour
● If you keep spare pastry cases in the freezer and use canned prunes, this dessert can be produced at short notice.

into the prepared bowl.

Cover with a circle of greaseproof or waxed paper greased with the remaining butter, then with a circle of foil, both pleated across the middle to allow for expansion. Tie with string and place in a large pan with enough boiling water to come about two-thirds up the sides of the bowl. Cover and steam for 3 hours, adding more boiling water as necessary. When cooked uncover and turn onto a plate. Serve immediately.

Cooking time: 3½ hours

Green Grape and Apple Pie

This delicious and unusual apple dessert is flavoured with cinnamon and nutmeg. Serve it with a bowl of plain whipped cream or with vanilla ice-cream.

SERVES 4–6
FOR THE PASTRY
275g/10 oz (2½ cups) flour
1.5ml (¼ teaspoon) salt
100g/¼ lb (½ cup) vegetable fat or lard (shortening) cut in small pieces
50g/2 oz (¼ cup) plus 5ml (1 teaspoon) butter, cut in small pieces
90ml (6 tablespoons) ice-cold water
1 egg, lightly beaten, for glaze
FOR THE FILLING
100g/¼ lb (½ cup) sugar
1.5ml (¼ teaspoon) salt
2.5ml (½ teaspoon) ground cinnamon
1.5ml (¼ teaspoon) grated nutmeg
2 large cooking apples, peeled, cored and thinly sliced
350g (¾ lb) seedless green grapes
15ml (1 tablespoon) cornflour (cornstarch) dissolved in 30ml (2 tablespoons) water
25g/1 oz (2 tablespoons) butter, cut into small pieces

First make the pastry. Sift the flour and salt into a large mixing bowl. Cut in the vegetable fat or lard and 50g/2 oz (¼ cup) of the butter. With your fingertips, rub the fats into the flour until the mixture resembles fine breadcrumbs.

Add 60ml (4 tablespoons) of the iced water and mix it in with the knife. Knead the dough with your hands until it is smooth, adding the remaining water if the

Scots Porridge Apples

This warming dessert is easy to make, economical and gives generous helpings. Serve it with thick, hot custard or, for a special occasion, whipped cream.

SERVES 6
225g (½ lb) plus 5ml (1 teaspoon) butter, melted
225g/½ lb (2⅔ cups) rolled oats
175g/6 oz (1 cup) soft brown sugar
1.5ml (¼ teaspoon) salt
8 medium-sized cooking apples, peeled, cored and thinly sliced
150ml/¼ pt (⅔ cup) water
1 large cooking apple, cored and thinly sliced but not peeled
30ml (2 tablespoons) strained apricot jam, warmed

Heat the oven to 180°C (350°F) gas mark 4. Use the 5ml (1 teaspoon) of butter to grease a large baking dish. In a medium-sized mixing bowl, combine the oats, sugar, salt, and the remaining butter, stirring well with a wooden spoon to blend.

Layer the oat mixture and peeled apple slices in the baking dish, beginning and ending with a layer of oat mixture. Carefully pour the water over the mixture. Place the unpeeled apple slices decoratively over the top of the pudding and, using a pastry brush, brush them with apricot jam.

Place the dish in the centre of the oven and bake for 40–50 minutes or until the top of the pudding is deep golden brown. Remove the dish from the oven and serve immediately.

Cooking time: 1 hour

Ohio Steamed Pudding

SERVES 4–6
15ml (1 tablespoon) butter
100g/¼ lb (1 cup) flour
7.5ml (1½ teaspoons) baking powder
5ml (1 teaspoon) mixed spice or ground allspice
4ml (¾ teaspoon) grated nutmeg
large pinch of ground cloves
50g/2 oz (1 cup) fresh breadcrumbs
1 large carrot, scraped and grated
1 small potato, peeled and grated
100g/¼ lb (⅔ cup) soft brown sugar
175g/6 oz (1 cup) raisins
175g/6 oz (1 cup) currants
juice and grated rind of 1 lemon
125ml/4 fl oz (½ cup) milk
1 egg, lightly beaten

Using half the butter, grease a 1.1L/2 pt (6 cup) pudding bowl. Sift the flour, baking powder, mixed spice or allspice, nutmeg and cloves into a large mixing bowl. Stir in the breadcrumbs, carrot, potato, sugar, raisins, currants and lemon juice and rind.

Pour in the milk and the egg and beat the mixture until the ingredients are thoroughly combined. Spoon the mixture dough is too dry. Form the dough into a ball and wrap it in greaseproof or waxed paper. Chill in the refrigerator for 30 minutes.

Grease a deep 23cm (9 in) pie dish with the 5ml (1 teaspoon) of butter. Divide the dough into two unequal portions and return the smaller portion to the refrigerator. On a lightly-floured surface, roll out the larger portion into a round large enough to line the pie dish. Lift the dough on the rolling pin and lay it over the pie dish. With your fingers, gently ease the dough into the dish. Using a sharp knife, trim the dough even with the outer rim of the pie dish. Set aside.

Heat the oven to 220°C (425°F) gas mark 7. To make the filling, in a medium-sized mixing bowl, mix together the sugar, salt, cinnamon and nutmeg. Add the apples and grapes and the cornflour (cornstarch) mixture and mix thoroughly. Turn the mixture into the pie dish, piling it higher in the centre. Dot the top of the filling with the butter. Dampen the pie rim with water.

Roll out the remaining portion of the dough into a circle about 3mm ($\frac{1}{8}$ in) thick and 30cm (12 in) in diameter. Place the dough over the filling. With a sharp knife, trim the top crust to within 6mm ($\frac{1}{4}$ in) of the dish edge. Tuck the overhanging dough under the edge of the bottom crust all around the rim and press down with your thumb and forefinger to seal the two crusts and to make a crimped design.

Brush with the beaten egg. With the knife, cut two small gashes in the centre of the top crust to allow steam to escape.

Bake the pie for 10 minutes. Reduce the oven temperature to 180°C (350°F) gas mark 4 and continue baking for 45 minutes or until the fruit is tender and the crust brown. Serve the pie hot.
Cooking time: 2 hours

Coriander Fruit Crumble

SERVES 4–6
5ml (1 teaspoon) butter
700g (1½ lb) cooking apples, peeled, cored and thinly sliced
255g (½ lb) fresh blackberries, washed
30ml (2 tablespoons) brown sugar
5ml (1 teaspoon) ground cinnamon
FOR THE TOPPING
100g/¼ lb (1 cup) flour
100g/¼ lb (½ cup) sugar
100g/¼ lb (½ cup) butter, diced
10ml (2 teaspoons) ground coriander

Heat the oven to 180°C (350°F) gas mark 4. Grease a 1.7L/3 pt (2 US quart) baking dish with the butter. Put the apples and blackberries in the baking dish and sprinkle with the brown sugar and cinnamon.

To make the crumble topping, put the flour and sugar in a medium-sized mixing bowl. Cut in the butter, then, using your fingertips, rub it into the flour and sugar until the mixture resembles breadcrumbs. Mix in the coriander.

Sprinkle the crumble on top of the fruit and bake in the oven for 45 minutes.
Cooking time: 1 hour

Grumble Pie

This delicious sweet pie, with a cinnamon-flavoured topping, will be very popular with children.

SERVES 6
FOR THE PASTRY
175g/6 oz (1½ cups) flour
5ml (1 teaspoon) fine sugar
large pinch of salt
50g/2 oz (¼ cup) butter, cut in small pieces
50g/2 oz (¼ cup) vegetable fat (shortening) cut in small pieces
15-30ml (1-2 tablespoons) ice-cold water
FOR THE FILLING
75g/3 oz (½ cup) raisins
175g/6 oz (1 cup) brown sugar
125ml/4 fl oz (½ cup) water
3 eggs, lightly beaten
FOR THE TOPPING
50g/2 oz (⅔ cup) stale cake crumbs
50g/2 oz (½ cup) flour
2.5ml (½ teaspoon) ground cinnamon
1.5ml (¼ teaspoon) ground ginger
50g/2 oz (¼ cup) butter, cut in small pieces

For the pastry, sift the flour, sugar and salt into a medium-sized mixing bowl. Cut in the butter and vegetable fat (shortening) then rub in until the mixture resembles fine breadcrumbs.

Add 15ml (1 tablespoon) of the iced water and, using the knife, mix it into the flour mixture. With your hands, mix and knead the dough until it is smooth. Add more water if the dough is too dry. Form the dough into a ball and wrap it in greaseproof or waxed paper. Place it in the refrigerator to chill for 30 minutes.

Heat the oven to 200°C (400°F) gas mark 6. Remove the dough from the refrigerator and, on a lightly-floured sur-face, roll it out to a circle about 6mm (¼ in) thick. Lift the dough on your rolling pin and lay it over a 23cm (9 in) pie dish. Gently ease the dough into the dish and trim the edges. Blind bake (*see page 61*) for 15 minutes. Reduce the heat to 180°C (350°F) gas mark 4.

For the topping, combine the cake crumbs, flour, cinnamon and ginger in a medium-sized mixing bowl. Rub in the butter until the mixture resembles fine breadcrumbs and set aside. In a small, heavy pan, dissolve the brown sugar in the water over moderate heat, stirring constantly. Reduce the heat to very low and beat in the eggs. Cook, stirring constantly, for 3–4 minutes or until the mixture thickens. Remove the pan from the heat and set it aside until the mixture cools.

Sprinkle the raisins over the bottom of the pastry shell. Pour the cooled sugar mixture over the raisins. Sprinkle the crumb mixture over the top. Return the pie to the oven and bake for 20–30 minutes, or until the topping is a golden brown. Remove the pie from the oven and serve at once.
Cooking time: 2½ hours

Aunt Rebecca's Rich Rice Pudding

This pudding comes from the Lake District in the north of England where a rich pudding of this sort was popular in the farmhouses and in the homes of the iron ore miners. Soaking the rice in milk overnight makes the pudding very rich.

SERVES 4
50g/2 oz (⅓ cup) pudding rice
700ml/1¼ pt (3 cups) milk
75g/3 oz (½ cup) raisins (optional)
25g/1 oz (2 tablespoons) fine sugar
25g/1 oz (2 tablespoons) butter, cut in pieces
pinch of nutmeg

Place the rice in a lightly-buttered oven-proof dish. Pour on the milk. Add the raisins and sugar. Leave to soak for about 8 hours or overnight.

Set the oven to 150°C (300°F), gas mark 2. Dot the butter over the dish and sprinkle with nutmeg. Bake on the lowest shelf in the oven for 2–2½ hours until the pudding is thick and creamy with a golden skin on top.
Cooking time: overnight soaking, then 2½–2¾ hours

Cakes and Teabreads

Frosted Walnut Cake

SERVES 8
75g/3 oz (6 tablespoons) butter
225g/$\frac{1}{2}$ lb (2 cups) flour
2.5ml ($\frac{1}{2}$ teaspoon) salt
10ml (2 teaspoons) baking powder
225g/$\frac{1}{2}$ lb (1 cup) fine sugar
2.5ml ($\frac{1}{2}$ teaspoon) vanilla extract
2 medium-sized eggs, separated
100g/$\frac{1}{4}$ lb (1 cup) walnuts, chopped
125ml/4 fl oz ($\frac{1}{2}$ cup) milk
small pinch of salt
FOR THE FROSTING
2 egg whites
350g/$\frac{3}{4}$ lb (1$\frac{1}{2}$ cups) sugar
75ml/5 tablespoons ($\frac{1}{3}$ cup) cold water
1.5ml ($\frac{1}{4}$ teaspoon) cream of tartar
2.5ml ($\frac{1}{2}$ teaspoon) vanilla extract
8 walnut halves

Heat the oven to 190°C (375°F) gas mark 5. Sift the flour, salt and baking powder into a bowl.

Cream the butter in a medium-sized bowl with a wooden spoon, add the sugar and vanilla and beat until light and fluffy. Beat in the egg yolks with a quarter of the flour. Add the chopped walnuts with half the milk, half of the remaining flour and mix again. Mix in the remaining milk and flour.

Whisk the egg whites with the salt until they form stiff peaks. Using a metal spoon, fold the whites into the cake mixture. Pour the mix into 2 greased 20cm (8 in) cake tins (pans).

Bake 35–40 minutes until a skewer inserted into the cakes comes out clean. Cool for 5 minutes in the tins, then turn onto a wire rack and leave to cool.

To make the frosting, put the sugar and water into a heavy-bottomed pan and stir over low heat until the sugar has dissolved. Stir in the cream of tartar and vanilla and bring to the boil. Boil hard for 2 minutes.

Meanwhile whisk the egg whites until stiff. Remove the syrup from the heat and allow the bubbles to subside completely. Pour the hot syrup onto the whisked egg white, beating at high speed all the time. Continue whisking at high speed until the frosting thickens, turns opaque and will coat a spoon. It should be almost cold.

Working quickly, pour about a third of the frosting over one cake, sandwich the other on top and pour over the remaining frosting. Spread the frosting with a spatula, dipping it from time to time into a jug of hot water to keep it warm and wet. Fluff the frosting over the top and sides of the cake and decorate with the walnut halves.
Cooking time: 1 hour plus cooling, then 10 minutes

Toffee Cake

SERVES 8
350g/$\frac{3}{4}$ lb (3 cups) flour
10ml (2 teaspoons) baking powder
100g/$\frac{1}{4}$ lb ($\frac{1}{2}$ cup) plus 5ml (1 teaspoon) butter, softened
175g/6 oz ($\frac{3}{4}$ cup) sugar
2 eggs, lightly beaten
150ml/$\frac{1}{4}$ pt ($\frac{2}{3}$ cup) milk
2.5ml ($\frac{1}{2}$ teaspoon) rum extract
FOR THE TOPPING
40g/1$\frac{1}{2}$ oz (3 tablespoons) butter, softened
15ml (1 tablespoon) flour
45ml (3 tablespoons) soft brown sugar
50g/2 oz ($\frac{1}{2}$ cup) finely chopped hazelnuts or pecans
2.5ml ($\frac{1}{2}$ teaspoon) ground ginger

Heat the oven to 180°C (350°F) gas mark 4. Use the spoonful of butter to grease an 18cm (7 in) cake tin or a 20–25cm (8–10 in) spring-form cake tin (pan). Sift the flour and baking powder together.

In a large bowl, cream the remaining butter, using a wooden spoon, until light and fluffy. Add the sugar and beat well until the mixture is smooth and creamy. Mix in the eggs, beating well until the ingredients are thoroughly combined.

Using a large metal spoon, fold in the flour and baking powder and mix well. Stir in the milk and rum and mix well until the mixture is smooth. Spoon the batter into the cake tin and smooth the top.

To make the topping, beat the butter, flour, sugar, nuts and ginger well until thoroughly combined. Spoon it on top.

Put the tin in the oven and bake for 1–1$\frac{1}{4}$ hours or until a skewer inserted into the centre of the cake comes out clean. Remove the tin from the oven and allow to cool for 10 minutes. Remove the cake from the tin and place it on a wire rack to cool.
Cooking time: 1$\frac{1}{2}$–1$\frac{3}{4}$ hours

Perth Ginger Loaf

MAKES 10–12 SLICES
100g/$\frac{1}{4}$ lb ($\frac{1}{2}$ cup) plus 5ml (1 teaspoon) butter, melted
125ml/4 fl oz ($\frac{1}{2}$ cup) black treacle or molasses
2 large eggs
225g/$\frac{1}{2}$ lb (2 cups) flour
7.5ml (1$\frac{1}{2}$ teaspoons) baking powder
7.5ml (1$\frac{1}{2}$ teaspoons) ground ginger
2.5ml ($\frac{1}{2}$ teaspoon) ground allspice
1.5ml ($\frac{1}{4}$ teaspoon) ground cinnamon
1.5ml ($\frac{1}{4}$ teaspoon) salt
100g/$\frac{1}{4}$ lb (1 cup) rolled oats
100g/$\frac{1}{4}$ pt ($\frac{2}{3}$ cup) sour cream
60ml (4 tablespoons) sultanas or raisins
30ml (2 tablespoons) chopped walnuts

Heat the oven to 180°C (350°F) gas mark 4. With the spoonful of butter lightly grease a 700g (1$\frac{1}{2}$ lb) loaf tin (pan). In a medium-sized mixing bowl, combine the remaining butter, treacle or molasses and eggs together, beating with a fork until they are well blended.

Sift the flour and baking powder into a large mixing bowl. Add the ginger, all-spice, cinnamon, salt and rolled oats and stir until well mixed.

Gradually add the butter mixture to the flour mixture, beating constantly until all the ingredients are well blended. Stir in the sour cream, then fold in the raisins or sultanas and walnuts. Spoon the batter into the prepared loaf tin. Bake the loaf for 1 hour or until a skewer inserted into the centre comes out clean.

Remove from the oven and set aside to cool in the tin for 10 minutes. Run a sharp knife around the edge of the loaf and turn it out on to a wire rack. Allow to cool slightly. It is equally good served warm or cold, cut into thick slices with butter.
Cooking time: 1$\frac{1}{4}$–1$\frac{1}{2}$ hours

This frosted walnut cake may look too good to be true, but the proof is in the eating.

Martha Washington Cake

Martha Washington cake is a one-egg cake sandwiched with jam and cream filling.

SERVES 8
FOR THE CAKE
50g/2 oz (¼ cup) plus 5ml (1 teaspoon) butter
225g/½ lb (1½ cups) plus 15ml (1 tablespoon) flour
225g/½ lb (1 cup) sugar
1 egg, lightly beaten
15ml (1 tablespoon) baking powder
2.5ml (½ teaspoon) salt
175ml/6 fl oz (¾ cup) milk
5ml (1 teaspoon) vanilla extract
FOR THE FILLING
1 egg yolk
15ml (1 tablespoon) sugar
10ml (2 teaspoons) cornflour (cornstarch)
125ml/4 fl oz (½ cup) milk
2.5ml (½ teaspoon) vanilla extract
50ml/2 fl oz (¼ cup) thick cream, whipped
350g (¾ lb) raspberry jam
30ml (2 tablespoons) icing (confectioners') sugar

Heat the oven to 180°C (350°F) gas mark 4. Use the spoonful of butter to grease a deep 23cm (9 in) round cake tin (pan). Dust the cake tin with the 15ml (1 tablespoon) of flour and knock out any excess.

In a medium-sized mixing bowl, cream the remaining butter and the sugar together with a wooden spoon until they are well mixed. Beat in the egg. Add the remaining flour, the baking powder and salt, a little at a time, alternately with the milk. Beat until the ingredients are well blended. Stir in the vanilla extract.

Pour the batter into the prepared cake tin. Put the tin in the oven and bake the cake for 35 minutes or until the top springs back when gently pressed with a fingertip.

Remove the cake from the oven and leave it to cool in the pan for 5 minutes. Then turn it out on to a wire rack to cool completely.

Meanwhile make the filling. In a small mixing bowl, beat the egg yolk, sugar and cornflour (cornstarch) together until they are well mixed. Scald the milk (bring to just under boiling point) over moderate heat. Stirring constantly, pour the milk slowly on to the egg mixture. Stir in the vanilla. Return the mixture to the sauce-

Martha Washington cake is a simple sandwich cake filled with jam and a creamy custard. Serve as a dessert or for tea.

pan. Place the pan over low heat and, stirring constantly, cook the custard for 6–7 minutes or until it is very thick, and smooth. Pour the custard into the small bowl. Cover with plastic wrap to prevent a skin forming and set aside until completely cold.

Fold the whipped cream into the custard. Again cover the bowl with plastic wrap and put it into the refrigerator to chill.

When the cake is cold, slice it in half with a large knife to make two layers. Spread the jam on one layer and spread the chilled custard mixture over the jam. Place the other cake layer on top. Sprinkle the cake with the icing (confectioners') sugar to serve.

Cooking time: 1¾–2½ hours

●For a simple dessert include 225g (½ lb) raspberries in the middle. Or use the whisked sponge on *page 246* and sandwich with this cream and raspberries.

Lazy Chocolate Cake

SERVES 8

25g/1 oz (2 tablespoons) plus 5ml (1 teaspoon) butter, melted
100g/¼ lb (1 cup) flour
1.5ml (¼ teaspoon) salt
5ml (1 teaspoon) baking powder
225g/½ lb (1 cup) sugar
2 eggs, lightly beaten
50ml/2 fl oz (¼ cup) milk
100g (¼ lb) dark (semi-sweet) chocolate (squares) melted
5ml (1 teaspoon) vanilla extract
5ml (1 teaspoon) grated orange rind
15ml (1 tablespoon) orange juice
75g/3 oz (1 cup) chopped hazelnuts or walnuts

FOR THE ICING

100g (¼ lb) dark (semi-sweet) chocolate (squares)
50g/2 oz (¼ cup) butter
15ml (1 tablespoon) cornflour (cornstarch)

Heat the oven to 190°C (375°F) gas mark 5. Lightly grease an 18cm (7 in) cake tin (pan) with the teaspoon of butter.

Sift the flour, salt and baking powder into a large mixing bowl. Stir in the sugar with a wooden spoon. Make a well in the centre and pour in the remaining butter, eggs and milk. Using a wooden spoon, gradually incorporate the flour mixture with the liquids, stirring until the mixture forms a smooth batter. Stir in the melted chocolate, vanilla extract, orange rind and juice, beating until they are well blended. Stir in the nuts.

Spoon the mixture into the prepared cake tin. Put the tin in the oven and bake the cake for 35–40 minutes, or until a skewer inserted into the centre of the cake comes out clean. Remove the cake from the oven and set aside in the tin for 10 minutes. Turn out the cake on to a wire rack to cool.

To prepare the icing, melt the chocolate in a heatproof bowl over a pan of boiling water. Add the butter and cornflour (cornstarch) and beat constantly until the mixture forms a smooth paste.

Remove the pan from the heat. With a spatula spread the icing over the cake. Leave to cool for at least 30 minutes before serving.
Cooking time: about 2 hours

Date and walnut loaf is excellent sliced and spread with butter or cream cheese.

Date and Walnut Loaf

MAKES 8–10 SLICES

5ml (1 teaspoon) butter
225g/½ lb (2 cups) self-raising flour
2.5ml (½ teaspoon) baking powder
5ml (1 teaspoon) salt
100g/¼ lb (⅔ cup) soft brown sugar
225g (½ lb) dates, stoned (pitted) and finely chopped
75g/3 oz (¾ cup) walnuts, chopped
1 egg, beaten
150ml/5 fl oz (⅔ cup) milk

Heat the oven to moderate 180°C (350°F) gas mark 4. With the butter lightly grease a 450g (1 lb) loaf tin (pan). Sift the flour, baking powder and salt into a medium-sized mixing bowl. Mix in the sugar, dates and walnuts.

Beat the egg with the milk, then stir into the flour mixture. Mix well until the batter is smooth. Turn the batter into the prepared loaf tin. Bake for 1–1½ hours, or until a skewer inserted into the centre of the loaf comes out clean.

Remove the loaf from the oven. Allow it to cool in the tin for 5 minutes. Run a knife round the edge of the tin and reverse the loaf on to a wire cake rack. Leave until the loaf is completely cold before serving.
Cooking time: 1¼–1¾ hours

Raisin Loaf

MAKES 10–12 SLICES

50g/2 oz (¼ cup) butter, cut into pieces, plus 5ml (1 teaspoon)
225g/½ lb (1 cup) sugar
225ml/8 fl oz (1 cup) milk
175g/6 oz (1 cup) sultanas or seedless raisins
225g/½ lb (2 cups) self-raising flour
1 egg, lightly beaten

Heat the oven to 180°C (350°F) gas mark 4. With the spoonful of butter lightly grease a 900g (2 lb) loaf tin (pan).

Put the sugar, milk, dried fruit and the remaining butter in a medium-sized pan and place over moderate heat. Gradually bring the mixture to the boil, stirring occasionally. Remove the pan from heat.

When the mixture has cooled, stir in the flour, a little at a time, until it is incorporated. Add the egg and beat all the ingredients thoroughly until they are mixed well. Spoon the mixture into the prepared loaf tin and place it in the oven. Bake for 1¼ hours or until a skewer inserted into the loaf centre comes out clean.

Remove from the oven and leave the loaf in the tin for 10 minutes. Turn out on to a wire rack to cool completely.
Cooking time: 1¾–2 hours

173

Banana Teabread

MAKES 10–12 SLICES

100g/¼ lb (½ cup) plus 5ml (1 teaspoon) butter, melted
175g/6 oz (1½ cups) flour
50g/2 oz (½ cup) rice flour
7.5ml (1½ teaspoons) baking powder
1.5ml (¼ teaspoon) salt
2.5ml (½ teaspoon) ground ginger
large pinch of ground allspice
100g/¼ lb (⅔ cup) soft brown sugar
30ml (2 tablespoons) ground almonds
3 eggs, lightly beaten
grated rind of 1 lemon
4 bananas, well mashed

Heat the oven to 180°C (350°F) gas mark 4. Use the spoonful of butter to grease a 450g (1 lb) loaf tin (pan). Sift the flour, rice flour, baking powder, salt, ginger and allspice into a large mixing bowl, mixing well to blend. Stir in the sugar and ground almonds.

In a small bowl, combine the remaining melted butter, the eggs and lemon rind, beating well to blend. Make a well in the centre of the flour mixture and pour in the liquid. Using a spatula or wooden spoon, gradually draw the flour mixture into the liquid until it is incorporated.

With a metal spoon, fold in the bananas and beat well to blend. Spoon the mixture into the prepared tin and place the tin in the centre of the oven. Bake for 1 hour or until the teabread is brown on top and a skewer inserted into the centre comes out clean. Remove from the oven and allow the teabread to cool in the tin for 5 minutes.

Remove the teabread from the tin and cool completely on a wire rack before serving.
Cooking time: 1¼–1½ hours

Regina Cake

SERVES 6–8

5ml (1 teaspoon) butter
2 eggs
175g/6 oz (¾ cup) sugar
50ml/2 fl oz (¼ cup) fresh orange juice
50ml/2 fl oz (¼ cup) pineapple juice
175g/6 oz (1½ cups) flour
10ml (2 teaspoons) baking powder

FOR THE SYRUP

225g/½ lb (1 cup) sugar
5ml (1 teaspoon) ground cinnamon
175ml/6 fl oz (¾ cup) water
50ml/2 fl oz (¼ cup) fresh orange juice

Heat the oven to 180°C (350°F) gas mark 4. Use the butter to grease a 900g (2 lb) loaf tin (pan).

Break the eggs into a large mixing bowl and, using a wooden spoon, gradually beat in the sugar. Stir in the orange and pineapple juices and continue stirring until the mixture is thoroughly combined.

Sift in the flour and baking powder and beat the mixture until it forms a smooth batter.

Turn the batter into the prepared cake tin and place in the centre of the oven. Bake for 40–45 minutes or until the centre of the cake springs back when lightly pressed with your fingertips, and it has shrunk away from the sides of the tin.

Meanwhile, prepare the syrup. In a small pan, dissolve the sugar and the cinnamon in the water and orange juice over moderate heat, stirring constantly. Bring the syrup to the boil and boil until it reaches 104°C (220°F) on a sugar thermometer or until a small spoonful of the mixture dropped into a small bowl of cold water forms a short thick thread. Remove the pan from the heat and keep warm.

Remove the cake from the oven and turn it out on to a wooden board. Using a sharp knife, cut the cake into serving pieces and place the pieces in a large shallow dish.

Pour over the warm syrup and set aside for 2–3 hours to allow the cake pieces to absorb the syrup before serving.
Cooking time: 50 minutes plus 2–3 hours soaking

Richmond Cake

MAKES 8 SLICES

225g/½ lb (2 cups) flour
10ml (2 teaspoons) baking powder
75g/3 oz (1 cup) ground almonds
175g/6 oz (¾ cup) plus 5ml (1 teaspoon) butter, softened
5ml (1 teaspoon) mixed spice or ground allspice
5ml (1 teaspoon) ground cloves
5ml (1 teaspoon) ground ginger
50g/2 oz (⅓ cup) soft brown sugar
125ml/4 fl oz (½ cup) dark treacle or molasses
4 eggs, slightly beaten
175g (6 oz) chopped candied peel

Heat the oven to 170°C (325°F) gas mark 3. Use the spoonful of butter to lightly grease a 20cm (8 in) cake tin (pan). Sift the flour and baking powder into a medium-sized mixing bowl. Stir in the almonds.

In a large mixing bowl, cream 175g/6 oz (¾ cup) butter with a wooden spoon until it is light and fluffy. Add the mixed spice or allspice, cloves and ginger, beating constantly. Beat in the sugar, then the treacle or molasses.

Beat the eggs into the butter mixture, one at a time, adding a large spoonful of the flour mixture with each egg. Continue beating until thoroughly blended.

Using a metal spoon, fold in the remaining flour mixture, then the peel. Stir until the ingredients are thoroughly combined. Turn the mixture into the prepared cake tin. Bake for 1¾–2 hours or until the cake is golden brown on top and a skewer inserted into the centre comes out clean.

Remove the tin from the oven and turn the cake out on to a wire rack to cool.
Cooking time: 2¼–2½ hours

Anise Fork Biscuits (Cookies)

MAKES 28

100g/¼ lb (½ cup) butter, softened
50g/2 oz (¼ cup) fine sugar
6.5ml (1 heaped teaspoon) aniseed (anise seed)
1 large egg, lightly beaten
150g/5 oz (1¼ cups) self-raising flour
a pinch of salt

Heat the oven to 180°C (350°F) gas mark 4. Cream the butter with a wooden spoon. Add the sugar and continue beating until the mixture is light. Mix in the aniseed (anise seed). Add the egg and mix well. Add the flour gradually with the salt and stir in well.

Shape the dough into small balls. Place them on a non-stick or lined baking sheet, leaving space between them. Using a fork dipped in water, flatten out each ball. Bake for 15 minutes.
Cooking time: 30 minutes

Chocolate Peanut Cookies

Soft brown sugar gives a butterscotch flavour to these cookies.

MAKES 5

75g/3 oz (¾ cup) self-raising flour
7.5ml (1½ teaspoons) cocoa powder
50g/2 oz (¼ cup) softened butter
65g/2½ oz (⅓ cup) soft brown sugar
1 small egg, lightly beaten
100g/¼ lb (¾ cup) unsalted shelled peanuts

Position the shelf just above the centre and heat the oven to 180°C (350°F) gas mark 4. Grease one large or two small baking sheets.

Sift the flour and cocoa. Cream the butter. Add the sugar and cream again. Add the egg and stir in the flour and cocoa, then the nuts.

Drop in small spoonfuls on to the prepared baking sheets 5cm (2 in) apart. Bake for about 15 minutes. Cool for 5 minutes then transfer to a wire rack.

Cooking time: 35–40 minutes

Isle of Wight Doughnuts

Traditional doughnuts, made on the Isle of Wight in the English Channel, are well-flavoured with spices. They were often made in vast quantities and drained on clean straw. Double the quantity if you have a freezer and freeze half the cooked doughnuts. They are excellent served hot from the pan, with butter.

MAKES 15
7g ($\frac{1}{4}$ oz) fresh yeast ($\frac{1}{2} \times \frac{3}{5}$ oz cake compressed yeast) or 5ml (1 teaspoon) dried yeast
25g/1 oz (3 tablespoons) plus 2.5ml ($\frac{1}{2}$ teaspoon) brown sugar
90ml/3$\frac{1}{2}$ fl oz (scant $\frac{1}{2}$ cup) lukewarm milk
15g/$\frac{1}{2}$ oz (1 tablespoon) plus 5ml (1 teaspoon) butter, melted
225g/$\frac{1}{2}$ lb (2 cups) flour
2.5ml ($\frac{1}{2}$ teaspoon) ground allspice
1.5ml ($\frac{1}{4}$ teaspoon) ground cloves
1.5ml ($\frac{1}{4}$ teaspoon) ground cinnamon
1.5ml ($\frac{1}{4}$ teaspoon) ground mace
25g/1 oz (2 tablespoons) currants
oil for deep-frying

Crumble the yeast into a small bowl and mash in the 2.5ml ($\frac{1}{2}$ teaspoon) sugar. Add 30ml (2 tablespoons) of the milk and cream the milk and fresh yeast together. For dried yeast, use all the milk and the spoonful of sugar. Leave the bowl in a warm place for 10 minutes until frothy.

Grease a large baking sheet with the teaspoon of butter. Sift the flour, allspice, cinnamon, cloves and mace into a large mixing bowl. Make a well in the centre and pour in the yeast mixture and the remaining milk, sugar and melted butter.

Using your fingers or a spatula, gradually draw the flour mixture into the liquids. Continue mixing until all the flour is incorporated and the dough comes away from the sides of the bowl. Shape the dough into a ball and cover it with a clean, damp cloth. Set it aside in a warm, draught-free place for 1–1$\frac{1}{2}$ hours, or until the dough size has doubled.

Turn the risen dough out on to a floured surface and knead it—stretching and rerolling it—for about 10 minutes, or until it is smooth and elastic.

Shape the dough into about 15 very small balls. Press a few currants into the centre of each ball with your thumb and roll the balls on a board so that the currants are completely enclosed. Put the dough balls on the baking sheet and cover them with a clean cloth. Set aside in a warm, draught-free place for 30 minutes.

Heat the deep-frying oil over moderate heat until it reaches 180°C (350°F) on a deep-frying thermometer, or until a small cube of stale bread dropped into the oil turns light brown in 60 seconds.

Drop the doughnuts into the oil, a few at a time. Fry them for 5–6 minutes, turning occasionally, or until golden brown.

With a slotted spoon, remove the dough-

Traditional Isle of Wight doughnuts are spicy inside; serve hot with butter.

nuts from the pan and place them on absorbent paper to drain. Keep them warm while you fry the remaining doughnuts in the same way. Serve piping hot.

Cooking time: 4 hours including 2 rising times

Anzac Biscuits (Cookies)

MAKES 24
50g/2 oz ($\frac{1}{2}$ cup) plain flour
50g/2 oz ($\frac{2}{3}$ cup) rolled oats
50g/2 oz ($\frac{1}{2}$ cup) desiccated (flaked) coconut
100g/$\frac{1}{4}$ lb ($\frac{1}{2}$ cup) fine sugar
75g/3 oz ($\frac{1}{3}$ cup) butter, cut in pieces
15ml (1 tablespoon) golden syrup or honey
2.5ml ($\frac{1}{2}$ teaspoon) bicarbonate of soda (baking soda)

Heat the oven to 150°C (350°F) gas mark 2. Lightly oil or grease 2 baking sheets. Sift the flour, combine with the other dry ingredients except the soda and set aside.

Melt the butter and syrup or honey together in a heavy-bottomed pan, stirring. Combine the bicarbonate of soda with 15ml (1 tablespoon) boiling water and blend into the syrup and butter, off the heat. Gradually mix in the dry ingredients.

Drop the mixture in small spoonfuls on to the baking sheets, spacing 7.5cm (3 in) apart. Bake in the centre of the oven for 20 minutes. Cool slightly then transfer to wire racks.

Cooking time: 35–40 minutes

Pickles and Chutneys

Pickles and chutneys are a marvellous way of turning surplus fruits and vegetables into delicious relishes, preserved with vinegar, that will spice bland flavours and enliven cold meals. If you have never made them before, try some of the following recipes first then devise your own, experimenting with different combinations of fruits, vegetables and spices. Make them in fairly small quantities, then, if they are not to your taste, you can adjust the spices and flavourings in the next batch.

The quality of your preserves depends on the right choice of ingredients, though bruised and slightly damaged fruits, such as windfalls, can be used when the damaged parts are cut away. The quality of vinegar is most important as this is what preserves them; it should have an acetic acid content of at least 5 per cent. It can be dark or clear, though white vinegar gives a better appearance to light coloured pickles.

The sugar can be white or brown. For light-coloured pickles it is obviously better to use white, but for dark, rich chutneys, brown sugar adds both colour and flavour.

Use whole spices for pickles as ground spices tend to cloud the vinegar. Tie them loosely in a cheesecloth bag which can be removed easily at the end of the cooking. Ground spices are used in most chutneys, as they blend in better with the mixture.

For pickles, the vegetables or fruit are left in identifiable chunks, but for chutneys, mixtures of fruit and/or vegetables are finely chopped. Before pickling the prepared vegetables are put into brine or sprinkled with salt. This is done to draw out some of the water which would otherwise dilute the vinegar and affect its preserving qualities. Brining is more gentle in action, but dry salt is recommended for vegetables such as marrow (squash) with a high water content. The time necessary for brining or salting is given in the recipes. With chutneys the brining is omitted, so that they can be made in one day.

When preserving with vinegar, it is important to use the right equipment. Pans of stainless steel, aluminium or unchipped enamel are suitable but avoid brass, copper or iron pans as they can give an unpleasant metallic taste to the chutney. For the same reason use sieves of hair or nylon. Always use a stainless steel knife for cutting up the ingredients and for stirring, a wooden spoon. If you make pickles and chutneys regularly, keep a wooden spoon for just that purpose. The flavour will eventually penetrate the wood and this could affect the taste of other cookery.

You do not need special jars, provided you use a cover that will prevent evaporation. Coffee jars, well washed and sterilized, with plastic screw tops can be used, so too can jam jars with clip-on or screw-top lids. If you use metal lids, make sure the vinegar does not come into contact with the metal or it will cause rusting. The lids should be laquered or fitted with a vinegar-resistant paper or card disc. Greaseproof or waxed paper and transparent jam covers are not suitable as they allow evaporation. Always label the jars as different chutneys and pickles look very similar once stored.

Home made pickles are cheaper – and nicer – than store-bought ones. The great majority of vegetables and some fruits can be used to make a tasty accompaniment to cold meat. Pickles are ready to eat within 3 weeks of being made.

Making Pickles

1. Put prepared vegetables into wet brine: use 50g/2 oz (3 tablespoons) salt and 575ml/1 pt (2½ cups) cold water for 450g (1 lb) vegetables. Cover and leave 24 hours.

2. If dry brining, layer prepared vegetables with salt—15ml (1 tablespoon) to each 450g (1 lb) vegetables—in a bowl. Leave 12–48 hours.

3. After the time given in the recipe, drain the vegetables and rinse well with water to remove salt. Dry on absorbent paper. Rinse and dry the jars.

4. Pack the vegetables to within 12mm (½ in) of jar top. Add spices and vinegar, making sure vegetables are covered. Cover with vinegar-proof lid and label.

5. For sweet pickles, prick whole fruit (so it will not shrivel). Cook in spiced vinegar until tender. For piccalilli, vegetables are also cooked in vinegar.

6. For sweet pickles and piccalilli, pour vegetables, fruit and liquid into warmed jars, filling to 6mm (¼ in) of the top. Cover, label and store in cool, dark place.

Making Chutneys

1. Roughly chop prepared fruit and vegetables. Put in the pan with 575ml/1 pt (2½ cups) vinegar per 450g (1 lb) vegetables and the sugar and spices.

2. If using watery vegetables, cook alone until they have given up the liquid, then add vinegar and other ingredients and continue cooking.

3. Bring slowly to the boil, stirring frequently. Simmer uncovered until ingredients are tender, the mixture thick and pulpy. Fill jars to within 6mm (¼ in) of top.

Maine Cauliflower and Tomato Pickle

The flavour of the pickle will improve if it is stored for about 6 weeks before using.

MAKES 2.7 KG (6 LB)

2 medium-sized firm cauliflowers, separated into florets

700g (1½ lb) firm tomatoes, quartered

4 medium-sized onions, coarsely chopped

175g/6 oz (¾ cup) salt

5ml (1 teaspoon) dry mustard

5ml (1 teaspoon) ground ginger

5ml (1 teaspoon) freshly ground black pepper

225g/½ lb (1¼ cups) soft brown sugar

5ml (1 teaspoon) pickling spices

575ml/1 pt (2½ cups) white wine vinegar

Arrange the vegetables in layers in a large deep dish, sprinkling equal amounts of the salt on each layer. Pour over enough cold water to cover the vegetables. Cover the dish with foil and set it aside in a cool place for 24 hours.

Drain the vegetables, discarding the liquid. Place the vegetables in a large colander and rinse them thoroughly under cold running water to remove the excess salt. Drain off the water, shaking the colander, and place the vegetables in a large saucepan.

Sprinkle over the mustard, ginger, pepper, sugar and pickling spices. Pour over the vinegar. Set the pan over moderate heat and bring the liquid to the boil, stirring frequently.

Reduce the heat to low and simmer, stirring occasionally, for 15–20 minutes, or until the vegetables are tender but still firm when pierced with the point of a sharp knife.

Remove the pan from the heat. With a slotted spoon, remove the vegetables from the pan and pack them into pickling jars. Pour in enough of the cooking liquid to fill each jar. Wipe the jars clean with a damp cloth and seal the jars with lids. Label and store them in a cool dry, dark place.

Cooking time: 24 hours brining time, then 1–1¼ hours

This pickle from New England, Maine cauliflower and tomato pickle, will add to the pleasure of eating leftover meat. Store it for 6 weeks before using, but eat it within 6 months of making, as pickles, unlike chutneys, go soft if stored too long.

Oriental Relish

A delicious relish to flavour any plain dish, stored in airtight jars in a cool place, it will keep for up to 6 months.

MAKES ABOUT 2.7KG (6 LB)

3 lemons

2.3kg (5 lb) canned tomatoes

10 medium-sized apples, peeled, cored and coarsely chopped

4 × 5cm (2 in) pieces fresh ginger root, peeled and finely chopped

30ml (2 tablespoons) mixed spice or ground allspice

900g (2 lb) sugar

450g (1 lb) soft brown sugar

Using a sharp knife, cut the lemons into quarters and remove any pips. Place the lemon quarters in a blender and process for 30 seconds. Alternatively, grate the lemon rind and chop the remaining pith and flesh very finely.

Place the blended lemons, tomatoes with the can juice, apples, ginger and mixed spice or allspice in a very large saucepan. Set the pan over high heat and bring the mixture to the boil, stirring constantly. Boil for 3 minutes. Reduce the heat to low and stir in both sugars. Simmer the mixture, stirring occasionally, for 1–1½ hours or until it is thick.

Remove the pan from the heat. Ladle the relish into clean, warmed jars. Cover and store in a cool dry place until ready to use.

Cooking time: 1¼–1¾ hours

Date and Banana Chutney

An unusual, spicy accompaniment to cold meat, this chutney is particularly good with cold pork.

MAKES 1.4KG (3 LB)

6 bananas, peeled and sliced

4 medium-sized onions, chopped

225g (½ lb) dates, stoned (pitted) and chopped

275ml/10 fl oz (1¼ cups) vinegar

5ml (1 teaspoon) curry powder

125g (¼ lb) crystallized ginger, chopped

2.5ml (½ teaspoon) salt

225ml/8 fl oz (1 cup) black treacle or molasses

Put the bananas, onions, dates and vinegar into a medium-sized saucepan and cook over a moderate heat until the onions are tender.

Remove the pan from the heat. With a wooden spoon, mash the mixture to a pulp. Alternatively, put the mixture in a blender and purée for 5 seconds. Add the curry powder, ginger, salt and treacle (molasses) to the mixture.

Return the pan to moderate heat. Cook, stirring occasionally, for 15–20 minutes, or until the mixture is a rich brown colour.

Remove the pan from the heat. Pour the mixture into clean, warmed jam jars. Place a circle of waxed paper over the chutney and seal each jar. Label the jars and store them in a cool, dry place until ready to use.

Cooking time: 1–1½ hours

Apple Chutney

The basic apple chutney may be served with almost any cold meat but it is particularly good with pork and duck. Chutneys improve with age; keep 3 months before eating.

MAKES ABOUT 1.8KG (4 LB)

1.8kg (4 lb) cooking apples, peeled, cored and finely chopped

450g (1 lb) sultanas (white raisins)

4 medium-sized onions, finely chopped

1 chilli (chilli pepper), chopped

15ml (1 tablespoon) mustard seed

45ml (3 tablespoons) lemon juice

45ml (3 tablespoons) chopped lemon rind

10ml (2 teaspoons) ground ginger

850ml/1½ pt (3¾ cups) vinegar

900g (2 lb) brown sugar

Put the apples, sultanas, onions, and chilli into a large preserving pan. Add the mustard seed, lemon juice, lemon rind and ginger. Pour in two-thirds of the vinegar. Place the pan over high heat and bring to the boil. Reduce the heat to low and simmer for 1–1½ hours, or until the mixture is soft and cooked.

In a small saucepan, dissolve the sugar in the remaining vinegar over moderate heat. Pour the vinegar-sugar mixture into the preserving pan and continue to cook, stirring constantly, until the chutney is thick.

Remove the pan from the heat and ladle the chutney into clean, warmed jam jars. Place a circle of waxed paper over the chutney and seal each jar. Label the jars and store in a cool, dry place until ready to use.

Cooking time: 3½–4 hours

Pennsylvania Dutch Mixed Chow-Chow

Various types of vegetables are cooked separately then stored in a pickling solution containing vinegar, sugar, mustard and mustard seed. The result is a marvellous pickle to serve with any type of cold meat.

MAKES ABOUT 1.6 KG (3½ LB)
350g (¾ lb) red or white kidney beans, soaked overnight in cold water and drained
4 green or red (bell) peppers, white pith removed, seeded and cut into 5cm (2 in) pieces
7.5ml (1½ teaspoons) salt
1 medium-sized cauliflower, trimmed and broken into small florets
450g (1 lb) French (green) beans, trimmed and cut into 5cm (2 in) lengths
450g (1 lb) canned sweetcorn, drained
1.1L/2 pt (5 cups) wine vinegar
175g/6 oz (1 cup) soft brown sugar
75ml (5 tablespoons) dry mustard
45ml (3 tablespoons) mustard seed
5ml (1 teaspoon) turmeric

Place the kidney beans in a medium-sized saucepan and add enough water just to cover. Place the pan over high heat and bring the liquid to the boil. Cover the pan and simmer for 1–1½ hours or until the beans are just tender.

Meanwhile, place the green or red peppers in a small saucepan. Pour over enough water just to cover and add 2.5ml (½ teaspoon) of the salt. Bring the water to the boil then reduce the heat and cook the peppers for 10 minutes or until they are tender but still firm. Drain the peppers in a colander. Set aside.

Cook the cauliflower florets in the same way for 8–12 minutes, and cook the French (green) beans, for 5–8 minutes.

When the kidney beans are cooked, drain them in a colander. Transfer them to a large mixing bowl and add the peppers, cauliflower florets, beans and corn, stirring well to blend. Set aside.

Put the vinegar, sugar, mustard, mustard seed and turmeric in a large saucepan over low heat. Cook, stirring constantly, until the sugar has dissolved. Increase the heat and bring the mixture to the boil. Reduce the heat to moderately low and add the vegetables to the pan. Cook the mixture, stirring occasionally so that all the vegetables are all well basted, for 5 minutes.

Remove the pan from the heat and ladle

Celery and Pepper Relish

For this relish, choose crisp, white autumn celery. The yellowish type of celery will not give such good results. When you have eaten all the celery you can re-bottle the vinegar to use again.

MAKES ABOUT 450G (1 LB)
2 heads (bunches) of celery
1 red (bell) pepper, seeded and cut into strips
1.7L/3 pt (7½ cups) white wine vinegar
10ml (2 teaspoons) salt
6 small pieces dried ginger root
6 blades of mace

Cut off the green tops and scrub the celery stalks. Dry on absorbent paper. Cut the stalks so they will come to within 12mm

An attractive feature of this celery and pepper relish is that the celery sticks are left almost whole. Eat it with brown wholewheat bread and cheese for lunch.

(½ in) of the top of the jars.

Put the vinegar and salt in a large pan. Tie the spices in a piece of cheesecloth. Boil the vinegar with the spices for 10 minutes. Add the celery stalks and pepper strips and boil for a further 5 minutes.

Strain off the vinegar and remove the spices. Rinse the jars in hot water and dry well. Pack the celery stalks upright in the jars with the pepper strips among them.

Pour the vinegar over the celery so that it is covered. Cover, label and store for 2 weeks before eating. Use the relish within 1 month of opening.
Cooking time: 1 hour

the pickle into clean, warmed preserving jars. Seal the jars and label them. Store in a cool, dry place until ready for use.
Cooking time: 2½ hours

Tomato Chutney

MAKES ABOUT 1.5KG (3 LB)

1.4kg (3 lb) tomatoes, blanched, peeled and sliced
2 green (bell) peppers, white pith removed, seeded and finely chopped
450g (1 lb) onions, sliced
450g (1 lb) cooking apples, peeled, cored and sliced
225g (½ lb) sultanas or seedless raisins
22.5ml (1½ tablespoons) mustard seed
30ml (2 tablespoons) salt
1 large piece ginger root, peeled and slashed
2.5ml (½ teaspoon) cayenne pepper
350g/¾ lb (2 cups) brown sugar
575ml/1 pt (2½ cups) vinegar

Combine all the ingredients together in a large preserving pan. Place the pan over high heat and bring to the boil. Reduce the heat to low and, stirring occasionally, cook for 2 hours, or until the chutney is very soft and thick. Remove the pan from the heat. With a slotted spoon, remove the ginger from the pan and discard it.

Ladle the chutney into clean, warmed jam jars. Place a circle of waxed paper over the chutney and seal each jar with a jam cover and a rubber band. Label the jars and store them in a cool, dry place until ready to use.
Cooking time: 2½ hours

Marrow (Squash) Pickle

MAKES 1.8KG (4 LB)

1 large marrow (squash), peeled, seeded and diced
450g (1 lb) onions, chopped
30ml (2 tablespoons) ground ginger
30ml (2 tablespoons) salt
30ml (2 tablespoons) turmeric
5ml (1 teaspoon) cloves
4 green chillis (chilli peppers), slit lengthwise and seeds removed
12 peppercorns
350g/¾ lb (2 cups) soft brown sugar
2.3L/4 pt (5 US pt) malt vinegar

In a large bowl, make layers of the marrow (squash) and onions, sprinkling each layer generously with the salt. Cover the bowl with a clean cloth and set aside for 9 hours or overnight. Drain off all excess liquid from the vegetables. Set aside.

In a large saucepan or preserving pan, combine the ginger, turmeric, cloves, chillis, peppercorns, sugar and vinegar. Bring the mixture to the boil over high heat, stirring occasionally. When the mixture comes to the boil, reduce the heat to low and simmer for 30 minutes.

Add the marrow and the onions and stir well to mix. Increase the heat to high and bring the mixture to the boil again. When it boils, reduce the heat to low and simmer the pickles, stirring occasionally, for 1½ hours or until it is thick.

Remove the pan from the heat. Using a ladle, spoon the pickle into warm dry jam or preserving jars, filling them right up to the top. Seal the jars, label and store in a cool, dry place.
Cooking time: overnight brining, then 2½–3 hours

Pear Chutney

Pear Chutney has a sharp, fruity flavour and goes well with any cold meat or cheese. Stored in a cool dry place, it will keep for several months.

MAKES ABOUT 1.8KG (4 LB)

1.4kg (3 lb) pears, peeled, cored and chopped
2 tart apples, peeled, cored and chopped
2 medium-sized onions, sliced
450g (1 lb) raisins
5ml (1 teaspoon) chilli powder
5cm (2 in) piece fresh ginger root, peeled and finely chopped
1 garlic clove, crushed
5ml (1 teaspoon) salt
2.5ml (½ teaspoon) grated nutmeg
12 cloves
juice and grated rind of 2 oranges
450g (1 lb) soft brown sugar
575ml/1 pt (2½ cups) white vinegar

Place all the ingredients in a very large saucepan and stir well with a wooden spoon. Set the pan over high heat and bring the mixture to the boil, stirring occasionally.

Reduce the heat to low and, stirring occasionally, simmer the chutney for 2½ hours or until it is thick.

Remove the pan from the heat. Ladle the chutney into clean, warmed jam jars.

Place a disk of vinegar-resistant paper inside the lid of each jar and seal. Label the jars and store them in a cool dry place until ready for use.
Cooking time: 3 hours

Orange Pickle

Orange pickle tastes delicious with roast goose or pork. Whole cardamom pods can be obtained from health food stores and some supermarkets. Keep the pickle for 2–3 weeks before eating, to allow it to mature.

MAKES ABOUT 1.8KG (4 LB)

6 oranges
5ml (1 teaspoon) salt
450g (1 lb) sugar
30ml (2 tablespoons) golden (light corn) syrup
175ml/6 fl oz (¾ cup) malt vinegar
450ml/16 fl oz (2 cups) water
seeds of 6 cardamoms
6 black peppercorns, crushed
2.5ml (½ teaspoon) ground cinnamon
1.5ml (¼ teaspoon) mixed spice or ground allspice
12 cloves

Put the oranges and salt into a large saucepan. Pour over just enough hot water to cover them and place the pan over moderate heat. Bring the water to the boil, then simmer for 50 minutes or until the oranges are tender. Drain the oranges and place them on a board to cool.

In a medium-sized saucepan, bring the sugar, syrup, vinegar, water, cardamom seeds, peppercorns, cinnamon, mixed spice or allspice and cloves to the boil over moderate heat, stirring constantly. Simmer the mixture for 8 minutes. Remove the pan from the heat and set aside to cool for 20 minutes.

Using a sharp knife, cut the orange into thin slices. Pour the sugar and vinegar mixture through a strainer into a large saucepan. Discard the flavourings. Add the orange slices. Place the pan over moderate heat and bring the mixture to the boil, stirring frequently. Reduce the heat and simmer for 20 minutes. Remove the pan from the heat and allow the mixture to cool for 5 minutes.

Ladle the pickle into 2 or 3 clean, warm jars. Place a disk of vinegar-resistant paper on top of each and cover with a lid. Keep any leftover vinegar for another use. Label the jars and store them in a cool, dry place.
Cooking time: 2¾–3 hours

181

Freezing Vegetables and Fruit

Freezing vegetables

Vegetables for the freezer should be picked at the peak of their season when young, tender and full of flavour. Harvest only what you can deal with at one time, because the shorter the time between picking and freezing the better. Do not forget to turn on the fast freeze switch a couple of hours before you start.

When you have cleaned and prepared your vegetables for freezing they need blanching. Blanching—scalding in boiling water—is done to halt enzyme activity. If it is not done there will be loss of colour, flavour and nutritional value during freezer storage. Blanch in a generous amount of boiling water—it should return to boiling 1 minute after the vegetables are added. If the time is longer, reduce the batch size. Bring back to a boil between each batch and time the vegetables according to the chart. Different vegetables need different times and it is important to get these right or quality is impaired.

Cool immediately after blanching, in a sink or bowl of water with ice cubes. You will need a large quantity, so prepare these ahead and store them in the freezer. Drain and pack produce.

If you want free-flowing vegetables, open freeze them first. To do this spread the blanched, cold vegetables onto foil-lined baking sheets and put into the freezer until hard; then tip them into a plastic bag, where they will remain separate. You can then just take out what you want, reseal the bag and return it to the freezer. Your vegetables can be stored in the freezer for up to a year; the chart gives details for different types. Cook them from frozen in the minimum of boiling salted water until just tender.

Freezing Vegetables

VEGETABLE and Storage Time	PREPARATION	BLANCHING and Cooling Times
Artichokes, Globe: 6 months	Remove coarse outer leaves, trim stalks and tips of leaves. Wash thoroughly.	Add 15ml (1 tablespoon) lemon juice to 1.15L/2 pt (5 cups) blanching water. 7–10 minutes. Drain upside down.
Artichokes, Jerusalem (Sunchokes): 3 months	Best frozen as a purée. Scrub, peel, cut up roughly. Cook until tender, sieve or blend.	
Asparagus: 1 year	Separate into thick, medium and thin stalks. Wash, trim, cut into equal lengths.	Thick: 4 minutes; medium: 3 minutes; thin: 2 minutes
Avocados: 6 months	Peel and mash or blend to a pulp. Add 15ml (1 tablespoon) lemon juice to each avocado.	
Beans: Broad (Lima): 1 year French (Green): 1 year Runner (Wax): 1 year	Shell. Wash, snip off ends. Wash, trim, string if necessary. Cut into chunks.	2 minutes 2 minutes 2 minutes
Beetroot (Beets): 6 months	Cook small baby beets whole until tender. Rub off skins.	
Broccoli: 1 year	Remove coarse stalks and large leaves. Wash in salt water.	Thick stalks: 4 minutes; thin stalks: 3.
Brussels sprouts: 1 year	Choose small firm sprouts. Trim stalks and bad leaves.	3 minutes
Cabbage: 1 year	Wash thoroughly and shred.	$1\frac{1}{2}$ minutes
Carrots: 1 year	Scrape, leave baby ones whole, dice or slice large ones.	Whole: 5 minutes; diced or sliced: 3.
Cauliflower: 6 months	Wash, break into florets of even size.	3 minutes. Add lemon juice as above.
Celeriac (Celery root): 6 months	Wash and peel. Cut into large dice.	4 minutes
Celery: 1 year	Trim, string and wash. Cut into 5cm (2 in) lengths.	3 minutes

Freezing Vegetables

1. Boil a large pan of water—about 4L/ 6–8 pt (1 gal). Put in 450g (1 lb) prepared vegetables. When water boils, start timing according to vegetable type.

2. Cool vegetables in water containing ice cubes for same amount of time that they were blanched. Drain in colander lined with absorbent paper. Shake dry.

3. Pack in bags, or in rigid containers for delicate vegetables. Open freeze peas and beans for a free flow, then pack when solid. Do your best to exclude air.

VEGETABLE and Storage Time	PREPARATION	BLANCHING and Cooling Times
Corn-on-the-cob: 1 year	Remove husks and threads. Trim ends.	Large: 8 minutes; medium: 6; small: 4.
Courgettes (Zucchini) and Summer Squash: 1 year	Wash, small young ones, trim ends. Cut into 1cm ($\frac{1}{2}$ in) slices.	1 minute or sauté them in butter until tender
Leeks: 6 months	Remove outer leaves, trim ends, wash well. Leave small ones whole, slice large ones.	Whole: 4 minutes; sliced: 2 minutes
Mushroom: 3 months	Wipe clean, do not peel. Button mushrooms can be left whole, large ones sliced.	Sauté in butter for 2 minutes
Onions: 6 months	Large: Peel and slice into rings or dip in batter. Small: Peel and leave whole.	Sliced: 1 minute; battered: fry until golden; whole: 4 minutes
Parsnips: 1 year	Peel and cut into fingers or dice.	2 minutes
Peas: 1 year	Must be young and tender. Shell.	1 minute
Mange-tout (Snow Peas): 1 year	Use while quite flat. Wash and trim ends.	2 minutes
Peppers (bell peppers) green, yellow and red: 1 year	Wash, cut out stems, remove seeds. Cut in halves, rings or thin slices.	Halves: 3 minutes; rings and slices: 2 minutes
Potatoes New: 3 months Mashed: 3 months Chipped (French fried): 6 months	Scrape. Slightly undercook. Freezes well as croquettes or Duchesse potatoes. Peel, cut into chips.	Part fry in deep fat for 2 minutes
Spinach: 1 year	Wash and trim stems. Cook then chop or purée.	
Swedes (Rutabagas): 1 year	Trim, peel, cut into cubes. Cook, sieve, freeze as purée.	3 minutes
Tomatoes: 1 year	Wash, fry and pack whole for use in stews and soups or cook, sieve and freeze as purée.	
Turnips: 1 year	Trim, peel, cut into cubes.	3 minutes

Freezing fruit

Most fruits freeze successfully. They should be fully ripe, unblemished and frozen as soon as possible after picking. The way you freeze them depends on the type of fruit and how you will use it when thawed.

Dry pack: this means fruit packed without either sugar or sugar syrup, but open frozen until solid and then bagged. It is the way to freeze fruit for people on a sugar-free diet; soft fruit where a syrup is not required; or fruit which is to be used later for jam.

Sugar pack: this is suitable for soft fruit such as raspberries from which the juice is easily drawn and where a small amount of syrup is required when the fruit is thawed. Mix the fruit and sugar gently together in a bowl allowing about 100g/¼ lb (⅓ cup) sugar to 450g (1 lb) fruit, though this can be adjusted depending on the tartness of the fruit and personal taste.

Sugar pack syrup: this is the best way to freeze non-juicy fruit, mildly-flavoured fruit and those which discolour easily. The syrup is made by heating sugar and water together until the sugar has dissolved, boiling it for 2 minutes then leaving it until cold.

Heavy: 500g/18 oz (2 cups) sugar to 575ml/1 pt (2½ cups) water

Medium: 275g/10 oz (1¼ cups) sugar to 575ml/1 pt (2½ cups) water
Light syrup: 225g/½ lb (1 cup) sugar to 575ml/1 pt (2½ cups) water

When freezing a large amount of fruit, make up the syrup in quantity beforehand, so you do not have to wait for it to cool. Keep it in the refrigerator, ready for use. You will need about 275ml/½ pt (1¼ cups) syrup to 450g (1 lb) fruit. Pack the fruit in rigid containers or preformed plastic bags in cartons; cover with the syrup, leaving about 1.2cm (½ in) headspace.

Purée pack: any well-flavoured fruit can be sieved and frozen as a purée. This is a good way of using up damaged or windfall fruit. Soft fruit can be puréed raw and sweetened, if liked, by stirring in sugar to taste until it has dissolved. Hard fruit should be cooked in the minimum of water with or without sugar, then pressed through a strainer.

Fruit for jam making: if you have not time to make jam when the fruit is in season, simply prepare and pack the fruit in suitable quantities and freeze it away until you have more time.

Storage time: fruit can be stored in the freezer for up to 1 year, purées for up to 6 months. For best results, thaw in the refrigerator in unopened packs. Fruit for stewing can be cooked from frozen over a gentle heat.

Freezing Fruit

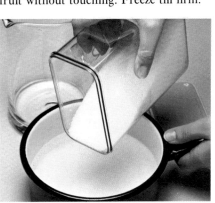

1. For dry pack fruit, line baking trays with waxed or non-stick paper. Spread out fruit without touching. Freeze till firm.

2. When solid, pack fruit in rigid containers or in polythene bags, squeezing out air. Fruit will be free flowing.

3. For sugar pack, mix together fruit and sugar, 100g (¼ lb) sugar to 450g (1 lb) fruit. Stand for 1 hour, cover and freeze.

4. Make sugar syrup in advance for hard fruit. Dissolve sugar in water then boil for 2 minutes. Match syrup to fruit.

5. Prepare fruit and two-thirds fill a rigid container. Strain cold syrup over fruit, leaving 12mm (½ in) headspace. Freeze.

6. Fruit purée can be frozen raw or cooked, sweetened or unsweetened. Place bag inside rigid container, fill, then freeze.

FREEZING FRUIT

FRUIT and Storage Time	PREPARATION	PACKING
Apples: 1 year sliced 8 months puréed	Peel, core, cut into 6mm ($\frac{1}{4}$ in) slices. Blanch 1 minute OR peel, core, slice, cook and sieve.	Open freeze then dry pack. OR purée pack.
Apricots: 1 year	Wash, halve and stone (pit).	Light syrup pack (add 1.5ml/$\frac{1}{4}$ teaspoon ascorbic acid to each 575ml/1 pt (2$\frac{1}{2}$ cups).
Bilberries and Blueberries: 1 year	Treat as currants.	
Blackberries: 1 year 6 months puréed	Wash only if necessary. Can also be cooked with sugar and sieved.	Open freeze then dry pack or dry sugar pack. OR purée pack.
Cherries: 1 year	Stalk, wash, dry and stone (pit).	Open freeze then dry pack or dry sugar sugar pack. OR purée pack.
Currants: black, red, and white: 1 year 6 months puréed	Stem, wash and dry or stem, wash, stew with sugar and sieve.	Open freeze then dry pack or dry sugar pack. OR purée pack.
Gooseberries: 1 year 6 months puréed	Wash, dry, top and tail OR cook with sugar	Dry pack OR purée pack.
Greengages: 1 year	Wash, halve and stone (pit).	As apricots.
Mandarins and Tangerines: 1 year	Peel, divide into segments.	Light syrup pack.
Melon: 1 year	Halve, remove seeds, peel and cut into cubes.	Dry sugar pack OR light syrup pack.
Peaches: 1 year	Skin, halve and stone. Slice if desired.	As apricots.
Pears: 1 year	Peel, quarter and core into acidulated water to retain colour. Cook lightly in the syrup.	Light syrup pack.
Pineapple: 4–6 months	Peel, remove eyes and core. Slice or dice.	Dry sugar pack OR light syrup pack.
Plums and Damsons: 1 year 6 months puréed	Wash and stone (pit), leave raw OR cook in the sugar syrup OR cook with sugar, sieve.	Medium syrup pack.
Raspberries: 1 year	Hull but do not wash. OR sieve to remove pips and sweeten.	Open freeze then dry pack OR dry sugar pack. OR purée pack.
Rhubarb: 1 year	Wash, remove leaves and white base and any strings. Cut into 2cm (1 in) chunks. Blanch 1 minute OR cook with sugar, sieve.	Open freeze then dry pack OR dry sugar pack. OR purée pack.
Strawberries: 1 year	Treat as raspberries.	

Winter

Soups and Starters

Bacon and Pea Soup

SERVES 6

50g/2 oz ($\frac{1}{4}$ cup) butter
4 lean bacon slices, diced
1 large onion, finely chopped
1 small carrot, diced
1 small turnip, diced
200g/7 oz (1 cup) dried or split green peas, soaked in water overnight
1.7L/3 pt (7$\frac{1}{2}$ cups) ham or bacon stock
1 bouquet garni
salt
freshly ground black pepper
150ml/$\frac{1}{4}$ pt ($\frac{2}{3}$ cup) milk

Melt the butter in a saucepan. Add the bacon and vegetables and fry until the onion is softened. Stir in the drained peas and stock and bring to the boil. Add the bouquet garni, then cover the pan and simmer for 2–2$\frac{1}{2}$ hours or until the vegetables have been reduced to a pulp.

Remove the bouquet garni, adjust the seasoning and stir in the milk. Reheat and serve.

Cooking time: overnight soaking, then 2$\frac{1}{4}$–2$\frac{3}{4}$ hours

● This soup can also be made with a gammon or ham hock. Omit the bacon slices and add the hock before the water. After cooking remove the hock from the soup with a slotted spoon, remove the meat from the bone, discarding the fat. Chop the meat and return it to the soup.

Bean and Tomato Soup

SERVES 6

25g/1 oz (2 tablespoons) butter
1 large onion, thinly sliced
400g (14 oz) canned tomatoes
100g/$\frac{1}{4}$ lb ($\frac{1}{2}$ cup) dried butter (lima) beans, soaked overnight
1 bay leaf
850ml/1$\frac{1}{2}$ pt (3$\frac{3}{4}$ cups) stock or water
salt
freshly ground black pepper

Melt the butter in a saucepan. Add the onion and fry until softened. Stir in the tomatoes with their juice and cook for a further 2 minutes.

Drain the beans and add to the pan with the bay leaf and stock or water. Bring to the boil, then cover the pan and simmer for 2–2$\frac{1}{2}$ hours or until the beans are tender. Discard the bay leaf.

Mash or blend the soup to a purée and return to the pan. Add seasoning and reheat.

Cooking time: 2$\frac{1}{4}$–2$\frac{3}{4}$ hours

Bread and Cheese Soup

Any mild, soft-textured cheese can be used for this soup.

SERVES 4–6

75g/3 oz ($\frac{1}{3}$ cup) butter
12 slices of French bread
12 slices of Fontina cheese
1.7L/3 pt (7$\frac{1}{2}$ cups) boiling homemade beef stock

Bean and tomato soup makes a warming start to any family meal in winter.

Stir in the stock and bring to the boil. Add the remaining ingredients, except the cheese, then cover the pan and simmer for 35–45 minutes or until the vegetables are tender. Discard the bouquet garni.

Heat the grill (broiler) to moderate. Pour the soup into a flame-proof tureen or individual flame-proof soup bowls and sprinkle over the grated cheese. Grill (broil) for 5 minutes or until the cheese has melted and is bubbling.

Cooking time: 55–65 minutes

Mussel and Tomato Soup

SERVES 6
2.2kg/2 qt (5 lb) mussels
15g/$\frac{1}{2}$ oz (1 tablespoon) butter
15ml (1 tablespoon) oil
2 large onions, chopped
2 garlic cloves, crushed
400g (14 oz) canned tomatoes
45ml (3 tablespoons) chopped parsley
7.5ml (1$\frac{1}{2}$ teaspoons) sugar
2.5ml ($\frac{1}{2}$ teaspoon) dried basil
2.5ml ($\frac{1}{2}$ teaspoon) ground coriander
salt
freshly ground black pepper
425ml/$\frac{3}{4}$ pt (1$\frac{3}{4}$ cups) fish or chicken stock
45ml (3 tablespoons) fresh white breadcrumbs

Scrub the mussels well and discard any which are not tightly shut or which do not close when tapped and any with broken shells. Scrape off the beards and scrub the shells. Then soak the mussels in clean cold water for 1 hour.

Melt the butter with the oil in a saucepan. Add the onions and garlic and fry until softened. Stir in the tomatoes with their juice, the parsley, sugar, basil, coriander and seasoning. Cook, stirring occasionally, until thick.

Meanwhile, put the stock in another saucepan and bring to the boil. Add the drained mussels in two batches. Cover the pan and cook until the shells open, shaking the pan. Remove the mussels with a slotted spoon. Discard any which are still closed. Remove the mussels from the shells and keep warm.

Stir the breadcrumbs into the tomato mixture, followed by the mussels. Strain the stock twice through cheesecloth inside a sieve to remove all grit, then stir into the mussel mixture. Heat through gently, then serve.

Cooking time: 1 hour 20 minutes cleaning, then 30 minutes

Heat the oven to 180°C (350°F) gas mark 4. Melt the butter in a frying-pan. Add the bread slices and fry until golden brown on both sides. Drain on absorbent paper.

Lay the bread slices on the bottom of an ovenproof tureen or individual ovenproof soup bowls and top with the cheese slices. Pour over the stock. Cook in the oven for 10 minutes or until the cheese has nearly melted.

Cooking time: 20 minutes

Beef Soup with Herb Dumplings

SERVES 6
1.1L/2 pt (5 cups) beef stock
1 onion, chopped
2 medium-sized carrots, diced
1 medium-sized potato, diced
1 celery stick, chopped
100g/$\frac{1}{4}$ lb ($\frac{1}{2}$ cup) cooked beef, diced or shredded
salt
freshly ground black pepper
FOR THE DUMPLINGS
50g/2 oz ($\frac{1}{2}$ cup) self-raising flour
salt and freshly ground black pepper
50g/2 oz (1 cup) fresh breadcrumbs
50g/2 oz ($\frac{1}{4}$ cup) shredded suet
5ml (1 teaspoon) dried mixed herbs
1 small egg, beaten

First make the dumplings. Sift the flour and seasoning into a bowl. Add the bread-

Herb dumplings in beef soup make an economical and filling meal-in-a-bowl.

crumbs, suet and herbs and mix well, then bind with the egg. Shape into walnut-sized balls.

Put the stock in a saucepan and bring to the boil. Add the vegetables and simmer for 5 minutes. Add the dumplings, cover the pan and simmer for a further 10 minutes.

Stir in the beef and seasoning and simmer, uncovered, for a final 5 minutes.

Cooking time: 30 minutes

Quebec Onion Soup

SERVES 4
100g/$\frac{1}{4}$ lb ($\frac{1}{2}$ cup) butter
5 large onions, thinly sliced
2 garlic cloves, crushed
1.1L/2 pt (5 cups) beef stock
2 medium-sized carrots, sliced
2 celery stalks, sliced
1 small turnip, diced
50g/2 oz ($\frac{1}{4}$ cup) cooked beef, finely chopped
2.5ml ($\frac{1}{2}$ teaspoon) dried thyme
1 bouquet garni
salt
freshly ground black pepper
125g/$\frac{1}{4}$ lb (1 cup) Cheddar cheese, grated

Melt the butter in a saucepan. Add the onions and garlic and fry until softened.

The combination of beef, pasta and vegetables in pepperpot beef soup makes a substantial family meal when served with hunks of fresh French bread.

Pepperpot Beef Soup

SERVES 4

350g ($\frac{3}{4}$ lb) beef shin, cut into 1.2cm ($\frac{1}{2}$ in) cubes

30ml (2 tablespoons) Worcestershire sauce

1L/1$\frac{3}{4}$ pt (4 cups) water

2 onions, chopped

2 carrots, cut into matchsticks

2 celery stalks, sliced

1 bouquet garni

15ml (1 tablespoon) tomato paste

salt

freshly ground black pepper

40g/1$\frac{1}{2}$ oz ($\frac{1}{2}$ cup) pasta shapes

15g/$\frac{1}{2}$ oz (1 tablespoon) butter

30 ml (2 tablespoons) flour

Put the beef in a plastic bag and sprinkle over the Worcestershire sauce. Close the bag and leave to marinate in the refrigerator for 12 hours, shaking the bag occasionally.

Pour the meat and sauce into a saucepan. Add the water and bring to the boil. Stir in the vegetables, bouquet garni, tomato paste and seasoning and simmer for 45 minutes. Stir in the pasta shapes and simmer for 30 minutes more or until the meat is tender. Discard the bouquet garni.

Mash the butter with the flour. Add a little of the hot liquid, then stir this mixture into the rest of the liquid in the pan. Simmer, stirring, until thickened.
Cooking time: 12 hours marinating, then about 1$\frac{1}{2}$ hours

Turnip Soup with Cheese Croûtes

SERVES 6

700g (1$\frac{1}{2}$ lb) turnips, cut into chunks

25g/1 oz (2 tablespoons) butter

25g/1 oz ($\frac{1}{4}$ cup) flour

1L/1$\frac{3}{4}$ pt (4 cups) chicken stock

salt

freshly ground black pepper

2 large egg yolks

150ml/$\frac{1}{4}$ pt ($\frac{2}{3}$ cup) cream

6 thick slices French bread

100g ($\frac{1}{4}$ lb) Cheddar cheese, cut into 4 slices

15ml (1 tablespoon) French mustard

Parboil the turnips in boiling water for 5 minutes. Drain well. Melt the butter in a clean pan. Add the turnips and brown lightly. Stir in the flour and cook, stirring, for 3 minutes. Gradually stir in the stock and bring to the boil, stirring. Cover the pan and simmer for 10 minutes.

Heat the grill (broiler) to high. Mash or blend the turnip mixture to a purée and return to the saucepan. Season to taste. Combine the egg yolks and cream. Stir in a little of the turnip mixture, then mix this into the rest of the turnip soup in the pan. Heat through, stirring, until thickened.

Toast the French bread on one side. Place a slice of cheese on each slice of bread and spread with the mustard. Grill (broil) until the cheese has melted.

Serve the soup with the cheese croûtes floating on top.
Cooking time: 35 minutes

Celery and Walnut Soup

This unusual soup is fairly inexpensive to make; walnuts and celery are both fairly strongly flavoured, so only small amounts are needed.

SERVES 4

50g (2 oz) shelled walnuts

275ml/$\frac{1}{2}$ pt (1$\frac{1}{4}$ cups) milk

575ml/1 pt (2$\frac{1}{2}$ cups) chicken stock

25g/1 oz (2 tablespoons) butter

1 small onion, finely chopped

2 celery stalks, roughly chopped

25g/1 oz ($\frac{1}{4}$ cup) flour

2 large egg yolks

150ml/$\frac{1}{4}$ pt ($\frac{2}{3}$ cup) thick cream

salt and freshly ground black pepper

chopped walnuts to garnish (optional)

Put the nuts in a blender or food mill and purée. Scald the milk and add the nuts. Cover and leave to infuse for 20 minutes. Set the stock over low heat.

Place the butter in a heavy-bottomed pan over low heat. Add the onion and sauté gently for 3 minutes. Add the celery and cook for a further 2 minutes. Stir the flour into the butter mixture and cook for 3 minutes. Stir in the stock and milk with walnuts off the heat. Bring to the boil, stirring. Simmer for 15 minutes.

Beat the eggs and cream together. Purée the soup in a blender or with a food mill. Return to the pan and season to taste.

Stir 30ml (2 tablespoons) of the hot soup into the egg and cream mixture. Set the soup over low heat and stir in the egg and

cream. Simmer the soup for 4 minutes, stirring from time to time before serving. Garnish with chopped walnuts if wished.
Cooking time: 1$\frac{1}{4}$ hours

Scotch Broth

SERVES 6

700g (1$\frac{1}{2}$ lb) mutton scrag or middle neck of lamb, trimmed of excess fat and chopped

1.7L/3 pt (7$\frac{1}{2}$ cups) water

salt and freshly ground black pepper

40g/1$\frac{1}{2}$ oz (3 tablespoons) pearl barley

3 small carrots, chopped

3 small leeks, chopped

2 small turnips, chopped

1 onion, chopped

2 celery stalks, chopped

chopped parsley to garnish

Put the lamb into a saucepan with the water and bring to the boil. Skim off the scum that rises to the surface. Add seasoning and the barley, then cover the pan and simmer for 30 minutes. Stir in the vegetables, re-cover the pan and simmer for a further 1$\frac{1}{2}$ hours.

Lift out the lamb with a slotted spoon and remove the meat from the bones. Shred the meat. Skim the fat from the surface of the soup. Return the meat to the soup and reheat. Sprinkle with parsley.
Cooking time: 2$\frac{1}{4}$ hours

Japanese Mackerel

SERVES 4

4 small mackerel, cleaned, skinned and filleted

125ml/4 fl oz ($\frac{1}{2}$ cup) water

10ml (2 teaspoons) sugar

30ml (2 tablespoons) dry sherry

30ml (2 tablespoons) soy sauce

2.5ml (1 in) piece ginger root, peeled and thinly sliced

15ml (1 tablespoon) lemon juice

Place the mackerel fillets in a large frying-pan, overlapping them slightly to make one layer. Add the remaining ingredients and bring to the boil. Cover the pan and simmer very gently for 10 minutes or until the fish flakes easily.

Transfer the fillets to a serving dish and strain over the cooking liquid. Serve hot or cold.
Cooking time: 15 minutes

French Potted Pork

MAKES ABOUT 350G ($\frac{3}{4}$ LB)

450g (1 lb) boned belly of pork
(pork shoulder), rinded

225g ($\frac{1}{2}$ lb) pork fat, diced

$\frac{1}{2}$ garlic clove, crushed

1 bay leaf

salt

freshly ground black pepper

60ml/4 tablespoons ($\frac{1}{4}$ cup) water

2.5ml ($\frac{1}{2}$ teaspoon) dried thyme

Heat the oven to 140°C (275°F) gas mark 1. Cut the meat into thin strips 2.5cm × 6 mm (1 × $\frac{1}{4}$ in). Put the meat and fat into a heavy oven-proof pot and stir in the garlic, bay leaf, seasoning and water. Cover the pot tightly and cook in the oven for 4 hours. Shake the pot occasionally to be sure the meat is not sticking.

Turn the contents of the pot into a strainer placed over a saucepan. Let all the melted fat drip into the pan. Discard the bay leaf. Tear the meat into very fine shreds using two forks. Mix in the thyme and adjust the seasoning. Press the meat into small pots, leaving about 1.2cm ($\frac{1}{2}$ in) headroom. Cool.

Warm the pan of fat over gentle heat if it has solidified, then strain through dampened cheesecloth inside a sieve. Cover the pots of meat with this clarified fat in two layers, then store in the refrigerator.

Cooking time: $4\frac{1}{2}$ hours plus chilling

Devils on Horseback

SERVES 4

8 large prunes

850ml/1$\frac{1}{2}$ pt (3$\frac{3}{4}$ cups) strong hot tea

30ml (2 tablespoons) oil

8 blanched almonds

salt

cayenne pepper

4 fatty bacon slices, cut in half crosswise

Put the prunes and tea in a saucepan and bring to the boil. Cover the pan and simmer for 30 minutes.

Meanwhile, heat the oil in a frying-pan. Add the almonds and fry until golden but not brown. Remove the nuts from the pan and coat them with salt and cayenne.

Heat the grill (broiler) to moderate. Drain the prunes. Slit them and take out the stones. Place an almond in each cavity. Stretch each piece of bacon with the back of a knife, then wrap a piece around each prune. Secure with wooden cocktail sticks (picks), if necessary.

Grill (broil) the devils for 10–15 minutes, turning occasionally. Serve hot.
Cooking time: 40–45 minutes

Walnut and Cauliflower Flan

SERVES 4–6

FOR THE PASTRY

150g/5 oz (1$\frac{1}{4}$ cups) plain flour

pinch of salt

50g/2 oz ($\frac{1}{2}$ cup) shelled walnuts, finely
chopped

50g/2 oz (4 tablespoons) butter

1 egg yolk

10ml (2 teaspoons) cold water

FOR THE FILLING

1 medium-sized cauliflower, in florets

275ml ($\frac{1}{2}$ pt) white sauce *(page 252)*

1 medium-sized egg, beaten

175ml/6 fl oz ($\frac{3}{4}$ cup) thin cream

30ml (2 tablespoons) soft brown sugar

50ml/2 fl oz ($\frac{1}{4}$ cup) cider vinegar

30ml (2 tablespoons) Dijon mustard

50g (2 oz) Mozzarella cheese, sliced

25g/1 oz ($\frac{1}{4}$ cup) shelled walnuts, chopped

1 tomato, blanched, skinned and chopped

To make the pastry sift the flour and salt into a mixing bowl and stir in the walnuts. Cut the butter into the mixture and rub in. Blend the egg yolk and water together in a cup and pour into the rubbed-in mixture. Cut the flour into the liquid with a spatula until the mixture forms a dough. Knead briefly until smooth, then wrap and chill in the refrigerator for 30 minutes.

Heat the oven to 200°C (400°F) gas mark 6. Roll out the pastry and line a 20cm (8 in) flan ring (tart pan). Bake blind (*page 61*) for 20 minutes. Meanwhile simmer the cauliflower florets in salted water for 10 minutes.

Make or heat the white sauce and pour it onto the beaten egg in a bowl. Add the cream, sugar, vinegar and mustard and stir. Strain the sauce back into the saucepan and heat through gently: do not boil.

Heat the grill (broiler) to medium. Remove the pastry case from the oven and transfer to an ovenproof serving plate. Arrange the cauliflower in the flan case and cover with the sauce. Arrange the cheese over the top and grill until the cheese has melted. Sprinkle chopped walnuts and tomato over the flan and grill 2 more minutes.
Cooking time: 1 hour 5 minutes

Game Pâté

SERVES 8–10

25g/1 oz (2 tablespoons) butter

30ml (2 tablespoons) oil

175g (6 oz) pig's or calf's liver, chopped

100g ($\frac{1}{4}$ lb) lean bacon, chopped

1 small onion, finely chopped

1 garlic clove, crushed

the meat from 1 medium-sized duck or
rabbit, cut into strips

30ml (2 tablespoons) seasoned flour

15ml (1 tablespoon) parsley, chopped

15ml (1 tablespoon) chives, chopped

2.5ml ($\frac{1}{2}$ teaspoon) dried tarragon

Melt the butter with the oil in a frying-pan. Add the liver, bacon, onion and garlic and fry for 10 minutes, stirring frequently. Remove the liver, bacon, onion and garlic from the pan with a slotted spoon and mince (grind) or finely chop together. Heat the oven to 180°C (350°F) gas mark 4.

Coat the meat strips with the seasoned flour. Return the frying-pan to the heat and heat the fat in it. Add the meat strips and fry until they are lightly browned.

Make a layer of half the minced liver mixture on the bottom of a greased pâté dish or terrine. Cover with half the meat strips and sprinkle with the parsley, chives and tarragon. Add the remaining meat strips and then the rest of the minced liver mixture. Smooth the top and cover.

Place the dish or terrine in a baking pan with enough water to come halfway up the sides of the dish and bake for 1$\frac{1}{2}$ hours, or until the pâté is well browned and has shrunk slightly from the sides of the dish. Cool completely before serving.
Cooking time: about 2$\frac{1}{4}$ hours plus chilling

Pâté Maison

MAKES ABOUT 1KG (2$\frac{1}{4}$ LB)

100g ($\frac{1}{4}$ lb) pig's or calf's liver, chopped

100g ($\frac{1}{4}$ lb) belly of pork or salt pork,
boned and chopped

225g/$\frac{1}{2}$ lb (about 1 cup) cooked rabbit
meat, shredded

225g ($\frac{1}{2}$ lb) pork sausagemeat

1 onion, chopped

25g/1 oz ($\frac{1}{2}$ cup) fresh breadcrumbs

1 medium-sized egg, beaten

15ml (1 tablespoon) milk

75ml/3 fl oz (5 tablespoons) brandy

salt

freshly ground black pepper

8–10 fatty bacon slices

Heat the oven to 180°C (350°F) gas mark 4. Combine the liver, pork, rabbit, sausage-meat, onion and breadcrumbs. Add egg, milk and brandy, season and stir well.

Line a greased 1.2L/2¼ pt (5 cup) pâté dish or terrine with all but 3 of the bacon slices. Spoon in the meat mixture and cover with the reserved bacon. Cover the dish tightly with foil and place in a baking pan. Surround with boiling water and cook in the oven for 1½ hours.

Remove from the pan and uncover. Put a clean foil on top of the pâté and weight it down. Stand in a pan of cold water and leave for 24 hours. Then scrape off the excess fat. Chill for at least 24 hours.

Remove the top bacon and turn the pâté out of the dish for serving.

Cooking time: 1¾ hours plus 36 hours chilling

Eggs Soubise

SERVES 6
425ml/¾ pt (1⅔ cups) milk
1 large onion, finely chopped
salt
freshly ground black pepper
40g/1½ oz (3 tablespoons) butter
40g/1½ oz (⅓ cup) flour
pinch of grated nutmeg
15ml (1 tablespoon) thick cream
30ml (2 tablespoons) top of pasteurized milk (light cream or half and half)
6 hard-boiled eggs, halved lengthwise
10ml (2 teaspoons) chopped parsley
5ml (1 teaspoon) paprika

Put the milk, onion and seasoning in a saucepan and bring to the boil. Simmer

Hard eggs coated in a creamy onion sauce are an original and economical starter for a dinner party.

for 15 minutes, then purée the mixture in a blender or through a food mill.

Melt the butter in a clean pan. Add the flour and cook, stirring, for 2 minutes. Gradually stir in the onion purée and bring to the boil, stirring. Simmer until thickened. Stir in the nutmeg, cream, and top of the milk (light cream) and cool.

Arrange the eggs, cut sides down, on individual serving plates. Spoon over the cold onion sauce and garnish with parsley and paprika. Refrigerate, covered, until serving.

Cooking time: 25 minutes, plus cooling time

Eggs and Cheese

Baked Potatoes with Egg

SERVES 4

4 large baking potatoes

15g/$\frac{1}{2}$ oz (1 tablespoon) butter

15ml (1 tablespoon) chopped chives

pinch of grated nutmeg

salt

freshly ground black pepper

60ml/4 tablespoons ($\frac{1}{4}$ cup) thick cream

4 eggs

Heat the oven to 190°C (375°F) gas mark 5. Prick the potatoes all over, then bake for 1$\frac{1}{2}$ hours or until tender. Cut the tops off the potatoes and scoop out the flesh, being careful not to break the skin. Mash the flesh with the butter, then beat in the chives, nutmeg, seasoning and cream. Gradually beat in the eggs. Stuff this mixture back into the potato skins, piling it up in the centre.

Return the stuffed potatoes to the oven to bake for a further 10 minutes or until the filling is lightly browned.
Cooking time: 2 hours

● For baked soufflé potatoes, mix 2 egg yolks and 8 chopped anchovy fillets into the mashed potato. Fold in 2 stiffly whisked egg whites and bake for 10 minutes.
● For sweet cheesy potatoes, add 100g/ $\frac{1}{4}$ lb (1 cup) grated Cheddar cheese, 15ml (1 tablespoon) chutney and 1 finely chopped celery stalk to the mashed potato. Bake 10 minutes.

Mince Eggs

SERVES 4

30ml (2 tablespoons) oil

100g ($\frac{1}{4}$ lb) minced (ground) beef

1 small onion, finely chopped

5ml (1 teaspoon) ground cardamon

4 large eggs

salt

freshly ground black pepper

Heat the oil in a frying-pan. Add the beef and fry until browned. Stir in the onion and cardamon and continue frying for 5 minutes. Meanwhile, beat the eggs with seasoning until just mixed.

Heat the grill (broiler) to high. Drain off all the fat from the pan, then spread out the meat mixture evenly. Pour the eggs over the meat and cook until the bottom of the omelet has set. Place the pan under the grill (broiler) and cook until the top is set.
Cooking time: 20 minutes

Eggs Florentine

This variation of a classic French dish makes a substantial lunch or supper.

SERVES 4

450g (1 lb) spinach, stalks removed

4 tomatoes, thinly sliced

100g ($\frac{1}{4}$ lb) cooked ham, cut into strips

50g/2 oz ($\frac{1}{4}$ cup) butter

pinch of grated nutmeg

salt

freshly ground black pepper

8 soft-boiled eggs

100g/$\frac{1}{4}$ lb (1 cup) Cheddar cheese, grated

30ml (2 tablespoons) grated Parmesan cheese

Heat the oven to 120°C (250°F) gas mark $\frac{1}{2}$. Cook the spinach in a covered pan without any water for about 7 minutes. Turn it and break it up every now and then with a wooden spoon. Drain well in a colander, pressing out all excess liquid, then chop the spinach.

Scatter the tomato slices and ham strips over the bottom of a greased ovenproof serving dish.

Melt the butter in a saucepan. Add the spinach, nutmeg and seasoning and mix well. Spread the spinach over the tomatoes and ham. Make 8 indentations in the spinach with the back of a spoon, then put the dish in the oven to heat through.

Heat the grill (broiler) to high. Place an egg in each indentation in the spinach. Sprinkle over the Cheddar cheese followed by the Parmesan. Grill (broil) until the cheese has melted and is golden and bubbling.
Cooking time: 15 minutes

Baked potatoes with egg makes an economical dish for a children's meal.

Parsnip Soufflé

SERVES 4
3 medium-sized parsnips, chopped
1 large onion, chopped
salt
freshly ground black pepper
1.5ml ($\frac{1}{4}$ teaspoon) ground cloves
60ml (4 tablespoons) thin cream
40g/1$\frac{1}{2}$ oz (3 tablespoons) butter
50g/2 oz ($\frac{1}{2}$ cup) flour
175ml/6 fl oz ($\frac{3}{4}$ cup) milk
4 egg yolks
5 egg whites

Heat the oven to 200°C (400°F) gas mark 6. Cook the parsnips and onion in boiling water until tender. Drain well, then purée the vegetables in a blender, or food mill. Add seasoning, the cloves and cream.

Melt the butter in a saucepan. Add the flour and cook, stirring, for 2 minutes. Gradually stir in the milk and bring to the boil, stirring. Remove from the heat and stir in the parsnip purée. Beat in the egg yolks.

Beat the egg whites until stiff, then fold into the parsnip mixture. Spoon into a greased 1.7L/3 pt (2 qt) soufflé dish. Place in the oven and reduce the heat to 190°C (375°F) gas mark 5. Bake for 20–30 minutes or until the soufflé has risen and is golden brown. Serve immediately.
Cooking time: 35–45 minutes

Indian-style Scotch Eggs

SERVES 4
550g (1$\frac{1}{4}$ lb) minced (ground) lamb or beef
2.5cm (1 in) piece ginger root, peeled and finely chopped
2.5ml ($\frac{1}{2}$ teaspoon) hot chilli powder
5ml (1 teaspoon) ground cumin
15ml (1 tablespoon) ground coriander
1 onion, finely chopped
2 garlic cloves, crushed
40g/1$\frac{1}{2}$ oz ($\frac{1}{3}$ cup) flour
5ml (1 teaspoon) salt
2.5ml ($\frac{1}{2}$ teaspoon) pepper
1 egg
8 hard-boiled eggs
oil for deep frying

Combine the meat, ginger, chilli powder, cumin, coriander, onion, garlic, flour, seasoning and egg, using your hands to mix the ingredients thoroughly. Divide the meat mixture into 8 portions and use each one to enclose a hard-boiled egg. Chill for about 30 minutes in the refrigerator until quite firm.

Heat the oil to 190°C (375°F) or until a cube of stale bread dropped in turns golden in 40 seconds. Fry the egg and meat balls, in batches, for 2–3 minutes or until a rich brown. Drain on absorbent paper and serve hot.
Cooking time: 4–6 minutes plus chilling and draining

Cauliflower, salami and tomato make an unusual cauliflower cheese.

Cauliflower Cheese with Salami

This is a sensible way of finishing up broken cheese crackers. If you have none, use dried brown breadcrumbs.

SERVES 4
1 cauliflower, broken into florets
50g/2 oz ($\frac{1}{4}$ cup) butter
8 thin slices salami
salt and freshly ground black pepper
225g ($\frac{1}{2}$ lb) tomatoes, sliced
50g/2 oz ($\frac{1}{2}$ cup) cheese, grated
50g/2 oz ($\frac{1}{2}$ cup) broken cheese crackers

Cook the cauliflower in boiling water for 8 minutes or until just tender. Drain well.

Heat the grill (broiler) to moderate. Liberally grease an ovenproof serving dish with 25g/1 oz (2 tablespoons) of the butter and arrange the cauliflower florets in the dish. Tuck the rolled salami slices between the florets and season. Cover with the tomato slices.

Combine the cheese and broken cheese crackers or breadcrumbs and sprinkle on top. Dot with the rest of the butter. Grill (broil) until the topping is golden brown and bubbling.
Cooking time: 20 minutes

Meat and Poultry

Steak and Kidney Pudding

SERVES 6

suet pastry *(page 243)*
30ml (2 tablespoons) flour
5ml (1 teaspoon) dried mixed herbs
salt
freshly ground black pepper
700g (1½ lb) chuck steak, cut into 1.2cm (½ in) cubes
225g (½ lb) ox (beef) kidney, cut into 1.2cm (½ in) cubes

Reserve one third of the dough then roll out the larger piece to a circle about 1.2cm (½ in) thick. Use to line a greased 1.4–1.7L/2½–3 pt (6–7 cup) pudding bowl (as shown on *page 243*), fitting the dough well to the bowl and overlapping the top.

Combine the flour, herbs and seasoning and use to coat the steak and kidney cubes. Put them into the lined bowl and fill up to two-thirds with water.

Roll out the reserved piece of dough, to a circle about 5cm (2 in) larger all around than the top of the bowl. Dampen the edges and press on this lid. Grease a piece of foil, and pleat across the centre to allow for expansion. Cover the bowl top and tie on securely with string.

Steam the pudding for 3 hours, adding more boiling water to the pan as needed.
Cooking time: 3½ hours

Spinach-stuffed Breast of Lamb

SERVES 6

175g/6 oz (¾ cup) cooked ham, shredded
100g/¼ lb (2 cups) fresh breadcrumbs
grated rind and juice of 1 large orange
175g (6 oz) spinach, finely chopped
1.5ml (¼ teaspoon) grated nutmeg
salt
freshly ground black pepper
1 small egg, beaten
2 × 1kg (2¼ lb) breasts of lamb, boned
25g/1 oz (¼ cup) flour
5ml (1 teaspoon) tomato paste
425ml/¾ pt (1⅔ cups) brown stock

Heat the oven to 180°C (350°F) gas mark 4. Combine the ham, breadcrumbs, orange rind, 15ml (1 tablespoon) of orange juice, the spinach, nutmeg, seasoning and egg.

Lay one breast of lamb on top of the other and sew the two ends and along one long edge to make a large pouch. Spoon the spinach mixture into the pouch and sew up to enclose it completely. Weigh the stuffed breasts. Put the meat in a roasting pan and roast for 30 minutes to each 450g (1 lb).

Transfer the meat to a warmed serving platter and keep warm. Pour off all but 30ml (2 tablespoons) of the fat from the pan and stir in the flour. Cook on top of the stove, stirring, for 2 minutes. Gradually stir in the remaining orange juice, the tomato paste and stock and bring to the boil, stirring. Simmer until thickened. Serve this sauce with the lamb.
Cooking time: about 2½ hours

Steak and kidney pudding is wrapped up in sustaining suet pastry.

Dutch Steak

SERVES 6

1.4kg (3 lb) braising steak, in one piece
salt and freshly ground black pepper
60ml (4 tablespoons) oil
2 medium-sized onions, sliced
2 medium-sized carrots, sliced
2 celery stalks, sliced
1 bay leaf
5ml (1 teaspoon) dried thyme
5ml (1 teaspoon) paprika
6 black peppercorns
275ml/½ pt (1¼ cups) beef stock

Heat the oven to moderate 180°C (350°F) gas mark 4. Rub the steak with seasoning. Heat the oil in a flameproof casserole or dutch oven. Put in the meat and brown on both sides. Remove from the pot.

Add the vegetables to the pan and fry until they are just golden. Stir in the remaining ingredients and bring to the

boil. Replace the meat in the pan then cover and place in the oven. Braise for $2\frac{1}{2}$ hours or until the meat is tender.

Transfer the steak to a warmed serving dish and keep hot. Strain the cooking liquid and return to pan. Boil briskly to reduce it, then pour over the meat.
Cooking time: 3 hours

Roast Marinated Pork Sparerib (Picnic Shoulder)

SERVES 6
1 large bay leaf, crumbled
15ml (1 tablespoon) dried thyme
7.5ml ($1\frac{1}{2}$ teaspoons) grated nutmeg
1.5ml ($\frac{1}{4}$ teaspoon) ground cloves or allspice
15ml (1 tablespoon) salt
freshly ground black pepper
1.4kg (3 lb) pork sparerib joint (picnic shoulder)
15ml (1 tablespoon) flour
275ml/$\frac{1}{2}$ pt ($1\frac{1}{4}$ cups) stock

Braising steak is cooked in one piece with selected vegetables for Dutch steak.

Combine the bay leaf, thyme, nutmeg, cloves and seasoning. If there is rind on the pork, cut it off and reserve. Rub the herb and spice mixture all over the meat. Cover and leave in the refrigerator for 24 hours.

Heat the oven to moderate 180°C (350°F) gas mark 4. Put the pork rind, if available, in a roasting pan and place the rack over it. Put the pork on the rack, fat side up. Roast for $2\frac{1}{4}$ hours or until the pork is cooked through.

Transfer the pork to a warmed serving platter and keep warm. Discard the rind and pour off all but 15ml (1 tablespoon) of fat from the pan. Stir in the flour and cook, stirring, on top of the stove for 2–3 minutes. Gradually stir in the stock and simmer, stirring, until thickened. Serve this gravy with the meat.
Cooking time: 24 hours marinating then $2\frac{1}{2}$ hours cooking

Welsh Layer Pudding

SERVES 4
suet pastry *(page 243)*
350g ($\frac{3}{4}$ lb) fatty bacon slices, diced
2 medium-sized leeks, thinly sliced

Set aside one-third of the dough. Divide the remaining dough into three portions, the smallest portion the size of a golf ball and the other 2 portions slightly larger.

Roll out the smallest portion to about 6mm ($\frac{1}{4}$ in) thick and press onto the bottom and against the sides of a greased 850ml/$1\frac{1}{2}$ pt (4 cup) pudding bowl. Cover with one-third of the bacon and leeks.

Continue making layers of dough and bacon and leeks in this way. Roll out the reserved one-third of the dough to make the lid. Cover with greased foil, pleated across the centre to allow for expansion *(page 243)*.

Steam for 2–$2\frac{3}{4}$ hours, replenishing the water when necessary.
Cooking time: about 3 hours

197

Roast Shoulder of Lamb Boulangère

A classic French roast, this shoulder of lamb is well within the budget for family eating.

SERVES 6
1.6kg (3½ lb) shoulder of lamb
salt
freshly ground black pepper
2 or 3 garlic cloves, cut into slivers
25g/1 oz (2 tablespoons) butter
15ml (1 tablespoon) oil
1 large onion, thinly sliced
900g (2 lb) potatoes, thinly sliced
275ml/½ pt (1¼ cups) stock
chopped parsley to garnish

Heat the oven to 180°C (350°F) gas mark 4. Rub the lamb all over with seasoning. Make incisions in the meat and insert the garlic slivers. Melt the butter with the oil in a frying-pan. Add the onion and fry until softened.

Make alternating layers of onion and potatoes in a large baking dish, seasoning each layer. Pour in the stock which should almost reach the top of the vegetables

Place the lamb on top.

Roast for 1¾–2¼ hours or until the lamb is cooked through. Serve with the vegetables garnished with parsley.
Cooking time: 2–2½ hours

Honey-glazed Chicken

A quick meal for hard-pressed mothers—and others too—grilled (broiled) chicken is a universal favourite.

SERVES 4
4 chicken portions
75g/3 oz (5 tablespoons) margarine
20ml (4 teaspoons) prepared mustard
60ml (4 tablespoons) honey

Heat the grill (broiler) to medium. Mash the margarine in a bowl with a fork and stir in the other ingredients. Prick the chicken all over with a fork to help the fat to flow and the baste to penetrate. Put the chicken in an ovenproof dish and spread the baste over the portions.

Grill (broil) close to the heat for 3 minutes on each side, then lower the pan and continue for a total of 25 minutes, turning the chicken and basting with the juices. Pour the basting juices over the vegetable with which the chicken is served.
Cooking time: 30 minutes

● If you prefer a spicier mix, omit the honey and add 5ml (1 teaspoon) each of soy sauce and prepared mustard, a dash of Tabasco or hot pepper sauce and 2.5ml (½ teaspoon) garlic salt to the margarine.
● Mango chutney can also be substituted for the honey, but avoid big bits of fruit.

Shoulder of lamb roasted with layers of potatoes and stock is a complete meal.

Turkey and Ham Pie

SERVES 4–6

50g/2 oz ($\frac{1}{4}$ cup) butter
1 medium-sized onion, chopped
4 celery stalks, chopped
25g/1 oz ($\frac{1}{4}$ cup) plain flour
150ml/$\frac{1}{4}$ pt ($\frac{2}{3}$ cup) milk
salt
freshly ground black pepper
juice of 1 lemon
225g/$\frac{1}{2}$ lb (1 cup) cooked turkey meat, diced
salt and freshly ground black pepper
100g/$\frac{1}{4}$ lb ($\frac{1}{2}$ cup) cooked ham, diced
550g (1 lb 2 oz) made weight frozen puff pastry, thawed (pastry for 2-crust pie)
beaten egg to glaze

Melt the butter in a saucepan. Add the onion and celery and fry until softened. Stir in the flour and cook, stirring, for 2 minutes. Gradually add the milk and simmer, stirring, until thickened. Remove from the heat and add seasoning to taste and the lemon juice. Leave to cool.

Heat the oven to 200°C (400°F) gas mark 6. Divide the pastry dough in half. Roll out one half on a lightly-floured surface to an oblong about 3mm ($\frac{1}{8}$ in) thick and transfer to a baking sheet. Fold the turkey and ham into the cold sauce. Spoon the turkey and ham filling onto the dough oblong and spread out to within 2.5cm (1 in) of the edges.

Roll out the other piece of dough to an oblong the same size and place over the filling. Dampen the edges and press together to seal. Pinch decoratively around the edge and make a slit in the centre. Brush all over with beaten egg.

Bake for 25 minutes or until the pastry is well risen and golden brown. Serve warm.
Cooking time: 45 minutes

Stuffed Braised Lambs' Hearts

SERVES 4

4 lambs' hearts
salt
20ml (4 teaspoons) oil
1 medium-sized onion, sliced
20ml (4 teaspoons) flour
275ml/$\frac{1}{2}$ pt (1$\frac{1}{4}$ cups) stock
10ml (2 teaspoons) mushroom ketchup (or steak sauce)
freshly ground black pepper
7.5ml (1$\frac{1}{2}$ teaspoons) lemon juice
FOR THE STUFFING
25g/1 oz (2 tablespoons) butter
1 small onion, finely chopped
40g/1$\frac{1}{2}$ oz ($\frac{3}{4}$ cup) fresh breadcrumbs
grated rind of 1 lemon
2.5ml ($\frac{1}{2}$ teaspoon) dried marjoram
20ml (4 teaspoons) fresh parsley, chopped
salt
freshly ground black pepper

Remove the muscular artery walls and any outside skin from the hearts. Trim away any excess fat. Snip with scissors down through the dividing wall inside each heart, cutting down almost to the base. Wash under cold running water, then soak in salted water for at least 30 minutes.

Meanwhile, make the stuffing. Melt the butter in a saucepan. Add the onion and fry until softened. Remove from the heat and mix in the remaining stuffing ingredients.

Heat the oven to 150°C (300°F) gas mark 2. Drain the hearts and dry with absorbent paper. Fill the cavities with the stuffing and secure with small skewers or wooden cocktail sticks (picks).

Heat the oil in a flame-proof casserole (dutch oven). Add the hearts and brown on all sides. Remove from the pot. Add the onion to the pan and fry until golden. Stir in the flour and cook, stirring, for 1 minute. Gradually stir in the stock and bring to the boil, stirring. Add the mushroom ketchup or steak sauce and seasoning and mix well, then return the hearts to the pan.

Cover the pot and place it in the oven. Braise for 2$\frac{1}{2}$ hours or until the hearts are tender. Skim any fat from the surface of the cooking liquid, stir in the lemon juice and serve.
Cooking time: 30 minutes soaking, then 3 hours cooking

Rolled Braised Beef

SERVES 6

1.4kg (3 lb) braising steak, in one piece
175ml/6 fl oz ($\frac{3}{4}$ cup) wine vinegar
2 bay leaves
6 black peppercorns, crushed
3 sage leaves (if available)
salt
25g/1 oz (2 tablespoons) butter
30ml (2 tablespoons) oil
2 large onions, thinly sliced
1 garlic clove, crushed
4 celery stalks, chopped
1 small turnip, chopped
175ml/6 fl oz ($\frac{3}{4}$ cup) beef stock

Cut the meat across the grain into three equal pieces. Pound each piece until it is thin, then lay the pieces on a work surface, slightly overlapping the edges. Roll up the meat like a Swiss (jelly) roll and tie securely with string.

Put the meat roll in a shallow dish and pour over the vinegar. Add the bay leaves, peppercorns, sage leaves and salt, then marinate for 2 hours, turning occasionally.

Drain the meat roll. Strain the marinade and reserve. Melt the butter with the oil in a saucepan. Add the meat roll and brown on all sides. Remove from the pan.

Add the onions, garlic, celery and turnip to the pan and fry until the onions are softened. Stir in the stock and reserved marinade and bring to the boil. Return the meat roll to the pan, then cover and simmer for 1–1$\frac{1}{2}$ hours or until tender.
Cooking time: 2 hours marinating then 1$\frac{1}{2}$–2 hours cooking

Greek Pot Roast

SERVES 6–8

45ml (3 tablespoons) oil

1.4kg (3 lb) brisket of beef, rolled and tied

3 medium-sized onions, finely chopped

4 garlic cloves, crushed

salt

freshly ground black pepper

15ml (1 tablespoon) sugar

5ml (1 teaspoon) ground cinnamon

3 cloves

1 bay leaf

150ml/¼ pt (⅔ cup) boiling stock

45ml (3 tablespoons) tomato paste

350g (¾ lb) spaghetti

15ml (1 tablespoon) oil

25g/1 oz (¼ cup) grated Parmesan cheese

Heat the oven to 150°C (300°F) gas mark 2. Heat the oil in a flameproof casserole (dutch oven). Add the meat and brown on all sides. Remove from the pot.

Add the onions and garlic to the pan and fry until golden. Stir in the seasoning, sugar, cinnamon, cloves, bay leaf, stock and tomato paste. Bring to the boil.

Return the meat to the pan. Cover the pot tightly and place it in the oven. Braise for 2–2½ hours or until tender.

Fifteen minutes before the meat is ready, cook the spaghetti in boiling salted water with the oil for 8–10 minutes, or until just tender. Drain well and keep hot.

Remove the meat and keep hot. Skim any fat from the cooking liquid.

Carve the meat into thick slices and arrange on a warmed serving platter surrounded by the spaghetti. Strain the cooking liquid over the meat and sprinkle the spaghetti with the Parmesan.
Cooking time: 2½–3 hours

Rabbit Goulash

SERVES 4

1.4kg (3 lb) rabbit, jointed

3 medium-sized onions, sliced

3 medium-sized carrots, sliced

2 celery sticks, sliced

400g (14 oz) canned tomatoes

15ml (1 tablespoon) tomato paste

2 garlic cloves, crushed

5ml (1 teaspoon) dried basil

2 bay leaves

150ml/¼ pt (⅔ cup) dry white wine or dry cider

10ml (2 teaspoons) paprika

salt

freshly ground black pepper

Put the rabbit joints in a heavy-bottomed saucepan and add the onions, carrots and celery. Mix the tomatoes with their juice, the tomato paste, garlic, basil and bay leaves and pour over the top. Add the wine, paprika and seasoning.

Cover the pan and bring to the boil, then simmer for 2 hours or until the rabbit is tender.
Cooking time: 2 hours

● Chicken can also be used for this dish.

Chinese Sweet and Sour Pork

It is worth planning to have left-over cold, cooked pork to make this universally-popular Chinese dish. Serve it with rice.

SERVES 4

350g (¾ lb) cold cooked pork, cut into 2.5cm (1 in) cubes

egg white batter *(page 245)*

oil for deep frying

FOR THE SAUCE

30ml (2 tablespoons) oil

1 medium-sized onion, grated

1 green pepper, chopped

20ml (4 teaspoons) cornflour (cornstarch)

275ml/½ pt (1¼ cups) chicken stock

30ml (2 tablespoons) tomato paste

225g (½ lb) canned apricot halves

50g/2 oz (⅓ cup) sultanas or raisins

15ml (1 tablespoon) honey

45ml (3 tablespoons) red wine vinegar

pinch of salt

2.5ml (½ teaspoon) ground ginger

Fry the onion in the oil in a frying pan for about 3 minutes. Add the pepper and cook for 3 more minutes. Blend the cornflour (cornstarch) with a little stock. Stir the stock, starch mix and tomato paste into the pan and cook, stirring until thickened.

Drain the apricots reserving the juice. Chop the fruit, then add the juice and the remaining sauce ingredients to the pan. Cover and simmer for 20 minutes. Add the apricots for the last 5 minutes.

Meanwhile heat the deep frying oil to 160°C (350°F) or until a bread cube will brown in under 60 seconds. Stir the pork cubes into the batter. Deep fry in batches for 4 minutes, turning and removing the fritters with a slotted spoon. Keep warm in a dish lined with absorbent paper.

Reheat the sauce, put the fried pork into a serving dish and pour the sauce on top.
Cooking time: 50 minutes

● This is a successful way of using up cold, cooked turkey.

Brisket of beef pot roast the Greek way is served with ribbon noodles and Parmesan.

Ham in Cider Sauce

This recipe can be used for a smoked ham of about 2.7–3.2kg (6–7 lb) weight, if you are lucky enough to get one, or for a cut of gammon. Corner gammon or a collar joint would be suitable.

The number of servings will depend on the size of the cut. The sauce is calculated for 6 people to eat the meat hot. Meat left from a larger cut will then be served later cold.

SERVES 6

1 gammon joint, tied with string, or a smoked ham, weighing not less than 900g (2 lb)
6 cloves
1 large onion, sliced
2 carrots, quartered
1 bouquet garni
40g/1½ oz (3 tablespoons) butter
400ml/14 fl oz (1¾ cups) cider
30ml (2 tablespoons) flour
50g/2 oz (⅓ cup) sultanas or raisins

Make small incisions in the ham and insert the cloves. Put the ham in a large saucepan with the onion, carrots and bouquet garni and almost cover with water. Bring to the boil and simmer, allowing 20 minutes to each 450g (1 lb) and 20 minutes over.

Remove from the heat and rest the ham in the liquid until cool enough to handle. Lift the ham from the liquid and peel off the skin.

Heat the oven to 180°C (350°F) gas mark 4. Score the fat in diamond shapes, put the ham in a roasting pan and dot with 15g/½ oz (1 tablespoon) of the butter. Pour 175ml/6 fl oz (¾ cup) of the cider around the ham. Bake, allowing 10 minutes to each 450g (1 lb) plus 10 minutes over. Baste occasionally with the pan cider.

Transfer the ham to a carving board and keep warm. Strain the cider into a jug.

Melt the remaining butter in a saucepan. Add the flour and cook, stirring, for 2 minutes. Gradually stir in the reserved cider plus the rest of the cider and the sultanas or raisins. Bring to the boil, stirring, and simmer until thickened.

Carve the ham and serve with the cider sauce.

Cooking time: 2 hours or more

● For a cold centrepiece, insert a clove at the corner of each diamond.
● A gammon slipper weighing about 700g (1½ lb), boiled as in this recipe and cooled in the stock, is the ideal meat to use in any recipe that requires a quantity of cooked ham. This will prove cheaper than buying slices from a delicatessen or supermarket.
● Ham stock is useful for cooking vegetables and as a base for soup. Do not use more than ⅓ stock in a soup as it tends to be salty.

Cornish Pasties

SERVES 6

1½ × shortcrust pastry *(page 240)*
1 small turnip, coarsely chopped
350g (¾ lb) lean beef, finely chopped
1 small kidney, skinned and chopped
1 large onion, finely chopped
4 medium-sized potatoes, diced
salt
freshly ground black pepper
beaten egg

Heat the oven to 200°C (400°F) gas mark 6. Roll out the pastry thinly and cut out 12 rounds, each 15cm (6 in) in diameter. Mix together the turnip, beef, kidney, onion, potatoes and seasoning. Divide this filling between the pastry rounds, placing it in a heap in the centres.

Cornish pasties were first made for the miners in the Cornish tin mines—as a convenient 'packed lunch' of meat and vegetables in a pastry envelope.

Heat the oven to 200°C (400°F) gas mark 6. Roll out the pastry thinly and cut out 12 rounds, each 15cm (6 in) in diameter. Mix together the turnip, beef, kidney, onion, potatoes and seasoning. Divide this filling between the pastry rounds, placing it in a heap in the centres.

Dampen the edges of the pastry rounds and fold over to make semi-circles. Press the edges to seal. Place the pasties on a baking sheet. Make a few cuts in the top of each and brush with beaten egg. Bake for 15 minutes, then reduce the temperature to moderate, 180°C (350°F) gas mark 4. Continue baking for 40 minutes. Serve hot or cold.

Cooking time: 70 minutes

● The quantity of potatoes can be reduced and more turnip used.
● Carrot or swede (rutabaga) can be used instead of turnip, or all four vegetables can be used to make up the equivalent amount of vegetable.

Boiled Beef with Lemon and Mushroom Sauce

SERVES 8

1.8kg (4 lb) silverside of beef (sirloin tip), rolled and tied
salt
60ml/4 tablespoons (¼ cup) oil
1 large onion, stuck with 3 cloves
1 bouquet garni
6 black peppercorns
thinly pared rind of 1 small lemon
850ml/1½ pt (3¾ cups) chicken stock
FOR THE SAUCE
75g/3 oz (⅓ cup) butter
30ml (2 tablespoons) flour
45ml (3 tablespoons) lemon juice
salt
freshly ground black pepper
100g (¼ lb) button mushrooms, quartered
1.5ml (¼ teaspoon) grated nutmeg
1 egg yolk, beaten
30ml (2 tablespoons) sour cream

Rub the meat all over with salt. Heat the oil in a large saucepan or dutch oven. Put in the meat and brown on all sides. Add the onion, bouquet garni, peppercorns, lemon rind and stock and bring to the boil. Cover the pan and simmer gently for 2½–3 hours or until the beef is tender.

Remove the beef from the pan and keep warm. Skim any fat from the cooking liquid, then strain the liquid and reserve 425ml/¾ pt (1⅔ cups).

Melt 25g/1 oz (2 tablespoons) of the butter in a clean saucepan. Add the flour and cook, stirring, for 1 minute. Gradually stir in the reserved cooking liquid and bring to the boil, stirring. Simmer until thickened. Add the lemon juice and seasoning and simmer for a further 5 minutes.

Meanwhile, melt the remaining butter in a frying-pan. Add the mushrooms and fry for 3 minutes. Drain on absorbent paper, then stir into the sauce with the nutmeg.

Combine the egg yolk and sour cream. Stir in a little of the hot sauce, then add this to the rest of the sauce in the pan. Cook very gently, stirring, for 3 minutes. Do not allow to boil.

Carve the meat into thick slices and serve with the sauce.

Cooking time: 3–3½ hours

● Substitute brisket for the silverside.

Tangy lemon and mushroom sauce is an excellent accompaniment to boiled beef.

Brains with Capers

This is a classic French dish, considered a great delicacy because of its smooth texture.

SERVES 6

3 sets of calves' brains
salt
freshly ground black pepper
225ml/8 fl oz (1 cup) beef stock
2 celery stalks, sliced
1 onion, halved
1 bay leaf
1.5ml (¼ teaspoon) dried sage
10 black peppercorns
100g/¼ lb (½ cup) butter
10ml (2 teaspoons) white wine vinegar
15ml (1 tablespoon) capers

Soak the brains in cold salted water for 20 minutes. Drain them and remove the membranes and veins.

Put the stock in a saucepan and bring to the boil. Add the brains, celery, onion, bay leaf, sage and peppercorns. Cover and simmer for 25 minutes.

Meanwhile, melt the butter in another saucepan. Cook until it is nut brown, but do not let it burn. Stir in the vinegar and capers.

Drain the brains and place in a warmed serving dish. Pour over the caper-butter sauce and serve.

Cooking time: 25 minutes

Turkey Fritters

SERVES 4

75g/3 oz (¾ cup) plain flour
salt and freshly ground black pepper
15g/½ oz (1 tablespoon) butter, melted
150ml/¼ pt (⅔ cup) warm water
5ml (1 teaspoon) curry powder
225g/½ lb (1 cup) cooked turkey meat, minced (ground)
10ml (2 teaspoons) grated lemon rind
2 large egg whites
oil for deep frying
50g/2 oz (½ cup) grated Parmesan cheese

Sift the flour into a bowl and stir in seasoning to taste. Make a well in the centre and put in the butter and water. Gradually mix the dry ingredients into the liquid to make a smooth, thick batter. Add the curry powder, turkey and lemon rind and mix well. Beat the egg whites until stiff and fold into the turkey mixture.

Heat the oil to 180°C (350°F), or until a cube of stale bread dropped in will turn golden in 60 seconds. Drop large spoonfuls of the turkey mixture into the oil and fry for 4 minutes or until golden. Drain on absorbent paper. Serve hot, sprinkled with the Parmesan cheese.

Cooking time: 20 minutes

Braised Birds with Cabbage

SERVES 6

25g/1 oz (2 tablespoons) lard
3 pigeons (large Rock Cornish game hens)
100g (¼ lb) fatty bacon slices, diced
2 carrots, diced
1 large onion, chopped
2 small, tight green cabbages, each cut into 4 wedges
575ml/1 pt (2½ cups) chicken stock
1 bouquet garni
salt and freshly ground black pepper

Heat the lard in a heavy-bottomed saucepan. Add the birds and brown on all sides. Remove from the pan.

Add the bacon and vegetables to the pan and fry until just coloured. Return the birds to the pan and bury them, breasts down, in the vegetables. Add the stock and bouquet garni and bring to the boil. Cover and simmer for 2½–3 hours or until the birds are tender. Discard bouquet garni.

Transfer the birds to a warmed serving platter and split each one in half. Surround with the vegetables and keep warm.

Boil the cooking liquid briskly to reduce. Season to taste and pour over the birds.

Cooking time: 3–3½ hours

Lamb and Turnip Parcels

SERVES 4

700g (1½ lb) boneless lamb, cut into 1.2cm (½ in) cubes
450g (1 lb) turnips, diced
1 medium-sized onion, finely chopped
grated rind and juice of 1 orange
10ml (2 teaspoons) dried thyme
salt and freshly ground black pepper

Heat the oven to moderate 180°C (350°F) gas mark 4. Combine all the ingredients. Divide the mixture between four 25cm (10 in) squares of foil and fold up the foil to enclose the meat mixture. Place the parcels on a baking sheet. Bake for 1¼ hours.

Cooking time: 1½ hours

Fillet Steaks in French Pastry

These rich succulent little steaks make a dinner party dish which serves a minute quantity of meat to each person—with style! It is also one of those convenient party dishes that can be fully prepared ahead and just pushed into the oven at the last moment. Beurre manié is made by combining equal weights of butter and flour or 15ml (1 tablespoon) butter with 30ml (2 tablespoons) flour.

SERVES 4
350-450g ($\frac{3}{4}$-1 lb) fillet steak (filet mignon), cut into 4 slices
15g/$\frac{1}{2}$ oz (1 tablespoon) butter
$\frac{1}{3}$ × economical liver pâté *(page 83)*
salt and freshly ground black pepper
1 egg, beaten, to glaze
FOR THE PASTRY
175g/6 oz (1$\frac{1}{2}$ cups) flour
pinch of salt
100g/$\frac{1}{4}$ lb ($\frac{1}{2}$ cup) butter, diced
1 medium-sized egg yolk
15ml (1 tablespoon) cold water
FOR THE SAUCE SOUBISE
225g ($\frac{1}{2}$ lb) onions, chopped
275ml/$\frac{1}{2}$ pt (1$\frac{1}{4}$ cups) milk
6 parsley stalks
1 bay leaf
2 peppercorns
15g/$\frac{1}{2}$ oz (1$\frac{1}{2}$ tablespoons) beurre manié
15ml (1 tablespoon) lemon juice
45ml (3 tablespoons) thick cream

Trim membrane and extra fat from the steaks. Heat the butter in a frying-pan over maximum heat until it has stopped frothing. (If it burns, tip it into a cup and start again). Sear the steaks for 1 minute on each side to seal the cut surfaces. Leave them on a plate to get cold.

Sift the flour and salt into the middle of a large bowl and make a well in the centre. Put the diced butter and egg yolk in the centre. Work butter and egg yolk together, plus the water, pulling in the flour. Work with your fingertips, dispersing the fat and liquid into the flour. When a ball of dough is formed, roll it round the bottom of the bowl to pick up all the flour and amalgamate it. Knead by pressing down on the ball with the heel of your hand to flatten it; gather it up again and press once more. Continue kneading until a smooth pastry is formed. Divide the pastry into four fat sausages, wrap in a plastic bag and chill in the refrigerator for 1 hour.

To make the soubise sauce, put the first 5 ingredients in a pan and simmer gently

for 25 minutes. Purée in a blender or through a food mill and return to the pan. Reheat and add the beurre manié, stirring well. Cook for 2 minutes.

Salt and pepper the cold steaks all over and spread the pâté on one side, dividing it between the four. Return to the refrigerator to firm up the pâté.

Roll out the pastry, and place the steak, pâté side down, in the middle of the pastry. Mould the pastry round the meat. Hold the parcel flat side down in the palm of your left hand and pinch the pastry round the top, pulling it and dampening the overlaps to seal. Do not leave any holes but enclose the meat completely. Cover all four steaks, then sit them, seams underneath, on a greased baking sheet. Prick the top of each with a fork, glaze with beaten egg and reserve in the refrigerator until needed—chill at least 45 minutes.

Heat the oven to 200°C (400°F) gas mark 6. Bake in the centre of the oven for 20 minutes until the pastry is golden brown. Reheat the sauce, adding the lemon juice and then the cream. Serve the sauce in a jug.

Cooking time: 45 minutes, 1$\frac{1}{2}$ hours chilling time, then 20 minutes

Sausages with Celeriac Purée

SERVES 4
225ml/8 fl oz (1 cup) water
2.5ml ($\frac{1}{2}$ teaspoon) dried marjoram
2.5ml ($\frac{1}{2}$ teaspoon) grated lemon rind
salt
freshly ground black pepper
450g (1 lb) potatoes, chopped
450g (1 lb) celeriac (celery root), sliced
1 onion, chopped
8 pork sausages
60ml/4 tablespoons ($\frac{1}{4}$ cup) hot milk
75g/3 oz ($\frac{3}{4}$ cup) Cheddar cheese, grated

Heat the grill (broiler) to moderate. Put the water, marjoram, lemon rind and seasoning in a saucepan and bring to the boil. Add the potatoes, celeriac (celery root) and onion and simmer for 20–25 minutes until the vegetables are tender.

Meanwhile, grill (broil) the sausages until they are brown on all sides and cooked through.

Purée the vegetable mixture in a blender and return to the saucepan. Add the milk and cheese and heat through, beating well. Spread out the purée in a warmed serving dish and arrange the sausages on top.

Cooking time: 40 minutes

Chinese Lemon Chicken

SERVES 4
1.8kg (3 lb) chicken, skinned and cut into 16–20 pieces through the bone
7.5ml (1$\frac{1}{2}$ teaspoons) salt
5ml (1 teaspoon) ground ginger
1 egg, beaten
100g/$\frac{1}{4}$ lb (1 cup) ground rice (rice flour)
oil for deep frying
juice of 1 lemon
15ml (1 tablespoon) chopped spring onions (scallions)
1 lemon, thinly sliced
FOR THE SAUCE
60ml/4 tablespoons ($\frac{1}{4}$ cup) chicken stock
30ml (2 tablespoons) dry sherry
1.5ml ($\frac{1}{4}$ teaspoon) salt
5ml (1 teaspoon) sugar

Rub the chicken pieces with the salt and ginger. Dip them in the egg, then coat in the ground rice (rice flour).

Heat the oil to 185°C (360°F), or until a small cube of stale bread dropped in turns golden in 50 seconds. Fry the chicken pieces, in batches, for 3–5 minutes or until golden brown. Drain on absorbent paper and keep hot.

Put all the sauce ingredients in a saucepan and bring to the boil. Arrange the chicken pieces in a warmed serving dish and pour over the sauce. Sprinkle with the lemon juice and spring onions (scallions) and garnish with the lemon slices.

Cooking time: about 25 minutes

Red Flannel Hash

SERVES 4
15g/$\frac{1}{2}$ oz (1 tablespoon) butter
1 large onion, finely chopped
450g (1 lb) potatoes, cooked and diced
450g (1 lb) cooked, peeled beetroot (beets), diced
450g (1 lb) (cooked) corned beef, diced
45ml (3 tablespoons) thick cream
salt
freshly ground black pepper

Melt the butter in a frying-pan. Add the onion and fry until softened. Stir in the remaining ingredients and cook, without stirring, for 5–8 minutes or until the underside is crusty.

Turn the hash over and cook the other side for 5–8 minutes until crusty. Slide the hash onto a serving platter and serve.

Cooking time: 15–20 minutes

Fish and Shellfish

Mullet with Tomatoes and Capers

SERVES 4

30ml (2 tablespoons) oil
3 large onions, chopped
2 garlic cloves, crushed
900g (2 lb) tomatoes, blanched, skinned, seeded and chopped
5ml (1 teaspoon) dried chervil
5ml (1 teaspoon) dried tarragon
1 bay leaf
1.5ml ($\frac{1}{4}$ teaspoon) dry mustard
15ml (1 tablespoon) capers
30ml (2 tablespoons) tomato paste
salt
freshly ground black pepper
1.8kg (4 lb) grey mullet, cleaned
1 lemon, thinly sliced
parsley sprigs

Heat the oil in a saucepan. Add the onions and garlic and fry until softened. Stir in the tomatoes, herbs, mustard, capers, tomato paste and seasoning. Cook for 30 minutes.

Heat the oven to 180°C (350°F) gas mark 4. Make three diagonal, parallel cuts in both sides of the fish and rub all over with salt. Place in a greased baking dish. Pour over the tomato sauce, then cover with foil. Bake for 35 minutes or until the fish will flake easily.

Discard the bay leaf from the sauce. Serve the fish garnished with lemon slices and parsley sprigs.

Cooking time: 65 minutes

Mussels with Lemon Sauce

SERVES 4

2$\frac{1}{2}$kg/5 pt (6 lb) mussels
50g/2 oz ($\frac{1}{4}$ cup) butter
2 shallots, finely chopped
1 bouquet garni
1.5ml ($\frac{1}{4}$ teaspoon) grated nutmeg
salt
freshly ground black pepper
juice of 4 lemons
15ml (1 tablespoon) flour

Scrub the mussels well and discard any which are not tightly shut or which do not close when tapped and any with broken shells. Scrape off the beards, then soak the mussels in clean, cold water for 1 hour.

Melt half the butter in a large saucepan. Add the shallots, bouquet garni, nutmeg and seasoning and cook until the shallots are softened. Stir in the lemon juice.

Drain the mussels and add in batches to the pan. Cook, shaking the pan, for 3 minutes or until the shells open. Remove the mussels from the pan with a slotted spoon and pile up on a dish. Keep warm. Strain the liquid through a cloth.

Melt the remaining butter in another saucepan. Add the flour and cook, stirring, for 1 minute. Gradually stir in the strained liquid and bring to the boil. Stir until thick then pour over the mussels.

Cooking time: 1$\frac{1}{2}$ hours initial cleaning, then 30 minutes

Mullet with tomatoes and capers is a most impressive dinner party dish.

Cheddar cod is a simple dish of cod steaks with a bubbling cheese topping.

Cheddar Cod

SERVES 4
4 cod steaks
100g/$\frac{1}{4}$ lb ($\frac{1}{2}$ cup) butter, melted
100g/$\frac{1}{4}$ lb (1 cup) Cheddar cheese, grated
15ml (1 tablespoon) French mustard
salt
freshly ground black pepper

Heat the grill (broiler) to moderate. Remove the centre bone from each cod steak. Place the cod steaks in the grill (broiling) pan and brush with half the butter. Cook for 5 minutes. Turn the steaks over and brush with the rest of the butter. Cook for a further 3 minutes.

Combine the cheese, mustard and seasoning. Spread this mixture over the steaks and grill for 5 minutes or until the top is golden and bubbling.
Cooking time: 15 minutes

Whiting in Apple Sauce

SERVES 4
50g/2 oz ($\frac{1}{4}$ cup) butter
30ml (2 tablespoons) flour
275ml/$\frac{1}{2}$ pt (1$\frac{1}{4}$ cups) apple sauce or purée
30ml (2 tablespoons) lemon juice
salt
freshly ground black pepper
1.5ml ($\frac{1}{4}$ teaspoon) grated nutmeg
4 whiting fillets, skinned and halved
50g/2 oz (1 cup) fresh brown breadcrumbs

Heat the oven to 220°C (425°F) gas mark 7. Melt 15g/$\frac{1}{2}$ oz (1 tablespoon) of the butter in a saucepan. Add the flour and cook, stirring, for 1 minute. Gradually stir in the apple sauce and lemon juice and bring to the boil, stirring. Simmer until thickened. Remove from the heat and stir in seasoning and the nutmeg.

Arrange half the whiting fillets in a greased baking dish. Pour over half the apple sauce and sprinkle with half the breadcrumbs. Repeat the layers, then dot the top with the remaining butter.

Bake for 20 minutes or until the fish flakes easily and the top is golden brown.
Cooking time: $\frac{1}{2}$ hour

● Use haddock instead of whiting.

Rock Salmon with Cayenne Sauce

SERVES 6
900g (2 lb) rock salmon fillets or salmon tail
10ml (2 teaspoons) lemon juice
2.5ml ($\frac{1}{2}$ teaspoon) paprika

Smoked Haddock Crêpes

SERVES 4

crêpe batter *(page 245)*
90ml (6 tablespoons) butter or oil for frying
225g (½ lb) smoked haddock fillets
25g/1 oz (2 tablespoons) butter
1 small onion, finely chopped
1 celery stalk, chopped
50g (2 oz) mushrooms, thinly sliced
150ml/¼ pt (⅔ cup) thick cream
salt and freshly ground black pepper
15ml (1 tablespoon) chopped chives
50g/2 oz (½ cup) Cheddar cheese, grated

Make 12 crêpes in the usual way *(page 245)* and keep them warm.

Poach the haddock for 10 minutes or until it flakes easily. Meanwhile, melt the butter in a frying pan. Add the onion, celery and mushrooms and fry for 4 minutes. Drain the vegetables.

Heat the grill (broiler) to high. Drain the fish. Remove the skin and flake the fish in a bowl. Add the fried vegetables, cream, seasoning and chives to the fish and mix well.

Divide the fish mixture between the crêpes and roll them up. Arrange in one layer in a greased flameproof serving dish. Sprinkle with the cheese and grill until the cheese has melted.

Cooking time: about 40 minutes

Fish Loaf

SERVES 4

450g (1 lb) white fish fillets, cooked, skinned and flaked
2 medium-sized potatoes, cooked and mashed
1 small turnip, cooked and mashed
2 hard-boiled eggs, chopped
150g/5 oz (⅔ cup) canned cream-style corn kernels
1 egg, beaten
1.5ml (¼ teaspoon) cayenne pepper
salt and freshly ground black pepper
10ml (2 teaspoons) chopped parsley
50g/2 oz (⅔ cup) dry breadcrumbs
50g/2 oz (½ cup) Cheddar cheese, grated
25g/1 oz (2 tablespoons) butter

Heat the oven to 190°C (375°F) gas mark 5. Combine the fish, potatoes, turnip, hard-boiled eggs, sweetcorn, beaten egg, cayenne, seasoning and parsley. Spoon into a greased 900g (2 lb) loaf tin (pan) and

smooth the top. Combine the breadcrumbs and cheese and scatter over the top. Dot with the butter, then bake for 45 minutes or until golden brown.
Cooking time: about 1 hour

Deep-fried Sprats (Sardines)

SERVES 4

50g/2 oz (½ cup) seasoned flour
grated rind of 1 lemon
450g (1 lb) sprats (fresh sardines)
oil for deep frying
parsley sprigs to garnish

Mix the seasoned flour with the lemon rind in a plastic bag. Tip in the fish in batches, then close the bag and shake until all are well coated.

Heat the oil to 185°C (360°F), or until a small cube of stale bread dropped into the oil turns golden in 50 seconds. Fry the fish in small batches for 2–3 minutes or until light brown. Drain on absorbent paper. Serve hot, garnished with parsley.

Fish Stew

SERVES 4

25g/1 oz (2 tablespoons) butter
350g (¾ lb) potatoes, sliced
2 large leeks, sliced
6 celery stalks, sliced
575ml/1 pt (2½ cups) fish stock or water
salt and freshly ground black pepper
400g (14 oz) canned tomatoes
150ml/¼ pt (⅔ cup) dry white wine or cider
225g (½ lb) coley or haddock fillets, skinned and cut into 5cm (2 in) cubes
2 large mackerel, filleted, skinned and cut into thick slices
2.5ml (½ teaspoon) dried marjoram
30ml (2 tablespoons) chopped parsley

Melt the butter in a saucepan. Add the potatoes, leeks and celery and cook gently, covered, until softened but not browned. Stir in the stock or water and seasoning and bring to the boil. Simmer, uncovered, until the vegetables are tender.

Add the tomatoes with their juice and the wine or cider and return to the boil. Stir in the fish and marjoram, then cover the pan and simmer for 10 minutes or until the fish flakes easily. Stir in the parsley and serve.

Cooking time: 45 minutes

FOR THE SAUCE

225ml/8 fl oz (1 cup) hot béchamel sauce *(page 252)*
60ml/4 tablespoons (¼ cup) thick cream
5ml (1 teaspoon) lemon juice
1.5ml (¼ teaspoon) cayenne pepper
15ml (1 tablespoon) chives, chopped
salt
freshly ground black pepper

Heat the oven to 190°C (375°F) gas mark 5. Place the fillets in a baking dish and sprinkle them with lemon juice.

Combine the sauce ingredients in a saucepan and bring to the boil, stirring. Pour over the fillets. Cover the dish and bake for 40–50 minutes or until the fish flakes easily. Sprinkle over the paprika and serve.

Cooking time: 45–55 minutes

● Any white fish may be used instead of rock salmon—which is not to everybody's taste. Try cod, haddock or whiting.

Rice and Pasta

Apple Noodle Pudding

SERVES 6
350g ($\frac{3}{4}$ lb) fine noodles
15ml (1 tablespoon) oil
30ml (2 tablespoons) sugar
1.5ml ($\frac{1}{4}$ teaspoon) salt
1.5ml ($\frac{1}{4}$ teaspoon) ground cinnamon
1.5ml ($\frac{1}{4}$ teaspoon) mixed spice
2 large cooking apples, peeled, cored and grated
50g/2 oz ($\frac{1}{3}$ cup) sultanas or raisins
2 eggs, beaten
30ml (2 tablespoons) milk
25g/1 oz (2 tablespoons) butter, melted

Heat the oven to 180°C (350°F) gas mark 4. Cook the noodles for 6–9 minutes in boiling water until cooked but firm. Drain and add the sugar, salt, spices, apples and raisins. Spoon into a baking dish. Combine the eggs and milk and pour over the dish. Finally sprinkle over melted butter. Bake for 45 minutes or until the pudding is firm and golden.
Cooking time: 55 minutes

Risotto Milanese

This classic Italian side dish or starter is also useful in left-over form for stuffing vegetables etc.

SERVES 6
1 medium-sized onion, chopped
75g/3 oz (6 tablespoons) butter
350g ($\frac{3}{4}$ lb) Italian rice
50g/2 oz ($\frac{1}{4}$ cup) white vermouth
1.1L/2 pt (5 cups) chicken stock
2 saffron strands (optional)
25g/1 oz (3 tablespoons) grated Parmesan cheese

Melt 50g/2 oz (4 tablespoons) of the butter in a large saucepan and add the onion. Cook for about 4 minutes over medium heat. Add all the rice and stir so that the grains are well coated with fat.

Add the vermouth and stir well. Add about 75ml/3 fl oz ($\frac{1}{2}$ cup) hot stock and stir. Cook until the liquid has been absorbed, then add a little more. Infuse the saffron strands in a cup of stock, if using. Continue to add the stock and to cook until it is absorbed. Use the saffron liquid last. Continue until all the stock has been absorbed and the rice is soft and creamy.

Stir in the remaining butter and the cheese and serve.
Cooking time: about $\frac{3}{4}$ hour

Lasagne

SERVES 4
225g ($\frac{1}{2}$ lb) lasagne
salt
15ml (1 tablespoon) oil
1$\frac{1}{2}$ × béchamel sauce *(page 252)*
100g/$\frac{1}{4}$ lb (1 cup) grated Parmesan cheese
FOR THE SAUCE
60ml (4 tablespoons) oil
1 medium-sized onion, chopped
1 garlic clove, crushed
1 medium-sized carrot, diced
1 celery stalk, diced
3 fatty bacon slices, diced
100g ($\frac{1}{4}$ lb) mushrooms, sliced
225g ($\frac{1}{2}$ lb) minced (ground) beef
1.5ml ($\frac{1}{4}$ teaspoon) dried oregano
1.5ml ($\frac{1}{4}$ teaspoon) dried basil
salt
freshly ground black pepper
400g (14 oz) canned tomatoes
45ml (3 tablespoons) tomato paste

First make the sauce. Heat the oil in a saucepan. Add the onion, garlic, carrot and celery and fry until softened. Add the bacon and mushrooms and fry for a further 5 minutes. Stir in the meat and fry until well browned.

Add the remaining sauce ingredients and mix well. Bring to the boil, then cover the pan and simmer for $\frac{1}{2}$ hour.

Heat the oven to 200°C (400°F) gas mark 6. Cook the lasagne in boiling salted water with the oil in two saucepans for 3–4 minutes. Drain in a colander. Spread out two-thirds of the lasagne on a towel to keep it separated.

Line a greased gratin dish or baking tin (pan) with the remaining lasagne. Pour over one-third of the sauce and spread out. Pour over one-third of the béchamel sauce, then sprinkle with one-third of the cheese. Cover with a layer of the lasagne. Repeat the layers, ending with Parmesan cheese.

Bake for 40 minutes or until heated through and the top is golden brown and bubbly.
Cooking time: 1$\frac{1}{2}$ hours

Steamed Meat and Pasta Pudding

SERVES 4
175g (6 oz) macaroni
15ml (1 tablespoon) oil
700g (1$\frac{1}{2}$ lb) minced (ground) pork
400g (14 oz) canned tomatoes, drained
100g ($\frac{1}{4}$ lb) frozen green beans, thawed
salt
1 garlic clove, crushed
freshly ground black pepper
30ml (2 tablespoons) tomato paste
2.5ml ($\frac{1}{2}$ teaspoon) dried thyme
1 egg, beaten

Cook the macaroni in boiling salted water with the oil for 10–12 minutes or until just tender. Drain, then mix with the remaining ingredients. Spoon into a greased 1.1L/ 2 pt (1 qt) pudding bowl. Cover with greased foil, making a pleat across the centre to allow for expansion.

Steam for 2 hours, replenishing the water when necessary. Serve hot.
Cooking time: 2$\frac{1}{4}$ hours

Special Macaroni Cheese

SERVES 4
100g ($\frac{1}{4}$ lb) macaroni
15ml (1 tablespoon) oil
salt
freshly ground black pepper
40g/1$\frac{1}{2}$ oz (3 tablespoons) butter
50g (2 oz) smoked fatty bacon slices, diced
1 small onion, finely chopped
40g/1$\frac{1}{2}$ oz ($\frac{1}{3}$ cup) flour
575ml/1 pt (2$\frac{1}{2}$ cups) milk
pinch of dry mustard
pinch of cayenne pepper
175g/6 oz (1$\frac{1}{2}$ cups) Cheddar cheese, grated

Cook the macaroni in boiling salted water with the oil for 10–12 minutes until tender.

Meanwhile, melt the butter in another saucepan. Add the bacon and onion and fry until the onion is softened. Stir in the flour and cook, stirring, for 2 minutes. Gradually stir in the milk and bring to the boil. Simmer, stirring, until thickened. Add the mustard, cayenne and seasoning, then stir in three-quarters of the cheese until melted.

Heat the grill (broiler) to moderate. Drain the macaroni and fold into the cheese sauce. Turn into a flame-proof serving dish. Sprinkle over the rest of the cheese and grill (broil) for 5 minutes or until bubbling.

Cooking time: 20 minutes

Vermicelli with Clams and Mussels

SERVES 4
1kg (2 pt) mussels
20 clams
75ml (5 tablespoons) olive oil
1 medium-sized onion, finely chopped
3 garlic cloves, crushed
800g (1 lb 14 oz) canned tomatoes
salt
freshly ground black pepper
350g ($\frac{3}{4}$ lb) vermicelli
15ml (1 tablespoon) vegetable oil
chopped parsley to garnish

Scrub the mussels and clams well and discard any which are not tightly shut or which do not close when tapped and any with broken shells. Scrape the beards off the mussels, then soak the shellfish in clean, cold water for 1 hour.

Heat 45ml (3 tablespoons) of the olive oil in a large saucepan. Add the onion and fry until softened. Stir in the garlic, tomatoes and their liquid and seasoning and simmer gently for 20–25 minutes or until thick.

Meanwhile, cook the vermicelli in boiling salted water with the vegetable oil until just tender—about 9 minutes. Drain and keep warm.

Drain the shellfish. Rinse out a saucepan and put in the shellfish. Cover them with a damp folded towel and put over low heat, shaking the pan at intervals. After 5–7 minutes they should be open. Remove the shellfish from the shells, retaining a few shells for garnish. Discard any shells which do not open at this point. Add the fish to the sauce.

Strain the cooking liquid through cheesecloth inside a strainer and add to the tomato sauce. Mix well and heat gently.

Heat the remaining olive oil and pour it into a shallow warmed serving dish. Add the vermicelli and toss to coat the strands with oil. Pour over the sauce, sprinkle with parsley and serve.

Cooking time: preparation and soaking for 1$\frac{1}{4}$ hours then 40 minutes

●Extra mussels can be used if clams are not available. Or use a few prawns (shrimp) or even 90g (3$\frac{1}{2}$ oz) canned tuna.

Nasi Goreng

SERVES 4
3 large eggs
60ml/4 tablespoons ($\frac{1}{4}$ cup) peanut oil
2 medium-sized onions, finely chopped
1 garlic clove, chopped
5ml (1 teaspoon) chilli powder
100g ($\frac{1}{4}$ lb) peeled prawns (shrimp)
100g/$\frac{1}{4}$ lb ($\frac{1}{2}$ cup) diced, cooked chicken
30ml (2 tablespoons) soy sauce
juice of $\frac{1}{2}$ lemon
5ml (1 teaspoon) brown sugar
225g/$\frac{1}{2}$ lb (1$\frac{1}{2}$ cups) cold, boiled long grain rice
2 firm tomatoes, sliced

Steamed meat and pasta pudding is served hot and makes a filling children's dish for cold winter days.

Break the eggs into a bowl and beat until frothy. Place 15ml (1 tablespoon) of the oil in a frying-pan about 20cm (8 in) in diameter. Set over high heat. Pour the beaten egg into the pan. Allow the bottom to set and become firm—about 2 minutes. Turn the omelet and cook it for a further 2 minutes. Keep the cooked omelet warm.

Pour the remaining oil in a large, heavy-bottomed frying-pan over medium heat. Add the onions, garlic and chilli powder to the pan and stir-fry for 1 minute.

Add the prawns (shrimp), chicken, soy sauce, lemon juice and sugar. Stir-fry for 2–3 minutes. Add the rice. Stir-fry for 2 minutes until the rice is heated through and coated with the fat.

Turn the rice into a heated dish. Cut the omelet into strips and make a lattice over the rice. Decorate edges with sliced tomato. Serve immediately with side dishes of fried onions and peanuts.

Cooking time: 20 minutes

●You will need about 65g/2$\frac{1}{2}$ oz (7 tablespoons) raw rice, if you have no cooked rice ready.

●Use beef or pork instead of chicken.

Vegetables and Salads

Cauliflower Bread

SERVES 6

2 medium-sized cauliflowers, broken into florets

700g (1½ lb) potatoes, quartered

15g/½ oz (1 tablespoon) butter

1.5ml (¼ teaspoon) cayenne pepper

salt

freshly ground black pepper

6 eggs

150g/5 oz (1¼ cups) Gruyère or Cheddar cheese, grated

Heat the oven to 180°C (350°F) gas mark 4. Cook the cauliflower florets in boiling salted water until tender, about 10 minutes. Meanwhile, cook the potatoes in boiling water until tender. Drain both vegetables well and purée through a foodmill into one saucepan. Add the butter, cayenne and seasoning and mash together.

Beat in the eggs one at a time, then stir in all but 45ml (3 tablespoons) of the cheese. Ladle into a greased 2.3L/4 pt (2½ qt) bowl, or a cake tin (pan) 19cm (7½ in) diameter and 7.5cm (3 in) deep. Cover tightly with foil.

Place the bowl in a baking pan, pour boiling water around it and bake for 1 hour.

Turn out the bread onto a warmed oven-proof serving dish. Sprinkle over the reserved cheese and return to the oven. Bake for 5 minutes or until the cheese has melted. Serve hot.

Cooking time: 1 hour 20 minutes

Serve cauliflower bread with grilled (broiled) steak or roast meat.

Cabbage with Curried Cheese Stuffing

SERVES 4

900g (2 lb) whole curly cabbage

30ml (2 tablespoons) oil

1 large onion, finely chopped

1 dessert apple, peeled, cored and finely chopped

15ml (1 tablespoon) curry powder

15ml (1 tablespoon) tomato paste

50g/2 oz (⅓ cup) long-grain rice

1 egg

salt

freshly ground black pepper

175g/6 oz (1½ cups) Cheddar cheese, grated

275ml/½ pt (1¼ cups) stock

Blanch the cabbage, stalk end up, in boiling water for 4 minutes. Drain and pat dry with absorbent paper.

Heat the oil in a frying-pan. Add the onion and apple and fry until softened. Stir in the curry powder and fry for a further 2 minutes. Remove from the heat and stir in the tomato paste, rice, egg, seasoning and cheese.

Carefully stuff the cabbage, inserting the filling between the leaves and pushing it well towards the base. Tie the cabbage in cheesecloth or with string and place in a heavy-bottomed saucepan. Pour the stock around it. Cover the pan and cook very gently for 3 hours.

Cooking time: 3¼ hours

Sweet and Sour Onions

SERVES 4

25 button onions, peeled

45ml (3 tablespoons) olive oil

75ml/3 fl oz (⅜ cup) port or red vermouth

75ml/3 fl oz (⅜ cup) red wine vinegar

30ml (2 tablespoons) soft brown sugar

25g/1 oz (2 tablespoons) raisins

salt

cayenne pepper

Cook the onions in a heavy-bottomed pan in the oil over low heat. Shake the pan so that the onions are browned on all sides. Add the port or vermouth and the vinegar

Celery, jugged with apples, bacon and walnuts makes a novel family supper dish.

and bring to the boil. Reduce the heat and stir in the brown sugar, raisins, salt and cayenne pepper. Cover and simmer for 15–20 minutes until the onions are tender and the liquid has reduced to a syrup. Serve the onions hot with their syrup.
Cooking time: 30 minutes

Brussels Sprouts with Honey and Orange Juice

SERVES 6
700g (1½ lb) Brussels sprouts
60ml/4 tablespoons (¼ cup) orange juice
25g/1 oz (2 tablespoons) butter
1.5ml (¼ teaspoon) mixed spice
1.5ml (¼ teaspoon) ground ginger
salt
freshly ground black pepper
60ml/4 tablespoons (¼ cup) clear honey

Put all the ingredients in a saucepan and mix well. Bring to the boil, then cover the pan and cook gently for 15–20 minutes or until the sprouts are tender.
Cooking time: 15–20 minutes

Jugged Celery

SERVES 6
8 lean bacon slices
10 large cooking apples, halved
450ml/16 fl oz (2 cups) water
30ml (2 tablespoons) sugar
pinch of ground cloves
2.5ml (½ teaspoon) grated nutmeg
salt
freshly ground black pepper
1 large head (bunch) of celery, cut into 10cm (4 in) pieces
50g/2 oz (½ cup) walnuts, chopped

Heat the oven to 180°C (350°F) gas mark 4. Lay half the bacon on the bottom of a small, greased casserole.

Put the apples in a saucepan with the water. Cook gently for 20 minutes or until the apples are very soft. Purée the apples through a strainer or food mill, discarding the peel, core and seeds. Add the sugar, spices and seasoning to the purée and mix well. Spoon the purée into the casserole.

Stand the celery pieces upright in the purée and sprinkle the walnuts on top. Cover with the remaining bacon. Bake for 1½–2 hours or until the celery is tender. Serve hot straight from the casserole.
Cooking time: 1¾–2¼ hours

Puréed Jerusalem Artichokes

SERVES 4
350g (¾ lb) Jerusalem artichokes, peeled and dropped into water containing vinegar
2 medium-sized onions, each stuck with a clove
45ml (3 tablespoons) thick cream
salt and freshly ground black pepper
40g/1½ oz (3 tablespoons) butter
25g/1 oz (½ cup) fresh wholewheat breadcrumbs

Cook the artichokes in boiling water for 10 minutes. Add the onions and simmer for a further 5 minutes or until the vegetables are tender.

Drain the vegetables and return to the pan. Dry for 1 minute over low heat, shaking the pan, then purée the vegetables in a blender or with a food mill. Return the purée to the saucepan and add the cream, seasoning and 15g/½ oz (1 tablespoon) of the butter. Mix well and keep warm.

Melt the remaining butter in a frying-pan. Add the breadcrumbs and fry quickly until browned. Turn the purée into a warmed serving dish and top with the breadcrumbs.
Cooking time: 20 minutes

Curried Chick Peas

SERVES 6

350g/¾ lb (2 cups) dried chick-peas, soaked overnight

1.4L/2½ pt (6 cups) water

40g/1½ oz (3 tablespoons) butter

5ml (1 teaspoon) cumin seed

1 medium-sized onion, finely chopped

2.5cm (1 in) piece ginger root, peeled and finely chopped

5ml (1 teaspoon) turmeric

2.5ml (½ teaspoon) ground cumin

5ml (1 teaspoon) ground coriander

5ml (1 teaspoon) garam marsala

1.5ml (¼ teaspoon) hot chilli powder

15ml (1 tablespoon) coriander leaves, chopped, if available

Drain the chick-peas and put into a saucepan with the measured water. Bring to the boil, then half cover the pan and simmer gently for 1 hour.

Melt the butter in another saucepan. Add the cumin seeds and fry for 1 minute. Add the onion and fry for 5 minutes, stirring occasionally. Stir in the ginger and continue frying until the onion is golden brown.

Combine the turmeric, cumin, coriander, garam masala and hot chilli powder with water to make a paste. Add to the onion mixture and fry for 3 minutes, stirring constantly. Pour in the chick-peas with their cooking liquid and bring to the boil, stirring. Cover and simmer gently for 30 minutes or until the chick-peas are tender. Serve sprinkled with coriander leaves, if available.

Cooking time: 1¾ hours

●If you have problems in getting the spices, substitute 15–20ml (3–4 teaspoons) curry powder.

Root Vegetable Casserole

SERVES 6

25–50g (1–2 oz) dripping

1 large onion, thinly sliced

850ml/1½ pt (3¾ cups) beef stock

225g (½ lb) leeks, cut into 2.5cm (1 in) pieces

1 bouquet garni

salt

freshly ground black pepper

225g (½ lb) parsnips, diced

225g (½ lb) carrots, sliced

225g (½ lb) potatoes, cut into chunks

Heat the oven to 160°C (325°F) gas mark 3. Heat the dripping in a flame-proof casserole (dutch oven). Add the onion and fry until softened. Stir in the stock and bring to the boil. Add the leeks, bouquet garni and seasoning.

Cover the pot and transfer to the oven. Cook for 10 minutes. Add the parsnips and carrots and cook for a further 10 minutes.

Stir in the potatoes and continue cooking for 35–40 minutes or until all the vegetables are tender. Discard the bouquet garni before serving.

Cooking time: 1–1¼ hours

Glazed Turnips

SERVES 6

25g/1 oz (2 tablespoons) butter

15ml (1 tablespoons) oil

700g (1½ lb) turnips, quartered

30ml (2 tablespoons) soft brown sugar

175ml/6 fl oz (¾ cup) chicken stock

Melt the butter with the oil in a saucepan. Add the turnips and cook for 5 minutes or until they are golden brown. Sprinkle over the sugar and cook for a further 5 minutes, stirring frequently.

Add the stock and bring to the boil. Cover and simmer for 30 minutes or until the turnips are tender but still firm and most of the stock has evaporated.

Cooking time: 40 minutes

Potato Casserole

SERVES 4

25g/1 oz (2 tablespoons) butter

2 shallots, chopped

2 celery stalks, chopped

1 garlic clove, crushed

900g (2 lb) potatoes, thinly sliced

225g (½ lb) carrots, thinly sliced

4 fatty bacon slices, diced

400g (14 oz) canned tomatoes

225ml/8 fl oz (1 cup) beef stock

10ml (2 teaspoons) paprika

1.5ml (¼ teaspoon) dried basil

salt

freshly ground black pepper

Melt the butter in a frying-pan. Add the shallots, celery and garlic and fry until the shallots are softened. Add the carrots and bacon and some of the potatoes. Fry until the potatoes are golden brown. Remove from the pan and fry the rest of the

potatoes. Return the vegetables to the pan. Add the tomatoes with their juice, the stock, paprika, basil and seasoning and bring to the boil. Cover the pan and simmer for 10 minutes or until all the vegetables are tender.

Cooking time: 30 minutes

Brussels Sprouts Polonaise

SERVES 4–6

700g (1½ lb) Brussels sprouts

40g/1½ oz (3 tablespoons) butter

50g/2 oz (1 cup) fresh breadcrumbs

2 hard-boiled eggs, finely chopped

30ml (2 tablespoons) chopped parsley

salt

freshly ground black pepper

Cook the sprouts in boiling salted water for about 8 minutes or until they are just tender. Meanwhile, melt the butter in a frying-pan. Add the breadcrumbs and fry until golden, stirring frequently. Stir in the eggs, parsley and seasoning to taste.

Drain the sprouts and pile up in a warmed serving dish. Sprinkle over the egg and breadcrumb mixture and serve.

Cooking time: about 10 minutes

Red Cabbage and Bacon Casserole

SERVES 4

22.5ml (1½ tablespoons) oil

1 large onion, sliced

6 fatty bacon slices, chopped

1 large cooking apple, peeled, cored and sliced

2 large potatoes, sliced

1 medium-sized red cabbage, shredded

7.5ml (1½ teaspoons) caraway seeds

30ml (2 tablespoons) lemon juice

15ml (1 tablespoon) wine vinegar

salt

freshly ground black pepper

275ml/½ pt (1¼ cups) chicken stock

15ml (1 tablespoon) brown sugar

Heat the oven to 180°C (350°F) gas mark 4. Heat the oil in a flameproof casserole (dutch oven). Add the onion and fry until softened. Add the bacon and fry until lightly browned. Stir in the remaining ingredients and bring to the boil. Cover the pot and transfer it to the oven. Braise for 2 hours or until the cabbage is tender.

Cooking time: 2¼ hours

Red Cabbage, Walnut and Apple Salad

SERVES 6

½ medium-sized red cabbage, cored and finely shredded

3 dessert apples, cored and chopped

8 spring onions (scallions), finely chopped

2 medium-sized carrots, thinly sliced

50g/2 oz (½ cup) shelled walnuts, chopped

FOR THE DRESSING

90ml/6 tablespoons (⅓ cup) olive oil

15ml (1 tablespoon) clear honey

juice of 1 lemon

30ml (2 tablespoons) wine vinegar

salt

freshly ground black pepper

2.5ml (½ teaspoon) caraway seeds

Combine the cabbage, apples, onions, carrots and walnuts in a salad bowl. Put all the dressing ingredients in a screw-top jar and shake well. Pour the dressing over the salad and toss. Chill for 30 minutes before serving.

Preparation time: 5 minutes plus 30 minutes chilling

Cooked Mushroom Salad

Serve this salad with cold meat. Raw, marinated mushrooms (page 134) are an alternative salad; omit the filling given in the recipe.

SERVES 3–4

1 medium-sized onion

30ml (2 tablespoons) olive oil

225g (½ lb) mushrooms

salt

freshly ground black pepper

45ml (3 tablespoons red wine or lemon juice

15ml (1 tablespoon) tomato ketchup

15ml (1 tablespoon) chopped parsley

Chop the onion finely and fry it in the oil over low heat until softened. Slice the mushrooms and add them to the pan. Cook for 8–10 minutes. Season well, add the wine or lemon juice and stir in the ketchup. Transfer to a dish and leave to cool. Chill in the refrigerator and serve with parsley sprinkled on top.

Cooking time: 1 hour including chilling

Wilted Lettuce Salad

SERVES 4

6 fatty bacon slices, diced

60ml/4 tablespoons (¼ cup) white wine vinegar

5ml (1 teaspoon) sugar

6 spring onions (scallions), chopped

salt

freshly ground black pepper

1 round (head Boston) lettuce, torn into pieces

Fry the bacon in a frying-pan until it is crisp and has rendered most of its fat. Remove from the pan with a slotted spoon.

Add the vinegar, sugar, onions and seasoning to the bacon fat in the pan and bring to the boil, stirring well.

Put the lettuce in a salad bowl. Pour over the hot vinegar mixture and toss well. Serve immediately, sprinkled with bacon.

Cooking time: 6 minutes

Red Cabbage and bacon casserole is a sweet and juicy accompaniment for rich meats.

Desserts

Cranberry Pie

SERVES 6

225g/½ lb (1 cup) fresh cranberries
225g/½ lb (1 cup) sugar
45ml (3 tablespoons) water
100g/¼ lb (½ cup) unsalted butter
65g/2½ oz (⅔ cup) flour
90g/3½ oz (1 cup) rolled oats
100g/¼ lb (⅔ cup) light brown sugar

Heat the oven to 160°C (325°F) gas mark 3. Put the cranberries, sugar and water in a saucepan and heat gently, stirring to dissolve the sugar. Remove from the heat.

Rub together the butter, flour, oats and brown sugar to form a soft sticky dough. Press half the dough into the bottom of a 20cm (8 in) pie dish. Spread over the cranberry mixture and top with the rest of the dough. Bake for 45 minutes or until the top is golden brown.
Cooking time: 45 minutes

Rolled oats and brown sugar make a crunchy topping for cranberry pie.

Honeycomb Mould

SERVES 4–6

15g/½ oz (2 tablespoons) gelatin
30ml (2 tablespoons) water
2 large eggs, separated
75g/3 oz (⅓ cup) fine sugar
425ml/¾ pt (1⅔ cups) milk
60ml/4 tablespoons (¼ cup) lemon juice

Put the gelatin to soak in the water in a small cup. Beat the egg yolks and sugar together until pale and frothy. Put the milk in the top of a double boiler and scald, then pour on to the egg yolk mixture, beating constantly. Return to the pan, add the softened gelatin and cook, stirring, until the custard thickens and the gelatin dissolves. Remove from the heat and stir in the lemon juice.

Beat the egg whites until stiff. Fold into the still warm custard, then pour into a rinsed out 1.1L/2 pt (1 qt) mould. Chill until set.
Cooking time: 15 minutes plus 3 hours setting time

German Cheesecake

SERVES 8

175g (6 oz) digestive biscuits (graham crackers), finely crushed
75g/3 oz (5 tablespoons) butter, melted
125g/¼ lb (½ cup) sugar
5ml (1 teaspoon) ground cinnamon
2 eggs, beaten
1.5ml (¼ teaspoon) salt
juice and grated rind of ½ lemon
125ml/4 fl oz (½ cup) thin cream
225g/½ lb (1 cup) cottage cheese
75g/3 oz (¾ cup) mixed nuts, chopped

Heat the oven to 180°C (350°F) gas mark 4. Combine the biscuit (cracker) crumbs, butter, 25g/1 oz (2 tablespoons) sugar and the cinnamon. Press all but 30ml (2 tablespoons) of this mixture onto the bottom and sides of a greased 20cm (8 in) sandwich tin (spring-form pan).

Combine the eggs, remaining sugar, the salt and lemon rind and juice. Stir in the cream, cheese and half the nuts and mix

well. Pour into the crumb case and sprinkle over the rest of the nuts and the reserved crumb mixture.

Bake for 35–45 minutes or until a skewer inserted into the centre comes out clean. Leave the cake to cool in the turned-off oven, with door open, for 10 minutes. Serve cold.

Cooking time: 40–50 minutes

Cherry Clafoutis

SERVES 6

175ml/6 fl oz ($\frac{3}{4}$ cup) milk
2 eggs
10ml (2 teaspoons) vanilla extract
75ml (5 tablespoons) icing (confectioners') sugar
105ml (7 tablespoons) flour
pinch of salt
550g (1$\frac{1}{4}$ lb) canned black cherries, drained and stoned (pitted)

Heat the oven to 180°C (350°F) gas mark 4. Beat the milk, eggs and vanilla together. Gradually beat in 60ml (4 tablespoons) of the sugar and the flour, spoonful by spoonful. Add the salt. Pour this batter into a greased baking dish about 19cm (7$\frac{1}{2}$ in) in diameter. Dry the cherries with absorbent paper and add them to the dish, spreading them evenly through the batter.

Bake for 50–60 minutes or until a knife inserted into the centre comes out clean. Sprinkle over the remaining sugar and serve warm rather than hot.

Cooking time: 1 hour 10 minutes

Prune Mousse

SERVES 6

225g ($\frac{1}{2}$ lb) prunes
about 575ml/1 pt (2$\frac{1}{2}$ cups) tepid tea
45ml (3 tablespoons) sugar
15g/$\frac{1}{2}$ oz (2 tablespoons) gelatin
30ml (2 tablespoons) port or red vermouth
julienne strips of orange rind
75ml/5 tablespoons ($\frac{1}{3}$ cup) thick cream, whipped
1 egg white
whipped cream for serving (optional)

Soak the prunes in twice their volume of tepid tea, overnight. Stone if necessary. Put the prunes, tea and sugar in a pan and

Cherries baked in a sweet batter make this classic French dessert, clafoutis.

simmer until tender—this will take about 10 minutes.

Remove the prunes from the heat and drain. Put 200ml/$\frac{1}{3}$ pt ($\frac{3}{4}$ cup) of prune juice into a clean pan and add the gelatin. Leave to soak for 5 minutes. Meanwhile purée the prunes through a food mill into a bowl. Stir in the port or vermouth.

Dissolve the gelatin over heat without stirring. Stir the gelatin liquid into the prune purée and taste for sweetness, adding more sugar if necessary. Leave to cool, then refrigerate.

Blanch the orange rind strips for 1 minute in boiling water, then refresh in cold water. Reserve.

When the prune liquid is on the point of setting, whip the egg white stiffly and fold into the mousse. Fold in the whipped cream and turn the mousse into individual dishes or a serving bowl. Chill until set—about 2 hours.

To serve, top with whipped cream if wished and garnish with the orange strips.

Cooking time: overnight soaking, 15 minutes, then 2 hours setting time

215

Pears with Chocolate Sauce

SERVES 4
575ml/1 pt (2½ cups) water
350g/¾ lb (1½ cups) sugar
1 vanilla pod
4 cloves
4 ripe dessert pears, peeled
FOR THE SAUCE
15g/¼ oz (2 tablespoons) cornflour (cornstarch)
275ml/½ pt (1¼ cups) milk
50g (2 oz) plain semi-sweet chocolate (squares)
25g/1 oz (2 tablespoons) sugar
15g/½ oz (1 tablespoon) butter

Put the water and sugar in a saucepan and heat stirring to dissolve the sugar. Add the vanilla pod and cloves.

Cut a small slice from the base of each pear to make it flat. Stand the pears in the pan, cover and poach for 15–20 minutes or until tender. Drain the pears and stand in a serving dish. Cool, then chill for 30 minutes.

For the sauce, mix the starch with a little of the milk to make a paste. Put the rest of the milk in a saucepan with the chocolate and sugar. Heat gently, stirring to melt the chocolate and dissolve the sugar. Pour a little of this hot liquid onto the cornflour mixture, then add to the pan. Cook, stirring, until thickened.

Beat in the butter in small pieces. Remove the sauce from the heat and pour over the pears. Serve immediately.
Cooking time: 20–25 minutes

Caramel Rice Mould

SERVES 5–6
125g/4½ oz (⅔ cup) sugar
75ml/3 fl oz (⅓ cup) water
575ml/1 pt (2½ cups) milk
150g/5 oz (¾ cup) short-grain (white) rice
2 large eggs, separated

Chilled pears with hot chocolate sauce is an impressive-looking dessert.

Put 75g/3 oz (⅓ cup) of the sugar and the water in a saucepan and heat, stirring to dissolve the sugar. Bring to the boil and boil until the syrup is light golden brown. Immediately tip the syrup into a greased and warmed 700ml/1½ pt (4 cup) mould and tip the mould round so the bottom and sides are coated.

Put the milk in a double boiler and bring to simmering point. Stir in the rice and remaining sugar. Simmer for 40–50 minutes, stirring occasionally, or until the rice is soft and has absorbed all the milk. Remove from the heat and cool for 15 minutes.

Beat the egg yolks into the rice mixture. Beat the whites until stiff and fold in. Turn into the caramel-lined mould and cover with foil. Steam for 1 hour or until the pudding is set.
Cooking time: about 2 hours

Spiced Apple Pie

SERVES 4

275ml/½ pt (1¼ cups) cider
3 cloves
7.5cm (3 in) cinnamon stick, crumbled
large pinch of grated nutmeg
700g (1½ lb) cooking apples, peeled, cored and sliced
grated rind of ½ orange
75g/3 oz (½ cup) brown sugar
½ × shortcrust pastry (page 240)
milk
fine sugar

Put the cider and spices in a saucepan and bring to the boil. Boil briskly until reduced by about two-thirds. Cool, then strain the cider.

Heat the oven to 200°C (400°F) gas mark 6. Pack half the apples into an 850ml/1½ pt (1 qt) pie dish and sprinkle with the orange rind and brown sugar. Cover with the rest of the apples, Pour in the cider.

Roll out the pastry to about 6mm (¼ in) thick and use to cover the pie. Decorate with the trimmings. Brush with milk and sprinkle with fine sugar. Bake for 20 minutes, then reduce the temperature to 180°C (350°F) gas mark 4. Bake for a further 40 minutes.
Cooking time: 1¼ hours

Orange Trifle

SERVES 6

6 thick slices sponge cake or trifle sponges
90ml (6 tablespoons) orange marmalade
175ml/6 fl oz (¾ cup) sweet sherry
425ml/¾ pt (1⅔ cups) milk
few drops of vanilla extract
1 whole egg
2 egg yolks
75g/3 oz (⅓ cup) fine sugar
6 oranges
rind and juice of 2 lemons
150ml/¼ pt (⅔ cup) whipping cream

Split each sponge slice into two layers and sandwich back together with the marmalade. Put the cakes on the bottom of a 20cm (8 in) diameter serving dish that is 10cm (4 in) deep. Sprinkle the cakes with the sherry and leave to soak for at least 3 hours.

Meanwhile make the custard. First warm the milk, adding the vanilla. Prepare a double boiler. Beat the eggs with half the sugar together in the top pan. Pour on the milk and cook gently, stirring all the time, for about 15 minutes until the custard is thick. Leave to get completely cold.

Grate the rind from 2 oranges and squeeze their juice. Segment the other oranges (*page 70*) and scatter the fruit segments over the cake.

Combine the grated orange and lemon rinds and juices, then add the remaining sugar and stir until dissolved. Whip the cream until thick and fold this and the fruit juice mixture into the cold custard. Pour this over the oranges in the dish.

Cover and chill for at least 2 hours. Remove from the refrigerator 30 minutes before serving.
Cooking time: ½ hour in total, plus 5 hours chilling in two periods

Currants are incoporated into the suet pastry for lemony Sussex pond pudding for additional flavour and texture.

Sussex Pond Pudding

SERVES 4

100g/¼ lb (½ cup) butter
grated rind and chopped flesh of 2 lemons
175g/6 oz (1 cup) soft brown sugar
¾ × suet pastry (*page 243*) with 50g/2 oz (⅓ cup) currants added

Cream the butter until softened, then beat in the lemon rind and flesh and sugar. Chill in the refrigerator until firm.

Roll out two-thirds of the dough to about 6mm (¼ in) thick and use to line a greased 850ml/1½ pt (1 qt) pudding bowl (*page 243*). Place the butter filling in the bowl and cover with the remaining dough.

Cover with greased foil, pleated in the centre to allow for expansion, and steam for 2–2½ hours, replenishing the water when necessary.
Cooking time: 2½–3 hours

Coffee Crumble

SERVES 4

15ml (1 tablespoon) flour
30ml (2 tablespoons) cornflour (cornstarch)
15ml (1 tablespoon) drinking chocolate powder (cocoa powder mix)
225ml/8 fl oz (1 cup) milk
225ml/8 fl oz (1 cup) black coffee
75g/3 oz (⅓ cup) sugar
50g/2 oz (¼ cup) butter
60ml/4 tablespoons (¼ cup) crushed digestive biscuits (graham crackers)
60ml/4 tablespoons (¼ cup) rolled oats

Heat the oven to 160°C (325°F) gas mark 3. Combine the flour, cornflour (cornstarch) and chocolate (cocoa) powder with a little of the milk to make a paste. Put the rest of the milk in a saucepan with the coffee and 60ml (4 tablespoons) of the sugar. Heat, stirring, to dissolve the sugar. Stir a little of this hot liquid into the chocolate paste, then add this to the remaining liquid in the pan. Bring to the boil, stirring until thickened. Pour the custard into a baking dish.

Rub together the butter, biscuits (graham crackers), oats and remaining sugar and scatter over the coffee custard. Bake for 20 minutes. Serve hot or cold.
Cooking time: 30 minutes

Apple and Hazelnut Galette

This is an ideal dinner party dessert.

SERVES 8

FOR THE PASTRY

175g/6 oz (1¾ cups) plain flour
pinch of salt
50g//2 oz (½ cup) ground hazelnuts
100g/¼ lb (½ cup) butter, diced
125g/¼ lb (½ cup) sugar
4 medium-sized egg yolks
grated rind 1 lemon

FOR THE FILLING

450g (1 lb) dessert apples, peeled, cored and sliced
15ml (1 tablespoon) apricot jam
grated rind of 1 lemon
15ml (1 tablespoon) chopped candied peel
30ml (2 tablespoons) sultanas or raisins
30ml (2 tablespoons) currants

FOR THE DECORATION

icing (confectioners') sugar
150ml/¼ pt (⅔ cup) whipped cream
8 whole hazelnuts

Sift the flour, salt and ground hazelnuts into a large bowl and make a well in the centre. Put the butter, egg yolks, lemon rind and sugar in the centre. Work the ingredients together with your fingertips until incorporated in a dough. Knead the dough until smooth by pressing with the heel of your hand then gathering it up again into a ball. Put in the refrigerator to chill for 1 hour.

Meanwhile, to make the filling, put the apples in the pan with the apricot jam and lemon rind. Simmer until soft. Add the dried fruit, simmer 5 more minutes, then cool.

Heat the oven to 190°C (375°F) gas mark 5. Divide the pastry in half and roll out into two rounds about 23cm (9 in) in diameter. Bake on two greased baking sheets for 10 minutes. While still warm, cut one round into 8 portions. Leave the pastry to get cold.

Spread the cold purée over the whole pastry round, then top with the cut round. Sift powdered sugar over the top. Use a star nozzle to pipe a rosette of cream on each portion. Top each with a whole hazelnut.
Cooking time: 2 hours including cooling time

● The pastry can also be sandwiched together with well-blotted sliced, canned peaches and 175ml/6 fl oz (¾ cup) whipped thick cream.

Apple Tapioca Pudding

SERVES 4

450ml/16 fl oz (2 cups) milk
50g/2 oz (⅓ cup) tapioca
50g/2 oz (¼ cup) sugar
2.5ml (½ teaspoon) ground allspice
2.5ml (½ teaspoon) grated lemon rind
15g/½ oz (1 tablespoon) butter
2 eggs, separated
450g (1 lb) cooking apples, peeled, cored and chopped
50g/2 oz (⅓ cup) sultanas or raisins
1.5ml (¼ teaspoon) grated nutmeg
30ml (2 tablespoons) soft brown sugar
2 egg yolks

Heat the oven to 180°C (350°F) gas mark 4. Put the milk in a saucepan and heat. Just before it boils, sprinkle over the tapioca. Bring to the boil and cook, stirring frequently, for 10 minutes or until thickened. Stir in the sugar, allspice, lemon rind and butter and cook, stirring, until the sugar has dissolved. Cool mixture slightly.

Cover the bottom of a greased 1.7L/3 pt (2 qt) baking dish with the apples and sprinkle them with the sultanas or raisins, nutmeg and brown sugar. Beat the egg yolks into the tapioca mixture and spoon this over the apples.

Bake for 30–40 minutes or until the top has set and is golden brown.
Cooking time: 50–60 minutes

Spotted Dick

SERVES 6–8

225g/½ lb (2 cups) flour
5ml (1 teaspoon) salt
30ml (2 tablespoons) fine sugar
10ml (2 teaspoons) baking powder
pinch of ground cloves
75g/3 oz (⅓ cup) shredded suet
100g/¼ lb (⅔ cup) currants
50g/2 oz (⅓ cup) sultanas or raisins
90-120ml (6-8 tablespoons) water
90ml/6 tablespoons (⅓ cup) strawberry jam
45ml (3 tablespoons) milk

Sift the flour, salt, sugar, baking powder and cloves into a bowl. Stir in the suet, currants and sultanas or raisins. Gradually add the water, kneading, to make a light and pliable dough.

Roll out the dough to an oblong 6mm (¼ in) thick. Spread with the jam, leaving a 6mm (¼ in) border clear. Brush this border with the milk, then roll up like a swiss (jelly) roll, pressing the edges together to seal.

Wrap loosely in foil, twisting the ends to seal. Steam, standing on a wire rack in a covered pan, for 2½ hours, replenishing the water when necessary.
Cooking time: 3 hours

Apple and Mincemeat Pudding

SERVES 4

25g/1 oz (2 tablespoons) butter
15ml (1 tablespoon) oil
100g/¼ lb (1 cup) flour
1 large egg
275ml/½ pt (1¼ cups) milk
45ml (3 tablespoons) mincemeat
1 medium-sized cooking apple, peeled, cored and chopped

Heat the oven to 200°C (400°F) gas mark 6. Put the butter and oil in a 20cm (8 in) diameter 10cm (4 in) deep baking dish.

Put the dish in the oven to heat for 8 minutes. Sift the flour into a bowl. Make a well in the centre and add the egg and one-quarter of the milk. Beat well together, then gradually beat in the rest of the milk.

Spread the mincemeat and apple on the bottom of the hot, greased dish. Pour in the batter. Bake for 20 minutes, then reduce the temperature to 190°C (375°F) gas mark 5. Continue baking for 40 minutes or until the pudding is risen and golden.

Cooking time: 1¼ hours

● Use finely chopped dates with apples.

Chocolate suet sponge and chocolate sauce form hidden layers beneath the topping in this chocolate meringue suet pudding.

Chocolate Meringue Suet Pudding

SERVES 4
75g/3 oz (¾ cup) self-raising flour
25g/1 oz (¼ cup) cocoa powder
50g/2 oz (¼ cup) fine sugar
50g/2 oz (¼ cup) shredded suet
2 medium-sized egg yolks
60ml/4 tablespoons (¼ cup) milk
FOR THE SAUCE
15g/½ oz (1 tablespoon) butter
100g (¼ lb) plain (semi-sweet) chocolate (squares)
15ml (1 tablespoon) milk
FOR THE TOPPING
2 medium-sized egg whites
50g/2 oz (¼ cup) fine sugar
15ml (1 tablespoon) granulated sugar

Heat the oven to 200°C (400°F) gas mark 6. Sift the flour, cocoa and sugar into a bowl and stir in the suet. Add the egg yolks and milk and mix to a soft dropping consistency. Bake in a greased 575ml/1 pt (2½ cup) baking dish for 20 minutes.

Meanwhile, put all the sauce ingredients in a saucepan and heat gently, stirring, until melted and smooth.

Remove the cake base from the oven and pour over the sauce. Increase the temperature to 220°C (425°F) gas mark 7.

For the topping, beat the egg whites until stiff. Fold in the fine sugar. Spread the meringue topping on the sauce and draw up into peaks. Sprinkle with the granulated sugar.

Bake for a further 2–3 minutes or until lightly browned. Serve at once.

Cooking time: ½ hour

Cakes, Scones and Biscuits

Economical Fruit Cake

MAKES 10–12 SLICES

225g/½ lb (1 cup) margarine
225g/½ lb (1¼ cups) soft brown sugar
275g/10 oz (2½ cups) flour
2.5ml (½ teaspoon) bicarbonate of soda (baking soda)
5ml (1 teaspoon) mixed spice
pinch of grated nutmeg
grated rind of ½ lemon
4 large eggs
a few drops of vanilla extract
a few drops of almond extract
15ml (1 tablespoon) marmalade
100g/¼ lb (⅔ cup) currants
225g (½ lb) each raisins and sultanas or 450g (1 lb) raisins

Heat the oven to 150°C (300°F) gas mark 2. Grease and line a deep 20cm (8 in) cake tin (pan). Tie a double thickness of brown paper around it.

Cream the margarine and sugar together until light and fluffy. Sift in the flour, soda and spices and fold in, with the lemon rind. Beat the eggs with the extracts and marmalade and add to the creamed mixture. Fold in the fruit until evenly distributed.

Pour into the cake tin. Level the top and make a slight hollow in the centre.

Put a thick piece of newspaper on a baking sheet and place the cake tin on the sheet. Bake for 4 hours. When the cake colours, cover with foil. Cool in the tin.
Cooking time: 4¼ hours

Singin' Hinny

SERVES 8

350g/¾ lb (3 cups) flour
2.5ml (½ teaspoon) baking powder
50g/2 oz (½ cup) ground rice (rice flour)
5ml (1 teaspoon) salt
50g/2 oz (¼ cup) butter
50g/2 oz (¼ cup) fine sugar
75g/3 oz (½ cup) currants
275ml/½ pt (1¼ cups) mixed thin cream and milk (half and half)

Sift the flour, baking powder, rice (rice flour) and salt into a bowl. Rub in the butter until the mixture resembles breadcrumbs. Stir in the sugar and currants, then gradually work in the liquid to make a soft but not sticky dough.

Knead the dough quickly and lightly. Roll out to a 23cm (9 in) circle that is 6mm (¼ in) thick.

Lightly grease a griddle or heavy-bottomed frying pan and heat very gently until really hot. Place the singin' hinny on the griddle and cook for 4–5 minutes or until risen and brown on the underside.

Turn over and cook for a further 4–5 minutes. Serve, cut into wedges, with butter.
Cooking time: about 15 minutes

Brandy Snaps

Inexpensive but elegant, brandy snaps can be filled with cream, plus a single crystallized fruit if you wish, for a party dessert.

MAKES 12

50g/2 oz (3 tablespoons) golden syrup or honey
50g/2 oz (¼ cup) fine sugar
50g/2 oz (¼ cup) butter
5ml (1 teaspoon) brandy (optional)
2.5ml (½ teaspoon) ground ginger
grated rind of ½ lemon
50g/2 oz (½ cup) plain flour

Heat the oven to 180°C (350°F) gas mark 4. Line two baking sheets with greaseproof or waxed paper and oil them. Put the syrup (honey), sugar and butter in a saucepan and heat gently, stirring until melted and well blended. Remove from the heat and stir in the brandy, ginger and lemon rind. Sift in the flour and fold in thoroughly.

Drop small spoonfuls of the mixture on to the lined baking sheets. Leave at least 10cm (4 in) between each brandy snap. Bake in two batches for 8 minutes each.

Working quickly while the brandy

Christmas cake does not have to be expensive: economical fruit cake is ideal when suitably decorated.

snaps are warm and malleable, shape them by rolling them, one at a time, around the oiled handle of a wooden spoon. If they become too crisp to roll, return them to the oven for a few minutes. Cool the rolled biscuits (cookies) on a wire rack.
Cooking time: 20 minutes

Apple Cakes

MAKES 36	
275g/10 oz (2½ cups) self-raising flour	
10ml (2 teaspoons) baking powder	
7.5ml (1½ teaspoons) ground cinnamon	
150g/5 oz (⅔ cup) soft margarine	
225g/½ lb (1 cup) fine sugar	
2 medium-sized eggs	
275ml/½ pt (1¼ cups) thick unsweetened apple purée or sauce	
25g/1 oz (3 tablespoons) raisins	
2 red-skinned apples, cored and thinly sliced	
lemon juice	

Heat the oven to 180°C (350°F) gas mark 4. Sift the flour, baking powder and cinnamon into a bowl. Add the margarine, sugar, eggs and apple purée (sauce) and beat until smooth. Fold in the raisins.

Divide the batter between 36 paper cases and place them on baking sheets. Bake for 20–25 minutes. Cool on a wire rack.

Dip the apple slices in lemon juice to prevent discoloration and use to decorate the cakes (see picture on *page 118*).
Cooking time: 45 minutes

Chocolate and Orange Cake

SERVES 6–8	
350g/¾ lb (3 cups) flour	
1.5ml (¼ teaspoon) salt	
10ml (2 heaped teaspoons) baking powder	
4 eggs	
175g/6 oz (¾ cup) fine sugar	
100g/¼ lb (½ cup) butter, melted	
finely grated rind of 2 oranges	
125ml/4 fl oz (½ cup) orange juice	
FOR THE BUTTERCREAM	
100g (4 oz) dark (unsweetened) chocolate, broken into pieces	
100g/¼ lb (½ cup) unsalted butter	
350g/¾ lb (3⅓ cups) icing (confectioners') sugar, sifted	
45ml (3 tablespoons) thick cream	

This chocolate and orange cake is filled and topped with a luscious chocolate-flavoured buttercream icing (frosting).

Heat the oven to 180°C (350°F) gas mark 4. Sift the flour, salt and baking powder. Beat the eggs and sugar together until frothy. Fold in the flour. Gradually beat in the butter, orange rind and orange juice.

Divide the cake mixture between two greased 20–23cm (8–9 in) sandwich tins (cake pans). Bake for 20–25 minutes or until the cakes spring back when lightly pressed in the centres. Cool 5 minutes in the tin then turn out onto a wire rack.

Meanwhile, make the buttercream. Melt the chocolate in a heavy-bottomed saucepan over low heat. Remove from the heat. Cream the butter with half the sugar, then beat in the melted chocolate and the cream. Gradually work in the rest of the icing (confectioners') sugar.

Sandwich the cold cakes together with about one-third of the buttercream, then use the remainder to cover the top and sides of the cake, fluffing up the cream decoratively.
Cooking time: 40 minutes plus cooling time

Nutty Fruit Scones

These scones (biscuits) will help to fill up a hungry party of children at the end of an afternoon. Bake half this quantity for one family.

MAKES ABOUT 30 SMALL SCONES
450g/1 lb (4 cups) flour
20ml (4 teaspoons) baking powder
5ml (1 teaspoon) salt
175g/6 oz (¾ cup) butter
50g/2 oz (¼ cup) fine sugar
225g (½ lb) sultanas or raisins
50g/2 oz (½ cup) flaked almonds
2 medium-sized eggs
about 60ml/4 tablespoons (¼ cup) milk
beaten egg to glaze

Heat the oven to 220°C (425°F) gas mark 7. Sift the flour, baking powder and salt into a bowl. Rub in the butter until the mixture resembles breadcrumbs. Stir in the sugar, fruit and half the almonds. Mix in the eggs with enough milk to bind to a soft dough.

Knead the dough until it is smooth and elastic. Roll out to about 12mm (½ in) thick, then cut into 5cm (2 in) circles. Place the circles on a baking sheet and glaze with beaten egg. Top with the rest of the almonds. Bake for 15 minutes and serve warm.
Cooking time: 25 minutes

● For quick family fruit scones, sift 225g/ ½ lb (2 cups) self-raising flour with 2.5ml (½ teaspoon) salt. Rub in 50g/2 oz (4 tablespoons) butter and stir in 25g/1 oz (1 tablespoon) fine sugar, 50g/2 oz (⅓ cup) dried fruit and about 150ml/¼ pt (⅔ cup) of milk. Pat into two rounds. Glaze with 15ml (1 tablespoon) honey and cut almost through to make each one into 4 wedges. Bake for 20 minutes.

Sponge Fingers

Quick to bake and put on the table, sponge fingers contain no butter and are therefore very cheap to make. Home-made sponge fingers can be used to line moulds for puddings, for trifles and, of course, as a snack.

MAKES ABOUT 30
3 medium-sized eggs, separated
65g/2½ oz (⅓ cup) fine sugar
few drops vanilla extract
65g/2½ oz (⅔ cup) flour
fine sugar to finish

Heat the oven to 180°C (350°F) gas mark 4. Grease 2 baking sheets and then dust well with flour and shake off the excess.

Cream egg yolks with the sugar until light and add the vanilla. Beat again. Whisk egg whites until stiff. Add a big spoonful of the whites to the creamed mixture, sifting over a little flour. Fold in. Continue folding egg white and flour together until all is incorporated. Put into a piping bag with an éclair nozzle and pipe out fingers on the baking sheet about 7.5cm (3 in) long, allowing 2.5cm (1 in) space between them. Sprinkle fine sugar along the top of each finger from a teaspoon. Bake 15–20 minutes until risen but firm. Remove with a flat knife and pack in an airtight container.
Cooking time: 20 minutes

● To serve sponge fingers as cakes, sandwich them with whipped cream or butter cream, then dip one end of each finger in melted chocolate then in chopped nuts. Allow to cool until set.
● The mixture may also be piped in circles. Sandwich these together with any of the following: bramble or other jelly, lemon curd, buttercream (*page 248*) or whipped, sweetened cream, flavoured with vanilla.

Chocolate Eclairs

Choux pastry beats even meringues as the cheapest form of pâtisserie. Two eggs and minute quantities of flour and butter can be turned into 8 large éclairs, for less money than you could buy a single one in a shop. The ingredients are so cheap that you can afford to experiment without having a special occasion.

French pastry cream is the traditional filling and this, too, is cheap; but you can use whipped cream if you prefer. If you do not have a piping nozzle, make buns instead of éclairs; dot the mixture in tablespoonfuls on the baking sheet.

MAKES 8
choux pastry (*page 244*)
425ml/¾ pt (1⅔ cups) confectioners' custard (*page 248*) OR 150ml/¼ pt (⅔ cup) thick cream whipped with 15ml (1 tablespoon) milk, 2 drops of vanilla extract and 5ml (1 teaspoon) fine sugar
25g/1 oz (2 tablespoons) fine sugar
75ml (5 tablespoons) water
75g (3 oz) plain (semi-sweet) chocolate

Heat the oven to 200°C (400°F) gas mark 6. Grease a baking sheet then dust with flour and shake off the excess.

Make the choux pastry (*page 244*) and fit an éclair nozzle to a piping bag. Stand the piping bag in a tumbler and pull back the wide part of the cloth bag outside the glass (see picture on *page 117*). Then fill the bag with choux pastry.

Pipe 8 éclairs on the baking sheet 10cm (4 in) long, allowing at least 2.5cm (1 in) between them. Bake in the top of the oven for 20 minutes, then reduce the temperature to 190°C (375°F) gas mark 5 and bake for a further 15 minutes.

Slit along the side of each éclair with a grapefruit knife and use the tip to scrape out any pastry inside that is still soft. Leave to cool.

Fill the cold éclairs, spooning in confectioners' custard or Chantilly cream, made by whipping the thick cream, with the milk and vanilla extract until it will hold its shape, then folding in the sugar.

For the topping, dissolve the fine sugar in the water and bring to the boil. Boil for 2 minutes without stirring. Meanwhile melt the chocolate in a wide bowl over hot water. Pour in the sugar syrup and stir. Hold the éclairs over the bowl and spoon chocolate over the top of each one. Allow excess chocolate to drip off. Leave on a plate to set. Refrigerate and serve within 5 hours.
Cooking time: 1 hour

Cheese Scones

MAKES 12–14
225g/½ lb (2 cups) flour
1.5ml (¼ teaspoon) salt
5 ml (1 teaspoon) dry mustard
20ml (4 teaspoons) baking powder
50g/2 oz (¼ cup) butter
100g/¼ lb (1 cup) Cheddar cheese, grated
about 150ml/¼ pt (⅔ cup) milk
milk for glazing

Heat the oven to 230°C (450°F) gas mark 8. Sift the flour, salt, mustard and baking powder into a bowl. Rub in the butter until the mixture resembles breadcrumbs. Stir in the cheese, then mix in enough of the milk to make a soft dough. Knead until smooth.

Roll out the dough to about 12mm (½ in) thick. Cut out 5cm (2 in) circles and place them on greased baking sheets. Brush each scone with milk and bake for 12–15 minutes. Cool on a wire rack.
Cooking time: 20–25 minutes

Rock Cakes

MAKES 6–8

225g/½ lb (2 cups) flour

10ml (2 teaspoons) baking powder

pinch of salt

2.5ml (½ teaspoon) mixed spice

2.5ml (½ teaspoon) grated nutmeg

50g/2 oz (¼ cup) butter

25g/1 oz (2 tablespoons) lard

75g/3 oz (½ cup) soft brown sugar

25g/1 oz (2 tablespoons) chopped mixed candied peel

75g/3 oz (½ cup) mixed dried fruit

grated rind of ½ lemon

1 medium-sized egg

milk

Heat the oven to 200°C (400°F) gas mark 6. Sift the flour, baking powder, salt and spices into a bowl. Rub in the fats until the mixture resembles breadcrumbs. Stir in the sugar, peel, dried fruit and lemon rind.

Add the egg and just enough milk to bind the mixture. It should be stiff. Divide the mixture into 6–8 portions and shape each into a slightly flattened ball. Place these on a greased baking sheet, 4cm (1½ in) apart.

Bake for 15 minutes or until pale golden brown and firm. Cool on a wire rack.

Cooking time: 20 minutes plus cooling time

The traditional shape for Scottish shortbread is known as 'petticoat tail': a triangular slice with a pretty fluted edge. In Scotland it is also made in special wooden moulds.

Scottish Shortbread

SERVES 6–8

100g/¼ lb (1 cup) flour

50g/2 oz (½ cup) rice flour

pinch of salt

50g/2 oz (¼ cup) fine sugar

100g/¼ lb (½ cup) butter

fine sugar to dredge

Heat the oven to 160°C (325°F) gas mark 3. Sift the flour, rice flour, salt and sugar into a bowl. Cut the fat into the flour, then knead the mixture to form a smooth dough. Press into a shortbread mould or 18cm (7 in) sandwich tin (cake pan) dusted with rice flour; then turn out onto a greased baking sheet.

If you used a tin (cake pan), flute the edges to make a frilly effect. Mark the shortbread into portions with a sharp knife. Bake for 45 minutes or until pale golden and firm. Cool on a wire rack, then dredge with fine sugar.

Cooking time: 50 minutes plus cooling time

Irish Soda Bread

This emergency bread can be made and consumed within 1 hour. Buttermilk can usually be obtained at health food shops and delicatessens.

MAKES 1 LARGE LOAF

700g/1½ lb (6 cups) flour

5ml (1 teaspoon) salt

10ml (2 teaspoons) bicarbonate of soda (baking soda)

25g/1 oz (2 tablespoons) margarine or lard

275ml/½ pt (1¼ cups) buttermilk or milk soured with 5ml (1 teaspoon) lemon juice

milk for glazing

Heat the oven to 200°C (400°F) gas mark 6. Sift the flour, salt and soda into a bowl. Rub in the fat until the mixture resembles breadcrumbs. Make a well in the centre and pour in the buttermilk or sour milk. Mix together with a knife, then lightly press the mixture together with your fingertips and shape into a ball.

Place the ball on a floured baking sheet and flatten slightly. Cut a deep cross on the top, then brush with a little milk.

Bake for 30–35 minutes or until the bread is risen and golden brown. Cool for at least 15 minutes before serving with butter.

Cooking time: 1 hour

Stews and Casseroles

The attraction of a stew or casserole, apart from its warming, stick-to-the-ribs qualities in the chill of winter, must be its convenience. Stews and casseroles are the epitome of one-pot cookery, and most can be left to cook while you get on with other things. Long, slow cooking also transforms less expensive, tougher meat into succulent, tender morsels.

Strictly speaking, a stew is cooked in a saucepan on top of the stove, whereas a casserole is baked in the oven. But the same principles of preparation apply to both.

For very tough, sinewy meat, such as beef shin or leg and lamb middle neck or scrag, the cold-start method of preparation is best. Cut the meat into chunks or strips, so that a large percentage of the surface area is exposed to the liquid, and remove all possible fat. Put the meat in a heavy-based saucepan or casserole and add vegetables, herbs, liquid and seasoning as specified in the recipe. Bring to the boil if stewing, or place in the preheated oven for a casserole. This is the ideal method of cooking tougher forms of offal and also pulses.

Less tough cuts of meat, such as beef clod (shoulder), sticking (sirloin tip), chuck, blade or skirt, lamb breast or shoulder, pork belly or hand (picnic shoulder) and stewing veal, and poultry and game are usually browned in fat before the prolonged cooking begins. This is called the fry-start method, and gives the dish a richer, more savoury flavour than the cold-start method. The meat is usually cut into chunks and then may be coated in seasoned flour before browning. The advantage of the flour is that the meat is really dry and so browns easily.

With the fry-start method, onions, if used, are also browned first. This is very important to the colour and flavour of the finished stew or casserole. Other vegetables may also be browned.

Careful heat control is necessary when stewing and casseroling. On top of the stove, keep the liquid at a gentle simmer—if the liquid is allowed to boil it will evaporate and the meat will shrink and toughen. Oven heat is easier to control, but ovens may vary, so inspect the casserole to be sure it is not bubbling hard. If it is, reduce the temperature. For both stewing and casseroling, use a pan, dutch oven or casserole with a tight-fitting lid to minimize the evaporation of the liquid during cooking.

At the end of the cooking, remove any fat from the surface of the stew or casserole using a skimmer, an ice cube to quickly reduce the temperature, or blot with absorbent paper.

Most stews and casseroles can be reheated; some are even improved in flavour. You can prepare them a day ahead, or enjoy the leftovers, or make two at the same time and freeze the one you do not need. In the latter case, add any cream or sour cream after thawing and reheating.

Beef stew with a rich sauce of herbs and walnuts is the first recipe of winter casseroles, given overleaf on page 226.

Stewing or Casseroling Meat

1. For very tough, sinewy meat, such as beef shin (shank) or leg and lamb middle neck or scrag (neck slices), use the cold-start method. Cut into 2.5cm (1 in) cubes.

2. Put the meat in a casserole with the vegetables, herbs and seasonings. Cover with cold liquid—up to 275ml/$\frac{1}{2}$ pt (1$\frac{1}{4}$ cups) per 450g (1 lb) meat. Season well.

3. Bring to the boil, cover tightly then lower the heat or transfer to the oven. Simmer gently, checking periodically; stew until tender—several hours.

4. For less tough cuts of meat, use the fry-start method. Cut the meat into 4cm (1$\frac{1}{2}$ in) cubes and shake in a bag with seasoned flour. Shake off excess flour.

5. Heat fat in a flameproof casserole or dutch oven. When very hot, add meat in batches and fry until browned all over. Remove from pot and keep warm.

6. Turn down the heat and fry chopped onions gently until softened. Stir in seasoned flour and cook gently, stirring continuously to make a brown roux.

7. Stir in the warmed stock gradually, off the heat. Return to the heat and bring to a boil, stirring constantly until the liquid thickens. Add herbs and flavourings.

8. Return meat to pot. Cover tightly. Lower heat and simmer on stove or transfer to low oven. Cook for 2–2$\frac{1}{2}$ hours until tender. Add vegetables after 1 hour.

9. Skim off any surface fat with a skimmer, or blot with absorbent paper or a slice of bread. Check meat is cooked, taste and adjust seasoning, then serve.

225

Beef Stew with Herbs and Walnuts

SERVES 6–8

| 1.4kg (3 lb) skirt (flank) steak, cut into 2.5cm (1 in) cubes |
| 75ml (5 tablespoons) seasoned flour |
| 50g/2 oz ($\frac{1}{4}$ cup) butter |
| 30ml (2 tablespoons) oil |
| 3 medium-sized onions, sliced |
| 2 garlic cloves, crushed |
| 1 large green (bell) pepper, cored, seeded and chopped |
| 50g/2 oz ($\frac{1}{2}$ cup) walnuts, finely chopped |
| 30ml (2 tablespoons) chopped parsley |
| 2.5ml ($\frac{1}{2}$ teaspoon) dried oregano |
| 2.5ml ($\frac{1}{2}$ teaspoon) dried thyme |
| 2 bay leaves |
| salt and freshly ground black pepper |
| 450ml/16 fl oz (2 cups) beef stock |
| 30ml (2 tablespoons) tomato paste |

Coat the steak cubes in the seasoned flour. Melt the butter with the oil in a saucepan. Add the steak cubes, in batches, and brown on all sides. Remove the steak cubes from the pan as they brown.

Add the onions, garlic and green pepper to the pan, with a little more oil if necessary, and fry until softened. Stir in the walnuts, herbs, seasoning, stock and tomato paste and bring to the boil.

Return the steak cubes to the pan and stir well, then cover the pan and simmer for 1$\frac{1}{2}$ hours or until the steak cubes are tender.
Cooking time: 2 hours

Liver, Bacon and Apple Hotpot

SERVES 4

| 700g (1$\frac{1}{2}$ lb) cooking apples, peeled, cored and thinly sliced |
| 2 medium-sized onions, thinly sliced |
| 700g (1$\frac{1}{2}$ lb) ox (beef) liver, thickly sliced and soaked overnight |
| 400g (14 oz) canned tomatoes, coarsely chopped |
| salt and freshly ground black pepper |
| 150ml/$\frac{1}{4}$ pt ($\frac{2}{3}$ cup) beef stock |
| 4 back bacon slices |

Heat the oven to 180°C (350°F) gas mark 4. Put about one-third of the apple and onion slices on the bottom of a casserole. Cover with half the drained liver slices, then half the tomatoes with their liquid. Season. Repeat the layers and finish with the rest of the apple and onion slices. Pour

in the stock and place the bacon on top. Cover the casserole and bake for 1$\frac{1}{2}$ hours.
Cooking time: overnight soaking, then 1 hour 35 minutes

French Rabbit Stew

SERVES 6

| 1.4kg (3 lb) rabbit, cut into serving pieces |
| 225g ($\frac{1}{2}$ lb) fatty bacon slices, cut into 5cm (2 in) strips |
| 2 medium-sized onions, sliced |
| 1 garlic clove, finely chopped |
| 3 large carrots, sliced |
| 15ml (1 tablespoon) Dijon mustard |
| FOR THE MARINADE |
| 225ml/8 fl oz (1 cup) dry white wine or dry cider |
| 225ml/8 fl oz (1 cup) chicken stock |
| 15ml (1 tablespoon) oil |
| 6 black peppercorns |
| 2 parsley sprigs |
| 1 bay leaf |
| 2 garlic cloves, crushed |
| 2.5ml ($\frac{1}{2}$ teaspoon) dried thyme |
| 5ml (1 teaspoon) salt |

Combine the marinade ingredients in a shallow dish. Add the rabbit pieces and turn to coat. Marinate for 12 hours, turning occasionally.

Heat the oven to moderate 180°C (350°F) gas mark 4. Drain the rabbit pieces and pat dry with absorbent paper. Strain the marinade and reserve. Fry the bacon strips in a flameproof casserole (dutch oven) until they have rendered most of their fat. Remove them from the pan. Add the rabbit pieces and fry until

A marinade of cider, carrots and mustard makes a rich sauce for French rabbit stew.

browned on all sides. Remove from pot.

Add the onions, garlic and carrots to the pan (with a little oil if necessary) and fry until softened. Stir in the reserved marinade and the mustard and bring to the boil. Return the rabbit pieces and bacon to the pot, cover and transfer to the oven. Simmer for 1 hour or until tender.
Cooking time: 12 hours marinating, then 1$\frac{1}{2}$ hours

Lamb and Kidney Hotpot

SERVES 4

| 700g (1$\frac{1}{2}$ lb) potatoes, thinly sliced |
| 700g (1$\frac{1}{2}$ lb) middle neck of lamb, cut into pieces and trimmed of excess fat |
| 2-4 lambs' kidneys, skinned, cored and halved |
| 1 large onion, thinly sliced |
| salt and freshly ground black pepper |
| 275ml/$\frac{1}{2}$ pt (1$\frac{1}{4}$ cups) chicken stock |
| 25g/1 oz (2 tablespoons) butter |

Heat the oven to 160°C (325°F) gas mark 3. Make alternate layers of potatoes, lamb, kidneys and onion in a casserole, beginning and ending with potato slices. Season each layer. Pour in the stock. Dot the top layer of potatoes with the butter. Cover the casserole tightly and bake for 1$\frac{1}{2}$ hours.

Uncover the pot and cook for a further 30 minutes or until the meat is tender and the top layer of potato is golden brown.
Cooking time: 2 hours

German Beef Stew with Dumplings

SERVES 4

90ml (6 tablespoons) oil

700g (1½ lb) chuck steak, cut into 2.5cm (1 in) cubes

450ml/16 fl oz (2 cups) beef stock

1 bay leaf

5ml (1 teaspoon) vinegar

salt

freshly ground black pepper

4 medium-sized potatoes, cubed

2 large onions, thinly sliced

chopped parsley to garnish

FOR THE DUMPLINGS

225g/½ lb (2 cups) flour

5ml (1 teaspoon) salt

pinch of grated nutmeg

2 eggs, beaten

175ml/6 fl oz (¾ cup) milk

Heat 60ml (4 tablespoons) of the oil in a saucepan. Add the beef cubes and brown on all sides. Add the stock, bay leaf, vinegar and seasoning and stir well. Bring to the boil, then cover the pan and simmer for 30 minutes. Add the potatoes and simmer for a further 45 minutes or until the meat is tender.

Meanwhile, make the dumplings. Sift the flour, salt and nutmeg into a bowl. Beat in the eggs, then gradually beat in the milk to make a smooth batter. Set aside for 10 minutes.

Drop walnut-sized spoonfuls of the dumpling batter into a pan of boiling water. After the dumplings rise to the surface, cook them for 3 minutes. Drain well. Stir the dumplings into the stew and cook for a further 10 minutes. Meanwhile, heat the rest of the oil in a frying-pan. Add the onions and fry until golden brown. Drain. Garnish the stew with the onions and chopped parsley.

Cooking time: 1 hour 45 minutes

Jamaican Beef Stew

SERVES 6

1.4kg (3 lb) stewing beef, cut into 2.5cm (1 in) cubes

50g/2 oz (½ cup) seasoned flour

50g/2 oz (¼ cup) butter

60ml/4 tablespoons (¼ cup) oil

2 onions, thinly sliced

1 green chilli, seeded and finely chopped

1 garlic clove, chopped

5ml (1 teaspoon) ground ginger

400g (14 oz) canned tomatoes

2.5ml (½ teaspoon) dried thyme

Coat the beef cubes with the seasoned flour. Melt the butter with the oil in a saucepan. Add the steak cubes, in batches, and brown on all sides. Keep the browned cubes warm.

Classic dumplings, potatoes and onions extend the beef in this German stew.

Add the onions, chilli, garlic and ginger to the pan and fry until the onions are softened. Return the beef cubes to the pan and stir in the thyme and the tomatoes with their liquid. Break up the tomatoes with the spoon. Cover and simmer very gently for 3 hours or until the meat is tender.

Cooking time: 3½ hours

● Pork may be used instead of beef.

Beef, Sausage and Bean Casserole

SERVES 8

450g (1 lb) dried blackeyed peas, soaked overnight

1.4L/2½ pt (6 cups) water

15ml (1 tablespoon) oil

450g (1 lb) pork sausages, cut into 2.5cm (1 in) pieces

2 large onions, finely chopped

2 garlic cloves, crushed

900g (2 lb) chuck steak, cut into 2.5cm (1 in) cubes

1 bay leaf

2.5ml (½ teaspoon) dried savory or sage

1.5ml (¼ teaspoon) dried marjoram

4 large tomatoes, skinned, seeded and chopped

175ml/6 fl oz (¾ cup) beef stock

salt

freshly ground black pepper

Drain the beans and put into a saucepan with the measured water. Bring to the boil, then lower the heat and simmer for ½ hour while preparing the meat. Drain the beans, reserving 350ml/12 fl oz (1½ cups) of the cooking liquid.

Heat the oven to 150°C (300°F) gas mark 2. Heat the oil in a frying-pan. Add the sausage pieces and fry until browned on all sides. Remove from the pan and put on one side. Pour off all but 45ml (3 tablespoons) of the fat from the pan. Add the onions and garlic and fry until softened. Transfer them to a casserole.

Add the steak cubes to the frying-pan and brown on all sides. Add to the casserole, then stir in the herbs, tomatoes and stock. Season to taste. Cover the casserole and cook in the oven for 2 hours.

Add the beans with the reserved cooking liquid and the sausage pieces to the casserole and mix well. Cook in the oven for a further 1 hour or until the steak cubes are tender.

Cooking time: 3½ hours

Beer Beef Pot Roast

SERVES 6–8

1.8kg (4 lb) silverside of beef (sirloin tip roast), rolled and tied
salt
freshly ground black pepper
60ml/4 tablespoons ($\frac{1}{4}$ cup) oil
4 leeks, thinly sliced
6 medium-sized parsnips, sliced
850ml/1$\frac{1}{2}$ pt (3$\frac{3}{4}$ cups) beef stock
1 bouquet garni
225ml/8 fl oz (1 cup) beer
7.5ml (1$\frac{1}{2}$ teaspoons) butter
7.5ml (1$\frac{1}{2}$ teaspoons) flour
parsley sprigs to garnish

Rub the beef all over with salt and pepper. Heat the oil in a heavy saucepan. Add the beef and brown on all sides. Put half the leeks and parsnips around the beef and cook for 8 minutes.

Pour in the stock and bring to the boil. Add the bouquet garni. Cover the pan and simmer for 2$\frac{1}{2}$–3 hours or until the beef is tender.

Remove the beef from the pan and keep warm. Skim any fat from the cooking liquid and strain into a clean saucepan. Add the remaining vegetables and bring to the boil. Boil for 20–25 minutes or until the liquid has reduced by half. Stir in the beer and return to the boil.

Mash together the butter and flour. Add a little of the hot liquid, then stir this mixture into the remaining liquid in the pan. Simmer, stirring, until thickened.

Carve the meat into thick slices and arrange on a warmed serving platter. Pour over the sauce and garnish with parsley.
Cooking time: 3$\frac{1}{4}$–3$\frac{3}{4}$ hours

● Root vegetables such as carrots, swedes or turnips may be used instead of the leeks and parsnips.

Pork, apples and sage are topped with a creamy ring of mashed potatoes.

Pork and Apple Casserole

SERVES 4–6

900g (2 lb) boned lean pork, cubed
2 medium-sized onions, chopped
2.5ml ($\frac{1}{2}$ teaspoon) dried sage
salt
freshly ground black pepper
2 medium-sized cooking apples, peeled, cored and thinly sliced
45ml (3 tablespoons) water
700g (1$\frac{1}{2}$ lb) potatoes
30ml (2 tablespoons) hot milk
25g/1 oz (2 tablespoons) butter

Heat the oven to 180°C (350°F) gas mark 4. Put about one-third of the pork cubes on the bottom of a greased casserole. Combine the onions, sage and seasoning to taste and sprinkle about one-third of this over the pork. Cover with one-third of the apple slices. Continue making layers in this way until the ingredients are used up. Sprinkle over the water.

Cover the casserole and cook in the oven for 2–2½ hours or until the pork is tender.

About 30 minutes before the pork is cooked, cook the potatoes in boiling salted water until tender. Drain well, then mash. Beat in the milk and butter with seasoning.

Spread the mashed potatoes over the pork mixture, roughing it up attractively with a fork. Return to the oven, uncovered, and cook for a further 15 minutes or until the potato topping is golden brown.

Cooking time: 2¼–2¾ hours

Hare in Sweet and Sour Sauce

SERVES 6
1 hare 1.8-2.3kg (4-5 lb) when skinned and paunched, cut into serving pieces
20ml (4 teaspoons) salt
50g/2 oz (½ cup) flour
2.5ml (½ teaspoon) black pepper
50g/2 oz (¼ cup) butter
15ml (1 tablespoon) olive oil
2 onions, finely chopped
2 carrots, scraped and sliced
bouquet garni
850ml/1½ pt (3¾ cups) beef stock
100g/¼ lb (¼ cup) canned cranberry sauce
175ml/6 fl oz (¾ cup) red wine

Place the hare pieces in a large mixing bowl. Cover the meat with cold water and add three-quarters of the salt. Leave the meat to soak for at least 1 hour. Drain the hare pieces in a colander and dry them thoroughly with absorbent paper. Dip the meat in seasoned flour to coat the pieces thoroughly on all sides. Shake off any excess flour.

Heat the oven to 170°C (325°F) gas mark 3. In a large flame-proof casserole (dutch oven), melt the butter with the oil over moderate heat. When the foam subsides, add the hare pieces in two batches and cook them quickly for 3–5 minutes, or until they are evenly browned on all sides. Remove the meat from the pan and set it aside.

Add the onions and carrots to the casserole and cook them, stirring occasionally, for 5–7 minutes, or until the onions are soft and translucent but not brown.

Replace the hare pieces in the pan and add the bouquet garni and the remaining salt and pepper. Pour in the stock and bring it to the boil. Cover the pan and transfer it to the oven. Simmer for 2½ hours, or until the hare is very tender when pierced with the point of a sharp knife.

Remove the pan from the oven. With tongs, remove the meat from the pan and place the pieces on a warmed dish. Keep them warm.

Strain the cooking juices into a measuring jug (cup). Pour 425ml/¾ pt (2 cups) back into the casserole and reserve the rest for soup. Add the cranberry sauce and wine. Heat gently then simmer for 5 minutes, stirring occasionally. Taste and add more salt and pepper if necessary.

Return the hare pieces to the pan and immerse in the sauce. Return the pan to the oven and simmer for a further 20 minutes.

Cooking time: 4½–4¾ hours

Pork and Bean Stew

SERVES 6
450g (1 lb) dried white haricot (navy) beans, soaked overnight and drained
60ml/4 tablespoons (¼ cup) oil
900g (2 lb) lean pork, cut into 5cm (2 in) cubes
2 medium-sized carrots, sliced
2 small turnips, quartered
2 medium-sized onions, sliced
2 garlic cloves, crushed
5ml (1 teaspoon) paprika
5ml (1 teaspoon) dried basil
salt and freshly ground black pepper
150g/5 oz (⅔ cup) tomato paste
575ml/1 pt (2½ cups) chicken stock

Put the beans into a saucepan, cover with fresh water and bring to the boil. Simmer for 1 hour.

Meanwhile, heat the oil in a frying pan. Add the pork cubes, in batches, and brown on all sides. Stir in the carrots, turnips, onions, garlic, paprika, basil and seasoning and cook for a further 5 minutes.

Drain the beans and return them to the saucepan. Stir in the pork mixture, the tomato paste and stock and bring to the boil. Cover the pan and simmer for 3½ hours or until pork and beans are tender.

Cooking time: overnight soaking, then 4½ hours

Cranberry sauce and wine mellow the strong flavour of hare for this distinctive dish.

Cassoulet

This traditional French casserole makes a warming two-meal dish for 4–5. It is also one of those convenient dishes that will wait in the oven for up to 2 extra hours without spoiling.

SERVES 8–10

550g/1¼ lb (2½ cups) dried haricot (navy) beans, soaked overnight

225g (½ lb) onions, chopped

6 large garlic cloves, halved

about 2.8L/5 pt (3 qt) unsalted stock

1 bay leaf

salt

freshly ground black pepper

350g (¾ lb) belly of pork or salt pork cut into 2.5cm (1 in) slices

450g (1 lb) boned shoulder of lamb, cubed

1 bouquet garni

400g (14 oz) canned tomatoes

225g (½ lb) salami, skinned and thickly sliced

30ml (2 tablespoons) tomato paste

175g/6 oz (3 cups) fresh breadcrumbs

5ml (1 teaspoon) dried oregano

5ml (1 teaspoon) dried thyme

Drain the beans and measure them in a measuring jug or cup. Pour them into a flameproof casserole (dutch oven) and stir in the onions and garlic. Measure the stock in the measuring jug (cup) and add twice the volume of beans to the casserole. Add the bay leaf and bring to the boil. Cover and simmer for 1 hour.

Heat the oven to 150°C (300°F) gas mark 2. Drain the beans and vegetables.

Season the bean mixture well and put a layer on the bottom of the pan. Cover with the pork, then make another layer of beans. Add the lamb and bouquet garni, then another layer of beans.

Break up the tomatoes with a fork, then add to the casserole with a little stock. Cover with the salami, then the remaining beans. Mix the tomato paste with a little stock and pour over the top. Add enough of the remaining stock to bring the liquid level with the top of the beans.

Combine the breadcrumbs and herbs and sprinkle half over the top layer of beans. Bake for 3 hours, checking the liquid level from time to time and adding more of the stock if necessary.

Push the crust that will have formed down into the beans, then sprinkle with the remaining breadcrumb mixture. Bake for a further 30 minutes.

Cooking time: overnight soaking and 1 hour cooking, then 3½ hours

Braised Oxtail with Celery

SERVES 6

2 oxtails, cut into pieces

10ml (2 teaspoons) salt

2.5ml (½ teaspoon) black pepper

50g/2 oz (½ cup) flour

75ml (5 tablespoons) olive oil

1 large onion, finely chopped

2 garlic cloves, finely chopped

175ml/6 fl oz (¾ cup) dry red wine

200ml/7 fl oz (1 cup) beef stock

400g (14 oz) canned tomatoes, coarsely chopped

30ml (2 tablespoons) tomato paste

1 bouquet garni

1 bunch celery, outer stalks discarded, washed and coarsely chopped

425ml/¾ pt (2 cups) boiling water

10ml (2 teaspoons) cornflour (cornstarch) dissolved in 15ml (1 tablespoon) cold water

Heat the oven to 170°C (325°F) gas mark 3. Sprinkle the oxtail pieces with seasoned flour. In a large frying-pan, heat half the oil over high heat. Brown the oxtail pieces evenly on all sides for 3–4 minutes. Transfer the oxtail to a large flameproof casserole (dutch oven) with tongs or a slotted spoon.

Add the rest of the oil to the pan. Add the onion, garlic and remaining salt and, stirring frequently, fry them over moderate heat for 5–6 minutes or until they are soft. Add the red wine to the pan. Increase the heat and boil the liquid until it has reduced by half, stirring occasionally.

Add the beef stock and cook for 1–2 minutes. Pour the onions and liquid over the oxtail in the pan. Using a wooden spoon, mix the tomatoes and their liquid, tomato paste and bouquet garni into the casserole. Bring to the boil over high heat. Remove the pan from the heat, cover and place it in the oven. Braise for 3½ hours.

Just before the end of this time, blanch the chopped celery in the boiling water for 5 minutes and drain it in a colander. Stir the celery into the casserole, re-cover the casserole and continue simmering for a further 30 minutes.

Remove the casserole from the oven and, with a metal spoon, skim the fat off the surface. In a small bowl, mix the cornflour (cornstarch) and water to a paste and stir into the sauce. Bring to the boil over moderate heat, stirring constantly, and cook for 2 minutes. Discard the bouquet garni before serving.

Cooking time: 4½ hours

Boston Baked Beans

SERVES 4

350g/¾ lb (2 cups) dried white haricot (navy) beans, soaked overnight

15ml (1 tablespoon) oil

1 large onion, sliced

5ml (1 teaspoon) dry mustard

10ml (2 teaspoons) black treacle or molasses

150ml/¼ pt (⅔ cup) tomato juice

30ml (2 tablespoons) tomato paste

10ml (2 teaspoons) soft brown sugar

275ml/½ pt (1¼ cups) stock or water

450g (1 lb) belly of pork or 100g (¼ lb) salt pork cut into 5cm (2 in) cubes

Drain the beans and put into a saucepan. Cover with fresh water and bring to the boil. Simmer for 1½ hours and drain.

Heat the oven to cool 150°C (300°F) gas mark 2. Heat the oil in a flameproof casserole (dutch oven). Add the onion and fry for 2 minutes. Stir in the rest of the ingredients, except the pork. Lay the pork on top.

Cover the pot and place it in the oven. Bake for 5 hours, stirring occasionally.

Cooking time: 1½ hours, then 5 hours

Sweet and Sour Pork Casserole

Hand and spring of pork (picnic shoulder) is lean but rather tasteless. Here the meat is given an oriental flavour with fruit as well as vegetables in a tangy sauce.

SERVES 6

30ml (2 tablespoons) oil

900g (2 lb) boned hand and spring of pork (picnic shoulder), cut into 2.5cm (1 in) cubes

420g (15½ oz) canned pineapple chunks

1 large onion, sliced

1 large green (bell) pepper, cored, seeded and sliced

2 celery stalks, sliced

60ml/4 tablespoons (¼ cup) wine vinegar

15ml (1 tablespoon) soy sauce

75g/3 oz (½ cup) soft brown sugar

salt

freshly ground black pepper

30ml (2 tablespoons) cornflour (cornstarch) dissolved in 30ml (2 tablespoons) water

Heat the oil in a saucepan. Add the pork cubes, in batches, and brown on all sides.

Remove the pork cubes from the pan as they brown.

Drain the pineapple and make up the can syrup to 275ml/½ pt (1¼ cups) with water. Add the liquid and pineapple chunks to the pan with the onion, green pepper, celery, vinegar, soy sauce, sugar and seasoning. Return the pork to the pan and mix well. Bring to the boil, then cover tightly and simmer gently for 1½ hours or until the pork is tender.

Skim any fat from the surface of the liquid in the pan. Add the cornflour liquid to the pan. Simmer, stirring, until thickened.

Cooking time: 1 hour 50 minutes

Salt pork is traditional for this famous dish of Boston baked beans; only a little is needed. If pork belly meat is used, quantities can be increased. Molasses, mustard and tomato juice make a rich, sweet sauce which soaks into the beans.

Salt Beef with Herby Dumplings

SERVES 6–8
1.4kg (3 lb) silverside (sirloin tip roast) or brisket of beef, soaked overnight if salted
15ml (1 tablespoon) soft brown sugar
150ml/¼ pt (⅔ cup) dry cider
1 small onion
4 cloves
4 black peppercorns
2 bay leaves
900g (2 lb) carrots, halved or quartered
FOR THE DUMPLINGS
100g/¼ lb (1 cup) self-raising flour
50g/2 oz (1 cup) fresh breadcrumbs
75g (3 oz) shredded suet (lard)
salt
freshly ground black pepper
5ml (1 teaspoon) dried thyme
1 large egg
25g/1 oz (4 tablespoons) plain flour

Drain the beef and pat dry with absorbent paper. Rub the sugar into the meat. Put the meat in a saucepan that fits it neatly and add the cider and just enough water to cover completely. Bring to the boil. Add the onion stuck with the cloves, the peppercorns and bay leaves. Skim off any scum, cover and simmer for 1¼–1½ hours.

Meanwhile, make the dumplings. Sift the self-raising flour into a bowl. Stir in the breadcrumbs, suet (lard), seasoning and thyme. Bind with the egg. Shape into 12 balls, then coat in plain flour.

Remove the meat from the pan and place in another saucepan. Ladle over some of the cooking liquid and keep warm. Bring the rest of the cooking liquid to the boil. Add the dumplings and carrots and cover the pan. Simmer for 10 minutes.

Drain the meat and place on a warmed serving dish. Drain the dumplings and carrots and arrange around the meat.

Cooking time: overnight soaking, then 1¾–2 hours

Cooking with Yeast

Bread-making is a satisfying process as it allows you really to come to grips with what you are cooking. The enticing smell of baking bread is sure to whet any appetite—even of the most determined slimmer!

In these days of the plastic-wrapped, commercially-baked loaf, homemade bread is becoming a thing of the past. This is a pity, because the flavour of commercial bread can never compete with that of homemade bread, and bread and yeast goods can be made at home for a fraction of their cost in the shops. There are no secrets to making bread, just a few points to remember.

Yeast makes doughs rise. It is a living plant, which needs food and comfort to carry out its duties: too hot water or milk will kill it: too cold will not awaken it. Test the liquid with a clean finger: it should feel comfortable, neither hot nor cold. As the yeast grows, it gives off carbon dioxide and it is this gas within the dough that raises it. As the gas expands, the elastic walls of the gluten in the flour stretch to form the risen structure.

Fresh (compressed) yeast is the easiest to use, but dried yeast, which is more widely available, may be substituted. Only half the amount of yeast specified in the recipe is needed when cooking with large quantities if you use dried instead of fresh. Use 10ml (2 teaspoons) dried yeast for $15g/\frac{1}{2}$ oz ($\frac{3}{5}$ oz cake) fresh yeast. There may be an expiration date stamped on the package. Add about 5ml (1 teaspoon) sugar to the lukewarm liquid to feed the yeast, then stir in the dried yeast. Leave in a warm place to become frothy—about 10 minutes. If the mixture does not froth at this point, discard it; the yeast is too old and the dough has no chance of rising.

Certain flours make bread-making easier and give better results. Strong plain flour, sometimes called bread flour, is best for bread as it will absorb more liquid than a soft flour. (In the US use all-purpose plain flour.) It will develop quickly into a firm elastic dough when kneaded, producing a larger volume and light texture when baked. Wholewheat flour gives a good nutty flavour, extra nutrients and close texture to bread. Mix it with at least an equal weight of strong plain flour for best results. Bread made entirely with rye flour is very dark and heavy. For lighter rye bread, less than half the flour used should be rye. Make a batter as described for crumpets (English muffins) and allow to rise in order to develop the yeast, then add the rye flour to make a dough. Put the dough in the tin (pan) for the second rise.

The most important element in flour for bread-making is gluten. This is formed when the protein reacts with water, and it gives the dough its elasticity. Gluten is strengthened by the addition of salt; without it you will have a sticky dough that is difficult to handle. (However, too much salt will inhibit the yeast and thus the rise.) Ascorbic acid (vitamin C) also strengthens the gluten (see quick-method bread, *page 234*). But more than anything else, kneading strengthens the gluten. By stretching the dough it becomes elastic and expands easily; this is necessary to hold in the gas bubbles that the yeast produces.

Kneading may be done by hand, in a food processor or with the dough hook of an electric mixer. By hand it will take about 10 minutes, with a machine about half that; follow the manufacturer's instructions. When sufficiently kneaded, the dough should no longer feel soft or stick to your fingers.

Put the dough to rise in a warm place, away from draughts—over or under a warm oven or in a linen cupboard. A plastic bag makes an ideal container but leave plenty of room for the dough to expand. Do not knot the bag but tie loosely with a tag. Let the dough rise until doubled in bulk. Dough made with wholewheat or rye flour will rise slightly less.

'Knocking back' after rising disperses any large air bubbles and restores the dough to its previous strong state. Shape the dough into loaves or rolls and put into an oiled tin (pan) as specified in the recipe. The dough should only half fill a loaf tin (pan) and must fit the bottom of the tin exactly to ensure an even upward rise. The final rise, or proving, when it acquires its loaf shape takes 40–50 minutes at 21°C (70°F) room temperature. The dough will almost double in size again.

Bread must be baked in a very hot oven. This heat kills the yeast, thus preventing the dough from rising further, and sets the gluten to make the framework of the bread. To test if a loaf or rolls are done, tip out of the tin and rap the bottom with your knuckles: the bread or rolls should sound hollow.

Bread-making is simpler than those who never do it imagine, but it can be quite time-consuming, because bread needs two rising periods, each of about an hour. Bread-making can be speeded up by including ascorbic acid with the yeast at the outset (quick-method bread, *page 234*). This type of bread is sometimes referred to as 'single-rise' bread, though this is not strictly correct, because it still needs a first rise of 5–10 minutes.

Bread rises in about an hour in a warm place; in a cold place it rises considerably more slowly. Cooks who do not want to spend their whole time in the kitchen may well find it more convenient to stop cooking and pack up when the bread is put to prove. If you put the bread in the refrigerator, well oiled on top and then lightly covered, it can be left from 15–24 hours to prove, as is convenient for you. It can then be baked at some point the next day when you return again to the kitchen. The unproven loaf can also be put straight into the freezer. Oil it when you remove it and it will prove if allowed 24 hours thawing time. Allow cold loaves to come to room temperature before putting them in the oven.

When yeast doughs contain dried fruit, for example currant buns, a slightly different method is adopted, because the sugar in the fruit could otherwise interfere with the yeast and the weight could retard the yeast's expansion. A batter is made with the yeast liquid and flour and the fruit and eggs are then incorporated afterwards. This type of yeast batter is also used for crumpets or English muffins.

Making Bread

1. Warm water to blood heat—test with a finger. Crumble in fresh yeast. With dried yeast, sprinkle in and add sugar. Stir with a fork and leave 10 minutes until dissolved, when the top will be frothy.

2. Put flour, salt and sugar in a bowl and cut in the fat until pieces are pea-sized. Rub in the fat with the fingertips until mixture resembles fine breadcrumbs. Make a hollow in the middle of the mixture.

3. Pour in the yeast liquid and gradually draw the flour into the liquid with a spoon to make an ever-thickening paste. When the dough binds and leaves the sides of the bowl, use your fingers to amalgamate it.

4. Turn the dough out of the bowl onto a floured surface. Knead the dough to make it elastic by pushing away with the heal of one hand, while using the other hand to steady the dough on the surface.

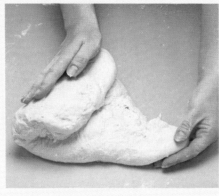

5. Give the dough a quarter turn (so that next time it will be stretched in a different direction). Roll up the dough and repeat kneading as before. Continue for 10 minutes with a regular, rhythmic action.

6. Shape the dough into a ball and put in a lightly-greased plastic bag, leaving plenty of room for expansion. Tie only loosely. Leave until the dough is doubled in bulk— 45–60 minutes in a warm place.

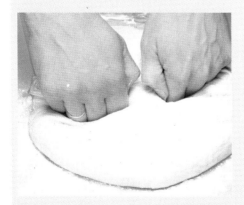

7. Remove the dough from the bag and punch it, on a floured surface, with your knuckles to remove any air bubbles. Knead again by stretching and rolling as before (see steps 4–5) for 1 minute.

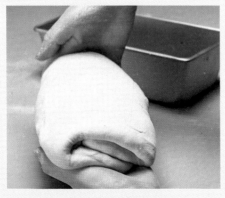

8. Shape the bread dough. Traditionally a rectangular loaf is stretched out then folded under in three, as shown. Put in the greased tin (pan) then knuckle it to ensure the corners are well filled.

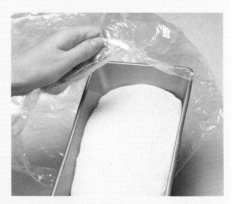

9. Put the tin (pan) back in the plastic bag. Tie loosely and leave in a warm place until proved—risen to the final shape. Brush with oil or add any topping before baking according to the individual recipe.

Traditional White Bread

MAKES 1 LARGE LOAF

15g/$\frac{1}{2}$ oz ($\frac{3}{5}$ oz cake) fresh yeast or 10ml (2 teaspoons) dried yeast plus 5ml (1 teaspoon) sugar
425ml/$\frac{3}{4}$ pt (1$\frac{2}{3}$ cups) lukewarm water
700g (1$\frac{1}{2}$ lb) strong plain flour (6 cups all-purpose flour)
15ml (1 tablespoon) salt
15g/$\frac{1}{2}$ oz (1 tablespoon) lard or shortening

Crumble fresh yeast into the water then stir, or alternatively, mix the yeast to a paste with a little water and then stir in the rest. With dried yeast stir the sugar into the water and sprinkle over the yeast. Stir with a fork until dissolved. Leave in a warm place until puffed up and frothy—about 10 minutes for dried yeast.

Sift the flour and salt into a bowl. Rub in the lard. Make a well in the centre and pour in the yeast mixture. Gradually draw the dry ingredients into the liquid with a wooden spoon and continue mixing until the dough comes away from the sides of the bowl, then use your hands to amalgamate it well.

Knead for 10 minutes, as shown on *page 233*, or until smooth and elastic. Put the dough in a greased plastic bag, loosely tied, then let it rise in a warm place for 45–60 minutes or until doubled in bulk.

Knock back the dough by punching it and knead again until smooth. Shape into a loaf and place in a 900g (2 lb) loaf tin (pan). Let it rise again, in the bag, for 1 hour.

Heat the oven to 230°C (450°F) gas mark 8. Bake the bread for 30–35 minutes. Turn out and cool on a wire rack.

Cooking time: about 2$\frac{3}{4}$ hours including rising

● This dough will make 3 pizzas. The second rise can be omitted.

Quick-Method Bread

MAKES 3 SMALL LOAVES

50g (2 oz) fresh yeast
850ml/1$\frac{1}{2}$ pt (3$\frac{3}{4}$ cups) lukewarm water
2 × 25mg ascorbic acid tablets ($\frac{1}{5}$ × 250mg vitamin C tablet), crushed
1.4kg/3 lb strong plain flour (12 cups all-purpose flour)
30ml (2 tablespoons) salt
10ml (2 teaspoons) fine sugar
25g/1 oz (2 tablespoons) butter or margarine

A newly-baked, crusty white loaf, from your own oven, is always a pleasure.

Mash the yeast with a little of the water, then stir in the rest of the water with the crushed ascorbic acid tablets. Whisk with a fork until dissolved.

Sift the flour, salt and sugar into a bowl. Rub in the fat until the mixture resembles breadcrumbs. Make a well in the centre and pour in the yeast mixture. Gradually draw the dry ingredients into the liquid with a wooden spoon and mix until the dough leaves the side of the bowl. Use your hands to amalgamate the dough into a ball.

Knead until the dough is smooth and elastic—about 10 minutes (or 4–5 minutes with the dough hook of an electric mixer). Leave, covered, to rise in a warm place for 5–10 minutes.

Punch back the dough and knead for 1 minute. Divide into portions and shape into loaves. Place in three 450g (1 lb) greased loaf tins (pans), or one 900g (2 lb) loaf tin and one 450g (1 lb) tin, then put in greased plastic bags and allow to rise for 45 minutes.

Heat the oven to 230°C (450°F) gas mark 8. Bake the bread for 30–35 minutes or until it is golden and well risen. Turn out onto a wire rack to cool.

Cooking time: total 1 hour 40 minutes

● As an alternative, this dough will make a 900g (2 lb) loaf and 20 small rolls. Bake the rolls on greased baking sheets for 10 minutes only.

● This dough is handy for homemade pizza. The quantity in the recipe will make a 900g (2 lb) loaf and 2 × 30cm (12 in) pizzas. Once shaped the pizza need only rest for as long as is needed to make the topping.

● If you have a freezer, make more pizzas and freeze them, topped or untopped, raw or baked as suits you.

Granary Cob

MAKES 1 LARGE LOAF

15g/$\frac{1}{2}$ oz ($\frac{3}{5}$ oz cake) fresh yeast or 10ml (2 teaspoons) dried yeast plus 5ml (1 teaspoon) sugar
425ml/$\frac{3}{4}$ pt (1$\frac{2}{3}$ cups) lukewarm water
350g ($\frac{3}{4}$ lb) granary meal (3 cups all-purpose plain flour)
350g ($\frac{3}{4}$ lb) whole wheat flour
15ml (1 tablespoon) salt
15g/$\frac{1}{2}$ oz (1 tablespoon) margarine
beaten egg or milk to glaze
oatmeal or cracked wheat

Mash fresh yeast with a little of the water, then stir in the rest of the water. Alternatively, add the sugar to the water and sprinkle on the dried yeast. Stir with a fork until dissolved. Leave in a warm place until puffed up and frothy.

Put the two flours into a bowl with the salt. Rub in the margarine. Make a well in the centre and pour in the yeast mixture. Gradually draw the dry ingredients into the liquid with a wooden spoon and continue mixing until the dough leaves the sides of the bowl. Work with your hands to amalgamate.

Knead (*page 233*) until the dough is smooth and elastic. Then put it in a greased plastic bag and leave to rise in a warm place for 40 minutes or until doubled in bulk.

Punch back the dough and knead until smooth. Shape into a ball and place on a baking sheet. Cover with a cloth and leave to rise in a warm place for 1 hour.

Heat the oven to 230°C (450°F) gas mark 8. Brush the dough with beaten egg or milk and sprinkle with oatmeal or cracked wheat. Cut a deep cross in the top of the dough. Bake for 30–35 minutes. Cool on a wire rack.

Cooking time: about 2½ hours, including rising time

●This dough will make 16 brown rolls. Bake them on a greased sheet for 10–15 minutes.

Oat Bread

MAKES 2 SMALL LOAVES
15g/½ oz (⅗ oz cake) fresh yeast OR 10ml (2 teaspoons) dried yeast plus 5ml (1 teaspoon) sugar
575ml/1 pt (2½ cups) lukewarm milk
50g/2 oz (¼ cup) soft brown sugar
75g/3 oz (5 tablespoons) butter, melted
700g/1½ lb (6 cups) flour
5ml (1 teaspoon) salt
350g/¾ lb (3¾ cups) rolled oats

Mash fresh yeast with a little of the milk. Add up to half the lukewarm milk, stirring to mix. Alternatively add the sugar to half the milk, sprinkle over dried yeast and stir with a fork. Leave in a warm place until the mixture is puffed up and frothy.

Scald the remaining milk, add the brown sugar and stir until the sugar has dissolved. Remove from the heat and allow to cool to lukewarm.

Sift the flour and salt into a bowl. Stir in the oats. Make a well in the centre and put in the yeast and milk mixtures. Gradually draw the dry ingredients into the liquid with a spoon and continue mixing until the dough comes away from the sides of the bowl. Amalgamate the dough well with your hands. Knead for 10 minutes or until elastic and smooth. Then leave to rise in a greased plastic bag in a warm place for 1¾–2 hours or until almost doubled in bulk.

Knead the dough for 4 minutes, then shape into two loaves. Put into greased 450g (1 lb) loaf tins (pans) and brush with the rest of the melted butter. Put the loaf tins into plastic bags and let rise for another hour or until the dough has risen to the tops of the tins (pans).

Heat the oven to 220°C (425°F) gas mark 7. Bake for 15 minutes, then reduce the temperature to 190°C (375°F) gas mark 5. Bake for a further 25 minutes. Cool on a wire rack.

Cooking time: about 4½ hours including rising

Caraway Knots

MAKES 20
425ml/¾ pt (1⅔ cups) milk
50g/2 oz (¼ cup) butter
900g/2 lb (8 cups) plain flour
15ml (1 tablespoon) salt
15ml (1 tablespoon) fine sugar
20g/¾ oz (1⅓ × ⅗ oz cakes) fresh yeast
10ml (2 teaspoons) lukewarm water
2 eggs
45ml (3 tablespoons) caraway seeds

Scald the milk (bring to just below boiling point) then remove from the heat. Add the butter and, when it has melted, set aside to cool to lukewarm.

Sift the flour, salt and sugar into a mixing bowl. Mash the yeast to a paste with the warm water, then add to the milk mixture with one of the eggs. Mix well.

Make a well in the centre of the dry ingredients and pour in the yeast and milk mixture. Mix to a smooth dough. Work in 30ml (2 tablespoons) of the caraway seeds, then leave, covered, to rise in a warm place for 1–1½ hours or until the dough has almost doubled in bulk.

Turn the dough on to a floured surface and knead for 5 minutes. Roll the dough into a 30cm (12 in) long roll and slice into 20 equal pieces. Roll one piece in your hands to make a rope about 35cm (14 in) long and shape it into a loop with its ends crossed. Turn the ends of the rope over again to make a twist at the base of the loop. Spread the tips of the two ends apart, bring over the loop to meet the tips and pinch the tips to the loop. Shape the remaining knots in the same way, then leave to rest for 10 minutes.

Drop the knots, two at a time, into a pan of boiling water. The knots will sink to the bottom and then rise to the surface and double in size. Drain the knots and place them on greased baking sheets. Leave to dry in a warm place for 15 minutes.

Heat the oven to 200°C (400°F) gas mark 6. Beat the remaining egg and brush all over the knots. Sprinkle them with the rest of the caraway seeds. Bake for 15–20 minutes or until golden brown. Cool on a wire rack and serve warm.

Cooking time: about 3½ hours including rising

These egg-glazed caraway knots are put into boiling water to make them rise.

Egg Bread

MAKES 1 ORNAMENTAL LOAF

15g/½ oz (¾ oz cake) fresh yeast or 10ml
(2 teaspoons) dried yeast plus 5ml
(1 teaspoon) sugar

175ml/6 fl oz (¾ cup) lukewarm milk

450g (1 lb) strong plain flour (4 cups
all-purpose flour)

15ml (1 tablespoon) fine sugar

7.5ml (1½ teaspoons) salt

2 eggs, beaten

15ml (1 tablespoon) oil

1 egg yolk beaten with 15ml
(1 tablespoon) cold water

30ml (2 tablespoons) poppy seeds

Mash fresh yeast with 10ml (2 teaspoons) of the warm milk. Alternatively, add the sugar to half the milk and sprinkle on the dried yeast. Stir until dissolved. Then leave in a warm place until the mixture is puffed up and frothy.

Sift the flour, sugar and salt into a bowl. Make a well in the centre and put in the yeast mixture, remaining milk, the eggs and oil. Gradually draw the dry ingredients into the liquid with a wooden spoon and mix until the dough comes away from the sides of the bowl. Amalgamate the dough well with your hands. Knead until it is smooth and elastic.

Divide the dough into three ropes about 30cm (12 in) long. Press the ropes together at one end, then loosely plait them in a braid. Place the loaf on a greased baking sheet and leave, covered, to rise in a warm place for 2–2½ hours.

Heat the oven to 220°C (425°F) gas mark 7. Brush the loaf with the egg yolk mixture and sprinkle with the poppy seeds. Bake for 10 minutes, then reduce the temperature to 190°C (375°F) gas mark 5. Bake for a further 25–30 minutes or until deep golden brown. Cool on a wire rack.
Cooking time: about 3¾ hours including rising

Orange Yeast Buns

MAKES 10–15

15g½oz (¾ oz cake) fresh yeast

30ml (2 tablespoons) lukewarm water

125ml/4 fl oz (½ cup) milk

175g/6 oz (¾ cup) butter

450g/1 lb (4 cups) flour

5ml (1 teaspoon) salt

2 eggs, beaten

125g/¼ lb (½ cup) sugar

75g/3 oz (⅔ cup) currants

grated rind of 2 large oranges

15ml (1 tablespoon) chopped mixed peel

1.5ml (¼ teaspoon) ground cinnamon

FOR THE ICING

225g/½ lb (2¼ cups) icing (confectioners')
sugar

30ml (2 tablespoons) orange juice

Mash the yeast and the water together, then leave in a warm place until the mixture is puffed up and frothy. Scald the milk in a saucepan and add 150g/5 oz (⅔ cup) of the butter. When it has melted, remove from the heat and allow to cool to lukewarm.

Sift the flour and salt into a bowl. Make a well in the centre and put in the yeast and milk mixtures and the eggs. Gradually draw the dry ingredients into the liquid with a spoon. Continue mixing until the dough comes away from the sides of the bowl. Knead the dough until it is smooth and elastic, then leave, covered, to rise in a warm place for 1–1½ hours or until almost doubled in bulk.

Knead the dough for 2 minutes. Roll it out into a square. Sprinkle with the sugar, currants, orange rind, peel and cinnamon. Roll up the dough like a Swiss (jelly) roll, then cut into 4cm (1½ in) slices. Place the slices close together, cut sides up, in a large greased baking tin (pan). Leave them to rise for 20 minutes.

Heat the oven to 190°C (375°F) gas mark 5. Bake the buns for 30–35 minutes or until golden brown. Cool slightly.

Meanwhile, make the icing. Combine the sugar and orange juice. Pour this icing

Orange yeast buns are like the traditional Chelsea buns. The addition of orange rind and juice gives them extra flavour.

over the buns on the baking sheet. Leave until they are cool enough to handle, then break them apart and cool completely on a wire rack.

Cooking time: 3 hours plus cooling time

Coffee and Walnut Yeast Ring

MAKES 24 SMALL BUNS
25g/1 oz ($\frac{1}{2}$ × 2 oz cake) fresh yeast
125ml/4 fl oz ($\frac{1}{2}$ cup) lukewarm milk
25mg ascorbic acid ($\frac{1}{10}$ × 250mg vitamin C) tablet, crushed
350g/$\frac{3}{4}$ lb strong plain flour (3 cups all-purpose flour)
5ml (1 teaspoon) salt
25g/1 oz (2 tablespoons) instant coffee powder
25g/1 oz (2 tablespoons) cornflour (cornstarch)
50g/2 oz ($\frac{1}{4}$ cup) butter or margarine
1 medium-sized egg, beaten
FOR THE FILLING AND COATING
50g/2 oz ($\frac{1}{4}$ cup) Demerara or granulated brown sugar
10ml (2 teaspoons) instant coffee powder
5ml (1 teaspoon) ground cinnamon
24 walnut halves
50g/2 oz ($\frac{1}{4}$ cup) butter, melted

Mash the yeast with a little of the milk, then stir in the rest of the milk and the crushed ascorbic acid tablet. Whisk with a fork until completely dissolved.

Sift the flour, salt, coffee powder and cornflour (cornstarch) into a bowl. Rub in the fat until the mixture resembles breadcrumbs. Make a well in the centre and add the egg and yeast mixture. Mix until the dough binds together.

Knead for 10 minutes, then leave to rise in a warm place for 10 minutes.

Meanwhile, mix together the brown sugar, coffee powder and cinnamon. Grease, line and grease again a 23cm (9 in) ring cake tin (pan), preferably a spring-form pan.

Divide the dough into 24 pieces. Place a walnut half in the centre of each and shape the dough around to enclose the walnut completely and form a ball. Dip the balls in the melted butter, then coat in the sugar mixture. Place the balls in the ring tin. Leave, covered, to rise in a warm place for 30 minutes.

Heat the oven to 200°C (400°F) gas mark 6. Bake for 30 minutes or until the ring is firm to the touch. Invert on a wire rack to cool. To eat pull the buns free.

Cooking time: 1$\frac{1}{2}$ hours plus cooling time

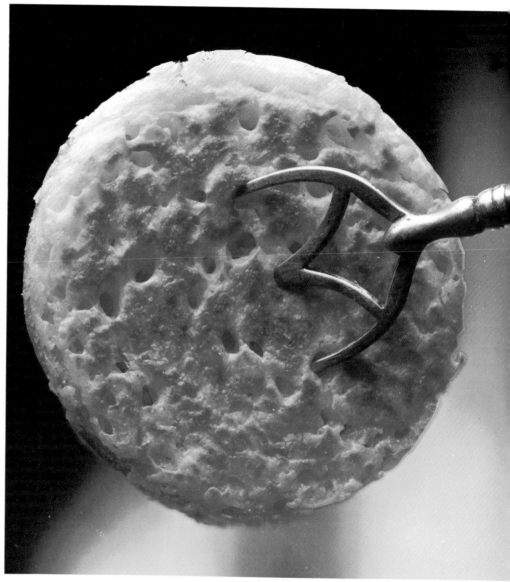

Crumpets (English Muffins)

Crumpets are eaten at tea or supper time. Traditionally, they should be toasted in front of an open fire, then stacked in a pile with a knob of butter on top. To make crumpets, you will need special rings.

MAKES 24
15g/$\frac{1}{2}$ oz ($\frac{3}{5}$ oz cake) fresh yeast
575ml/1 pt (2$\frac{1}{2}$ cups) lukewarm milk
450g/1 lb plain flour (4 cups all-purpose flour)
2.5ml ($\frac{1}{2}$ teaspoon) salt
1 egg
75g/3 oz (6 tablespoons) butter, melted

Mash the yeast with 30ml (2 tablespoons) of the milk, then leave in a warm place

Crumpets (English muffins) should be toasted and eaten with lots of butter.

until the mixture is puffed up and frothy.

Sift the flour and salt into a bowl. Make a well in the centre and put in the yeast mixture, remaining milk, the egg and one-third of the butter. Beat the ingredients together to make a smooth batter. Leave to rise in a warm place for 45 minutes.

Grease a large griddle, baking sheet or heavy iron frying-pan and the crumpet rings with some of the remaining butter. Heat well on top of the stove. Spoon enough batter into each ring to fill it one-third full and cook gently for 5–6 minutes or until the tops are set and full of holes and the bottoms are golden brown. Cool on a wire rack. Toast before serving.

Cooking time: about 1$\frac{1}{4}$ hours

Currant Buns

MAKES 14 BUNS

FOR THE BATTER

150g/5 oz strong plain flour (1¼ cups all-purpose flour)
5ml (1 teaspoon) fine sugar
10ml (2 teaspoons) dried yeast
15g/½ oz (⅗ oz cake) fresh yeast
225ml/8 fl oz (1 cup) lukewarm milk

FOR THE DOUGH

300g/11 oz strong plain flour (2¾ cups all-purpose flour)
5ml (1 teaspoon) salt
50g/2 oz (¼ cup) butter or margarine
1 medium-sized egg, beaten
175g (6 oz) mixed dried fruit
50g (2 oz) mixed peel

FOR THE GLAZE

beaten egg
fine sugar

For the batter, sift the flour and sugar into a bowl. Sprinkle or crumble in the yeast and make a well in the centre. Add the milk, beating with a wooden spoon to make a smooth batter. Leave in a warm place until frothy and bubbly.

For the dough, sift the flour and salt into a bowl. Rub in the fat until the mixture resembles breadcrumbs. Mix in the dried fruit and peel. Add with the egg to the batter in stages, beating well while the mixture is still liquid. Incorporate the last bit by working it with your hands.

Knead for 10 minutes or until smooth and elastic. Let the dough rise in a greased plastic bag in a warm place for 1 hour or until doubled in bulk.

Knead the dough and divide into 14 equal pieces. Roll into balls and arrange on 2 greased baking sheets leaving 2.5cm (1 in) between the buns. Leave, covered, in a warm place to rise for 40–50 minutes.

Heat the oven to 200°C (400°F) gas mark 6. Brush the buns with beaten egg, sprinkle with fine sugar and bake on the centre shelf of the oven and shelf above centre for 15–20 minutes. Leave the buns on the trays for 5 minutes then transfer to a rack to cool.

Cooking time: 2¾ hours

●Use all currants, raisins or sultanas instead of the mixed dried fruit.

Kuchen, a cake from Germany, is ideal for a mid-morning snack with coffee.

Kuchen

MAKES 1 LARGE LOAF

15g/½ oz (⅗ oz cake) fresh yeast
15ml (1 tablespoon) lukewarm water
225g/½ lb strong plain flour (2 cups plain flour)
2.5ml (½ teaspoon) salt
1.5ml (¼ teaspoon) ground ginger
2.5ml (½ teaspoon) grated lemon rind
30ml (2 tablespoons) sugar
150ml/¼ pt (⅔ cup) lukewarm milk
50g/2 oz (¼ cup) butter, melted
1 egg, beaten

FOR THE TOPPING

50g/2 oz (⅔ cup) digestive biscuits (graham crackers), crushed
30ml (2 tablespoons) sugar
5ml (1 teaspoon) ground cinnamon
50g/2 oz (¼ cup) butter, softened

Mash the yeast and the water together, then leave in a warm place until the mixture is puffed up and frothy.

Sift the flour, salt and ginger into a bowl. Stir in the lemon rind and sugar. Make a well in the centre and put in the yeast mixture, milk, butter and egg. Gradually draw the dry ingredients into the liquid

with a spoon and continue mixing until the dough leaves the sides of the bowl. Knead until the dough is smooth and elastic, then leave to rise in a warm place for 1–1½ hours or until almost doubled in bulk.

Knead the dough for 3 minutes. Shape into a loaf and place in a greased 900g (2 lb) loaf tin (pan). To make the topping, combine all the ingredients until the mixture resembles breadcrumbs. Sprinkle over the loaf, then leave to rise for 30 minutes.

Heat the oven to 180°C (350°F) gas mark 4. Bake for 40–45 minutes or until the topping is golden brown and slightly crunchy. Turn out to cool on a wire rack.
Cooking time: 2 hours 50 minutes plus cooling time

Orange Savarin

SERVES 8

20g/¾ oz (1⅓ × ⅗ oz cake) fresh yeast or 15ml (1 tablespoon) dried yeast plus 7.5ml (1½ teaspoons) sugar
45ml (3 tablespoons) warm milk
30ml (2 tablespoons) orange juice
175g/6 oz strong plain flour (1⅞ cup all-purpose flour)
pinch of salt
20g/¾ oz (1 tablespoon) fine sugar
3 medium-sized eggs, beaten
75g/3 oz (6 tablespoons) butter, softened
grated rind of 1 orange
FOR THE SYRUP
225g/½ lb (1 cup) granulated sugar
150ml/¼ pt (⅔ cup) orange juice
150ml/¼ pt (⅔ cup) water
30ml (2 tablespoons) brandy or rum (optional)
TO FINISH
60ml (4 tablespoons) marmalade jelly
15ml (1 tablespoon) water
275ml/½ pt (1¼ cups) thick cream
210g (7½ oz) canned mandarin oranges, drained

Cream fresh yeast in a bowl with the milk and the orange juice. Alternatively, add the dried yeast and sugar to the liquid and stir until dissolved; allow to stand 10 minutes. Stir in 50g/2 oz (½ cup) flour and blend until smooth. Leave in a warm place until frothy—about 20 minutes.

Stir in the remaining flour, salt, sugar, beaten eggs, softened butter and orange rind. Beat together 3–4 minutes.

Pour into a greased 23cm (9 in) savarin ring and level the top. Put in a greased plastic bag and leave in a warm place until

Anchovy and olive pizza can be baked in a square shape on a baking sheet if you do not own a round pizza tray or plate.

the dough has risen to the top of the tin (pan)—about 40 minutes.

Heat the oven to 200°C (400°F) gas mark 6. Bake for 35 minutes. Turn out onto a wire rack, then invert the savarin, so the flat side is uppermost. Arrange a bowl under the rack.

To make the syrup, put the sugar, orange juice and water in a small pan and dissolve the sugar. Bring to the boil and boil for 2 minutes.

Prick the savarin all over with a fork. Add the brandy or rum, if using, and spoon the hot syrup over the savarin until the base is saturated. Turn over the savarin, rounded side uppermost, and spoon over more syrup. Spoon up the syrup from the bowl and continue until the cake has absorbed all the syrup. Leave to get cold.

To make the glaze, boil the marmalade jelly with the water until dissolved. Brush this over the savarin. Pipe the whipped cream round the base of the cold savarin. Decorate at intervals with the mandarin orange segments. Put the remaining cream and orange segments inside the ring.
Cooking time: 2 hours plus cooling time

● In winter serve the savarin plain or with cream piped round the base of the cake.
● In summer the ring can be filled with a compôte of fruit, such as cherries. Pass a jug of pouring cream with the dessert.

Anchovy and Olive Pizza

SERVES 4

⅙ × quick-method bread dough or ⅓ × traditional white bread dough
800g (1 lb 12 oz) canned tomatoes, drained
salt
freshly ground black pepper
pinch of sugar
5ml (1 teaspoon) dried oregano
175g (6 oz) Mozzarella cheese, thinly sliced
50g (2 oz) canned anchovy fillets, drained and oil reserved
12 small black olives

Knead the dough lightly, then roll out to a 30cm (12 in) circle. Place on a greased baking sheet and press up the outer edge of the dough circle to make a rim.

Put the tomatoes in a saucepan with the seasoning, sugar and half the oregano. Break up the tomatoes with a spoon then simmer, stirring frequently, until thick. Spread the tomato mixture over the dough base. Arrange the cheese slices on top to cover, then make a lattice of anchovies on the cheese. Put an olive in the centre of each square. Leave to rest for 30 minutes if you have time; this is not essential.

Heat the oven to 230°C (450°F) gas mark 8. Drizzle over the oil from the can of anchovies and sprinkle with the rest of the oregano. Bake for 20–25 minutes or until risen and bubbling.
Cooking time: about 1 hour

Cheaper to make than buy

Shortcrust

Shortcrust is the one pastry that everyone should make at home. Flaky and puff pastry require an investment in time and are therefore best bought frozen, but shortcrust is quick to make, cheap and, what is more, extremely versatile. There are very few dishes—vol au vents is one example—in which shortcrust will not do as effectively as another pastry. Shortcrust makes excellent two-crust or single-crust pies and is the perfect pastry for lining every type of tart or flan. It will stand unsupported on a baking sheet to make pasties, turnovers and sausage rolls.

Unlike most other types of pastries, this can also be flavoured (see recipes on the opposite page) to provide the perfect complement to the filling.

Leftover trimmings of shortcrust will make a variety of useful biscuits (cookies) or nibbles to eat with drinks. A larger quantity of leftover shortcrust might make a small flan (tart) to be baked immediately and filled later.

Use a smaller quantity of pastry to make a few tiny tarts. Turn plain or sweet tarts into a dessert by adding jam or fruit; turn plain or cheese-flavoured pastry cases into an appetizer or picnic item by adding cooked vegetables or diced ham, plus mayonnaise. For a hot dish, combine the filling with white sauce and a little tomato purée, pile into the pastry and heat through.

Making Shortcrust Pastry

225g/$\frac{1}{2}$ lb (2 cups) plain flour
2.5ml ($\frac{1}{2}$ teaspoon) salt
125g ($\frac{1}{4}$ lb) butter or margarine, diced
about 40ml (8 teaspoons) cold water

The secret of success with this versatile pastry is to keep it cool. When rubbing in, lift up the fat and roll it over the tops of your fingertips, with your thumbs pressing from above, then let it drop back into the bowl. Chill the pastry in the refrigerator before rolling out and shaping.

Shortcrust keeps well. The wrapped dough will store in the refrigerator for 10 days or in the freezer for 6 months. To thaw frozen pastry, remove the wrappings, allow 2 hours at room temperature for the basic quantity. Baked, but unfilled pastry cases of every type will freeze for 6 months.

1. Sift the flour and salt into a mixing bowl. Add the fat and use a palette knife or spatula to cut it into the flour until it is in pea-sized pieces.

2. With the fingertips, rub the fat into the flour, lifting it up high and rubbing it with your thumbs on top. Let it fall back into the bowl to keep cool.

3. When it resembles even breadcrumbs, sprinkle on half the water and stir with a knife, until it clings together.

4. Add a little more water, as necessary, and with your hands, draw the dough together into a ball, picking up the crumbs.

5. Place the dough on a work surface and knead lightly until smooth. Wrap and chill dough for 30 minutes before using.

240

Rich Shortcrust

Slightly more difficult to handle, because it is shorter—that is, it contains more fat and therefore crumbles more easily—this short-crust is the best for pie toppings and for party food. Do not omit the resting period or you may have problems when shaping.

225g/½ lb (2 cups) plain flour
2.5ml (½ teaspoon) salt
175g/6 oz (¾ cup) butter or margarine
about 40ml (8 teaspoons) cold water

The method is identical to that given for shortcrust pastry on the opposite page. Quantities needed are those given below.
Preparation time: 40 minutes, including resting time

● Small quantities of herbs (dried or well chopped fresh ones) can be added to pastry for a pastry base but not to top a pie.

Sweet Rich Shortcrust

Perfect for fruit tarts and summer desserts of all sorts, this pastry should be used as a lining but not as a topping.

The basic quantity will line 2 × 9-hole tart tins or 2 × 23cm (9 in) flan tins or rings (quiche pans). For economy, when you want to make only half the quantity, the egg yolk can be omitted. However the basic recipe will keep for a week in the refrigerator and 3 months in the freezer. The baked but unfilled case can also be kept for up to 2 days in an airtight container.

Trimmings of sweet pastry make excellent quick cookies for serving with fruit purées, ice-creams etc. Cut shapes or cut into strips and brush with milk, then sprinkle over sugar, chopped nuts or a few chocolate drops and bake.

225g/2½ cups) plain flour
pinch of salt
10ml (2 teaspoons) caster sugar
175g/6 oz (¾ cup) butter or margarine
1 medium-sized egg yolk
10ml (2 teaspoons) cold water

Make in the same way as shortcrust (see opposite) stirring the sugar into the dry ingredients. Stir the egg yolk and water together and add to form the dough. Knead then wrap and chill for 30 minutes.
Preparation time: 40 minutes, including resting time

● Ground nuts can be used to replace part of the fat in this recipe, but you must include the egg yolk. Use 125g/¼ lb (1 cup) flour, 40g/1½ oz (3 tablespoons) fine sugar, 50g/2 oz (¼ cup) butter, 1 egg yolk and 10ml (2 teaspoons) water with 25g/1 oz (¼ cup) ground almonds, hazelnuts or walnuts. This quantity will line a 20cm (8 in) tart tin or ring or a 9-hole tart tin.

Cream-cheese Shortcrust

Any soft, creamy cheese, such as curd cheese, Philadelphia or Petit Suisse, can be used to replace part of the fat for a cheese pastry. Like hard-cheese shortcrust this is perfect for quiches and all savoury tarts. The quantities obtained from the basic recipe are the same as for hard-cheese shortcrust.

225g/½ lb (2 cups) plain or wholewheat flour
1.5ml (¼ teaspoon) paprika
1.5ml (¼ teaspoon) salt
75g/3 oz (5 tablespoons) butter or margarine, diced
100g (¼ lb) cream cheese
1 medium-sized egg yolk
10ml (2 teaspoons) water

Sift the dry ingredients into a bowl and cut in the fat and cream cheese with a metal spoon or spatula. Rub in the mixture lightly with your fingers until it resembles rather greasy breadcrumbs. Blend together the egg yolk and water in a cup and stir into the mixture. When a ball is formed, knead the dough lightly, then wrap and chill for at least 30 minutes.
Preparation time: 45 minutes, including resting time

Hard-cheese Shortcrust

This makes an excellent base for a vegetable flan (tart), especially when this is to form the main course and extra protein is needed. Do not use it for a topping. It will line 2 × 20–23cm (8–9 in) rings or will line up to 9 × 10cm (4 in) Yorkshire pudding moulds.

Economical nibbles for eating with drinks can be made from the trimmings; cut into shapes or small sticks and brush over with egg and milk before baking. These will keep for 3 weeks in an airtight container but do not freeze well.

225g/½ lb (2 cups) plain or wholewheat flour
1.5ml (¼ teaspoon) mustard powder
1.5ml (¼ teaspoon) black pepper
1.5ml (½ teaspoon) salt
175ml/6 oz (¾ cup) margarine, diced
75ml/3 oz (¾ cup) finely grated cheese
1 medium-sized egg yolk
10ml (2 teaspoons) water

Sift the dry ingredients into a bowl, add the grated cheese and stir in. Add the fat and rub in. Blend the water and egg yolk together in a cup, then scrape them into the rubbed-in mixture. Use a metal spoon or spatula to blend the liquid into the dough. When it forms a ball, knead it briefly with your hands to form a smooth dough. Wrap and chill the dough in the refrigerator for 30 minutes before rolling.
Preparation time: 45 minutes, including resting time

● For a cheaper version, omit the egg yolk and use 40ml (3½ tablespoons) water. This is useful when you only want to make up half the quantity.

QUANTITIES OF SHORTCRUST PASTRY NEEDED FOR QUICHES, PIES AND TARTS

TIN (PAN) SIZE	18–20cm (7–8 in)	23–25cm (9–10 in)	28–30cm (11–12 in)	
Pastry for lining				
quantity basic pastry	½	¾	1	
servings for appetizer	4–6	8–9	10–12	
servings for main course	3–4	6–8	9–10	
Two-crust pies				
quantity basic pastry	1	1½	2	
SMALL TART TINS	6-hole	9-hole	12-hole	4 × 10cm (4 in) tarts (Yorkshire pudding moulds)
Single crust				
quantity basic pastry	⅜	½	¾	½
Two-crust pies				
quantity basic pastry	¾	1	1¾	1

Making and using Hot-water Crust Pastry

450g/1 lb (4 cups) strong plain (bread) flour

pinch of salt

100g/½ lb (½ cup) lard or shortening

200ml/¼ pt plus 4 tablespoons (⅔ cup) water

A small raised pie, full of meat and eaten with salad, is the perfect portable meal. It is not difficult to do—and it is very cheap.

There are two different types of pie. A big mould is lined inside, then filled and baked. You can use a special mould or loaf tin (pan), but a spring-release, loose-bottomed cake tin (pan) is the easiest. For small pies the pastry is modelled on a jar (sometimes a cake tin) and, when set, is reversed and the jar removed. The pie is filled and baked free-standing on a baking sheet.

QUANTITY OF PASTRY NEEDED	
Mould size Cake tin (pan)	Proportion of pastry
19 × 7.5cm (7½ × 3 in) serves 8–10	1
16.5 × 7.5cm (6½ × 3 in) serves 6	¾
Loaf tins (pans)	
1kg (2 lb) serves 8–10	1
500g (1 lb) serves 4–6	½
Small pies	
modelled on 6 × 450g (1 lb) jars; one each, serves 6	1
modelled on 2 × 10cm (4 in) wide jars; ½ each, serves 4	½

1. Sift flour and salt into a bowl. Put lard and water into a small pan and heat until the lard has completely melted. Bring to the boil.

2. Pour the liquid into a well in the centre of the dry ingredients. Stir into the flour, then work with your fingers to form a dough.

3. Using one hand, pinch and knead the dough until it is smooth, crack-free and silky in texture. Cover in plastic wrap then a damp glass-towel. Rest 20 minutes.

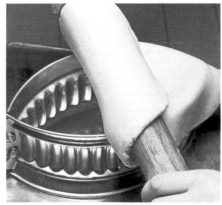

4. To line a big mould, such as a cake or loaf tin (pan), roll out to wider and longer than the mould, then drape over the mould. Push pastry into a bag inside.

5. Press pastry into the corners at the bottom of the mould. Move upwards, pressing flat anything resembling a pleat, so the thickness is uniform. Fill and top.

6. To make a little pie, use an upturned, floured jar as a model. Roll out a patty of dough and mould it around the jar base. Press, flattening out all pleats.

7. Cover the jars with a damp cloth and refrigerate for 2 hours. Reverse onto a baking sheet and remove the jars. Fill and pinch the lids in place to bake.

Making and using Suet Pastry

225g/½ lb (2 cups) self-raising flour or
225g/½ lb (2 cups) plain flour plus 15ml
(1 tablespoon) baking powder

2.5ml (½ teaspoon) salt

125g (¼ lb) shredded or grated suet

150ml/¼ pt (⅔ cup) water

This traditional form of pastry is far cheaper than shortcrust. It is economical, easy to use and difficult to make a mistake with. It is the perfect pastry for cold weather dishes.

Suet pastry is used for sweet or savoury rolls—rolled up like a Swiss (jelly) roll; the basic quantity will make a 20 × 25cm (8 × 10 in) rectangle, which will feed 4. Half the quantity of pastry will make dumplings for 6; cook these in a stew for the last 20 minutes and serve instead of potatoes.

QUANTITIES OF PASTRY NEEDED		
Bowl size and servings	Proportion of pastry	Steaming time
850ml–1L/ 1½–2 pt (4–5 cups) serves 3–6	¾–1	2½–3 hours
1¼–1½L/2½– 3 pt (6–8 cups) serves 6–10	1½–2	3½–4½ hours

Suet pastry is primarily used for lining the bowl for a steamed pudding. This is an easy way to produce a meat dish completely enclosed in pastry.

1. Sift the dry ingredients into a large bowl. Add the suet and mix lightly with a knife or spatula and until the two are thoroughly incorporated.

2. Make a well in the centre and add the water. Stir and cut until the mixture is blended, then use your hands to pull the ingredients together to make a ball.

3. On a floured work surface, knead the dough by pressing it out with your knuckles, then folding it up again. Continue until the dough is smooth.

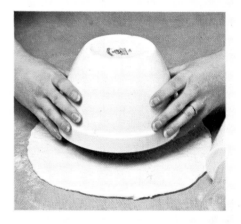

4. To line a bowl, reserve ⅓ dough for the lid. Grease the bowl and roll out the larger piece 5cm (2 in) larger all around than the bowl rim.

5. Sprinkle the pastry circle well with flour. Fold it in half then fold again to form a triangle. Put the point of the triangle in the bowl, touching the bottom.

6. Open the pastry carefully without stretching it. Shape into the bowl bottom and smooth the sides with your fingers, pressing out the pleats. Fill almost to top.

7. Fold the rim inwards over the filling. Dampen and cover with the rolled pastry lid. Grease and pleat a foil cover, then tie on with string below the bowl rim.

Making and using Choux Pastry

65g/2½ oz (⅔ cup) plain flour
2 medium-sized eggs, beaten
50g/2 oz (¼ cup) butter or margarine
pinch of salt
150ml/¼ pt (⅔ cup) water
few drops of vanilla extract
(for sweet pastry)

Choux pastry is the world's cheapest form of pâtisserie. Far from being difficult to make, it is particularly easy, because it is never handled; even people with hot hands who find other pastries difficult will find choux easy. There is no rolling out.

Its one disadvantage is that baked choux must be eaten within 5 hours; the light, puffy creations loose their crispness and taste of cardboard if kept too long. Baked choux does freeze, filled or unfilled; and the piped,

raw pastry can be open-frozen and then baked immediately before use.

Choux is usually sweet, but is also delicious when filled with savoury mousses based on mayonnaise or béchamel sauce. You can also add cheese to the basic pastry (see fish gougère, page 43.

The quantity of pastry will make 8 éclairs, 6 large choux buns (cream puffs), about 20 tiny profiteroles or 2 × 20cm (8 in) rings. Bake choux above the centre in the oven at 200°C (400°F) gas mark 6 for 20 minutes, then at 190°C (375°F) gas mark 5 for 15 minutes: 5 minutes less on each temperature for profiteroles.

Choux pastry can also be deep fried. Use the sweetened version for fluffy beignets— serve with vanilla sugar. Instructions are given in cheese aigrettes (page 88).

1. Sift the flour onto a piece of paper and put ready. Whisk the eggs lightly. Put the butter, salt and water in a pan.

2. Bring the water to the boil so that the butter melts. Off the heat tip in all the flour at once. Beat until smooth.

3. Return the pan to low heat and beat vigorously for 1–2 minutes until the water evaporates and the dough forms a ball.

4. Take the pan off the heat and cool for 2 minutes. Beat in the eggs a little at a time and the vanilla if using.

5. For éclairs, pipe 10cm (4 in) oblongs onto a greased, floured baking sheet. Cut off the pastry with a wet knife. Space them at 2.5cm (1 in) intervals.

6. For cream puffs dot on a heaped tablespoon of the pastry. Use a second spoon to scrape the pastry free from the spoon. Space at 5cm (2 in).

7. For a ring, pipe round a 20cm (8 in) marked ring, or arrange tablespoonfuls of pastry round the ring. This will give a bun-effect when cooked.

Crêpes

MAKES 12–15 CRÊPES
225g/½ lb (2 cups) strong plain (bread) flour
pinch of salt
4 medium-sized eggs
425ml/¾ pt (scant 2 cups) cold liquid, half milk and half water
60ml/4 tablespoons (¼ cup) melted butter
90ml (6 tablespoons) oil for frying

Sift the dry ingredients into a bowl. Make a well in the centre. Whisk the eggs lightly together and add the liquid. Stir, then pour into the dry ingredients, stirring the liquid into the flour as you do so.

When smooth, gradually blend in the melted butter. The batter should resemble thin cream. Strain the batter and leave to rest, covered in the refrigerator, for 2 hours, but not more than 8 hours before cooking. Whisk again before use.

A quick method of making the batter is to combine all the ingredients and whisk together in a blender.

To cook the crêpes, wipe a medium-sized frying-pan or crêpe pan with a little oil. Place over medium heat until the pan is hot. Lift the pan from the heat and pour in about 60ml (4 tablespoons) batter. Tilt the pan so the batter covers the bottom. Return to heat and cook for about 1 minute until light brown underneath. Turn the crêpe over with a fish slice or spatula and cook the other side. This first crêpe is a test, adjust the quantity of batter and the cooking time as necessary. Keep the crêpes warm on a heated plate, layed with greaseproof or waxed paper, while you cook remaining batter.

The side cooked first should be the inside—the side cooked second is usually more attractive, so spoon the filling on to this side.

Cooking time: 10 minutes plus 2 hours rest for the batter, then 25 minutes to cook the crêpes

●A rather plainer mix, yielding 12–15 crêpes, can be made using the same quantity of flour, but 2 eggs only, with 575ml/1 pt (2¼ cups) milk. If however, the crêpes are to be grilled (broiled) before serving, it is essential to include the melted butter in the basic recipe.

●Additions can be made to the batter to flavour it, for example small quantities of grated cheese or apple, or herbs or spices, according to the filling.

●Filled crêpes are often glazed; a more imaginative way to finish them is to make spring rolls and deep fry them. It is important to fold the sides of the crêpe over the filling and then roll up the crêpe to make a secure parcel. Roll in beaten egg then seasoned flour. Chill for 30 minutes to firm up. Deep fry at 180°C (350°F) for 5 minutes, in batches.

Sweet Crêpes

For sweet crêpes you can use half of either the basic crêpe batter or the plainer crêpe mix, adding 15ml (1 tablespoon) fine sugar. The ingredients in this recipe gives a richer result and it is best if the crêpes are to be reheated

MAKES 6–8 CRÊPES
150g/5 oz (1¼ cups) plain flour
15ml (1 tablespoon) caster sugar
3 egg yolks
75ml (5 tablespoons) butter, melted
125ml/4 fl oz (½ cup) milk
125ml/4 fl oz (½ cup) water
45ml (3 tablespoons) concentrated orange juice
30ml (2 tablespoons) clarified butter for frying *(page 95)*

The method is the same as given for crêpes.
Cooking time: 10 minutes plus 2 hours for the batter, 25 minutes to cook the crêpes

Egg White Batter

This light batter can be used for every type of deep frying: it is always puffy and golden. Use it to cover cubes or cold meat, cauliflower florets or cubes of cheese to make an emergency supper. Make the basic batter ahead and add the egg whites before using.

100g/¼ lb (1 cup) plain flour
pinch of salt
30ml (2 tablespoons) oil
150ml/¼ pt (⅔ cup) cold water
2 large egg whites

Sift the flour and salt into a bowl. Make a well in the centre. Pour in the oil and water and gradually incorporate the flour with a spoon. Mix the batter to the consistency of thick cream. Rest for 30 minutes.

Whisk the egg whites until stiff but not dry. Fold the batter into the whites and use immediately to coat food for deep frying. In many cases it is best to dredge the food lightly with additional flour before dipping in batter, so that the batter sticks on.
Preparation time: 35 minutes.

●Stir grated cheese into the batter and deep fry spoonfuls for an attractive appetizer. These can also be served on cocktail sticks (picks) or as a garnish for meat.
●For dessert, coat apple slices or soaked prunes filled with an almond and deep fry. Serve with vanilla sugar and/or grated chocolate.

Yeast Batter

Yeast batter has a distinctive flavour and is particularly suited to fruit fritters. Allow enough time when making the batter to let it rest before using.

100g/¼ lb (1 cup) plain white flour
pinch of salt
175ml/6 fl oz (¾ cup) water
15g/½ oz (¼ × 2 oz cake) fresh yeast or 10ml (2 teaspoons) dried yeast plus 2.5ml (½ teaspoon) fine sugar
15g/½ oz (1 tablespoon) butter, melted

Sift half the flour and salt into a bowl. Crumble the yeast into the warm water. If using dried yeast, stir in the sugar. Leave for 10 minutes, until frothy.

Make a well in the sifted flour and pour in the yeast. Stir to make a smooth paste. Cover and leave in a warm place for 20–30 minutes, until bubbles appear on the surface.

Beat in the remaining flour, water and the butter, adding flour and water alternately. Beat until smooth. The batter is then ready to use.
Preparation time: 45 minutes, including resting time.

●For a fruit dessert, macerate cubed fruit in lemon juice or alcohol. Then batter and deep fry.
●For deep fried onion rings, push out the onion into rings and blot dry. Batter them and deep fry until puffed and golden.

Rolling a Sponge

1. Cover a glasscloth with greaseproof or waxed paper and sprinkle on fine sugar. Invert the baked sponge onto the cloth, then peel off the lining.

2. Trim all edges, make a cut halfway through the cake 2.5cm (1 in) from the end and parallel. Spread jam or jelly then press over the edge firmly.

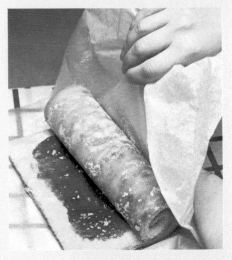

3. Holding down the cake with one hand, grip the paper with the other and use it to roll the cake. Hold the paper round the roll a few seconds to set the cake.

Whisked Sponge

This is the classic light, puffy sponge which gave the type of cake this name. It is an excellent choice for budget-conscious cooks because it contains no butter—unlike the better-known creamed sponge.

The basic quantity will make 3 × 18cm (7 in) layers or 2 × 20cm (8in) layers. Altnernatively it will make a large Swiss (jelly) roll, 33 × 23cm (13 × 9in) before rolling or a 30cm (10in) sponge base for fruit. All of these are versatile cakes.

75g/3 oz (¾ cup) plain flour
3 large eggs
75g/3 oz (5 tablespoons) fine sugar

Heat the oven to 180°C (350°F) gas mark 4 and grease the baking tins (pans). Prepare a double boiler.

Sift the flour twice. Put the eggs in the top of the boiler and whisk. Add the sugar and then whisk over hot not boiling water until the mixture thickens. Continue until the whisk leaves a trail in the mixture. Remove from the heat and continue whisking until pale and thick.

Carefully but quickly fold in one-quarter of the flour. Incorporate this, then fold in the rest in the same way.

Pour immediately into the prepared tins and bake; do not open the oven door during baking. For an 18cm (7 in) cake

allow 20–25 minutes, for a 20cm (8 in) cake or allow 25–30 minutes and for a 30cm (10 in) one allow 30–35 minutes. When cooked, the cake should feel firm to the touch. Turn out and cool on a wire rack. Fill when cold, then store in an airtight container. This cake should be eaten within 24 hours as it stales rapidly. *Cooking time:* 40 minutes plus cooling

● A sponge base, covered first with confectioners' custard (*page 248*) or whipped cream, will turn a small quantity of expensive fruit into a spectacular dessert. Ice-cream can also be used. Use ⅔ basic recipe

for a 20cm (8 in) sponge base. Try to top the cake as near to eating time as possible; sponge stales quickly in the refrigerator.
● For a Swiss (jelly) roll, grease, line then grease again the pan. Fill the tin then bake at a higher temperature, 200°C (400°F) gas mark 6 for 8–10 minutes. Details of rolling the cake are shown in the pictures. Swiss (jelly) rolls can be filled with ice-cream, thick fruit purée or lemon curd plus whipped cream.

A whisked sponge base makes a wonderful dessert filled with fruit or ice-cream.

Swiss Meringue

Meringues are a Godsend to the money-conscious cook, because they look and taste wonderful and yet demand very little in the way of ingredients. They are an obvious choice when entertaining numbers. Egg whites are often left over, especially in the mayonnaise season. Meringues will store 2 weeks in an airtight container.

Swiss meringue is the easiest to make and, depending on how it is cooked, it will make two quite different types. It will make a marshmallowy topping or, alternatively, crisp dry meringue. Piped stars or spooned shells are pale cream and either chewy or completely dry when baked. Use them for decorating, or pair with whipped cream. Large circles of dry meringue can also be made; sandwich with buttercream, ice-cream or whipped cream plus fruit.

Meringue using 2 egg whites will make 24 small stars or a 20cm (8 in) circle or will top a dessert 18cm (7 in) in diameter.

2 large egg whites, at room temperature
pinch of salt or cream of tartar
100g/¼ lb (½ cup) fine sugar

Heat the oven to 110°C (225°F) gas mark 4. Prepare 2 baking sheets, lining them with greaseproof or waxed paper or foil and then greasing well.

Add the salt or cream of tartar to the egg whites and whisk. A hand-held electric whisk or balloon whisk or rotary beater will give you a much bigger volume of egg white than a table-top electric mixer. Whisk until the whites stand in stiff peaks.

Add half the sugar whisking slowly until it is absorbed. Fold in the remaining sugar in two stages, using a metal spoon or spatula. Spoon or pipe immediately on to the prepared baking sheets and bake on the lowest shelf of the oven for 2–3 hours. The meringues should colour faintly. At the longer time they will be completely dry, at the shorter faintly chewy.
Cooking time: about 3 hours.

●Meringue topping for both hot and cold desserts is also made with this meringue. For American chiffon topping—useful with an electric mixer—reduce the amount of sugar by half. Cook at 200°C (400°F) gas mark 7 for 7–10 minutes to set the outside but leave the inside soft. This topping is celebrated on baked Alaska and lemon meringue pie, but can be used to disguise many desserts that are not quite big enough for the number of people.

Making and using Italian Meringue

250ml/9 oz (2⅓ cups) icing (confectioners') sugar
4 large egg whites
pinch of salt
3 drops of vanilla essence

This meringue is cooked while being made. As a result, it can be used as a topping for a tart that is not to be cooked. Alternatively, it can be piped and then baked, when it will set to a shape.

You can also pipe nests to hold fruit or loops, simple flowers or stars for spectacular dessert decorations. For a children's party, pipe numbers or a tray of letters—one for each child—for next to no cost.

Italian meringue keeps beautifully—at least 2 weeks in an airtight container, 6 months in a freezer.

1. Heat the oven to 110°C (225°F) gas mark ½. Prepare a double boiler with tepid water. Put the egg whites in a large bowl and whisk until foamy but not until stiff or in peaks.

2. Whisk in the icing (confectioners') sugar, a teaspoon at a time. Add the vanilla. Whisk over low heat until the meringue thickens—about 8 minutes. The whisk should leave a thick trail.

3. Fit a piping bag with a 12mm (½ in) star or éclair nozzle. Stand the bag in a jug or glass and turn back the top of the bag all around. Half fill it with meringue. Holding the top together, press firmly.

4. For fruit nests, line a baking sheet with greaseproof or waxed paper and mark 10cm (4 in) circles. Fill in the circles, piping from the centre outward. (Pipe shapes following a pencil line.)

5. Using a 12mm (½ in) star nozzle if possible, pipe a rim round the top outside of each circle. Bake for about 2 hours until white and dry. Fill with fresh fruit or ice-cream.

Basic Sweet Sauce

This sweet sauce can be served hot or cold : if serving cold, omit the butter. The liquid can be milk, fruit juice, the liquid in which dried fruit or fruit has been soaked or cooked, or the syrup left over from canned fruit, made up with water.

MAKES ABOUT 275ML/½ PT (1¼ CUPS)
275ml/½ pt (1¼ cups) milk, fruit juice or water
15g/½ oz (2 tablespoons) cornflour (cornstarch) or 7g (1 tablespoon) arrowroot
25g/1 oz (2 tablespoons) granulated sugar
flavouring
15g/½ oz (1 tablespoon) butter (optional)

In a mixing bowl mix the starch with 30ml (2 tablespoons) of the cold liquid. Stir until blended. Add the sugar to the remaining liquid in a saucepan. Dissolve the sugar and bring the mixture to the boil.

Remove the pan from the heat and, stirring all the time, gradually pour the hot liquid on to the starch. Return to the heat and cook for a few minutes. Add the flavourings. Serve cold if wished. If serving hot, stir in the butter just before serving.
Preparation time : 10 minutes

● To flavour and vary the sauce, add any of the following: a few drops of vanilla extract, 5ml (1 teaspoon) nutmeg or mixed spice, 30ml (2 tablespoons) jam or marmalade, grated rind of ½ orange or lemon or 30ml (2 tablespoons) rum, brandy sherry or liqueur. For a slightly richer version, add 30ml (2 tablespoons) cream.
● For chocolate sauce, melt 50g (2 oz) plain chocolate in milk. Alternatively, mix 15ml (1 tablespoon) cocoa powder into the milk.
● For coffee sauce add 15ml (1 tablespoon) instant coffee to the starch, and continue with the basic sauce.
● For a butterscotch sauce, dissolve 125ml/¼ lb (⅔ cup) brown sugar in half the liquid (milk or water). Add 25g/1 oz (2 tablespoons) butter and the thinly pared rind of ½ lemon. Bring to the boil and simmer 5 minutes. Strain into a clean pan and discard the rind. Blend the starch with the remaining water and continue the recipe.
● For orange sauce, use 275ml/½ pt (1¼ cups) orange juice, made up from concentrate or canned, and omit the sugar. Flavour with 5ml (1 teaspoon) grated rind.

● For a sharp lemon sauce, use the juice of 1 lemon and make up the rest of the liquid with water. Flavour with 5ml (1 teaspoon) grated lemon rind.

French Buttercream

This quick-to-make butter cream makes a rich filling for a classic sponge and is very attractive with whisked sponge, which itself contains no butter. It takes flavouring well and is also one of those convenient fillings which go on the outside of the cake as well as hidden inside. It pipes perfectly and will hold in place a decoration of chopped nuts or chocolate strands on the sides of a cake.

TO SANDWICH AND COVER AN 18CM (7 IN) CAKE
175g/6 oz (¾ cup) unsalted butter, softened
50g/2 oz (½ cup) icing (confectioners') sugar
2 medium-sized egg yolks
30ml (2 tablespoons) liqueur or 5ml (1 teaspoon) vanilla extract

Put the softened butter in a warm bowl and beat until smooth. Sift the icing (confectioners') sugar and add to the butter with egg yolks and flavouring. Beat all the ingredients until smooth. Chill before use.
Preparation time : 5 minutes plus chilling

Mock 'Cream'

You can make this cream and use it safely to replace cream in any cold dessert set with gelatin. It makes an excellent pouring cream for fruit.

MAKES ABOUT 275ML/½ PT (1¼ CUPS)
125g/¼ lb (½ cup) unsalted butter, diced
150ml/¼ pt (⅝ cup) milk
2.5ml (½ teaspoon) gelatin
10ml (2 teaspoons) cold water
5-10ml (1-2 teaspoons) sugar (optional)

Put the butter in a pan with the milk and heat gently, but do not boil. Turn off the heat and stir until the butter has melted. Soften the gelatin in the water in a cup, then pour on a little of the butter and milk mixture. Mix well then return to the pan and add the sugar if using.

Pour the mixture into a blender and whisk for ½ minute. Pour into a bowl and chill for 8 hours.
Cooking time : 5 minutes, then about 8 hours setting

● For an inexpensive, fluffy topping, rather like Italian meringue, use 1 spare egg white. Whip the white until stiff peaks are formed. Stand a jar of golden syrup or honey in hot water until liquid, then pour 15ml (1 tablespoon) syrup on to the egg white, whipping continually. Use immediately.
● Alternatively, whip the egg white and mash a banana. Add the banana purée to the white, beating until absorbed.

Confectioners' Custard

This cream, called crème pâtissière in France, is the filling found in éclairs and all sorts of choux pastry. Creamy and delicately flavoured, it is an excellent substitute for whipped cream in any cake or dessert, and is often the first choice, though it will not pipe. Use it to layer a whisked sponge or to fill a pastry case that is to be topped with fruit. Use the basic quantity where a recipe specifies 150ml/5 fl oz (⅔ cup) cream.

MAKES ABOUT 425ML/¾ PT (2 CUPS)
25g/1 oz (¼ cup) plain flour
10ml (2 teaspoons) cornflour (cornstarch)
275ml/½ pt (1¼ cups) milk
2 medium-sized egg yolks
50g/2 oz (¼ cup) fine sugar
1 medium-sized egg white
few drops of vanilla extract

Prepare a double boiler. Sift the flour and cornflour (cornstarch) together into the top pan. Add a quarter of the milk and mix until smooth. Combine the yolks and sugar and stir into the flour paste.

Put the remaining milk into a saucepan and bring to the boil. Pour it on to the egg mixture, stirring continuously. Put the pan over the boiling water and cook, stirring all the time, until the mixture thickens. Leave it to cool.

Whisk the egg white until stiff. Fold the white into the warm custard and return the pan to a low heat for 2 minutes, stirring. Fold in any flavouring. Leave until cold before using. Fill the cake or pastry as near as possible to eating time, so that it does not become soggy.
Cooking time : 10 minutes plus cooling

● Flavour the custard to match the dessert, using any of the following: 50g (2 oz) melted chocolate, 10ml (2 teaspoons) strong coffee, grated rind of a small orange or lemon or 15ml (1 tablespoon) rum, brandy or liqueur.

Yogurt

Nutritious yogurt has become increasingly popular in recent years. It is easy to buy but cheaper to make at home. Use it for both sweet and savoury dishes and as a cheap (and less fattening) substitute for cream.

To start off you will need a culture. Use plain, unpasteurized yogurt if you can buy it; otherwise buy a packet of culture at a healthfood shop. You can then reserve a little yogurt from each batch to act as the culture for the next. After 3 months start again. Because home-made yogurt is not pasteurized, it continues to develop even in the refrigerator. It will therefore taste slightly sharper as it gets older.

To keep your yogurt culture going, you need to make it regularly. Reserve 10 minutes for making it on the same day each week and buy extra milk. The first batch is slower—about 8 hours—after that batches will take about 5 hours.

Like bread, yogurt needs warmth to grow. A yogurt machine will provide warmth and little pots, but it cheaper to collect a set of empty pots—and to use a linen-drying cupboard or a big vacuum flask (Thermos) to provide steady warmth.

Cleanliness is very important. Boil up water in the saucepan you will use for the milk and pour this into the jug, bowl, vacuum flask or jars and on the whisks and spoons you will use.

● For a quick dessert add any of the following to yogurt: honey, red berries, mashed banana, cooked or puréed fruit, molasses, golden syrup, brown or white sugar. Pour sweetened yogurt over fruit.
● Use thickened yogurt (see recipe) as a substitute for cream or sour cream in any dish that is to be cooked. Use it to replace half the cream in any cake filling, mousse or cold pudding.
● Make yogurt salad dressing (*page 77*).
● For a savoury dip add mustard and seasoning and mix with any of the following: chopped olives, minced or finely chopped green peppers, chopped anchovies, pickles, smoked cod or haddock plus a little mayonnaise, shellfish, chopped cucumber or onion.
● For an easy gratin topping for a baked dish, mix together 275ml/½ pt (1¼ cups) thickened yogurt (see recipe), 2 large eggs, 25g/1 oz (¼ cup) plain flour, seasoning and 30ml (2 tablespoons) grated cheese. Bake for 30 minutes in a moderate oven.

Making Yogurt

| 575ml/1 pt (2½ cups) pasteurized, homogenized or ultra heat treated milk |
| Or 125g/¼ lb (¾ cup) dried skimmed milk made to 575ml/1 pt (2½ cups) with water |
| Or 275g/½ pt (1¼ cups) evaporated milk made to 575ml/1 pt (2½ cups) with water |
| 30ml (2 tablespoons) unpasteurized plain yogurt or ½ packet yogurt culture |

● A thick yogurt can be made initially in 2 different ways. Either boil the milk until it reduces to ⅓ the original volume, or add 100g/¼ lb (¾ cup) skimmed milk powder to the milk.
● Thicken made yogurt with 7.5ml (½ tablespoon) cornflour (cornstarch), made to a paste with milk for each 275ml/ ½ pt (1¼ cups) yogurt. Bring to the boil, stirring, then simmer for 10 minutes.

1. First sterilize your equipment. Make additions first. Bring the milk to the boil and simmer for 5 minutes. (Or reduce the milk for thickened yogurt.)

2. Cover the pan and stand in cold water to cool. The milk should be 46°C (115°F) on a thermometer and not colder than bloodheat: touch the side of pan to test.

3. When the milk is lukewarm, mix a little with the starter, then mix this into the milk, whisking well to disperse. Pour into jars if using a machine.

4. Alternatively, if using a warm environment, pour into a bowl and cover with plastic wrap then wrap and keep warm. Or use a Thermos. Leave 8 hours.

5. Transfer yogurt from a vacuum flask or Thermos to a bowl or pots. Chill the yogurt at least 1½–2 hours before using or making any additions.

Making Mayonnaise

2 large egg yolks
2.5ml ($\frac{1}{2}$ teaspoon) Dijon mustard
2.5ml ($\frac{1}{2}$ teaspoon) salt
15ml (1 tablespoon) vinegar or lemon juice
275ml/$\frac{1}{2}$ pt (1$\frac{1}{4}$ cups) olive oil or half and half olive and corn oil

Home-made mayonnaise is superior to the best commercial varieties. Never hurry when making it. Take the eggs from the refrigerator early to warm to room temperature. Stand the oil in a jug of hot water and then the sauce will blend easily.

Curdling is usually caused by adding the oil too fast. Start again with a fresh egg yolk and beat in the curdled mixture after the sauce emulsifies. Mayonnaise will keep 1 week in the refrigerator, covered.

1. Beat the egg yolks lightly. Add the mustard, salt and vinegar or lemon juice and mix well together.

2. Whisking all the time, add the oil drop by drop: a bottle with a notched cork will restrict the flow.

3. Carry on adding oil and whisking all the time until the mixture thickens. Then mix in a steady trickle of oil.

4. Keep beating. If mayonnaise becomes too thick, thin it down a little with lemon juice or a little vinegar.

5. The finished mayonnaise should hold its shape. Taste for seasoning and add a little pepper if desired.

Green Mayonnaise

Enliven cold white fish, a hard-boiled egg or potato salad with this colourful sauce.

30ml (2 tablespoons) frozen spinach purée
$\frac{1}{2}$ bunch of watercress leaves
15ml (1 tablespoon) parsley
a few fresh tarragon leaves
275ml/$\frac{1}{2}$ pt (1$\frac{1}{4}$ cups) mayonnaise

Simmer the spinach and herbs in a little water. Drain, squeeze dry and purée the mixture. Leave until cold, then fold into the mayonnaise.

Preparation time: 10 minutes, plus chilling

Aioli

Serve this piquant sauce with vegetable salads that have been cooked and cooled.

1-2 garlic cloves, chopped
1 large egg yolk
salt
150ml/$\frac{1}{4}$ pt ($\frac{2}{3}$ cup) olive oil

Crush the garlic cloves with the salt to make a paste. Beat the egg yolk well and beat in the garlic. Proceed as for mayonnaise.

Preparation time: 5 minutes.

Sauce Tartare

This famous sauce is not strictly a mayonnaise but is close to it. It is the classic accompaniment to deep-fried shellfish.

yolks of 2 hard-boiled eggs
20ml (4 teaspoons) Dijon mustard
15ml (1 tablespoon) lemon juice
150ml/$\frac{1}{4}$ pt ($\frac{2}{3}$ cup) olive oil
salt
white pepper
5ml (1 teaspoon) each of finely chopped chives, parsley and capers
1 small gherkin, finely chopped
30ml (2 tablespoons) thick cream

Press the hard-boiled egg-yolks through a strainer with a wooden spoon into a bowl. Work in the mustard and lemon juice to make a paste. Add the oil in drops and complete like a mayonnaise. Make the other additions, then chill.

Preparation time: 10 minutes plus chilling

Making Hollandaise Sauce

45ml (3 tablespoons) dry white wine or white wine vinegar
125g/$\frac{1}{4}$ lb ($\frac{1}{2}$ cup) unsalted butter
2 large egg yolks
salt
white pepper
10ml (2 teaspoons) lemon juice

This classic French emulsion sauce is always served warm. It is the best accompaniment to new or steamed vegetables for the perfect hors d'oeuvre. Serve it with hot salmon or to make more modest fish steaks worthy of a party. Keep it warm in a Thermos flask if made ahead.

● Add a little orange juice for serving with shellfish, a little cream and sherry to serve with chicken or broccoli.

1. Place white wine or vinegar in a pan. Boil and reduce to 30ml (2 tablespoons). Leave to cool. Prepare a double boiler.

2. Cut off a quarter of the butter. Cut this into small pieces. Melt the remaining butter. Pour into a jug and keep warm.

3. Off the heat, beat the yolks lightly in the top of the double boiler. Whisk with a balloon or sauce whisk.

4. Whisk in the vinegar. Add half the butter and return the pan to the boiler. The water must simmer but not boil.

5. Whisk the mixture. When it becomes smooth and forms a light cream, whisk in the remaining diced butter, off the heat.

6. Off the heat start adding the melted butter, drop by drop at first and whisk the mixture all the time.

7. When half the butter has been incorporated, pour in the rest in a steady dribble, whisking all the time.

8. Season with salt and pepper and stir in the lemon juice. Transfer to a sauceboat and serve lukewarm.

Making White Sauce and Béchamel

½ small onion, chopped
½ small carrot, chopped
½ celery stalk, chopped
275ml/½ pt (1¼ cups) milk
bay leaf
25g/1 oz (2 tablespoons) butter
25g/1 oz (¼ cup) flour
salt and white pepper
pinch of nutmeg or mace

These two white savoury sauces can be used to dress meat, fish and vegetables.

● To flavour add any of the following: 50g/2 oz (½ cup) grated cheese plus 2.5ml (½ teaspoon) prepared mustard; 50g (2 oz) mushrooms sautéed or 225g (½ lb) onions sautéed in butter and puréed (optional); 15ml (1 tablespoon) chopped parsley.

1. For béchamel, put the vegetables in a pan with the milk and seasonings. Bring to simmering. Remove from heat, stand for 30 minutes. Strain.

2. To make a roux, melt the butter in a pan. Off the heat add the flour and stir in. Return to the heat and cook for 2 minutes, stirring continually.

3. For a white sauce, warm the milk (omit the vegetables in step 1) in a separate pan. Heat through for easing blending but on no account let it boil.

4. Off the heat add a little warm milk to the roux. Stir vigorously until blended. Add the remaining milk, stirring all the time.

5. Return to the heat, stirring all the time. Bring to the boil. Add seasonings then cover and cook over a low heat for up to 5 minutes.

Stock

Stock cubes have their useful place in every kitchen. You will, however, pay for the bones when you buy boned meat, so it makes sense to use them, while home-made stock adds individual flavour to food. Any cooking liquid is better than water: use vegetable water and in particular that used for cooking or soaking pulses. Improve the made stock by reducing it.

Meat stock can be kept covered in the refrigerator for up to 10 days but should be boiled up every 3 days. You can also freeze the reduced stock in ice cube trays. Store the cubes in plastic bags and use as required.

2.25kg (5 lb) meat bones and trimmings
2 large onions, chopped
1 carrot, sliced
1 leek, sliced (optional)
2 celery stalks, sliced
bouquet garni
6 black peppercorns
salt

Put the bones and vegetables into a large saucepan and add 3.35L/6 pt (7 pt) water. Bring to the boil and remove the scum with a slotted spoon. Add the bouquet garni, peppercorns and a very little salt.

Cover and simmer for 3 hours, skimming and topping up with water as necessary. Then strain.

Degrease the stock, preferably by leaving it to stand overnight and then removing the cold layer of fat. When ready to use, reboil the stock, reducing it substantially. Check the seasonings.
Cooking time: 3½ hours minimum

● For brown stock, fry the bones and vegetables for 15 minutes at the beginning.
● For chicken stock, use a boiling fowl or 2 chicken carcasses.

Vegetable Stock

350g (¾ lb) vegetable peelings, such as outer stalks of celery, watercress stalks, parsley stalks, tomato and mushroom peelings and green parts of leeks
1 large onion
3 peppercorns
bouquet garni
salt

Put all the ingredients into a sacepan and add 1.1L/2 pt (1 qt) cold water. Bring to

the boil and simmer for 1½ hours. Strain, reduce and adjust seasoning to taste.
Cooking time: about 1½ hours

● For brown vegetable stock, fry the vegetables in a little dripping before cooking.

Aspic

Meat, poultry or fish stock, if made with enough bones, should all set to a good aspic. Include a pig's trotter (foot) when making meat stock; these are very inexpensive. Jellied home-made stock will save the money spent on cans of jellied consommé.

Let the strained stock chill overnight to remove the fat and check its setting strength. If the jelly is thin and the quantity large, boil uncovered to reduce it by a quarter, then chill it once more.

If there is no hope of its setting, calculate 15ml (1 tablespoon) gelatin for each 700ml/1¼ pt (3 cups) of stock. Sprinkle the gelatin over the stock and reheat, stirring to dissolve, then cool and place in the refrigerator once more before use.

Court Bouillon

Fish is cooked or poached in a court bouillon. It adds flavour to fish and can be used in sauces to be served with fish, or for soup.

| 1.1L/2 pt (1 qt) water |
| bouquet garni |
| 1 carrot, chopped |
| 1 onion, chopped |
| 1 leek, chopped |
| 10 peppercorns |
| 30ml (2 tablespoons) white wine vinegar |
| 3 cloves |
| salt |

Put all the ingredients into a saucepan and bring to the boil. Simmer for 30 minutes, uncovered. Strain and check seasoning before use.
Cooking time: 40 minutes

● Fish is always improved by the inclusion of wine in the cooking liquid.
● For a concentrated fish stock add 450g (1 lb) fish trimmings and fish bones and heads to the pan.

Tomato Sauce

This sauce can be served hot or cold, with meat, pasta, savoury pancakes and vegetables. It will keep for 4–5 days in the refrigerator. In winter use canned tomatoes and dried herbs. Basil is particularly good with tomatoes but when it is not available fresh, thyme or parsley can be substituted.

Make this sauce when there is a glut of overripe or damaged tomatoes. Store it in the freezer in convenient quantities—use empty commercial pots, such as cream pots.

MAKES 1.4L/2½ PT (6 CUPS)
1kg (2¼ lb) ripe tomatoes, blanched, skinned and roughly chopped
half a garlic clove, chopped
1 onion, chopped
2 celery stalks, chopped
salt
freshly ground black pepper
5ml (1 teaspoon) fresh basil, thyme or parsley, chopped

Put the tomatoes in a large, heavy-bottomed saucepan. Add the garlic, onion, celery and a little seasoning. Put the pan over medium heat and bring to the boil stirring.

Cover the pan, reduce heat and simmer for ¾ hour. Stir occasionally to break up the tomatoes. If you want a smooth sauce, press through a strainer into a clean pan. Add basil and check seasoning. Serve hot or as required.
Cooking time: about 1 hour

Tomato Ketchup

Tomato ketchup appears on most tables when bacon and eggs or hamburgers are served. Make your own—it is delicious with sausages, hamburgers or shepherds pie.

The sauce will keep, covered with plastic, in the refrigerator for up to 14 days. Boil it up again after 7 days. It freezes well.

MAKES ABOUT 575ML/1 PT (2½ CUPS)
700g (1½ lb) fresh or canned tomatoes, drained
5ml (1 teaspoon) pickling spice
150ml/¼ pt (⅔ cup) chicken stock
1 small onion, chopped
5ml (1 teaspoon) freshly chopped parsley
pinch of fresh thyme
bay leaf
freshly ground black pepper
salt
25g/1 oz (2 tablespoons) butter
15g/½ oz (2 tablespoons) flour
30ml (2 tablespoons) malt vinegar
2.5ml (½ teaspoon) sugar

Skin, halve and seed tomatoes if using fresh. Place in a heavy-bottomed pan with the stock. Grind the spices in an electric grinder or with a pestle in a mortar. Add the onion and herbs to the pan. Season to taste and simmer, covered, for 1 hour. Strain into a bowl. Wash out the pan, then melt the butter in it. Off the heat, stir in the flour. Return to the heat and cook for 2 minutes. Off the heat gradually incorporate the tomatoes, vinegar and sugar.

Return to heat and cook for 5 minutes. Serve either hot or cold.
Cooking time: 1 hour 10 minutes

Curry Spice

This general-purpose curry powder and paste can be used wherever a mild curry flavour is called for.

MAKES 50G (2 OZ)
1 nutmeg
20g (¾ oz) cardamom seeds (7-8 pods)
7g/¼ oz (1 big tablespoon) whole cloves
7g/¼ oz (1 tablespoon) cumin
2.5ml (½ teaspoon) chilli powder or half a dried chilli
20g/¾ oz (3 tablespoons) ground cinnamon
pinch of ground mace

FOR A PASTE
15ml (1 tablespoon) oil
10ml (2 teaspoons) vinegar

Grate the nutmeg so that you can have a good pinch of powder. Place the cloves and cumin in a grinder and grind them or crush them with a pestle and mortar. Grind the chilli if necessary. Mix all the ingredients together.

To make a paste heat the oil in a small pan. Stir the vinegar into the curry powder, add this to the pan and cook for 3–4 minutes until a paste is formed. Cool and store in an airtight jar.
Preparation time: 5 minutes

Making a Bouquet Garni

In winter a packet from the supermarket will have to do, but in spring and summer a fresh bouquet garni is quickly made. Make 2–3 and keep them in a box in the refrigerator. Provided it is completely dry, they will last up to 10 days.

sprig of fresh thyme
few sprigs of fresh parsley
bay leaf

Tie into a bunch with cotton thread or fine string and leave a long end. Tie this on to the saucepan handle so that you can easily remove the herbs at the end of cooking.
Preparation time: 2 minutes

● If dried herbs are used, make small bundles of cheesecloth.

1. Use fresh herbs when available. Simply tie them in a bundle and drop in the sauce. Remove before serving.

2. When fresh thyme is not available, use dried, or dried mixed herbs. Tie up in a small square of cheesecloth.

Forcemeat and Stuffings

Stuffing is a way of stretching meat. It can be used inside a boned roast, in a pocket in the meat, or rolled up inside individual slices. In a bird it is usually stuffed inside the neck skin. Balls of stuffing can be cooked round a roast, or added to a stew when the meat is inadequate for the number of people eating. If the weight of meat per head is very small it is best to use a forcemeat which contains meat, usually sausagemeat or bacon. Other stuffings have a higher proportion of breadcrumbs or suet (lard).

FOR SAUSAGE FORCEMEAT
175g (6 oz) sausagemeat
50g/2 oz (1 cup) fresh breadcrumbs
15ml (1 tablespoon) parsley, chopped
1 small onion, finely chopped
1 fatty bacon slice, finely chopped
1 large egg, beaten
salt
freshly ground black pepper

FOR LEMON STUFFING
grated rind of 1 lemon
100g/¼ lb (2 cups) fresh white breadcrumbs
50g/2 oz (¼ cup) soft butter, margarine or grated suet (lard)
15ml (1 tablespoon) chopped parsley
2.5ml (½ teaspoon) dried mixed herbs
salt
freshly ground black pepper
pinch of nutmeg
1 large egg, beaten

Combine the ingredients for either recipe and use as required.
Preparation time: 5–10 minutes

Marinades

A marinade serves 2 useful functions: the acid in it helps to break down the meat, thus tenderizing it and helping to reduce cooking time. It also adds richness and flavour to the dish. Salt is never included because it would draw the juices out of the meat. Simple marinades are rubbed into the meat with the fingers, and, if there is enough, can be used as a baste for grilled (broiled) meat.

Liquid marinades are used for soaking meat, which is turned regularly in the liquid. The liquid is then usually added to the dish to make the sauce. Wine is an obvious choice, but as it is not cheap, alternatives are suggested. If vegetables are included and the

meat is to remain in the marinade for 24 hours or more, the vegetables must be cooked, or they might turn sour.

FOR SIMPLE LEMON MARINADE
45ml (3 tablespoons) lemon juice
45ml (3 tablespoons) olive oil
2.5ml (½ teaspoon) dried thyme
freshly ground black pepper
1 bay leaf, crumbled

FOR SPICY VINEGAR MARINADE
125ml/4 fl oz (½ cup) olive oil
125ml/4 fl oz (½ cup) white wine vinegar
1 garlic clove, crushed
5ml (1 teaspoon) ground black pepper
5ml (1 teaspoon) Worcestershire sauce
5ml (1 teaspoon) paprika

Combine the ingredients for either of these marinades and rub into meat for grilling (broiling) etc. Leave 1–5 hours, turning the meat and spooning the marinade back over the meat. Use the marinade as a baste if desired.
Preparation time: 2 minutes

FOR 5 HOUR WINE MARINADE
1 large onion, finely chopped
150ml/¼ pt (⅔ cup) wine or vermouth—red or white according to the meat—or sherry
5ml (1 teaspoon) dried thyme
1 bay leaf, crumbled
4 parsley stalks
30ml (2 tablespoons) olive oil
4 bruised allspice berries

FOR 24 HOUR WINE MARINADE
1 medium-sized onion, chopped
1 garlic clove, crushed
1 medium-sized carrot
60ml (4 tablespoons) olive oil
275ml/½ pt (1¼ cups) wine
150ml/¼ pt (⅔ cup) wine vinegar
1 bay leaf
bouquet garni
12 peppercorns, crushed

For the second of these wine marinades, cook the vegetables until soft in the olive oil. Combine the marinade ingredients for either recipe and pour over the meat in a dish. Turn the meat 2–3 times, spooning the marinade over. Use the marinade to make the sauce for the dish.
Preparation time: up to 10 minutes

● For a quick, emergency marinade use water with a dash of malt vinegar in it; this is better than not marinating at all. Store meat in this liquid in the refrigerator.

Mincemeat

Mincemeat is traditionally associated with a British Christmas, but is useful for a variety of purposes. Enclose it in pastry for Christmas pies, use it for stuffing baked apples, mix it with stewed fruit in a hot dessert, serve it hot with ice-cream or make small sandwiches with it and batter and deep fry them for a hot dessert (see mincemeat fritters). Traditional mincemeat contains suet (lard) and needs about 4 weeks to mature.

Mincemeat is cheaper if it contains a higher proportion of fresh fruit to dried fruit. This can be made on the day of eating or can be kept for about 2 weeks.

FOR TRADITIONAL MINCEMEAT
MAKES ABOUT 1.4KG (3 LB)
100g (¼ lb) shredded beef suet (lard)
250g/9 oz (1½ cups) sultanas and raisins, mixed
175g/6 oz (1 cup) currants
100g/¼ lb (1 cup) mixed peel, chopped
50g/2 oz (½ cup) almonds, chopped
175g/6 oz (¾ cup) brown sugar
1 medium-sized cooking apple, peeled, cored and finely chopped
grated rind and juice of 1 lemon
2.5ml (½ teaspoon) mixed spice
125ml/4 fl oz (½ cup) brandy, medium-dry sherry or Marsala

FOR LAST-MINUTE MINCEMEAT
MAKES ABOUT 700G (1½ LB)
100g/¼ lb (⅔ cup) currants
150g/6 oz (¾ cup) sultanas and raisins, mixed
15g/½ oz (1 tablespoon) candied peel, chopped
15g/½ oz (2 tablespoons) almonds, shredded
25g/1 oz (1 tablespoon) glacé cherries, chopped
100g/¼ lb (½ cup) sugar
grated rind and juice of ½ lemon
1 medium-sized cooking apple, finely chopped
100g (¼ lb) grapes, seeded, skinned and roughly chopped and/or 1 banana, mashed
15ml (1 tablespoon) brandy

Combine all the ingredients. Store traditional mincemeat in sealed jars. Keep for 1 month before eating. Keep last-minute mincemeat covered in a bowl in the refrigerator for 2 hours minimum. It will keep for 48 hours if containing banana and otherwise for 2 weeks.
Preparation time: 10–20 minutes

Chocolate Fudge

MAKES 700G (1½ LB)

450g/1 lb (4 cups) granulated sugar
60ml/4 tablespoons (¼ cup) cocoa powder
50g/2 oz (3 tablespoons) honey
150g/5 oz (⅝ cup) butter
150ml/¼ pt (⅔ cup) milk
few drops vanilla extract

Grease a 28 × 23cm (11 × 9 in) flat tin (sheet pan) or an 18cm (7 in) square cake tin (pan). Put the sugar, cocoa, honey, butter and milk into a small heavy-bottomed saucepan over gentle heat. Stir with a wooden spoon until the sugar has dissolved and the cocoa is absorbed.

Bring to the boil, then boil until a temperature of 116°C (240°F) is reached, or a sample dropped into cold water will make a soft ball.

Take the pan off the heat and add the vanilla. Beat the fudge until thick and creamy. Pour into the prepared tin (pan) and mark it off in squares, then leave to set. When cold, break it up and store in an air-tight container.
Cooking time: 20 minutes plus cooling

Toffee

MAKES 700G (1½ LB)

350g/¾ lb (1¾ cups) brown sugar
225g/½ lb (1 cup) butter
200g/7 oz (⅔ cup) golden syrup or honey
juice of half a lemon

Brush the sides and bottom of a heavy-bottomed pan with oil. Add all the ingredients. Set over low heat and bring to the boil without stirring.

Oil a 28 × 23cm (11 × 9 in) flat tin (sheet pan) or 20cm (8 in) square cake tin (pan). Boil the mixture until it reaches a temperature of 143°C (290°F) on a thermo-meter or until a little dropped into cold water will set and crack between your fingers. Pour the mixture into the pre-pared tin.

When barely set, mark into squares with a knife. When set, break with a knife or a mallet.
Cooking time: 20 minutes plus cooling

● For half the weight of treacle toffee, use ⅓ of the sugar and ¼ of the butter with 150g/5 oz (½ cup) treacle (molasses).

Chocolate fudge and treacle toffee are two delicious sweets (candies) to make.

Light Fudge

MAKES 700G (1½ LB)

450g/1 lb (4 cups) fine sugar
150ml/¼ pt (⅔ cup) evaporated milk
50g/2 oz (¼ cup) butter
150ml/¼ pt (⅔ cup) milk
few drops of vanilla extract
15ml (1 tablespoon) flavourless oil

Put the fine sugar, evaporated milk, butter and milk in a heavy-bottomed pan. Heat, stirring until the sugar has dissolved. Boil to a temperature of 115°C (240°F) on a sugar thermometer, or until a little dropped into a cup of cold water forms a soft ball. Stir in the vanilla extract. Brush a 18cm (7 in) square tin with the oil. Pour in the fudge and leave about 2 hours to set. Mark into squares.
Cooking time: 20 minutes plus cooling

● For raisin fudge, add 50g/2 oz (⅓ cup) raisins.

Toffee Apples

MAKES 5
5 green dessert apples
225g/½ lb (1 cup) soft light brown sugar
25g/1 oz (2 tablespoons) butter
5ml (1 teaspoon) malt vinegar
15ml (1 tablespoon) golden syrup or honey
75ml/3 fl oz (⅜ cup) water

Wash the apples and remove the stalks. Pat dry but do not polish or rub them. Spear each apple at the stalk end with a wooden stick, pushing it along the core.

Put the sugar, butter, vinegar and syrup or honey in a large heavy-bottomed saucepan and add the water. Place over low heat, stirring constantly until the sugar has dissolved. Increase the heat to moderate and bring to the boil, without stirring. Boil for 10–15 minutes until a temperature of 150°C (300°F) is reached, or until it turns dark brown and a sample dropped into water is crisp and will crack between your fingers—the 'hard crack' stage.

Remove the pan from the heat and set aside for about 5 minutes to allow bubbling to subside and the toffee to cool. Oil some foil, ready to receive the apples and put ready a large bowl of cold water.

Tilt the pan slightly to one side and lower an apple into the toffee. Turn it around once until it is coated and then, twisting it to keep the toffee in place, plunge into the cold water to cool a moment. Stand on the foil and dip the other apples. Allow to cool for 2 hours.

Cooking time: ¾ hour plus 2 hours setting

Butterscotch

MAKES 550G (1¼ LB)
450g/1 lb (4 cups) granulated sugar
275ml/½ pt (1¼ cups) water
1.5ml (¼ teaspoon) cream of tartar
75g/3 oz (5 tablespoons) butter, diced
few drops of vanilla extract

Grease a 28 × 18cm (11 × 7 in) flat tin (sheet pan) or a 20cm (8 in) square cake tin (pan) with oil.

Dissolve the sugar, over low heat, in the water. Stir in the cream of tartar. Bring to the boil without stirring until a temperature of 116°C (240°F) is reached on a sugar thermometer, or until a little dropped into a cup of cold water forms a soft ball.

Remove the pan from heat and stir in the butter. Return to the heat and boil to a temperature of about 136°C (276°F), without stirring. Add the vanilla and boil to a temperature of 168°C (334°F), when a sample dropped into water will set very hard and crisp—the 'hard crack' stage. Pour the mixture into the prepared tin and, with an oiled knife, mark off into butterscotch oblongs. When completely cold break into shapes and wrap.

Cooking time: 45 minutes plus cooling

Quick Peppermint Creams

MAKES ABOUT 20
275g/10 oz (2⅔ cups) icing (confectioners') sugar
1 egg white
few drops of peppermint extract
drops of green food colouring

Sift 225g/½ lb (2¼ cups) icing (confectioners') sugar into a bowl. Beat the egg white and gradually stir this into the sugar until smoothly blended. Stir in the peppermint extract.

For green and white creams, divide the mixture into 2 and work green colouring sparingly into one half.

Sift the remaining sugar over a work surface and roll out the mixture to a 1cm (⅜ in) thickness. Using a 2.5cm (1 in) petit four or cookie cutter, stamp out the rounds. Leave the creams spread out to dry for 2 hours, then turn them over to dry the other side. Leave a further 2 hours before transferring to an airtight container. It is best to layer waxed paper between the peppermint creams.

Cooking time: 15 minutes, then 4 hours setting

Easy Coconut Ice

MAKES 500G (1LB 2 OZ)
15ml (1 tablespoon) flavourless cooking oil
250g/9 oz (2⅓ cups) icing (confectioners') sugar, sifted
150ml/¼ pt (⅔ cup) condensed (evaporated) milk
175g/6 oz (1⅔ cups) desiccated (shredded) coconut
few drops of pink food colouring

Brush a 28 × 23cm (11 × 9 in) flat tin (sheet pan) or 20cm (8 in) square cake tin (pan) with the oil.

Put the condensed (evaporated) milk in a bowl and stir in the sifted sugar and the coconut. Press half the mixture into the tin (apn). Add the pink food colouring to the remaining mixture. Stir quickly and spread on top of the first mixture. Cut into squares when cold.

Cooking time: 15 minutes plus cooling

● Alternatively, for coconut fingers set the mixture, pink on one side white on other, in ice-cube tray, with dividers removed.

Marshmallows

MAKES 450G (1 LB)
450g (1 lb) fine sugar
25g/1 oz (1 tablespoon) golden syrup or honey
275ml/½ pt (1¼ cups) water, divided
30ml (2 tablespoons) gelatin
2 large egg whites
few drops of vanilla extract
few drops of pink colouring
15ml (1 tablespoon) cornflour (cornstarch)
30ml (2 tablespoons) icing (confectioners') sugar

Line a 23cm (9 in) square tin (pan) with greaseproof or waxed paper and oil it. Put the sugar and golden syrup or honey in a large, heavy-bottomed pan with 150ml/¼ pt (⅝ cup) water. Set over low heat and boil until it reaches 130°C (266°F) on a thermometer, or until a sample dropped into cold water will crack between the fingers.

Soak the gelatin in 2 spoonfuls of water in a heatproof cup, then dissolve over low heat. Add water to make up to 150ml/¼ pt (⅝ cup). Add this to the hot syrup.

Whisk the egg whites until stiff. Pour the hot syrup on to the whites in a thin stream, whisking all the time.

Add the colouring and flavouring and whisk until thick. Pour into the prepared tin (pan). Leave exposed to air for 24 hours. Cut into squares. Sift the sugar and starch together then toss the marshmallows in this mixture.

Cooking time: 20 minutes then 24 hours setting, plus 5 minutes

● For pink and white marshmallows, separate into two batches and colour one one.

● For walnut marshmallows, add up to 50g/2 oz (¼ cup) chopped walnuts.

Cheese Straws

Make these nibbles when entertaining a party. They are very small, so do not be misled by the quantity. Make them up to 3 days in advance, and keep them in an air-tight container. Give them to the children for 'break-time' snacks instead of sweets.

MAKES UP TO 100
125g/¼ lb (1 cup) plain flour
salt
pinch of cayenne pepper
50g/2 oz (¼ cup) butter, diced
50g/2 oz (½ cup) Cheddar cheese, grated
1 large egg yolk
15ml (1 tablespoon) water
beaten egg to glaze
poppy seeds
sesame seeds
celery seeds

Grease 2–3 baking sheets. Sift the flour together with a pinch of salt and cayenne pepper. Cut in the butter and then rub in until the mixture resembles even-sized breadcrumbs. Stir in the cheese.

Beat the egg yolk with the spoonful of water. Add the flour and press the mixture into a dough with your fingers. Knead until smooth. Wrap and chill for 30 minutes.

Roll the pastry thinly to a rectangle. Trim edges. Brush with beaten egg and divide into 3 rectangles. Sprinkle each one with a different-flavoured seed. Cut the pastry into strips, 6mm (¼ in) wide then cut each strip into 6.5 cm (2½ in) lengths. Twist each straw and place on a greased baking sheet. Chill for 10 minutes. Heat the oven to 200°C (400°F) gas mark 6.

Bake the pastry for 10–12 minutes until lightly brown. Leave to cool. Refresh for 1–2 minutes in the oven before serving.
Cooking time: ¾ hour

Digestive Biscuits (Graham Crackers)

MAKES 30
125g/¼ lb (1 cup) plain flour
225g/½ lb (1¾ cups) wholewheat flour
2.5ml (½ teaspoon) salt
75g/3 oz (5 tablespoons) butter or margarine
75g/3 oz (5 tablespoons) lard or shortening
25g/1 oz (2 tablespoons) fine sugar
1 medium-sized egg
60ml/4 tablespoons (¼ cup) water

Heat the oven to 200°C (400°F) gas mark 6. Grease a large baking sheet. Sift the two flours and salt together. Tip the bran from the sifter back into the flour.

Cut the butter and lard into the dry ingredients then rub in the fat until the mixture resembles breadcrumbs. Stir in the sugar. Whisk the egg and water together. Make a well in the centre and pour in the egg mixture. Using a fork, draw the dry ingredients into the liquid. Work the mixture into a dough and knead until crack free.

Turn the dough out on to a lightly-floured surface. Use a rolling pin to roll the dough 6mm (¼ in) thick. Using a floured 5cm (2 in) cutter, cut out the dough. Re-roll the trimmings as necessary. Arrange on the prepared baking sheet.

Bake just above the centre of oven for 15 minutes. Leave to set then transfer the crackers to a wire rack to cool.
Cooking time: 30 minutes plus cooling.

● For a sweeter cracker, double the amount of sugar.

Water Biscuits

These biscuits can be served with cheese. They are much cheaper to make than any crackers you can buy.

MAKES 24
125g/¼ lb (1 cup) plain flour
pinch of salt
25g/1 oz (2 tablespoons) butter or margarine
30ml (2 tablespoons) water

Heat the oven to 200°C (400°F) gas mark 6 and grease a large baking sheet.

Sift the flour and the salt into a bowl. Cut the fat into the flour then rub in until mixture resembles even-sized bread-crumbs. Make a well in the centre and add the water. Using a fork draw the mixture in together. Knead gently until free of cracks.

On a lightly-floured surface roll out the dough 6mm (¼ in) thick. Use a floured 5cm (2 in) cutter to cut the biscuits. Re-roll the trimmings as necessary.

Roll the biscuits again to make thin 10cm (4 in) rounds. Transfer to the baking sheet. Bake just above the centre of the oven for about 8 minutes. Leave the biscuits on tray for 5 minutes then transfer to wire rack to cool.
Cooking time: 25 minutes plus cooling

Crisps (Chips)

Popularly known as 'crisps' or 'chips', these wafer-thin potatoes were first created as an accompaniment to game. They can still be served this way, as a side dish for 6 people. They also make an excellent nibble to serve with drinks and are far cheaper made at home than bought.

700g (1½ lb) potatoes, peeled
oil for frying
salt

Cut the potatoes into paper-thin slices, using a mandolin or the shredder blade on a food processor.

Soak the potato slices in a bowl of cold water for 60 minutes. Drain the potatoes and wrap in absorbent paper inside a towel. Leave to dry for 20 minutes.

Heat the oil in a deep fat fryer to 180°C (350°F) or until a bread cube takes 60 seconds to brown. Fry the potato slices, a few at a time to keep them separate. Remove the slices as soon as the bubbling stops. Set aside and continue with the remaining potato slices.

Heat the oil to 200°C (400°F) and put several batches of chips in and fry a second time until golden brown. Drain on absorbent paper and sprinkle with salt before serving.
Cooking time: 1¾ hours, including soaking

Devilled Almonds

Make your own devilled nuts to eat with drinks before dinner. Other nuts can be prepared in the same way.

SERVES 4
225g (½ lb) whole almonds
sea salt
1.5ml (¼ teaspoon) cayenne pepper
1.5ml (¼ teaspoon) curry powder
1.5ml (¼ teaspoon) chilli powder

Blanch the almonds by soaking in boiling water for 3 minutes and then popping the nuts out of their skins. Split by inserting a knife between the two halves and then toast in a moderate oven for 10–15 minutes. Alternatively, stir them in a frying-pan without any fat over a moderate heat until evenly browned. Grind over the sea salt and dust with the remaining spices. Shake the nuts to spread the seasoning.
Preparation time: 25 minutes

Index